To Karoline von Oppen

ACKNOWLEDGEMENTS

Heartfelt thanks to:

Andrew Davies, for a grand act of help quite literally incredible (by which I mean that the few people who know of it find it extremely hard to believe); **John Holme, Tim Walton** and **Richard Percival** for proving that in time of trouble, old friendships are priceless; **Philip Pullman**, for much encouraging warmth and practical support; **Nick Cohen**, for passing his intellectual mine detector over the most dangerous chapter; **James Meek**, for straight-talking advice on narrative structure; **Dr Peter Thompson (Sheffield University)** and **Prof. Karen Leeder (New College, Oxford)**, for countless debates and acts of hospitality; **Prof. Stefan Szymanski (University of Michigan)** for suggesting the chapter on sport; **Elke Bechthold**, for material from her unpublished thesis; **Dr Matt Fitzpatrick (Flinders University)**, for a discussion of Australian Germanophobia; **Karl von Oppen**, for conversations at his dinner table about Bismarck; lastly but firstly, **my mother, Mrs Janet Hawes née Fry**, who (apart from everything else) can read nineteenth-century German letters which entirely defeat me.

The following institutions, and the people named within them, have all provided help well beyond what might reasonably have been expected:

Oxford Brookes University, and in particular Dr Simon Kövesi, and Prof. Anne-Marie Kilday for the sabbatical and funding; the Bonn City Museum, and in particular Dr Ingrid Bodsch, for all the time and help given to someone who approached them without introduction in pursuit of a case unknown to them; the University of Heidelberg Library, and in particular Anna Vollner, for so very kindly providing the illustrations from *Kladderadatsch* and *Der Wahre Jacob*; Simplicissimus.com, and in particular Dr Hans Zimmermann, for doing the same with that wonderful material; the staff of the Secret State Archive (GStA PK), Berlin for guidance through their labyrinth; the staff of the SCOLAR rare books collection at Cardiff University; and for many kindnesses, the librarians of Balliol, Worcester and Hertford Colleges, Oxford.

At Simon & Schuster, Colin Midson and Mike Jones had the bravery to commission this book on a rather scanty pitch, and Mike the patience to see it through; Jo Whitford coped remarkably with a horribly complex task and Juliana Foster saved me from many dreadful solecisms. My agent, Caspian Dennis at Abner Stein, was a rock throughout.

CONTENTS

PROLOGUE:
AN UNCOMFORTABLE
EXCAVATION

No nation has ever been given so long to make so momentous a choice: by the time Archduke Franz Ferdinand was assassinated in Sarajevo on 28 June 1914, the line-up of the next major European war, its geographical flashpoint and the vast decision that would one day face Britain, had all been perfectly clear to thinking men for thirty-five years.*

The great question of our modern history is not how or why precisely this long-foreseen European war did indeed at last come about, but why Britain came to take the side she did, turning what would have been a relatively swift and comparatively un-traumatic victory for Germany and Austria-Hungary into that defining cataclysm of our times, the breaking of empires and the womb of horrors, the Great War.

The trouble is that the facts in this case lie below what professional archaeologists – I was once one – call a *destruction layer*: one of those melancholy, and literally dark, lines in the earth which mark the violent end of a settlement, a city, perhaps an entire civilisation. In the case

---

* 'Today Prussia confronts her colossal neighbour as the effective protector of the dual monarchy' (*The Times*, 22 September 1879); 'What would we do in the event of an attack by France and Russia upon Austro-Hungary and Germany? This is the question eagerly debated at Berlin. The resolute action of England would turn the scale in favour of peace or war. It may now settle the destinies of nations' (*Examiner*, 7 February 1880).

of the Great War the physical evidence of destruction is practically limited to that single, gigantic scar across northern France and Belgium,
the Western Front, the most concentrated charnel house in all military
history. But that was just the start. By the time the yet more terrible
aftershocks had been visited on all Europe, the world of July 1914 was
sealed off by a physical, cultural, and perhaps psychological destruction
layer so profound that truth has simply yielded to myth.

Our current national myth about 1914–18 is that of the entirely
meaningless, self-generating massacre, as seen in *Oh! What a Lovely
War* or *Blackadder*, set off by a more or less random assassination,
fought between rival European empires of more or less equal wickedness, run by generals of more or less equal inhumanity. This view has
been taken up by masterful storytellers, for whom it has been pay dirt
in the shape of tales like *Birdsong, The Ghost Road* and, most recently,
that veritable tsunami of Great War schmaltz, *War Horse*. As the
centenary of Britain's most far-reaching decision comes around, we
have become a nation which, rather than seeking the truth, and hence
a possible lesson in it, likes nothing better than to drown the imagined
sorrows of anyone we can remotely claim as a relative who took part
in this allegedly pointless and unfathomable tragedy.

Our actual historians are not, of course, entirely blind to the obvious
fact that Britain freely chose to line up against Germany. But their story,
too, is fascinating for what it says about us today. They all seem to agree
that things were essentially fine between Britain and Germany until
at least 1890.[1] Then, so goes the tale, the unstable Kaiser Wilhelm II,
having kicked out the cunning but essentially sane old Prince Bismarck,
went into cahoots with Admiral Tirpitz, who, like him, had a bizarre
love-hate relationship with Englishness.* The two deployed Germany's
new industrial might to supercharge her previously almost non-existent
navy. The Tirpitz Plan thus led – gratuitously, almost overnight and
more or less all by itself – to Britain lining up against Germany: 'Anglo-

---

* While planning to deter/browbeat/defeat the Royal Navy (depending on how you interpret
his thoughts), Tirpitz sent his daughters to Cheltenham Ladies' College. And Wilhelm's first wish
on escaping his own rebellious subjects in 1918 was for 'a good cup of English tea'.

German hostility dates from its inception' is the plain declaration of our greatest military historian, John Keegan.[2]

Since this thesis roundly blames the German leaders of 1897–1914, you might well imagine that it is a British version of the past. In fact, it was born in the 1960s in Germany, where it is now simple orthodoxy to see a *Grab for World Power* under Wilhelm II as the root cause of the *War of the English Succession*.[3]

The tale of Wilhelm, Tirpitz & Co. is comfortable to Britons because it clearly blames the Germans; it is comfortable to Germans because it clearly blames a *certain kind* of German – the scar-faced, sabre-rattling kind, who, like Prussia itself, quite simply no longer exists.

Blaming the Tirpitz Plan for everything thus preserves the idea, so fashionable in modern Britain, of a British Empire which was generally a Good Thing, if perhaps incompetently or pusillanimously run; and it preserves the idea, so essential to modern Germany, of a country whose naturally 'Western' path was deformed by the failure of its citizenry to resist a right-wing, war-mongering elite.[4]

In short, everyone today, in Britain and in Germany, and further afield, is pleased by a saga whose very modern moral rings out loud and clear, chiming so nicely with our happy view of events like the so-called Arab Spring: if only the Good Democratic People keep power away from the Bad Reactionary Cliques, all manner of things will be well and nation will speak peace unto nation.

Unfortunately, there is a problem with this comforting tale: that old devil, the detail.

One striking artefact lies in the Prussian Secret State Archives for 4 November 1899. At this time, virtually no one, even in Germany, had worked out the true extent or aim of Admiral Tirpitz's plotting, but there he is, informing the Staatsministerium, the innermost sanctum of Wilhelmian decision-making, that 'the present antipathy towards England is convenient for the strengthening of the fleet'. The gun could hardly be smoking more obviously: Tirpitz's plan for a mighty German navy did not *initiate* popular Anglo-German hostility, but deliberately *used* it. As Christopher Clark puts it in *The Sleepwalkers*: 'it was above all the sequence of peripheral clashes with Britain that *triggered* the decision' (my italics).[5] In short: the Tirpitz Plan only ever existed, and was only ever politically viable, because the Anglo-German rivalry had by then already begun to bite.

So this is the great question: when did that fatal sequence of Anglo-German clashes really start?

By 1900, the *New York Times*, which had no earthly reason to spin things, could see that feelings between the British and the Germans – not the *governments*, the *peoples* – were already almost out of control:*

ANGLOPHOBIA IN GERMANY.

The public has lost no opportunity of manifesting antipathy toward Great Britain. In music halls the portrait of the Queen, thrown on a biograph screen, has been hooted. In public meetings the English have been denounced as a nation of bandits. In yellow papers, like the Anti-Semite Staatsburger Zeitung . and the Deutsche Tageszeitung, the expression of anti-British sentiment has often bordered on hysteria. In Dresden and other places English residents have been insulted.

Four years earlier, when the Tirpitz Plan had not yet even been devised, let alone undertaken, the same paper was already printing headlines like this:

German Hatred of England Displayed in a Surprising Fashion.

GERMAN HATRED OF ENGLAND.

---

* The *New York Times*, 8 April 1900. Of course, this could just have been re-typed. But there's nothing like the actual look of the past to remind us that before all the stories, there are *facts* in history. This may seem pretty obvious, but over the past few decades an amazing number of otherwise sane and clever people have given time to a bizarre mixture of German nineteenth-century idealist philosophy and French eighteenth-century salon wordplay which seeks, in effect, to persuade us that there are no such things. So this book will occasionally present the artefacts exactly as they were.

A decade still further back, in 1885, the *New York Times** was telling its readers about

ENGLISH HATRED OF GERMANY.

Back, still further: in 1879 it was already being claimed in the German press that Britain's underhand financial muscle was being systematically employed to thwart honest German enterprise in Samoa:†

> daß augenscheinlich eine englische Intrigue den Zusammenbruch der Firma herbeigeführt habe, um ihre Factoreien bei Abwickelung der Geschäfte in englische Hände zu bringen; das Londoner Haus Baring Brothers, welches die letzte Godeffroy'sche Tratte nicht honorirt und dadurch den Sturz direkt veranlaßt habe, soll das Werkzeug in dieser Intrigue abgegeben haben.

Before that old chestnut of inevitable conflict due to capitalist rivalry is wheeled out, let's see a couple of pictures which really are worth many thousands of words, from the early mid-1870s and from each side of what was then still widely called the German Ocean.

These pictures date from the 1870s – that is, from a time when not one of the stock explanations for the Anglo-German rivalry works. In Disraeli's heyday, Germany could still not launch a serious ironclad without importing both design and technology from Britain (the flagship of her navy in 1878 had been built from keel to masthead on the Thames); Germany had still not even tried to get a single colony; and

---

* *New York Times*, 18 January 1885/22 June 1896/16 November 1896.
† *Vossische Zeitung*, 11 December 1879. 'apparently, an English intrigue brought about the collapse of the firm so that its factories would be brought into English hands after the winding-up. The London house of Baring Brothers, which, by refusing to honour the last draft on Godeffroy & Co., directly caused its fall, is said to have been the tool of this intrigue'. From now on, a modern font will be used for translations from the German, but it's worth remembering that this is how they all looked in their day. While most people in the world can pick up and read the newspapers of their ancestors with little trouble (producing that entrancing combination of apparent familiarity and sudden, vast distance), the average modern German finds almost all German printed matter from before 1918 functionally illegible. The more you consider this cultural fact, the profounder it becomes. Since gothic type resists all digital search-engines, it also means that going through old German newspapers is still real, eye-killing work.

the balance of trade was still so massively in Britain's favour that the only German export to Britain which anyone noticed was the Germans themselves, who came as political asylum seekers and/or cheap labour. Yet by then – as we'll see – highly influential German media dons were telling legions of readers that their most profound enemies were these decadent, yet somehow still cunningly hegemonic Englanders, while the most respectable British journals discussed the chances of war with, and even invasion by, these brutish, yet somehow almost superhumanly efficient Teutons. The popular images were already in place on both sides: the Hunnish, jackbooted, spike-helmeted, clenched-fisted thug, and the slippery, cunning, inhumanly ravenous, Jew-ish octopus – the very same images, that is, which would appear again and again in the propaganda of the deadly century to come.*

---

* It's widely assumed that Britons only started thinking of Germans as like Huns after Wilhelm publicly urged his troops to act like Attila's men in quelling the Boxer Rebellion. In fact, as with so much else in this story, that fatal image was born decades earlier. See p. 130.

So how far do we really have to go back? When and why did Britain and Germany really start to be so at odds?

Let's start this uncomfortable excavation exactly half a century before the great destruction began. 1864: Wilhelm was a mere boy, second in line to the throne of one German state among many; Tirpitz was an obscure lieutenant in a miniscule navy; and Great Britain, the industrial, financial and naval hegemon of Earth, was, to her own amazement, on the verge of war with Germany. Not with *Prussia*: with *Germany* . . .

PART ONE (1864):
THE SETTING OF THE TERMS

If England is resolved upon a particular policy, war is not probable. If there is, under these circumstances, a cordial alliance between England and France, war is most difficult; but if there is a thorough understanding between England, France, and Russia, war is impossible.

Disraeli, House of Commons, 4 July 1864

Trouble in paradise

Britain in 1864 was as confident as America in 1994.* The existential challenges of the previous decade were history: Russian ambition had been bloodily tamed in the Crimean War, India was once again firmly in British hands after the great trauma of the Mutiny and France's brief technological edge in ironclad warships had been so comprehensively annulled that Lord Palmerston's wildly over-engineered coastal forts (virtually indestructible, they may still be visited from Cork to Dover) were being called his follies before they were even finished.

There were problems on the peripheries, true: in Jamaica, General Eyre was putting down the rebellion with rather troubling zeal; the rambunctious Irish had bred a violent new group called the Fenians – or was it Feenians? Perhaps it derived from some classical Phenians? – and it seemed possible that the United States, now fully geared-up for war in body and mind, might be tempted to apply to the 49th parallel the same logic which it was remorselessly imposing upon the Mason–Dixon line.

But these were mere details, for mid-Victorian Britain was not only the richest and most potent country on Earth, it also had a matchless sense of how it had become so. Britons had a story about themselves like no one else had. The tale had been gloriously told them by Lord Macaulay, the great historian of British Progress.† In 1864 they were,

---

* The power of the Royal Navy in the mid-nineteenth century is a remarkably exact parallel to that of the USN/USAF/USMC after 1989: in both cases, the 'Anglo-Saxon' country, having no serious worldwide opposition, is widely able to intervene at will in distant nations at a handily low cost in domestic body-bags. Then as now, cultures inured to heavy losses in land campaigns, and not possessed of the necessary technology, claimed that this was a sort of cheating, which only worked because the 'Anglo-Saxons' somehow managed to combine essential cowardliness and decadence with inhuman ruthlessness and limitless money. The intellectually vacant outrage about drone-strikes is merely the most recent version of this.

† Macaulay is also the man who, more than any other, is responsible for the fact that the most populous democracy on Earth, India, conducts its public business in English.

almost to a man, as convinced as Donald Rumsfeld in 2003 that humanity would soon universally choose the self-evidently superior British ways of personal liberty, constitutional reform and trade's increase – prompted by a judicious dose of high-tech, low-risk military persuasion where necessary.

The finest proof of this muscular pudding lay in that vast new market which had been prised open by a short but fiery lesson in the reach of the British Empire and the inadvisability of trying to stem the inevitable march of free trade, even if it included opium.[6]

> **We are committed to trading relations with the extreme East, which are to compensate, and which do in a great measure compensate, the falling-off of our commercial relations with the West. The opening up of China is undoubtedly one of the most obvious causes of that wonderful, and to many inexplicable, prosperity which, amid the dangers of Europe and the convulsions of America, seems to settle in lieu of other sunshine upon these islands.**

And what were the dangers of Europe in 1864? The answer is simple, though perhaps surprising to us, so lost has historical truth become in later myth: Britain was, as a speaker in the House of Commons put it roundly, 'on the verge of a war with Germany'.[7]

The poor relations

It seemed ridiculous. Britain was used to looking at Germany as a sort of poor, backward and rather comic relation.

The word 'relation' is almost meant literally. Right up until 1914, the newspapers, essayists, cartoonists and even the topmost diplomats of Britain and Germany – men like Bismarck and Lord Haldane – often described the other nation in terms of more or less distant family. Terms like 'cousins' or 'relations' were common on both sides, even when – often, especially when – the subtext was by no means friendly. No one on either side ever spoke about the French or Russians in this way.*

The literal relatedness of the British and German royals was just the visible tip of this strange, deep and mutual feeling that Britons and Germans really *ought* to be like one another. This sounds very positive, but it also meant, of course, that if they *weren't*, something was very wrong indeed: there is no fight like a family fight.

To Victorian Britons, Germany's role in the future unfolding of the world was clear. She was to sort herself out, unite, and adopt the pre-destined British ways of her older, wiser and infinitely stronger relation. Protestant Prussia, Britain's helpmeet in the epochal triumphs of 1759 and 1815, would presumably lead the way, but would then be peaceably merged into a new, British-style United Germany, run by a real par-liament. This was the so-called Coburg Plan, beloved of the Prince Consort, himself, of course, a German. After his untimely death, the Queen clove to the Dear One's vision.

At present, however, Germany remained a hopeless mess of tiny countries, like Thackeray's comic Pumpernickel, scarce ten miles wide, with its absurd court, its gorgeous but entirely useless officers and its western frontier ludicrously bidding defiance to Prussia.[8] This Prussia was the most go-ahead German state, but even Prussia was hardly respectable: *The Times* warned that marrying Albert's and Victoria's own daughter (another Victoria) to the Prussian Crown Prince was making a connection with 'a paltry German dynasty'.[9]

If even the Prussian royal house was paltry, Henry Mayhew, co-founder of *Punch*, could only hope to make the poverty and backwardness of Germany in general imaginable to his readers by comparing it with that most irredeemably wretched of countries, Ireland:

---

* Though the British frequently did of the Americans – 'brethren' was reserved for them alone – and, to a lesser extent, vice versa, until Woodrow Wilson snappily told everyone to stop it.

Gadflies in summer never swarmed in such number about a dung-heap; nor vermin infested so profusely the rags of Irish beggars; such greedy parasitical animalcules were never seen in a magnified drop of dirty water; no insects at the time of a 'great blight' ever covered the land so thickly, or ravaged it so thoroughly, as the horde of petty swaggering bogtrotter potentates in this miserable, under-fed, and over-taxed – ground-down and used-up – ill-conditioned and well-plucked – luckless, lifeless, spiritless, hopeless, and penniless – befuddled, beleaguered, and benighted old Fatherland, or rather old Great-grandmother-land, of Germany.[10]

Many Britons, or at least many Londoners, saw the truth of this every day, because London was well supplied with Germans, drawn there by those simple but timeless dreams which still draw foreigners ceaselessly to London: freedom and money.

For most, then as now, it was simply money. Germans in 1864 were so much poorer than Britons that even if they were no longer sold en masse to the British Army, as they had been in the previous century (to the outrage of Irish and American patriots, in whose ballads the despised Hessian hirelings of King George III often figure), British employers could still draft them in another capacity: as cheap labour to keep costs down.

Karl Marx, himself of course a London German asylum seeker, and one kept from penury only by Friedrich Engels's helpfully intimate connections to the evils of capitalism, fulminated against this example of mid-Victorian globalisation:

Defeated in England, the masters are now trying to take counter-measures ... secretly they sent agents to Germany to recruit journeymen tailors, particularly in the Hanover and Mecklenburg areas ... The first group has already been shipped off. The purpose of this importation is the same as that of the importation of Indian COOLIES to Jamaica, namely, perpetuation of slavery ... No one would suffer more than the German workers themselves, who con-stitute in Great Britain a larger number than the workers of all the other Continental nations. And the newly-imported workers, being completely helpless in a strange land, would soon sink to the level of pariahs.[11]

The idea that cheap German labourers outnumbered the workers of all the other Continental nations was not a fantasy of Marx's. We can see this from a remarkable set of figures given in the *Daily News*:[12]

FOREIGNERS IN LONDON.

The Society of Friends of Foreigners in Distress—in other words "the great Society"—so frequently referred to at the German Benevolent Association previously described, differs considerably from the latter. Its scope is more extensive and its range more catholic. It confers small pensions, has almshouses for 24 inmates, as well as affords temporary assistance to distressed foreigners of every nationality. During last year 23 applicants from Africa; 4 from the United States; 3 from South America; 69 from Belgium; 14 from Denmark; 214 from France; 1,633 from Germany, including the 15 subdivisions coming under that general head; 1 from Greece; 215 from Holland; 2 from the Ionian Islands; 68 from Italy; 1 from Portugal; 141 from Russia; 6 from Spain; 29 from Sweden and Norway; 48 from Switzerland; and 1 from Turkey, were relieved.

German girls, lured from grinding rural poverty by promises of respectable work in a London paved with gold, were always to be found selling themselves around Leicester Square. Ragged-trousered street-bands of German buskers were such an infestation that the authorities, besieged by complaints from Dickens and Carlyle among many others, tried to suppress them by means of the 1864 Street (Metropolis) Music Act. This failed to stop the impecunious brass players of Germany coming to Britain or entering – ultimate sign of assimilation – the unwritten dictionary of London rhyming slang ('German bands' = 'hands').

Britons at home thus came across Germans in various not very flattering ways and would have looked down with pity or irritation at yet another 'thin, under-sized German lad such as we see every day in the streets'.[13]

These Germans, of course, had some attractive qualities. Their colourful, sentimental Christmas festivities, imported by the late Prince Regent, were just starting to really catch on. Some Londoners enjoyed watching, and even taking part in, their curious, quasi-military gymnastic displays. And they were the antithesis of the other great Victorian immigrant labour force, the Irish: though almost as cheap to hire, the Germans who came to London were good Protestants, famously sober, educated and respectful.

But the most agreeable thing to Britons about these poor, undersized, oppressed Germans was that they openly admired – adored! – the cousins who had so generously or conveniently found a place for them.

The Germans look up, the British look down

Everyone knew that the Good Germans longed simply to unite and to become like Britain. Their liberal politics was a direct import, stamped 'Made in England' for all to see, as was their progressive economics. The leading theoretical light of German liberalism was an old Etonian, John Prince Smith, who later embraced Bismarck as a Reichstag MP and who seems to have believed, in a way that put even Adam Smith to shame, that achieving universal free trade really was *all* that mattered in the world. Sometimes the imitation of Britain was literal and even illegal: Krupp, whose wares were later to become a byword for deadly German quality, at first tried to flog his inferior products by mendaciously labelling them 'best English steel'.[14]

The greatest German novelist of the day, Gustav Freytag, a public liberal, had the hero of his Europe-wide bestseller *Debit and Credit* be a good man trying to become a British-style, English-speaking businessman, to the gratification of his decent boss, a man of 'thoroughly English aspect'. Britain is the *good* foreign example in the book, which was a great favourite of the Crown Prince and Princess, whereas the French, Poles and Jews are bad influences on Germany.[15] The future high priest of Anglophobia, Heinrich von Treitschke, at first looked up to Britain with wide eyes as the land where social castes had been overcome by a healthy, organic union of the aristocracy and the middle classes.[16] Looking back, Treitschke wrote bitterly: 'What German liberal did not, in youth, dream the splendid dream of a natural alliance between free England and a free Germany?'[17]

German liberals sometimes even felt more German in Britain than in Germany. In London, among other Germans and 'surrounded by a bit of salt water', a German might delight so much in true, free German living as to forget reality, 'go down to the Thames, take a ship and journey across the green North Sea and so up the gloomy Elbe to Magdeburg, maybe even to Dresden, where he starts to speak openly – and gets thrown out of Germany again'.[18]

This love was so strong that in 1856 a still rather obscure conservative politician and newspaperman complained despairingly to a friend of the way the Germans seemed hopelessly at the mercy of cultural Englishness:

> The stupid admiration of the average German for Lords and Guineas, the anglomania of parliament, of the newspapers, of sportsmen, of landlords and of presiding judges. Even now, every Berliner feels himself elevated if a real English jockey talks to him and gives him the chance to grind out the crushed fragments of the Queen's English. How much more so it will be when the First Lady of this land is an Englishwoman?[19]

The trouble was that as the undoubted top nation, Britons took such adoration in their stride and, like most over-adored countries or beings, did not return the compliment. The Germans might be some kind of relations, but by God they were poor and stunted ones. Sir Robert Morier, the best-informed and best-connected of all Victorian

British diplomats, and a deep lover of liberal Germany, tried to explain to Britons that his work was hamstrung by 'the contempt for every thing German which is universally, in Germany, ascribed to all English statesmen'.[20]

Britons' 'contempt for every thing German'. Here is a charge which will ring down the following decades. Forty years later, the British were still being begged by some of their more insightful compatriots to drop their 'lofty superiority' and 'amused contempt' for Germany.[21] Why would England not treat Germany as a fully equal *Kulturvolk*? Kaiser Wilhelm II and his chancellor, von Bülow, as well as countless pamphlets and individuals, were still asking this question on the eve of 1914. One very informed Victorian observer spoke of 'the infinite number of bad jokes perpetrated by English comic writers and artists between the years 1840 and 1866 upon German manners and customs, politics and characteristics in general. There is no offence that a North German is more prone to resent, and less inclined to forgive, than a joke'.[22]

Clearly, being beastly to the Germans, or at any rate making fun of them and then accusing them of not being able to take a joke, was not born in the twentieth century and did not (sadly for profound psychologists) come out of deep fear or rivalry. Britons felt about the Germans rather in the way the French feel today about the Belgians: amusement at a harmless but ridiculous cousin. They did not *dislike* the Germans – they just could not take them seriously.

To moralising Victorians, it seemed likely that it was the Germans' own fault that they were disunited, backward and poor: Britons were practical men of business and politics, whereas the Germans were – the PM, Lord Palmerston, said it himself – a 'nation of damned professors'. The British thus showed Germans little respect, even when being a literal professor was exactly what was needed: the first German explorers in Africa, graciously permitted to accompany a British expedition at their own expense, knew themselves fitted by excellent German scientific education for the task, but found that 'we, who risk our own fortunes as well as our lives, are acknowledged neither as member of this English expedition, nor as gentlemen, but merely as servants'.[23]

The fact was that Britons simply found the Germans they met at home, political refugees or economic migrants, who looked up so openly, so hopelessly and with such theorising to Britain's constitution, to her navy, and to her empire, rather absurd.

The other way that Britons met Germans made things even worse: you can hardly respect a nation of entertainingly backward locals and unctuous hoteliers. For our ancestors had a unique new national hobby – like many of their hobbies, it was later to become universal among prosperous folk – which they called 'holyday-making', and the main place they made their 'holydays' was Germany, whither (as the *Standard* put it) 'transit is now so easy and expeditious that you may breakfast one day in London and on the following take your *déjeuner* in the Fatherland'.

The horrors of a German holyday

It's very easy to imagine the way Victorian Britons were seen by mid-century Germans: all you have to do is think of the stock comedy figure of the American tourist in post-war Europe.

Beef-fed Britons were physically larger than poor Germans, they dressed themselves in bizarre travelling clothes – plaid trousers were inexplicably fashionable – and they all went around with exactly the same guide book, 'the red-bound Murray', which told them what to see and how to get there, and which could make or break hoteliers in a single season. It was famously quipped that Englishmen went to Europe with Murray to tell them what to see, and Byron to tell them how to feel about it. They were known to be the great internationalist traders of the world, and to care nothing about what they traded to whom, for their only religion was money.

They were also notorious for refusing to learn foreign languages. What was the point? All cultures were as one, language was just a tool for communication and trade, and since English was self-evidently the most useful language for that, it was 'manifest that the time cannot be very far distant when other nations will be constrained to use it, for the mere convenience of intercourse with the rest; and, consequently, though Germans, French, and Russians may cling as hard as the Welsh and Irish to their ancient forms of speech, they are assuredly doomed to be extinguished by our own'.[24] There was certainly no point in learning *German*, which was spoken by no one outside Germany other than in Windsor Palace, and which was filled with 'grammatical foolery and absurd inflectional differences'.

GERMAN WITHOUT A MASTER.
Scene :—*Railway Terminus, Cologne.*
English Tourist (ignorant of the German language) :—" Hi ! Porter, can you speak English ?"
Porter :—" Nein, Herr."
English Tourist :—" Then can you tell me who does ?"

Britons' sense of their own, and of their country's, superiority was literally proverbial. According to an 1867 dictionary of German sayings, if you wanted another way of describing somewhere as heavenly, you might say, 'Hier kann ein Englander England vergessen!' ('An Englishman can forget England here!').

Most importantly for any tourist industry, Britons were rich – often in that new-rich way that was still rare in a continent where Money was still generally Old. They were also much fussier than Germans about superficial things like cleanliness and comfort, leading later nationalists to proclaim that when the English said 'civilisation' they meant 'soap' rather than real *Kultur*.

Murray's omnipresent guide book gives its readers stark warning about what they can expect in this strange and backward land:

One of the first complaints of an Englishman arriving in Germany will be directed against the beds. It is, therefore, as well to make him aware beforehand of the full extent of the misery to which he will be subjected on this score. A German bed is made only for one; it may be compared to an open wooden box often hardly wide enough to turn in, and rarely long enough for an Englishman of moderate stature to lie down in.[25]

Henry Mayhew, in our very year of 1864, struggled even to find words
which could describe to his fellow Britons that horror of all inexplicable German horrors, that 'huge, squabby-looking, flabby, bolster-like
coverlet' – the execrable duvet:

> The natives sleep in "cribs" but little bigger than orange-boxes, where
> sheets and blankets are unknown and where each individual slum-
> berer has to roll himself up in the superincumbent feather-bed to
> prevent being left in a state of Adamhood during the night.[26]

Coleridge himself declared that he 'would rather carry his blanket
about him like a wild Indian, than submit to this abominable custom'.[27]
And then there was the all-pervading smoking of Germany:

HOLYDAY MAKERS.

(FROM OUR OWN CORRESPONDENT.)
WIESBADEN, AUG. 15.

I got into a coach the other day at Coburg,
which was to convey me from the hotel to the
station. The vehicle was constructed to carry four
inside, and we had already our complement—myself and a sort of Thuringian bumpkin in the back
seat, and opposite to us two young and comely
women, a married lady and her sister, as I thought,
about whose ladylike appearance there could be no
mistake. Just as we were starting, a youngster,
or *junker*, looked in, a man of prepossessing appearance, with good features, a sanguine complexion, and
the bright expression of a *" witziger kopf,"* a wag
agreeably to the German notions of waggery. He
looked in, and the ladies, with whom he was evidently a favourite, with many an " *Ach !*" and an
"*Herr Je,*" hastened to make as much room between
them as enabled him to squeeze in. The fair companions gathered up their ample folds to the best of
their abilities, and apologized for the inconvenience
he had to endure from the pressure of their poor

crushed crinolines. "*Ach ! was sagen Sie, meine Damen,*" said the gallant spark, ogling to the right and left; "*Ich bin hier wie im Paradies.*" And his grin and his leer were certainly like those of Mephistopheles between two angels. He had his stump of cigar in his mouth, and he went on during the whole journey, with one puff here and a drollery there, lavishing his incense on those two deities, who stood that and the ashes and the sparks and worse, well knowing that in this country "Love me, love my cigar" is the motto; and that men are only to be had on those terms, or not to be had at all.

"Beast!" I fancy I may hear some of our own fair young ladies at home exclaim, as the disgusting but true and commonplace picture is laid before them. I quite agree with you, my dear girls; but it is just as well you should be forewarned

When they were not being downright beastly, even the grandest of locals were objects of mockery for rich, modern British tourists:

It requires a somewhat lengthy residence in the country before you can make out whether the *kellners* at the principal hotels are, one and all, grand dukes of the farm-yard principality, or the Grand Duke himself one of the expensively-got-up gentry to whom you have lately given some five *groschens* as "drink-money" upon settling your account ... In appearance this small mole-hill despot is as about as dignified as a linen-draper's shopman in the British metropolis, delighting to wear the turban cap known as the "pork-pie hat," which at the time of our quitting London was popular with every cheese-monger's apprentice.[28]

The pride of these wretched German nobles astonished well-off but untitled Britons. Sabine Baring-Gould waxed indignant at their feudal snobbery in 1879:

An Englishman is somewhat impatient to find barons abroad as thick as blackberries and looking equally ragged ... I have known a lady refuse to allow her daughter tó dance with sons of some of our first county families, and heirs to baronetcies, because they bore no "von" before their surnames and therefore could be no gentlemen.[29]

The proudest state of Germany was of course Prussia, which Britain had vastly strengthened in 1815 by presenting her with parts of the Rhineland.* Despite this friendly diplomatic history, Prussia proper was simply not on the British itinerary. After all, one guide book warned that 'the traveller arriving here for the first time feels as if he had left behind him everything that gives charm to existence'.[30] And as for Berlin itself, the *Saturday Review* of October 1865 gives scant encouragement to the Victorian city-break traveller, being at first quite unable to find words sufficient to express its scorn:

> Few English travellers whom neither public nor private business deprives of their freedom of choice are in the habit of losing their way to the City of the Plain, the oasis of stone and bricks in a Sahara of sand. Those who have been unfortunate enough to be deluded into a visit to Berlin are habitually silent as to their experiences of the Prussian capital.

Things in Berlin were so backward that the visitor would not even find that most basic necessity of life to a civilised Englishman, clubs. He would have to make do with 'coffee-houses and pastry-cooks' shops', but 'even the most sympathetic narrative of their glories, as in the case of most other institutions in the Intellectual City, runs a risk of proving as flat as the desert which surrounds it, and as insipid as the scum-topped beverage in which its citizens take so singular a delight'.

Best stick to Murray, for if you strayed from the tourist trail you might find yourself faced with hideously authentic German food:

---

* The Prussians had not actually wanted the Catholic Rhineland at all as a reward for their belated fight against Napoleon. They had wanted more of what *really* mattered to them, right up to the end: Poland. But Russia wanted that too, so the Prussians got 'Rhenish Prussia' as consolation prize and the British congratulated themselves on their cunning at having thus created a natural bulwark against France.

We could *not* eat, though we had been some time in Germany, that mud-coloured, sour and heavy cold-dumpling which the *Deutschers* call bread and which is generally about the same consistency and inviting appearance as papier-mache and of about the same specific gravity too – ay! and as easy of digestion as argillaceous ironstone besides.[31]

Worse, you might end up having not only to eat like a German, but with the Germans:

The common practice among German gentlefolks at dinner is to pin the meat down to the plate with the fork held straight up, while the handle is clutched firmly in the fist, and then to proceed to hack the slice of meat into so many little dice, the knife being held the while by the blade, rather than the handle, in the same manner as a countryman cuts at his bread and bacon. After this, the knife is thrown down on the table, and the fork removed to the right hand, by which means, the pieces are raised one after the other to the mouth; whereupon the fork is laid aside, so that the gravy may be duly lapped up with the knife; and, when this elegant process is finished, bits of bread are thrown into the plate, and the fork once more resumed, in order to mop up every particle of grease remaining on the platter.[32]

So with the certainty of meeting appalling beds, inedible food and ghastly manners, and with the capital city so utterly uninteresting, why on earth did Britons go to Germany at all?

Sublimity, roasted marmots and cricket

The Victorians on their holidays were every bit as determined to find things awe-inspiring as their descendants are to find them awesome, and they went to south-west Germany for much the same reasons which draw their great-great-great-grandchildren to South America or South-East Asia.

As the most thoroughly urbanised, leisured and moneyed people in the world, middle-class Britons could leave their Pooter-ish homes or offices and, in about the same door-to-door time as a modern long-haul flight, find themselves per reliable schedule amid sublime natural grandeur, exotic, pre-industrial native customs and decent hotels. Where else could you find, within twenty-four hours of Waterloo, 'the highest refinements of civilisation combined with the aspects of an Asiatic wilderness, studded here and there with the ruins of noble chateaux'?[33]

Just as modern first-worlders find the Day of the Dead in Mexico and suchlike irresistible, Victorian Britons sought out in backward Germany agreeably frisson-making attractions of that gothic and Catholic sort which progress had abolished in Britain.* *The Times*'s 'Holyday-Maker' columnist advises its readers:

> seek the solitude of those weird mountain lakes, the Mummelsee, the Wildsee, &c., visit the ruins of Ebersteinburg, of the Yburg, of the Windeck, of 100 other castles, abbeys, and nunneries, listen to the legends handed down among the peasantry for centuries ... And then the ghosts! Where shall we look for the dark side of nature with better chance of success than in the deep gloom of these fir woods? Singing and sighing ghosts, sneezing ghosts, screeching ghosts, mass-saying, bell-ringing, dancing and ban-quetting ghosts; wild huntsmen, the White Lady, a sister, belike, of the dread apparition of Berlin, Bayreuth, and other places, the bearer of tidings of death or calamity to the Princes of Baden as to other privileged reigning houses; or the Black Lady, that Fran Jutta of the Alte Schloss, near at hand, an unnatural monster, poi-soner of her own sons from avarice, now doomed to haunt the scene of her crimes to the end of time. All these uneasy souls, flit-ting about like bats, the rustle of their long trailing garments

---

* At home, Victorian Britons met almost only Protestant northern Germans, whereas they took their holydays largely in Catholic regions. This was no doubt one of the factors which made 'the Germans' hard for Britons to understand, for the depth of the Catholic/Protestant divide in Germany was profound in the nineteenth century. Even today, Germans speak of the River Main as an important cultural border, and historians of the future may see the shift of the German capital from the largely Catholic, once-Romanised Rhineland (Bonn) to what used to be Prussia (Berlin) as the subliminal precursor to an epochal shift in Germany's focus.

blanching the cheeks, the stare of their stony eyes curdling the blood in the beholder's veins.

As a contrast, the wonder-working images, the blessed Liebfrau of the cloister of Lichtenthal, to whose shelter the terrified nuns flocked as a band of lawless marauders were storming at their cell.

Another guide paints his picture of dubious Catholic delights as colourfully as any modern hack describing the irresistibly backward rites of, say, Peru:

> We know not if our readers, in their summer visits to Germany, have extended their wanderings to the Alpine district of Upper Styria: if not, we would recommend them, on their next tour, should they happen to have a taste for the romantic, the picturesque and the wonderful, not to neglect such a world-wide celebrity as the miraculous Maria of the Zell ... though we would not recommend any traveller of high moral feelings to come within its precincts on any of the great festivals, as the scenes he would witness would excite in him a feeling of disgust, never to be effaced.[34]

But the writer clearly assumes that the stomach of the good British Protestant will remain adventurous even after such irresistibly disgusting displays of Popery, for the book then helpfully suggests the finest dining to be had in the region: 'above all, if he would really enjoy a delicacy, let him have a marmot stuffed with aromatic herbs and roasted entire'.[35]

Most awe-inspiring and sublime of all, of course, were the Rhine and the Alps. The Rhine was so familiar to Britons that it was often called simply 'the German River'. Dwarfing any British waterway, it offered a regular succession of suitably breathtaking vistas from comfortable modern steamships.

> We linger heart-chained upon the crumbling ruins, where the ivy of centuries sheds its inexhaustible poetry, and listen to the mystic breathings of the past, rising from a hundred hills. The Englishman feels this deeply, but with his undemonstrative nature leaves such

impressions unuttered or, fearful of ridicule, turns the weapon against his heart in self-destruction and wends his way among beautiful things, making a humorous tale of them.

In other words, British travellers wandered jollily around ruins and monuments, 'doing the Rhine', making facile comments as they ticked off the requisitely sublime sights listed in Murray.

The other great thing, then as now, about exotic and backward places was that your money went much further. By the mid-century the annual invasion of Germany was within the reach of so many Britons that Murray itself sounded a warning: 'Many vulgar and half-witted Englishmen think, if they leave home with money they can command anything; that it is mean to be civil ... the Summer Tourist – many of whom, without any intention of doing wrong, contribute in no inconsiderable degree to bring us into contempt.'

By the 1860s, British tourists in Germany were so numerous that they were starting to annoy other British tourists. More fastidious Britons doing the Rhine were the first people ever to think up that wishful distinction, so popular today, between mere tourists and real travellers. They used exactly the same arguments that today's self-designated 'independent travellers' and 'adventurers' employ to make it clear that they are really, honestly *not* just more tourists:

A GLIMPSE AT WESTPHALIAN CITIES.

IT is a happy moment for the real traveller, as distinguished from the mere tourist, when he fairly feels himself out of the reach of his own countrymen. The real enjoyment and the real benefit of travel do not begin as long as you are in a region frequented by Englishmen, where you are liable to see English faces, to be spoken to in the English tongue, and to be half amused and half provoked at more or less successful attempts at adaptation to English ways. Till all this is left behind—English faces, English talk, and above all, English prices—one is not fairly in foreign parts. It is pleasant to feel oneself thrown on one's own resources, to live with the natives and as the natives, and to have to get on as one can with the real language of the country. A town thoroughly infested by tourists loses its own nationality without getting any other in exchange. And the thought is none the less true because it is somewhat selfish, that objects of the highest interest lose half their charm when all the world has seen them as well as oneself.

Like any modern *Lonely Planet* writer, the *Graphic*'s expert likewise urges his compatriots to find the *real* Germany, which he has helpfully recce'd in advance for them, where 'the foot of the wandering Englishman has scarcely ever trodden, and where, in consequence, a conversation book is almost a necessity'. He promises that such bold and genuine travellers will be rewarded by a sort of First Contact with cultural sights of incredible and even erotic strangeness:

> Our last sketch (No. 7) represents one of the numerous pleasure-gardens in the neighbourhood of Wurzburg, which are devoted principally to wine and beer-drinking. Will our fair readers be horrified if we tell them that here the ladies of Germany are to be seen imbibing liberal quantities of the delicious beverage; yes, positively in open daylight drinking beer in a public garden?

If you actually entered daringly into the social world of the locals, you might get a glimpse of something even more thrilling, 'the cotton ball-dresses of the fashionable *Frauleins* being cut with low necks, after the manner of the girls at some sailor's brothel in England, and the skins of the dear creatures as greasy and shiny as those of *Esquimaux*, rather than civilized Europeans.'[36]

If the sight of socially respectable women openly drinking beer by daylight in public gardens and displaying their sweaty décolletage, bordello fashion, was not enough for them, bored young Englishmen, then as now in search of dangerous physical activities rather than mere sightseeing, however titillating, had only to follow the German River to its source to find excitements of a kind either simply unavailable or punitively expensive back in the crowded, low-hilled Workshop of the World. They were as yet spared the notion, which has since made so much money for so many, that 'extreme sports' require special clothing or safety equipment:

> A man may pass six weeks in the Alps and get first-rate climbing for from £40 to £50, and he will require no outfit for the purpose except clothes, which he must have anywhere, and a few oddments in the

way of alpenstocks and the like, which cannot cost more than a few
shillings. What amount of exciting outdoor exercise could such a
man get in England at the same price? Six weeks' grouse-shooting or
deerstalking would do as well, no doubt, or perhaps even better; but
it would cost at the very least twice or three times as much, and
would involve all manner of trouble in making arrangements, and a
good deal of expense in the way of guns, dogs, &c.; whereas you may
leave London on Monday night, and be at the Eggischhorn or the
Riffel on the Friday, without asking leave of any human creature, and
without even making up your own mind about it till the Sunday
evening.[37]

Chaps ready to have a crack at the 'still-virgin Matterhorn' in tweeds
and decent brogues thought little of walking roughshod over local sen-
sibilities. Whether or not the British thought of themselves as mere
tourists, there is not much doubt what the Germans – those who were
not actually making their fortunes out of the 'English milch-cows'[38] –
thought of them. In one notorious case, a very well-connected British
officer, one Captain Macdonald, was arrested on the Prussian railways
following a dispute with a German about which seat was whose, and
the judge in Bonn felt moved to declare that 'the English residing or
travelling on the Continent were notorious for the rudeness, impudence and blackguardism of their conduct'.[39] When the British
residents of Bonn objected en masse and in writing to this accusation,
he fined the lot of them into the bargain, for daring to question
Prussian justice.

However, such rather brusque policing no more deterred Victorian
Britons from holidaying in, or at least passing through, the Prussian
Rhineland than it does modern Westerners from visiting, say, Thailand:
the tourist's eternal motto is that of Goethe's Egmont: 'Better a little lack
of freedom than a great disorder.'

After all, the British were in Germany to enjoy themselves, not to take
political notes. Once the sights were done and the sublime adequately
experienced, they preferred to remain unmolested by Germans, for, as
one guide confessed, 'The English traveller carries abroad with him

something of the Pharisee. He thanks God he is not as these foreigners; he does not put his knife in his mouth, he does not talk noisily.'[40]

At Homburg, or Baden, or Wiesbaden, or Ems, British visitors, promised *The Times*, will find a home from home, where they can escape such things: 'There are English houses here where English tastes and habits are consulted, and even English prejudices humoured; tables for English guests to sit at, gardens and *allées* for English saunterers to stroll in; meal times set apart for the English almost exclusively.'

Readers of the *Standard* were assured, on 25 August 1865, that at Homburg, 'English abound', that they would find 'celebrities in fashion, politics and science', and that even their servants would be properly catered for: 'At our hotel a table d'hote is provided for the English servants, of which about 60 sit down daily.' It was best to bring your own servants, after all, whatever the expense, for 'when we first came to the land, we were beset with the insane idea that it was possible to get the Thuringian maids to conform to English notions of cleanliness and propriety'.[41]

Once the British had sat down, decent servants and all, and made themselves at home, the first thing they did was, of course, organise their leisure time in the unique national way.

To us, the notion of organised sporting events is so familiar that it is hard to imagine just how strange a phenomenon this once was to non-Britons. Most well-bred Continentals still thought the notion of gentlemen engaging in violent physical games bizarre indeed.* Hunting and shooting was one thing, but gentlefolk otherwise dressed, and demanded that they be portrayed by their hired artists, in such a way as to emphasise the smallness and delicacy of their hands, feet, shoulders and suchlike: muscles, like tanned faces, were for the peasants who could hardly avoid getting them. Still, invested as it was with all the prestige of the *Pax Britannica*, British sporting culture in Victoria's heyday was as irresistibly attractive to some foreigners as American popular culture was in Eisenhower's. The nimbus of Britishness,

---

* In fact, the love of posh British males for contact sports was surprising even to British non-gentlemen: *General Jack's Diary* of 1915 records with amusement the outrage of the BEF's Other Ranks, who knew only 'association football', when their officers subjected them to the rough-housing of that bizarre minority sport, 'rugby football'.

though, tended rather to exercise its magnetism from the top down.*
The German correspondent, evidently a native, of the *Daily News*
writes on 3 August 1865:

> English sport is becoming the fashion with our aristocracy. Last week
> a cricket match of an All England eleven against the rest of Europe
> was played at Hombourg, where the season is now at its height, but
> it failed to attract the curiosity of the public; the peculiarities of the
> game are so little known in this country, and therefore very few per-
> sons are competent to judge of the respective merits of the cricketers.

The report of this unique England vs Europe cricket match in *The
Times* records that 'foreigners cannot yet be brought to understand
what they term *ce jeu feroce des criquettes*'. Indeed, not all the bemused
foreigners seem to have fully understood even the most basic and
ferocious fact of cricket: 'The prevailing impression amongst them
seems to be that the ball must be soft, consequently they are vastly
amused when anyone is struck by it.' This confusion between gentle,
gentlemanly pastimes and genuine, violent British sport led to an
unpleasant afternoon at the crease for one Anglophile Russian who
joined a scratch XI: 'He got terribly knocked about and afterwards
expressed his conviction that pursuits of the mind were preferable.'

Of course, not everyone was happy with the way the British simply
expected that everything should be done as if at home. Three days later,
at the races at Frankfort-on-the-Maine, as it was then called, 'complaints were heard that everything was arranged according to the
English taste and carried on in the English style'. But such comments
were hardly calculated to deter British visitors who, like today's upmarket Anglo-Saxon tourists, wanted foreignness, thrills and exoticism ...
up to a point.

> They limit themselves pretty much to each other's company, sit down
> to long breakfasts and still longer dinners, at their own late hours,

---

* As it still does, to the infinite cheer of London's elite estate agents.

and keep up a lazy, harmless, and *tant soit peu* drowsy talk about the last set come in or the last party gone off; about the merits and charges of various hotels, the best route to Zermatt, Bishop Colenso, the cattle disease, Bismarck, the gout, the waters, the waiters ...

In short, in the mid-1860s, the Rhineland and the Black Forest ticked for Victorian Britons exactly the boxes which prosperous folk today check when selecting foreign holidays: it was easy and safe to get to, your money went a long way and you could buy the guide books in advance; it was scenically spectacular, stuffed with ancient buildings and picturesquely backward, but not so as to actually threaten your health; it was efficiently policed; it offered outdoor activities you simply could not find, even if you could afford them, back home; it guaranteed hotels with proper comforts, delivered by a well-primed local tourist industry; you could even find your own national sports and spot celebrities from back home.

As for the natives who happened to populate the romantic picture, it was perhaps just as well not to look too closely: Henry Mayhew had just cast his unflinching gaze on the world of *London Labour and the London Poor*, but even he was shocked by Germany:

Now, to those who are in the habit of hurrying through Germany at the same rate as the Queen's messengers – and whose knowledge of the natives is consequently limited to such as are seen in Anglicized hotels – the view here given of the national character may appear somewhat harsh and prejudiced. Heaven knows we have seen poverty and wretchedness enough in our own land ! – for years we made the study of it, and the investigation of all its phases, a special vocation; nor did we fear, in order to work our purpose out, to fraternize with London beggars, and to mingle for many a day and night with London thieves. But we tell you, reader, we never saw such wretchedness, such squalor, such rude housing, such meanness in beggary, such utter want of truth and friendship in the terrible struggle to live, in the darkest dens, nor among the least luckless of the vagrants congregated in the British metropolis, as are to be found even in the families of the middle-class citizens of Saxony.[42]

How could one profitably expect to have any meaningful intercourse with such backward and wretched folk? If you were very lucky, you might fall in with 'Anglicised and accomplished Germans'[43] but in general the best a decent Englishman in Germany could do, if he insisted on leaving the tourist trail, was to act as a benevolent but strict schoolmaster on the road of progress, and

> to hold such a plain-speaking looking-glass in the face of these starv-
> ing, cringing, swaggering German folk, that they shall see themselves
> in the same despicable guise as an English gentleman beholds them;
> and feel how much they have to achieve – how much they have to
> learn – how much they have to alter, before they can pretend to take
> rank among the civilized nations of Europe.[44]

Perhaps one could also try to make them understand 'that from our little island-country the principles of enlightened humanity and government radiate like beams from a star'.[45]

Little wonder, then, that Britons were taken entirely aback when, in 1864, they found the whole of their favourite holiday destination up in arms – and themselves in the line of fire.

A confusing war

The war of 1863–4 (strictly speaking, it was two different wars) is always known as the Prussian-Danish or Dano-Prussian War today, which just shows how hindsight distorts history. We call it that because, to us, from here, it seems to fit neatly into a series of three with the Austro-Prussian and Franco-Prussian wars. No one, anywhere, called it that at the time, for the very good reason that the Prussians were at first nothing whatever to do with it.

The Schleswig-Holstein Question is still a byword for complexity among specialists in international law. Could a Danish king also be a German grand duke? Is a country's rule to be decided by hereditary claim? If so, in the male or female line? By established international treaty? By linguistic and cultural 'belonging', irrespective of whether or not its inhabitants actually want to 'belong'? By plebiscite? Or by mere *force majeure*? Palmerston famously claimed that only three people in the world had ever understood the Question: 'The Prince Consort, who is dead, a German professor, who has gone mad, and I myself – who have forgotten it.'

But however complex the Question seemed to Britons, to many Germans it was very simple: most of the Holsteiners and a substantial minority of the Schleswigers were Germans, but the Danes were trying to make out they were all Danish. Germany was having none of it. Not Prussia. *Germany*.

> The enthusiasm in favour of Schleswig-Holstein spreads to every country where there are Germans, or where the German language is spoken. Volunteers have arrived from the Russian provinces on the Baltic; they are being enrolled amongst the German residents in Paris; and numerous addresses to the committee from the towns of Switzerland by German residents and Swiss, promise every assistance in furtherance of the national ends.[46]

This is where things may start to feel very strange to us. For the Germans who invaded Schleswig-Holstein were not Prussian militarists at all. In fact, these particular Germans were the most hated and hating *enemies* of the Prussian court. They were liberal nationalists, and their dream was of a united, democratically governed Germany, based on the stillborn ideas of the 1848 revolution. They wanted to incorporate Schleswig and Holstein into the German Confederation, and they were certain that the royal, reactionary powers, led by Austria and Prussia, would betray the national cause and do a deal with the King of Denmark in the name of princely solidarity.

> The language of the papers is violent in the extreme. They openly accuse Austria and Prussia of treason to the Fatherland, and even commercial papers appeal to the public to abstain from Austrian and

Prussian loans, and from furnishing money for the subjection of
their countrymen.[47]

Here is the voice of German liberalism as it looked then:

> Die Regierung König Wilhelm's
> weigert sich, die Beschlüsse des Abgeordnetenhauses
> auszuführen. Wohlan, Du preußisches Volk! nimm
> Du, was jene zu thun sich sträubt, „in die eigene
> Hand" und führe die Beschlüsse Deiner Volksver-
> tretung aus mit allen Mitteln!

King William's government refuses to carry out the decisions of
parliament. Very well, you Prussian *volk*! Do what they refuse to do,
take things "into your own hands" and carry out the decisions of
your representatives with all the powers at your disposal!*

It's important to get this straight: this bold, liberal newspaper does *not*
mean, as we might suppose, that the *volk* should rise up in the name
of peace and poor little Denmark and overthrow the warmongering
Prussian court; on the contrary, it means that the *volk* should ignore
the reactionary Prussian monarchy and insist on invading Schleswig-
Holstein.

We have somehow come blithely to assume that people who call
themselves liberals and struggle against entrenched domestic elites for
a national democracy that will truly express what they see as the will
of the people must also be at heart pacific, tolerant and no threat to
their neighbours. This was no more necessarily true of the German liberals in 1864 than it is today of, say, the Syrian rebels.

We still find this muscular sort of national liberalism confusing. The
Victorian Britons certainly did, so it needs looking at carefully.

* *Freiburger Zeitung*, 20 January 1864.

The confusing German liberals

British liberalism in mid-Victorian times is very easy for us to imagine. We have merely to think of the USA in the halcyon years after 1989. Without any serious geopolitical rival, scornful of any alternative theory of progress, their homeland militarily impregnable, Britons happily imagined that the further liberalism extended in the world, the wider still and wider would be set the bounds of spiritual Englishness.

It was all so clear. The Royal Navy, able for half a century to laugh at or blow out of the water any possible challenger, would confine itself to abolishing the slave trade and enforcing free trade. Worldwide political reform would take place with minimal violence, the backward parties seeing that the game was up and throwing in the towel without too much last-ditchery, as seen in Britain's very own Glorious Revolution.* The world, liberated from oppressive regimes and irrational customs duties, would Buy British. History would end in peace, plenty and freedom for all.

The hungry, harassed, oppressed German liberals looked at Britain and wanted all they saw there. Being Victorian liberals, they too believed that prosperity and liberty were inextricably linked, and they were so fixated on Britain that they assumed such progress to require the whole British package, including a big navy and an overseas empire.[48]

They were, though, by no means inclined to gradualist reform. Schooled in Hegel's dialectics, they believed that progress came about through conflict, uprising and passionate, armed revolt, like that of 1813 against Napoleon. Hegel was no mere theoretician, either: he specifically lambasted the illusory 'freedom' of the British-style parliamentary system and crooned of 'the all-sustaining, all-resolving will of the State'.[49]

---

* This 'Whig History' of Britain somewhat downplayed the facts that the war between king and parliament had devastated Britain in the seventeenth century, that the Jacobites had scared the britches off Georgian England and its wee German lairdie as late as 1745, and that Ireland had been the scene of mind-numbing butcheries in 1789–90.

This was the most profound ideological difference between German and British liberalism, the root of what was to become the great culture clash of the Victorian world: the role of the state *vis à vis* the individual.

To British liberals, it was axiomatic that the less the pimply minions of bureaucracy interfered with, and taxed, the lives and businesses of the people, the better. Things in Germany were very different. There, as a Victorian observer put it, 'the principle of individualism has never attained the acceptance which it enjoys in England'.[50] While the German liberals did not accept Hegel's own handily prize-winning thesis that the current Royal Prussian State was the ultimate expression of the world spirit, and hence the end of history, they had no objection to the general idea that state power was an essentially more rational way of ordering things.[51] Many was the Young Hegelian who subscribed to the heady – or, as Nietzsche said in *Twilight of the Idols*, beery – vision of the ideal state as 'the power of reason actualising itself as will'.[52] Even Lassalle, Marx's great early rival as leader of the German workers, declared roundly that 'the State is God'.[53]

The most striking example of this essentially different attitude to state power was that the Prussian and German liberals did not in the least share the instinctive dislike of their British friends for having large numbers of soldiers hanging about the place. The most heated dispute in the Prussian Parliament in the early 1860s was on the question of who should man, and control, the barracks in Prussia – but that the barracks should be manned was not in dispute. The liberals disliked the Prussian Army not because it was a standing army, but because it was a strutting one: instead of a royal, professional, aristocratically run army, they were enthusiasts for an even bigger, parliamentary-run, short-service, militia-style army which was to be of and for the entire people, the *Landwehr* – the very name of which was loathed by all good Prussian military men.

British observers warned that 'be the natural qualities of the Teuton what they may, a vast military system cannot be imposed upon a nation without leaving a deep impress upon its character; and that to pass a whole people through a national army is not to civilize the military, but to militarize the civilian'.[54]

This profound, though in 1864 still largely hidden, ideological chasm between British and German conceptions of liberalism was driven at bottom by the simple fact that the British already *had* what the Germans *wanted*.

British liberals, sated, imagined that things were now more or less all for the best, and simply needed the wisely hesitant tinkerings of reform; hungry German liberals were convinced that radical change must ultimately be for the better, even if it might be violent in the moment.

It's no coincidence that radical Germans were among Darwinism's very earliest adopters, as Darwin himself gratefully noted.[*] They were the great revisionists of Europe, the dynamic and modernising force intent on re-drawing our mental, social and political maps, the better to agree with what they saw as scientific revelations. Karl Marx – who, of course, also venerated Darwin – is merely the most famous and extreme propagator of this basic philosophy, which was very widely held indeed in the Germany of his day.

This was the great fault line between British and German liberalism: a basically positive view of the state combined with a radicalism based on allegedly natural laws.

What is the German's fatherland?

The most far-reaching of the supposed laws beloved of German liberals was the one which said that all people who spoke the same language belonged together, and were essentially different from everyone else, being linked by deep, if mysterious, roots of collective experience, and that in order to live fully they must have their own, politically distinct state. This theory goes largely unquestioned today, and is particularly important to so-called 'small nations', but it was

---

* In March 1861, scarcely a year after *On the Origin of Species* was published, he wrote: 'The support which I received from Germany is my chief ground for hoping that our views will ultimately prevail' (Peter Watson, *The German Genius*, Simon & Schuster, London, 2010, p. 427).

once a brand-new idea, developed in Germany as a last, desperate redoubt of national survival.

If there is one thing worse than a vast and terrible war, it is a war which is vast, terrible and inconclusive. By the end of the seventeenth century, most parts of Europe had had their gunpowder plots and civil wars, their reformations and regicides, their unions and partitions, their inquisitions, their St Bartholomew's Day massacres, and so on, and had more or less bloodily worked out arrangements whereby the government and the people of a certain political territory generally spoke the same language and overwhelmingly followed the same rite of Christianity. People who spoke French and Spanish lived in places called France and Spain and were almost certainly Catholic; people who spoke Swedish and English lived in places called Sweden and England and were almost certainly Protestants.

In Germany, though, the Thirty Years War was fatally indecisive, despite having laid the country utterly to waste in a way whose brutal completeness is hard to exaggerate: most experts agree that it devastated the place, and its people, far more thoroughly even than all the bombs, tanks and massacres of 1944–5.

After the peace of sheer exhaustion that was agreed in 1648, there was a broad space of Europe which was generally admitted to be vaguely German, but which was split into countless tiny states, none of which had 'Germany' in their title, and in each of which the official state religion was Catholic or Protestant, depending entirely on the individual ruler. By two of the normal yardsticks of modern European nationhood – defined location and shared confession – the Germans simply did not know who they *were*.

Dazzled by the French hegemony of the long eighteenth century, Germany's ruling houses and aristocrats aped French manners, mulcted their citizenry to build ruinously expensive copies of Versailles, and even took to speaking French among their own. In the 1770s, middle-class German thinkers began to rebel, and to look to England for other models – but then things got even worse. After Austerlitz and Jena, all Germany lay prostrate before Napoleon; her undisputed cultural leader, Johann Wolfgang von Goethe, proudly wore the Légion d'honneur given to him personally by the man he publicly called 'my Emperor'.*

With their backs to the wall, German thinkers concentrated on the only thing left: it did not matter, they claimed, what you believed, or under whose rule you lived – it only mattered what you *spoke*.

If your mother tongue was German, you thought and felt German, hence you *were* German. And since the rulers of Germany were so Frenchified and even francophone, the real mighty fortress of Germanness was to be found not in the cultural elite, but in the language, the stories, the ways of the everyday *volk*. This conflation of the ancient Greek concepts *ethnos* (roughly: 'the nation') and *demos* (roughly: 'the common people') remains among the most troublesome innovations in modern thought.[†] Almost every deep thinker on Earth now seems to accept the idea that 'folk-stories', whether those of our own ancestors or of Australian aborigines, are not mere relics of an entertaining or shocking rural idiocy, but a source of deep, forgotten, pre-rationalist wisdom: certainly, there are times when the worship of Modernity needs a shot across the bows, but it is worth remembering that the adoration of 'folk wisdom' was more or less entirely invented by German Romantics of the late eighteenth and early nineteenth centuries, for very specific reasons.

So the idea that all Germans – that is, everyone who spoke any dialect of German – naturally belonged together was originally a last-ditch defensive plan for the cultural survival of a threatened nation. Unfortunately, it was riddled with strange implications as soon as it was applied to a real, post-Napoleon Europe in which there were very many Germans being threatened with cultural extinction by no one at all and kept apart only by their own princelings.

Where did the Germans who spoke East Frisian stop and the Flemings or eastern Dutch, who spoke something remarkably similar,

---

* Napoleon I was a genuine fan of Goethe: he declared that *The Sorrows of Young Werther* had been his favourite book in youth and that he had read it six or seven times.

† Michael Mann argues that this is the root of 'The Dark Side of Democracy'. In German history the most modern, and famous example of the glide from one meaning to another came in 1989: East German demonstrators at first wanting merely to reform East Germany carried banners appealing to the government on the socialistic grounds that 'We are the Common People!' ('Wir sind das Volk') but within days were swamped in the nationalistic cry 'We are one People!' ('Wir sind ein Volk').

start? What of a place like Prague, whose political allegiance, visible culture and street names were all German, even though its population was fast becoming Slavic? What of Schleswig and Holstein? What of the Baltic states, which had never been politically German and where the vast majority of people had never been Germans, but where a particular caste of German military aristocrats had run things for over six centuries? At least some of the Alsatians and Lorrainers spoke German and their lands had once undeniably been part of that sort-of-Germany, the Holy Roman Empire, so should they not be Germans again, once the liberals' longed-for new Reich actually came into being? Surely the Dutch (and, handily enough, their empire) were really Deutsch?

One thing was certain: the liberal notion of Germany's natural and scientific borders extended to the mouth of the Rhine and across its banks, to the Baltic states and the banks of the Danube – sometimes beyond even that. One prominent liberal of 1848 'proclaimed that he would only accept a Prussian hereditary emperor on condition of an immediate declaration of war that would carry the borders of Germany to the shores of the Black Sea'.[55] To most radical Germans, famously including Karl Marx until quite late in his career, it was perfectly obvious that the 'world-historical' people, the people who were driving things forward in Middle Europe, were they themselves. Therefore, the best thing for progress would be for the 'non-historical peoples' of the region to embrace the future and *become* Germans – i.e. make sure that their children's first language was German – as quickly as possible. This was exactly the choice made by so many middle-European Jews after 1870. The alternative was to mess with the inevitable unfolding of progress by succouring or re-inventing backward, doomed non-cultures like Judaism, Polishness or Czechness – thus becoming not merely an enemy of Germany, but a gratuitous block to History Itself.

With this vague equation of Germandom and progress, the intellectual construct of German liberalism allowed for huge cloudy symbols of some even greater unification which would embrace not only everyone who could conceivably be called German at present, but also anyone at all imbued with the true, inner essence of Germandom.[56] As the incessantly quoted couplet by Emanuel Geibel put it:

And thus the German spirit may
　　heal all mankind, some future day.*

And why not? The German liberals had, right before their eyes, a concrete example of a vast conglomerate of peoples welded into a single belonging by a great act of liberal-national willpower, which spawned free trade, parliaments, progress, cricket pitches, naval bases and race courses everywhere it went, as inevitably as the legions of Rome had brought forth bath houses, roads and hypocausts: the British Empire.

Well? Germany was clearly related to Britain in terms of linguistic-cultural heritage, and was a long-time ally of Britain, with twice the population: why should she not one day be equally great in every respect?[57]

The dream of a navy

The British thing which the German liberals wanted most of all was a big navy.

The 1848 all-German revolutionaries in the Frankfurt Parliament were notoriously unable to agree on anything. But, in fact, they did agree almost to a man on one thing: the need for an imperial fleet. The President of that doomed assembly cut short debate on the issue simply because, he said, the arguments were already so well known. The vote came in a sole voice short of a unanimous 'yea'.[58] In a glorious piece of reverse logic, a pamphlet of 1861 declared that since only a united Germany could bring about a German navy, the existence of a German navy would be proof of a united Germany.[59]

The liberals remained obsessed with their non-existent navy after the defeat of the 1848–9 revolution.† In 1865 Bismarck himself

---

* 'Und es mag am deutschen Wesen/Einmal noch die Welt genesen' (author's translation).
† Historians have ignored the plain evidence of their eyes on this question. Even Paul Kennedy's magisterial *Rise of the Anglo-German Antagonism* tells us that by 1880 only nameless 'other nationalists' in Germany had even begun 'to speculate upon the acquisition of colonies and a navy' (p.36). This is quite extraordinarily off the mark, and it really does make you think that even the best historians have blinded themselves by looking too much at Tirpitz.

declared that the German Navy had been 'the most important object of public debate for more than twenty years'.[60] He put this insight into tactical practice with his usual cunning, and transferred the tiny Royal Prussian Navy to the North German Confederation in 1867, causing – as well he knew it would – rejoicing among his erstwhile enemies that was out of all rational proportion to the actual event: one of their leaders announced that 'Germany has at least attained unity on the sea'.[61]

The vision of a mighty German navy was especially strong among one special community of Germans: the liberal émigrés in Britain. These political exiles were exposed at first hand to the full glories of British liberalism *triumphans* and their enthusiasm meant that when national agitation for a powerful navy revived in the early 1860s, it was German voices from London that led the way:

> On the free soil of England, under the ennobling influence of Britons' sense of their power and pride, at the sight of a fleet which unfurls its flag to protect and nurture this land; when we feel the daily shame of our powerlessness and unprotectedness, then we understand the full importance of the Movement [i.e. for a navy] in our homeland.[62]

> In England, which in its internal freedom and its outward expansion is so unique among nations, the German truly feels the shame which results from the shattering and division of our fatherland.[63]

England's glory was not to do with the English being better than the Germans: it was simply the result of a geographically natural impulse to seafaring. This theory was hailed in the 1990s as a wonderfully new explanation of the alleged historical fact (which now seems a little doubtful) that seagoing and free-marketing countries attain world power and others (i.e. China) do not, so it's worth hearing the 1869 version:

> When one thinks how irresistibly the English people were pushed into the way of trade and seafaring by their oceanic situation, one sees in

this grand display no moral achievement but simply the self-evident result of circumstance ... Germany too has a coast with great ports and though as yet we have no navy, we too have a mighty merchant fleet on every river and on all the oceans ... Perhaps it is simply that we have thus far sadly lacked a national government which will take marine matters seriously and address the lack of a German fleet.[64]

If Germany only had a truly *national* government which cared about her lack of a fleet, she might do just as well as Britain.

The heady vision of one day being real equals with their superb, world-bestriding, ocean-going Anglo-Saxon cousins could inspire liberal German navalists of the fractious 1860s to Wagnerian fantasies even when writing articles on such apparently mundane subjects as 'The German School of Seamanship in Hamburg'. Germany might be as yet divided and weak, but if you looked at things rightly, she already had a sort of racial stake in things which needed simply to be realised, and which no one could prevent – not even England. The double edge of the writer's feelings towards his supposed relations is perfectly obvious:

Despite the insistence of England against the fortification of Kiel, Germany will in a short time possess a fleet, a powerful fleet ... The Germanic race is destined by fate to rule the world. She is physically and mentally privileged above all other races, and half the Earth is virtually subject to her. England, America and Germany: these are the three branches of the mighty Germanic tree.[65]

There was, quite simply, no break at all in the continuity of this liberal desire for a mighty fleet. In 1899, when the fatal Second Navy Law was being debated in the Reichstag, one of the most potent voices in its favour was that of Johannes Versmann, political boss of the famously free-thinking, free-trading, Anglophile, anti-Prussian Free State of Hamburg, who had publicly championed such a fleet ever since 1861.[66] In those same debates, Prince Hohenlohe reminded foot-dragging liberals in the Reichstag that the revolutionaries of

1848 had longed for a big fleet and that the demand 'arose from the people'.

Of course, it comes as a surprise to think that the German *liberals* might have been the great instigators of the Anglo-German rivalry. Liberals are supposed to be a Good Thing, after all, are they not? Victorian Britons assumed that people who struggled against their feudal elites intended gratefully to fit in with the beneficent rules of the *Pax Britannica* (which, in truth, had itself been established through buccaneering aggression, economic might and sheer fire-power). It would take another three decades for it truly to dawn on Britons that those loudly Anglophile German liberals saw themselves not as the sidekicks of the British Empire, but as its heirs.

This subterranean history of German liberalism, as inconvenient to us today as it was baffling to the Victorians, has been lost on today's historians, who happily blame the whole Anglo-German antagonism on those villains straight from central casting, the scar-faced, sabre-rat-tling Prussian Junkers.

So who were these Junkers really, and what did they want?

The Bad Germans?

The Prussian Junkers were not a class, but a caste. They dwelled as extended families in isolated and often virtually self-sufficient Big Houses, most of which are now mere ruins in Poland, or even Russia, laying down the law to a peasantry not simply dirt poor but often actually foreign by nation and religion. They thus saw with peculiar clarity that without their very own state to back them up, they were doomed. And since they did not copy the ruthlessly property-concentrating British scheme of primogeniture, there were an awful lot of them with nothing much to their names apart from vast pride and ancient titles. The Royal Prussian Army was the one thing that made their individual lives financially sustainable and their caste's future secure.

A writer explained things in Prussia to his fellow Victorian Britons thus:

> As all the sons of a count are born counts and all his daughters countesses, the result is remarkably numerous nobility, richer in title than in worldly goods ... endeavouring to make up by stern uncompromising hauteur for the real grandeur in which it is deficient ... All nobles enter the army and have to work too hard at their profession to have leisure for amusement, even if they had the spare capital, which considering that the majority are as poor as rats, they certainly have not.[67]

The Times agreed: Germany had 'an aristocracy at once poor and well-educated, and disdainful of any work but that of then public service. The sons of a German Baron would scorn to become Traders, or even, as a rule to enter any of the more intellectual professions. They go into the Army as a matter of course.'[68]

The army the Prussian Junkers went into was a very special one. Thanks to the legendary reputation it was soon to win, it is very easy to forget that in 1864 the Prussian Army struck terror into absolutely no one except its own recalcitrant citizens.

Since Waterloo, the British, French, Austrian, Russian and even the new Italian armies had all done full-scale, pitched and bloody battle against respectable European opposition; the Prussian Army had merely policed the Prussian people and made the other North Germans nervous. Its sole attempt at the usual military activities had resulted in a retreat from confrontation with Austria at the memorably named Humiliation of Olmütz. For half a century, the only real purposes of the Prussian Army had been to keep its country quiet and its gentry in employment.

The Junkers were a famously narrow-minded lot, and Britain was not even in their line of sight. They only wanted to keep their Prussia strong, the price of their grain up, their liberals down, their Russian neighbours onside and their *volk* tugging its collective forelock – for the word '*volk*' meant, to the Junkers, simply the hoi polloi, German or Polish, Catholic or Protestant, not a deep and mystical well of national whatnot. They wished neither to emulate nor to overtake Britain, and remained to the end essentially uninterested in – quite often, actually opposed to – an overseas empire or a big navy.*

In fact, the idea of a mighty Imperial German Navy was not only nothing to do with the Junkers, it was such an obsession to German liberals *precisely because* it was nothing to do with the Junkers.

A naval officer does not spend his life in a barracks town, bossing the sons of the people about, ruining their daughters, clanking around in spurs, poor but overweening, daring any mere prosperous civilian to look him in the eye or cross his path: he boldly flies the flag in safely far-off lands, paving the way for trade and colonisation. And he must be more than just a gentleman. The Prussian Army, like some other armies until very recently indeed, could happily make use of junior officers whose main qualifications were breeding, manners and an eagerness to risk their necks. But a modern *navy* was utterly different. If you wanted your steam-powered, iron-cased leviathans to even make the next port, never mind engage an enemy vessel at extreme range, there was simply no place on board for officers without at least some degree of real, modern, technical education.

Non-Junker, all-German, British-style, trade-oriented, modernising, imperial and technocratic: the navy was the perfect stuff of liberal-nationalist dreams.

So the fact is that when it comes to the roots of the great Anglo-German confrontation, we can pretty well leave the Junkers out of it. They were a selfish, brutal and personally murderous lot if their Prussian toes were remotely trodden on; their militarism infected all German society after 1870; but they *cannot* be blamed for the rivalry with Britain which turned the European war of 1914 into the Great War.

---

* On 22 March 1898, when Wilhelm II announced to his Staatsministerium that he wished to make Admiral Tirpitz a Prussian minister of state, Miquel, the Minister of Finance, objected vainly on the grounds that 'the Navy Office is, of all the Imperial bodies, the one which has the least to do with Prussian interests'. Wilhelm himself complained more than once that Prussian generals treated every penny spent on *his* navy, which he commanded all the time, as one taken from *their* army, of which he was commander in chief only in time of war.

In that story, the central question is this: what transformed the mid-Victorian German liberal admiration of England into the almost pathological dislike which is traced in the pages of Heinrich Mann's immortal satire *Man of Straw*?*

There's no mystery here, for the tragedy started at a quite identifiable moment. In late 1863, liberal German dreams of a British-style future came up against something that was already real and existing: liberal Britain itself.

The grand disillusion of 1864

The German liberals regarded Schleswig and Holstein as naturally German, and were ready to make them so by force of arms. At this time, however bizarre it may sound to us, they feared that Bismarck, whom they called 'the Junkers' minister', would simply restore the hated status quo given half a chance, thus betraying the quest for the grail of German unity. They also assumed that Britons – the great sponsors of national liberation movements in Europe, after all – would naturally support their admiring German cousins.

They were wrong. When Britons watched the invasion of Schleswig-Holstein by the Confederate German forces – no Prussians at all were at first involved – they did not see fellow liberals trying to give a natural, scientifically justified and progressive new shape to the old, irrational, feudal map of Europe. They saw, rather, a small country just across the sea being bullied by a large country which intended to tear up a solemn international treaty mainly, so Lord Palmerston and the future Lord Salisbury both already suspected, in order to gain a naval base in Britain's very backwater.[69]

So, for once, liberal Britain did not support a movement for national unity in Europe, but instead backed a treaty which was, to liberal

---

* Niall Ferguson rightly cites this great book as a splendid source, but wrongly dates it to 1918 (*The Pity of War*, p. 17). Actually, it began to appear in 1914, making it a truly extraordinary act of artistic insight, not one of mere hindsight.

Germans, self-evidently unjust and unnatural. Britain hoped that Austria and Prussia, as 'responsible powers', would intervene to 'take matters out of the hands of the democracy', democracy being still a Bad Thing in 1864, and 'transfer them to European diplomacy'.[70] In pursuit of these hopes, Britain's liberal politicians loudly, if vaguely, signalled that the *Pax Britannica* wished to maintain the London Protocol of 1852.

Liberal Germans felt horribly betrayed by the power to which they had always looked up. Like all unrequited love, that of Germany for liberal Britain could switch easily to hate:

> England will hardly undertake an 'over-hasty step' against Germany without the support of France. We entertain far greater fear of Austria and Prussia than we do of the English threats ... England is the only Power which has to fear the union of the Duchies with Germany, because such an union offers the possibility of Germany rising to a naval power dangerous to English supremacy.[71]

British liberals were completely unprepared for this outburst of hostility. Suddenly, it seemed that these rather absurd Germans might actually consider themselves as potential rivals to Britain herself:

> The great majority of the German nation believe the honour and interests of their country to be inextricably involved in the triumph of the Augustenburg succession. They think that the opponent cause is firmly maintained only by England, which does so, say the more excited and unreasonable partisans of Prince Frederick, mainly because she dreads the commercial rivalry of Germany should she become possessed of the ports and coasts of Schleswig and Holstein. This will excite a smile in England, but it is an article of faith with numbers of Germans.[72]

The English might smile, but the Germans were furious. It was now plain that John Bull was merely self-seeking, for all his universalist cant. He would happily break his own rules if it meant preventing free competition from a united Germany.

Not only was John Bull a hypocrite – he was also, it turned out, a fat and impotent one. Britain's policy was memorably described by Disraeli as 'menaces never accomplished and promises never fulfilled', because when Prussia and Austria entered the fray together, Britain's bluff was resoundingly called. For a heady moment, it seemed to German nationalists that all Germans were at last united in one cause, with Britain the only power trying – vainly! – to block her legitimate aspirations.

Here are some images from that summer taken from the liberal *Kladderadatsch*, the Berlin equivalent of *Punch*:

Russell. Ich steh' dir bei, Hannemann, wenn sie dir was thun wollen. Aber erst werd' ich sie recht aufschreien; vielleicht thun sie dir dann nichts — was mir noch viel lieber wäre.

The title is 'Russell in the Lion-skin, or Don't Take Fright'. Inside his lion-skin, whose belt reads 'Britannia', the Foreign Secretary, Lord Russell (with a large bank-account book at his back and trading wares stacked behind him), says: 'I shall stand by you, Hannemann [i.e. the Danish leader] if they do anything to you. But first I'll roar really loudly, and then maybe they won't do anything – which I would like much better.'

This one is entitled 'The Effects of a Shot' and is ironically subtitled 'Dedicated to his long-time friend John Bull by Michel'. The caption reads: 'What smashes through entrenchments and destroys walls will surely be able to tear up a little sheet of paper!'

An asthmatic John Bull/British Lion (as ever with his trading wares in sight and backed by *The Times* as tattered scarecrow) bemoans the fact that 'I can open my mouth as wide as I like, no one listens to me!'

„So oft es sich trifft, daß ein Gentleman auf offener Straße von einem Lumpen beleidigt, und dieser von Ersterem gezüchtigt wird, wird man finden, daß der Pöbel stets für den Lumpen Partei ergreift."

(Aus dem Englischen des Fielding.)

Henry Fielding is quoted against his own countrymen: 'Whenever a gentleman [i.e. Germany] is insulted in a public street by a ruffian [i.e. Denmark], and drubs him for his pains, you will find that the rabble [John Bull, *Punch* and *The Times* as fishwife] always takes the ruffian's side.'

John Bull (to the amusement of Napoleon III) is given a Germanic black eye when, *The Times* under his arm, he tries to intrude on the 'Theatre of War – Private Function'.

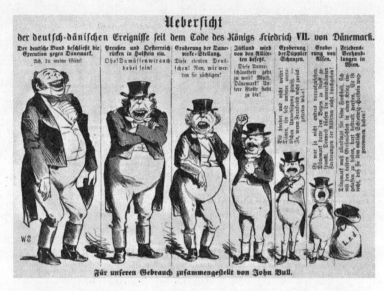

In this 'Overview of German–Danish relations since the death of King Frederick VII of Denmark, arranged for our use by John Bull', Britain's position over the seven frames is: (i) amused disbelief that mere Germany would dare challenge Denmark, (ii) outrage that she has been excluded by Prusso-Austrian action, (iii) threatening to punish 'these wretched Germans', (iv) promising naval support to Denmark, (v) blaming France for not supporting her, (vi) swiftly back-pedalling, and (vii) the revelation of Britain's real nature – a mere hypocritical sack of money which, to maintain trade, will desert its allies and trim whichever way the wind blows.

The liberal readership of *Kladderadatsch* clearly enjoyed the spectacle of overbearing, arrogant Britain being brought down a peg or two by a suddenly almost united Germany. The seminal *Prussian Yearbook*, at this time still resolutely liberal, declared that 'England is now deservedly a wretched and hateful example', but that 'even in these days of righteous outrage about England's policy on the Schleswig-Holstein Question, Germans will not be distracted from learning from the wielder of the trident when it comes to the building-up of sea-power'.[73]

There was one very non-liberal man for whom this sudden change in liberal perceptions of Britain was absolute meat and drink. He was to be the decisive actor in the Anglo-German drama for the next twenty-five years: Otto von Bismarck.

The press baron vs his internal Englanders

Before Bismarck was much else of note, he made himself a master of that new phenomenon which was changing Victorian politics as radically, as rapidly and as unpredictably as social media are changing our own: the mass-read newspaper.

Just how much his extraordinary career depended on his systematic manipulation of the press has largely gone forgotten.[74] It was perfectly clear to the pressmen of Victorian Britain, though. One of the greatest of them, Frederick Greenwood, founder of the *Pall Mall Gazette*, described Bismarck's tactics in a way which any decent twenty-first-century political spin doctor would immediately recognise: 'Carefully to put aside this or that document, carefully to reserve this or that "revelation," for publication in the newspapers at the right moment, is a habit with Prince Bismarck, and one of his best known methods of working.'[75]

It all started in the revolutionary year of 1848. Realising that the winds of change were blowing, and that the press was their medium-to-be, Bismarck helped to found the *Neue Preussische Zeitung*. Always known as the *Kreuz-Zeitung* because of the Iron Cross on its masthead, it was aimed specifically to counteract democratic ideas: it was to be an organ agitating with ruthless severity against revolution and democracy, and it hoped to spread a sort of one-nation monarchical Prussianism.[76] Next, in the 1850s, Bismarck was a central figure in the cabal responsible, under General von Manteuffel, for spiking, bribing and cajoling the newly abundant German press.

Britain offered him the clearest example of the power of this new force: in a letter of 1 February 1856, he wrote that in Britain 'the press-pack run the country' ('die Pressbengel führen das Regiment'). Almost his first act on taking power in 1862 was to set up his very own press organ, the *Provincial Correspondence*, whose title and distributive model were both lifted directly from Britain. Despite the unpromising title, this journal was centrally important to Bismarck's campaign. Where the British version was merely a governmental fact sheet, sent out across the whole land, Bismarck's was a political instrument. Funded directly by government, and controlled personally by Bismarck, the *Provincial Correspondence* had a print run of 150,000 copies weekly, which made it by a country mile the biggest newspaper in all divided Germany. Just as importantly, it was able directly to supply the columns and indirectly to guide the editorial line of many other German newspapers.

Government money to spend on the press came officially and openly to Bismarck as *Ministerpräsident* of Prussia. How he disposed of it was up to none but him. It included a large budget for the dissemination of official government announcements in the press: by awarding, withholding or shifting these lucrative adverts, he could reward or punish editors and owners. The system was described in detail a little later by *The Times*:[77]

> Prince Bismarck is known to have the unlimited command of several metropolitan newspapers, some official and acknowledged, others unofficial and unacknowledged, but all of them equally deriving their cue from the great Premier. To guard against misconstruction, let it be clearly understood that the organs coming under the latter category are not necessarily dependent upon the Prince's bounty. They are, on the contrary, the property of private individuals eager to oblige the Prince, and anxious to build up a political future for themselves with a profusion of printers' ink. Yet as none of these papers have a sufficient party to back them, or a public to subscribe and advertise in them, their serving as a mouthpiece to the leading Minister is their sole *raison d'être*.

When Victorian journalists talked about Bismarck, they meant exactly what they said: *Bismarck*, the man himself, not some vague gang of his supporters or a government department working under his name. And they were perfectly right, for he personally micro-managed both the organs he controlled directly and the many others he was able to influence or bribe.

Just how hands-on Bismarck's involvement was can be seen in his dealings with the one-time radical liberal and future doyen of German anti-Semitism, Wilhelm Marr. In January 1864, Marr claimed that he would and could, for 2,000 thalers, turn a certain newspaper into a supporter of Prussia's annexationist plans in Denmark. The offer was made through a coded newspaper advert, and Bismarck replied in kind before allowing Marr to call on him in person. No grant was awarded at the meeting – but somehow the money then appeared at Marr's disposal and the paper duly began to advocate Bismarck's plans.[78]

Not content with his substantial government funding, in 1866 Bismarck expropriated the gold reserves from the conquered state of Hanover to expand his bribery of the press. The Guelph Fund, as it was known – it was more often called simply 'the reptile fund' – was a colossal sum, equal to about 3 per cent of all the British government's annual spending at the time.[79] Money like that could buy an awful lot of column inches, and Bismarck himself ensured that all receipts were burned annually, making the payments impossible to trace and keeping the fund officially non-existent, though widely known of, until 1893.[*][80]

Bismarck was so obsessed with the press because, as one of our greatest academic historians puts it, he 'refused to be trapped into counter-revolutionary adventures no longer sustainable in the more complex bourgeois society Germany was becoming'.[81] In normal English: Bismarck realised that the days were gone when one could settle the hash of the German Diet in Frankfurt or the Prussian Parliament in Berlin by simply sending in one's loyal, royal, rural troops to crush the urban radicals. It had worked in 1848, and Bismarck, right to the end, never quite dropped the attractive idea of a military coup d'état, but in his heart he knew that if it came to that pass again, his side might well lose.

Things had gone too far: the German longing for national unity and reform was now an irresistible force. If royal Prussia did not ride that wave, the liberal nationalists would, and the feudal Prussia that

---

* It was later suspected that after Bismarck's fall, Kaiser Wilhelm used the Guelph Fund for his personal extravagances. See *Boston Evening Transcript* 16 September 1897.

Bismarck loved would simply disappear from the face of the earth, dissolved into Germany – just as Prince Albert had planned.

This danger stared Bismarck in the face at every meeting of the Prussian Crown Council, for his very own future sovereign, Crown Prince Friedrich, married to the vociferously British daughter of Victoria and Albert, was openly inclined to a liberal, constitutionalist Greater German future – so openly that Bismarck at times clearly suspected Friedrich of virtually acting under orders from Britain, via his wife or Sir Robert Morier.*

From 1864 until 1888, Bismarck was obsessed with neutering this Anglophile liberalism in Germany.

The fatal theory

Bismarck was able to call upon a uniquely sophisticated and prestigious theoretical underpinning for his campaign.

None other than Hegel himself, that great mystificator of the Forces of History and suchlike, who is still adored by all who love making up grand theories about culture and politics, had, when feeling more earthly, developed two practical ideas which were extraordinarily helpful to Bismarck.

The first Hegelian proposition was that if you allowed mere 'resolutions issuing from majorities' to interfere with the 'all-resolving, all-sustaining will of the State' in central matters like the annual budget – in other words, if you allowed parliament to control the executive – 'there would no longer be any government, only parties';[82] the second was that the Royal Prussian State was an 'organic' whole – so long as nothing 'from outside' was lodged within that body politic.

---

* It has to be said that this was not merely paranoia. Friedrich was indeed very close to Morier and their meetings were at times of a pretty clandestine nature – at one time of great diplomatic sensitivity, Friedrich and Morier met for several hours at a railway station in the (vain, naturally) attempt to evade Bismarck's spies.

Together, these two notions vouchsafed the incendiary argument that German liberals, if excessively liberal – e.g. if they tried to control the budget – were, in a profound sense, not really *German* at all.*[83]

This article from the *Kreuz-Zeitung*, pregnantly titled 'Shylock's Deed', makes precisely that argument:

> We are not yet nearly torn apart enough, not dissolved enough, not decadent enough, to take any pleasure or interest in this parliamentary mechanism. Though we have a parliament, we are no parliamentary *volk*; we are and will stay a monarchical *volk*, no matter how many constitutional babblers come to us from outside, to enjoy Prussia's blessings, no matter how many constitutional babblers, who will remain forever outsiders amongst us, stick their literary noses into our business.[84]

It is fairly obvious which nation was meant by 'outside'. To Bismarck, Britain was the patron saint, or even the actual sponsor, of this deadly liberal Enemy Within – and thanks to Hegel's arguments, the German liberals could be accused of being some sort of spiritual quasi-Englanders. It was a tactic Bismarck and his would-be heirs would use again and again over the next four decades – and it was to take German politics into very muddy waters indeed.

Bismarck leaps on the bandwagon

To Bismarck, the German liberals' sudden indignation at Britain, their long-time model, was a heaven-sent opportunity. It gave him the chance to show that, as Hegel had argued, British-style parliamentary liberty was fundamentally foreign to Germany.

---

* These notions are still central to every dictator who fears genuine democracy: 'opponents must be traitors not only to the ruling clique or family, but to the nation' (Nick Cohen, the *Observer*, 10 June 2012).

The level of anti-British invective in Bismarck's very own *Provincial Correspondence* in the summer of 1864 was so extraordinary that it is tempting to believe that Bismarck would have welcomed an actual shooting war. After all, he said on the very battlefield of Düppel that he was not afraid of England, and that a foreign war would be less risky than the threat of an internal German revolution.[85] This was an age when forms were adhered to rigidly and the mere suggestion of a public diplomatic rebuff (as manufactured by Bismarck in 1870) could be a *casus belli*. If statements like this had come openly from the Chief Minister of Prussia, rather than being handily disguised as journalistic opinion, Britain would have felt obliged to respond with physical measures:

The Hopes of the Danes

Which since the start of the war have been especially based on the idea of help from England, have been bitterly disappointed. After the English ministers had declared for weeks that England would come to Denmark's aid should the war break out again, they have now left their protégé completely in the lurch and have explained to their parliament that there is no reason to become involved in the war. As if to mock themselves, they add: if the Prussians should bombard Copenhagen and take away the Danish king as a prisoner, England would then at least have to ponder whether the time to interfere had not come. In all Europe there is but one voice of scorn and derision at England's behaviour – once so arrogant, now so wretched. The Poles last year and this year the Danes having been so perfidiously encouraged by English ministers into baseless hopes, people will at last see clearly what worth they may set on such friendship.[86]

A few weeks later, Bismarck's paper proclaimed the need for, and fudged the difference between, a Prussian-German fleet in language calculated to appeal to liberals, and which is almost an exact pre-echo of that used by Kaiser Wilhelm II thirty years later:

A Great Cause for Guilt

If only Prussia had a greater fleet! This is a wish which echoes around all Prussia and Germany, and which doubtless falls as a great weight of guilt into many a soul in our Fatherland.

How many costly sacrifices would we have been spared and how much more secure still would be our hopes of eventual success against Denmark, if we had, as well as our wonderful Army, sea-power which could powerfully chase the Danes into the heart of their land.

Only if Prussia already had a larger fleet could the scorn of our cunning enemy be fully broken! ... We could impose, in Copen-hagen, the peace over which we are now forced, in London, to haggle and deal over with an ill-inclined Europe.

But why do we still not have the fleet we need? The simple answer is: **because the best attempts of the government have been lamed and hamstrung, here too, by the plans and plots of the so-called Progressive Party in parliament.**

Bismarck's message was ringingly clear: Britain, however much she might champion other national liberation movements, would hypo-critically oppose German unification for fear of a competitor. And however powerful she had been, and thought she still was, Britain was now in fact too weak, too cowardly or too money-obsessed to back her clear and public wishes with bold deeds, even when the con-flict was just across the seas of which she grandly claimed exclusive dominance.

Now, what kind of a model was a country of hypocritical, cowardly shopkeepers for any self-respecting German nationalist? If you wanted national unity, true Germanness and a powerful navy, why not look nearer to home – to heroic Prussia?

The scene set

The year 1864 has largely been lost in the more dramatic smoke of later history, but set the scene for what was to follow in a remarkably precise way.

German notions about Britain which we might usually call 'Wilhelmian' are seen here, fully formed, well before Wilhelm was out of short trousers. In the Berlin press of 1864, John Bull is already portrayed as a money-bagged braggart with no guts for real action, and the British Lion is already a paper tiger, a moth-eaten, wheezy beast with a big mouth but no teeth.

As for Britons, the year 1864 ended with a lurking sense of shame. *Punch* tried to reassure its readers that Germany was simply not worth bothering about to the extent of actual war.*

Jack on the Crisis. 'Blow it, Bill! We can't be expected to *fight* a lot o' lubberly swabs like him. We'll *kick* 'em, if that'll do.'

* Compare the depiction of this German with that from 1902, on p. 368. The character the two British tars are mocking is a typical Victorian caricature, not of a Prussian militarist, but of a bespectacled, physically unprepossessing German. This image of Germans as individually unimpressive, unsporty types, however mighty their army and its organisation might be, seems to have been locked into British minds, or at least into *Punch's* mind, for it remains exactly the same almost forty years later.

But more clear-sighted observers saw the truth. The future Lord Salisbury wrote publicly that 'under a more heroic minister, and in a less self-seeking age, it is probable that England would have preferred the risk, whatever its extent, to the infamy of betraying an ally, whom she had enticed into peril'.[87] The shame of Britain was evident right across the Atlantic, where the *New York Times* gloatingly contrasted Britain's decadence with the sad but at least manly Civil War still raging at home: Old England was 'isolated, humiliated, ridiculed and disgraced – caricatured in the windows of every print-shop in Europe'.[88]

Queen Victoria herself plumbed new levels of unpopularity for her unveiled lobbying against war with Germany, and when the Prussian King awarded her second son, Alfred, the Order of the Black Eagle – whether by way of thanks for keeping England out of the war it is impossible now to say – *Fun* pointed the finger at Gladstone[89] for sending Alfred to meet the 'royal butcher' William, and a widely syndicated poem from *Punch* suggested how people felt about the whole business:

TAKE BACK THY ORDER

Black Eagle, murder's proper meed!
Well doth its colour match the stain
Of guilt, that dyes that coward's deed
Who females slew and infant Dane,
Black Eagles are for blackguards right,
White feather who with black combine.
No English Prince shall be a Knight
Of such black Chivalry as thine.

But the most fateful thing was the way popular opinion on both sides of the German Ocean in late 1864 was ready to see profound, national conspiracies at work.* This became clear following one of the most celebrated murders of the age.

Mr Briggs' Hat

In 1864, Franz Müller, one of those poor German tailors mentioned by Marx, who had come to Britain in search of work, was accused of, and hanged for, the murder of a prosperous and elderly City worker on the 9.45 p.m. from Fenchurch St Station.

The case (wonderfully recreated in Kate Colquhoun's *Mr Briggs' Hat*) quickly became about far more than just a murder. In Britain, the activities of the German Legal Protection Society, which tried to overturn the verdict, were mocked from the first as attempts to 'fool the British public with cock and bull stories',[90] but soon became seen as unwarranted, and perhaps suspicious, interference with the British judicial system:

TUESDAY, NOVEMBER 8, 1864
THE GERMAN SOCIETY AND MULLER

The German Legal Protection Society seems to us to be a very curious institution in such a country as ours, so curious that we wonder how and why it ever came to exist ... There are a great number of Germans in England, and so there are a great many Scotchmen and Irishmen; but we have not yet heard of a Scotch or an Irish Legal Protection Society. We do not imagine that Germans are more liable to criminal charges, or in greater peril when they fall under them, than the natives of these islands. They are tried with as much impartiality as though

---

* Of course, 'published opinion' and 'public opinion' are not the same thing. But then, how else are we to tell? The newspapers which people chose freely to buy by the thousand (or even, later, the million) in these years as part of their daily lives are surely the best signs of their opinions that we have. Schopenhauer said that newspapers are the second hands on the clock of history and modern political spinners certainly assume that the media is a reliable indicator of the way the wind is blowing.

they were not Germans, and are not sentenced, when they are found
guilty, to heavier punishments than other people, so we do not see why
the Germans need a legal protection more than the members of other
races, which seem to do without such an institution.

The *Era*[91] ran a spoof letter which expressed those 'send them home'
feelings which will always arise when a penniless immigrant murders
a prosperous native:

German Legal Protection Society.

MR. EDITOR.—Sir,—Allow me to suggest to the German Legal
Protection Society (1), that they should get up the evidence for
their countryman, Herr Köhl, before the trial instead of after; 2.
that "Criminal Protection Society" would be a more appropriate
title; 3, that inasmuch as the King of Prussia and Duke of Saxe-
Coburg urged the Queen by telegraph to save Muller's life, they
deserve to be elected President and Vice-President of the Society;
4, that a subscription be raised to enable all the Germans most
likely to need the aid of the Society to return to their own country.
I shall be happy to contribute   A KREUZER.

This clever satire from *Punch* – it would hardly seem out of place in
Private Eye today – mixed the case of Müller with scorn for Teutonic
philosophising and outrage about Denmark. It was so widely syndicated that almost every literate Briton must have read it, and it's worth
noting that, already, Britons clearly assumed that German naval ambitions were what really lay behind the Danish war:

APOLOGY FOR THE GERMAN SOCIETY.

BY HERR VON SCHWEPENBIER.
(From *Punch*.)

The spectacle of Germans loving one another out-and-
out, and sticking fast to one another through thick and
thin, notwithstanding aught that one another may have
done to anybody else, dumfounds Englishmen with angry
bewilderment. A clear explanation of this mystery shall
therefore be offered to the beef-headed ones.

The common sonship of Fatherland unites all Germans
in the paramount bond of a brotherhood of transcendental
holiness. Every German individual unit is as one of the
molecules of a mass of matter united with the cohesiveness
of wax. Hence the homogeneity of the German people.

Every German has an inner subjective self, of divine
essence, and an outer objectivity into which the subjective
occasionally passes, and, having there awhile submitted
itself to the appetites and the impulses, returns into its
pure ipseity, none the worse for having perhaps been engaged in picking pockets or cutting throats in the mean-
time.

It is in the state of objective consciousness that the
great German nation, as one man, actuated by an acquisi-
tive enthusiasm, rushes in overwhelming force on a neighbouring State, and dismembers it of two provinces necessary to complete the idea of German unity, and realise a
German fleet. What if, in the execution of that exploit,
they kill and mutilate any number of the antagonists who
offer them resistance? For when Germany has returned
from the objective into serene subjectiveness, what has
been has ceased to be in the thoughts of Germans, and is
not any more, so they innocently wonder to hear themselves accused of robbery and murder.

So when, in a momentary excursion from the inner of
moral consciousness, the German mind, rendered for the
time objective by the attraction of a watch and chain, or a
portemonnaie, impels the German hand to grab those
articles, and to knock their owner on the head for brevity
and precaution, the German, having satisfied his objective
craving, retires into his subjective tranquillity, and re-
sumes his habitually mild and gentle demeanour. The
assassination and robbery which his objective personality
has committed are a mere episode of his essential life.
They are dismissed from his subjective mind, and he goes
about as light-hearted as though nothing had happened.
He and his countrymen regard those acts as the work of a
past entity, and not his present own. They, therefore,
think it monstrously cruel to hang him on the ground that
he is guilty of them. The inner I of the German ever
retains its essential purity unsullied, under all circumstances, and, consequently, his brothers use their utmost
endeavours to prevent brutal foreigners from putting out
his I, as if he were a common objective ruffian, by the
capital punishment of stretching his neck, for the trifling
offence of cracking an old gentleman's skull, by the way.

It is hoped that this elucidation of a sentiment which
has been blindly mistaken for the mutual sympathy of
rascals may prove satisfactory.

If the British were thoroughly irritated by the case, the Germans were incandescent. They too believed that the Müller case revealed deep truths. Having just been told that Edward Albert, the Prince of Wales, had drunk a toast with his Guards officers to the destruction of the German forces in Denmark, they thought they knew exactly why Müller had been condemned.[92] The *Guardian*'s correspondent ventured out into the streets of Berlin to report back home:

THE MULLER SENSATION IN BERLIN.

BERLIN, Nov. 14.

Fearful has been the sensation created in Berlin since yesterday (Sunday) morning, by the telegram from London announcing the fact that Muller was to be hanged at eight o'clock a.m. to-day. In the Prussian provinces, and, indeed, throughout Germany in general, the excitement of the public is doubtless equally intense. Wherever one goes, Muller is all the talk. In the beerhouses and *cafés*, in the reading-rooms and restaurants, in public places of assembly, in private circles, and in the streets, the conversation turns almost exclusively on this one topic. The words "judicial murder," "hatred of the English against the Germans," "atrocious butchery of an innocent man," "revenge for political humiliations,"—these and similar expressions are in everybody's mouth. Vengeance is vowed on England in retaliation for the foul crime she is about to commit. No epithet is too strong or too black to characterise the base cruelty and criminality attributed to the British Government for determining upon the death of a man who is now firmly believed by most people in this country to be completely innocent of the crime with which he has been charged and for which he stands condemned.

This newspaperman himself is in no doubt as to who is to blame: responsibility rests 'entirely with the German press ... the theory that the poor German tailor was about to fall victim to the supposed national and political animosities of the English people'.

Here is an early example of that vicious circle so familiar to us by now: a media war. The British press sent back (in order to enthral its public) lurid accounts of how the German press (in order to enthral *its* public) was fanning the flames:

Monday Evening.

Since writing the above, I have been out into the town
again in order to see how things look. The public excitement, as I soon found, so far from slackening, has gone on
increasing to an intensity beyond all description. I found
the reading-rooms and beer-houses into which I looked
crowded with people all talking about Muller, and awaiting
with the utmost impatience the arrival of the evening papers,
which were expected to contain a telegram from London respecting his fate. Such a feverish state of agitation and excitement I never saw a German public in before. In one
large reading room where I was sitting, as the earliest evening papers (the *National* and *Börsen Zeitung*) arrived, a
breathless stillness came over the assembled public, which
had been excitedly discussing the matter the moment
before, and one could almost hear every man's heart
beat as the waiters handed out the papers containing the
momentous news. The intelligence flew like wildfire
round the hall. "He's hanged!" went from mouth to
mouth. A sickening feeling seemed to overpower every
heart, and then followed an outburst, a howl of
bitterness and fury, rage and indignation at the perpetra-
tion of that which all felt to be a horrible tragedy, a judicial murder. I thought it prudent on my own part to retire very speedily from the scene. In the momentary irritation of the public I shall not be surprised to hear of their
committing some excesses in their frenzy. If some Englishman is lynched or maltreated it will be to me no matter
of astonishment in the least ; nor should I be at all startled
to find that a frenzied mob had vented its displeasure by
sacking the British Legation in the Leipsiger Platz.

Fifty years before Sarajevo, the relationship between Britons and
Germans had changed almost overnight. The Germans, who had for
decades looked to England as the beacon of progress, now saw her as
determined to block the advance of German unity. The *Illustrirte
Zeitung* (originally cloned from the *London Illustrated News*) declared
in the foreword to its 1864 compendium that the year had shown 'the
new beginnings of German war-capability at sea', which was 'a strong
promise to all who are aware of the preconditions of our future
national greatness', but had also showed Germans 'the selfishness of our
relations across the Channel in its most hateful form'. Having clearly
been made aware of just how much Henry Mayhew scorned Germany,

it then offered readers a double-page spread of anti-British social vignettes by way of reply.

As for the ruling order of Britons, the great debate in the House of Commons on 4/5 July 1864 sums things up. Speaker after speaker lined up to announce that the government should have 'told the German people that the moment they attacked Denmark they must expect to have England for a foe', that 'the credit of England is destroyed', that in order to 'get Kiel as a German port', 'Prussia has mocked, bearded, and almost threatened us', and that 'twelve months ago we greeted the Germans as our friends and allies, but now such is the infamy with which they stand, self-branded ...' To cap it all, Disraeli himself stood to say that in the face of German warmongering, what was needed was 'a thorough understanding between England, France, and Russia'.

Precisely half a century before Sarajevo, the terms had been set.

PART TWO (1865—6):
THE LAST SUMMER BEFORE
BISMARCK

The entente cordiale

Every generation assures itself, with self-importance or self-pity, that it lives in times of unprecedented change. On the eve of the 1865 general election, Britons were certain of it:

> The *Times*, reviewing the six years which have passed since the present Parliament assembled, points out the remarkable changes which have occurred in the interval. Europe, India, and America have been absolutely revolutionized, and the England of that day is not easily recognized. It now sounds like a joke to say that at the last "appeal to the country" we were horribly afraid of a French invasion, and were preparing to defend ourselves with enormous wooden fighting ships, built in prodigious haste. We had no ironclads, no volunteer force, no rifled cannon. Money was at 2½ per cent., and there were no Finance Companies, no new banks, no monster hotels, and no underground railways.

But our ancestors did not fear change. They embraced it. The march of things continued at a dizzying pace. The entire world waited for news of the *Great Eastern* as she attempted to lay the monstrous cable beneath the Atlantic which would, though it sounded like one of M. Verne's fantastic tales, enable instantaneous communication between the Old World and the New. Meanwhile, life in London had been palpably transformed by Bazalgette's new sewers; they having opened for business of the unmentionable sort in April, even this summer's unusual heat brought no repeat of the Great Stink. That was progress for you, up close and personal.

Politically, all was well, and only getting better. The American Civil War had ended, re-opening those markets, and it was now clear that the victorious US Army was not going after Canada next; Britain could congratulate herself on having avoided an ill-advised involvement in the progress of 'the other branch of the Anglo-Saxon race'.[93] Best of all was the revived Entente Cordiale with France. Thousands of British visitors were headed to Cherbourg, swamping the holiday accommodation for miles around, to witness the unprecedented visit of the Royal Navy's finest ships as *allies* of France: Portsmouth was already putting itself *en fête* to welcome the French fleet in return. Now *that* would have shown those, wretched, troublesome Germans, last year!

> Had England and France – we mean of course the Governments – been upon cordial terms the Dano-German war would not have broken out. Denmark would not have been despoiled, to the eternal disgrace of England ... The flame of German patriotism would have burnt itself out at once if a French army of observation had taken up a position on the Rhine, and an English fleet made its appearance in the North Sea and the Baltic.[94]

But, in fact, even the backward Germans were at last catching up with progress, for by the summer of 1865, the political struggle in Prussia (and by extension, Germany) seemed to have reached an absolute head, and in a way which British writers and readers could readily understand.

Driven from the field by an elephant

The state of affairs in the Prussian Rhineland, as the British holiday invasion of 1865 began, was truly extraordinary.

When liberal MPs and councillors committed the foul crime of arranging a dinner in Cologne during the parliamentary recess without official permission, the Prussian police and army moved in at dawn on 22 July to close the famous Gürzenich Hall to all-comers, politicians or not.* The liberals moved forthwith to the open-air restaurant of the nearby Cologne Zoo, which was outside the old city walls and hence

---

* A month earlier, the young Nietzsche proudly described to his mother and sister how he had sung there, sporting the black, red and gold hat-band of his liberal student society.

had a notionally separate mayor, amid much singing and speechifying about freedom and backed by a noisy crowd of ordinary Rhineland folk who did not have the vote but certainly had voices. There, infantry and hussars surrounded them and the authorities, surely for the first and only time in Europe since the days of Rome, mobilised a handy elephant to help drive the elected representatives of the people from the field.[95] Thereafter, merely to call out the name of the liberals' ringleader, Johann Classen-Kappelmann, in public was declared illegal in every Prussian territory.

All of Germany was agog at the almost insane implications of the affair. Berlin's version of *Punch*, the liberal *Kladderadatsch*, mocked both the paranoia of the authorities and the proverbially gullible English tourist in Cologne:

Scene am Rhein.

Fremdenführer. Das ist das Rathhaus.

Engländer. That is very fine! Kann man nicht auch seben Bürgermeister?

Fremdenführer. O ja! Rufen Sie 'mal: „Classen-Kappelmann! Hurrah! Classen-Kappelmann!"

Engländer (schreit). Cläffen-Käppelmänn! Hurreh! Cläffen-Käppelmänn!

(Der Bürgermeister des Orts kommt sosort außer sich herbeigestürzt.)

Engländer. O, that is wonderful! Was kostet das?

Fremdenführer. Gar nichts; das wird hier alles bei uns umsonst gemacht!

Scene on the Rhine

Tourist Guide:	That is the Rathaus.
Englander:	That is very fine! [In bad German:] Can one not also Bürgermeister see?
Tourist Guide:	Oh yes! Just shout out 'Classen-Kappelmann! Hurrah! Classen-Kappelmann!'
Englander (screams):	Classen-Kappelmänn! Hurrah! Classen-Kappelmänn! [He naturally gets his umlaut wrong.]

The Bürgermeister immediately comes diving out, beside himself.

Englander:	O, that is wonderful. [In German:] How much is that?
Tourist Guide:	Nothing at all. We do that for nothing here in Germany!*

The liberal *Freiburger Zeitung* declared that 'a regime which makes itself so appallingly laughable must surely have had its day'[96] and senior figures on the nationally influential magazine *Die Grenzboten*, which had tentatively begun the epochal swing towards an alliance with Bismarck, quickly and publicly drew back: '[We] are giving Bismarck up completely; there can be no question of recognising him after the events in Cologne.'[97]

This was serious politics, elephants or no. Karl Marx, himself safely plotting amid the liberal British, who of course never handed political exiles over to anyone for any reason whatever, wrote sulkily to Friedrich Engels on 18 August (after first asking 'Fred' for money, as usual) that everyone in Germany was too busy adoring this mere Cologne liberal, Classen-Kappelmann, to make any true political advances. Bismarck hit back at the liberals with all the press power at his disposal, and his papers, too, spoke the language of class warfare, scorning 'these well-fed bourgeois with their big mouths'.[98]

Not for the last time in German history, liberals who wanted British-style, open and conscious politics in Germany managed to earn the distinction of being called 'bourgeois' by those from both extremes who claimed to have a hotline to the real, if unvoiced, interests of 'the people'.

To Britons, this was a conflict one could easily understand and where the Good and Bad Germans were plain to see. Stout parliamentarians refusing to grant their absolutist king his military budget? Elected representatives being locked out of their own meetings by force of arms? Taxes being collected illegally despite parliament? The most

---

* In German, the same word can mean both 'for free' and 'pointless'. The Englander in the scene assumes, of course, that anything can be had for money.

advanced trading cities in uproar against backward, feudal royal authority? To a country taught their history by Lord Macaulay, this was quite obviously the eve of the English Civil War all over again, and the *Pall Mall Gazette* compared Bismarck to Charles I's favourite from the days of ship money, who ended his life on the executioner's block:

> A franker confession that the people are nearly unanimous against the Government, but that the Government fears the people less than it fears the KING, it would not be easy to produce from the mouth of any Minister since the time of STRAFFORD.

The German liberals were clearly trying to fulfil their allotted mission by repeating British history. The paper worried only that these professorial German liberals might not be up to real, riotously libertarian British-style politics:

> If they could get up anything like the sort of demonstration that carried our Reform Bill, the Government would give way before it, and the popular will would be achieved. But they can't, and, as we believe, less for want of genuine popular sympathy, than for want of a good crowd in every great city that the educated liberals can set in motion, and that won't feel conscious and awkward in the unpleasant work of impeding gentlemanly civilians in their duties, smashing the windows of reactionary officials, and generally diffusing a wholesome physical terror among the enemies of popular rights.

German liberals were not impressed when British liberals 'with their usual half-understanding of the situation in Germany' advised them that 'after Cologne we should treat Bismarck's regime not to articles and speeches, but to cobble-stones and threshing-sticks'.[99] In civilised, once-Roman, liberal Cologne, if you genuinely took to the streets, you would be facing not ramshackle feudal levees but the Prussian Guards, farm-boys recruited from the brutal marshlands and forests of eastern Germany.

In their parliament, though, the liberals pressed until things came to a head and Bismarck actually challenged their leader to a duel before storming out of parliament. The *Morning Post* found the spectacle hard to credit:

There is something which sounds so strange to our ears in the
notion of a Prime Minister leaving the House of Parliament in a tow-
ering passion and declaring openly that it is his intention to seek
personal satisfaction from a political opponent who has used his
Parliamentary privilege to make some caustic comments on the
Minister's veracity, that we have some difficulty in realising the possibility of such an occurrence taking place.[100]

Grub Street was loud in praise of these newly muscular German
liberals.[101]

> The flippant impertinence with which Herr VON
> BISMARCK addressed the Chamber was deservedly rebuked by
> Herr VIRCHOW, the reporter to the Committee, in the telling and
> exhaustive speech by which he closed the debate. So provoked
> was the Minister at the castigation he received, that he threatened
> to call Herr VIRCHOW personally to account for the sharp things
> he had said of him, which, he observed, were calculated to settle
> the difficulty between the Ministry and the House in the manner
> of the Horatii and Curiatii. This empty vapouring, however, was
> put a stop to by the President, and Herr VON BISMARCK left the
> Chamber in evident anger.
>   It is impossible not to admire the conduct of the Prussian
> deputies on this occasion.

The article concludes, approvingly if a mite condescendingly, that if the
Prussian deputies 'continue in their present course they will nobly earn
the ascendancy in the fatherland to which they are known to aspire'.*

Good for the Good Germans! They were doing what they ought to,
at last, and becoming British. No reason, then, to think twice about this
year's holiday – especially when Queen Victoria herself was going to
Germany, retinue and all.

---

* Virchow, the heroic liberal doctor and MP – he is regarded by many as the very founder of
modern pathology as well as of the concept of social medicine – whom Bismarck indeed challenged to a duel, was said to have refused pistols and suggested instead that two sausages be
prepared, one of them injected with deadly bacilli. The duellists would then have to publicly eat
their hats or their *wurst*. One way or another, the duel never took place and Virchow, though
browbeaten into apologising to Bismarck, survived to win the further honour of being attacked
in Houston Stewart Chamberlain's poisonous anti-Semitic tracts of later decades (as the leading German anthropologist, Virchow dared maintain that all Europeans were 'mongrel races'
and that this might actually be a Good Thing from a biological point of view).

The royal connection

Queen Victoria was off to Coburg, to unveil a statue to the memory of her beloved Albert (a German, of course) and to introduce to his future subjects her second son, who, about to reach his majority, was now to be formally accepted as heir apparent to the throne of Saxe-Coburg. He was being educated in German, naturally, in Bonn, as had his father been, partly in order that he might, upon his succession, better 'direct the affairs of this small but not unimportant German principality'. The columns in the London press devoted to what Dickens, in *Bleak House*, mockingly calls 'the fashionable intelligence' were for weeks concerned almost exclusively with the progress.

THE QUEEN'S VISIT TO GERMANY.
MONUMENT TO THE PRINCE CONSORT
AT COBURG.

FROM OUR SPECIAL CORRESPONDENT.

COBURG, Aug. 25.

The trip might seem to prove the argument of the many historians who claim that there were deep and positive roots between Britain and

Germany, some kind of Victorian-style Special Relationship, some default setting of natural alliance, at this stage and for decades to come. But anyone who believes that royal visits, elite contacts and the upmarket holiday trade decide the friendship of nations – in other words, that what is reported in the *Fashionable Intelligence* of 1865 or in *Harper's Bazaar* today actually affects or expresses foreign policy – is deluded.

For a start, the British press was by no means so starry-eyed about royalty as it is today. Many respectable Britons in 1865 openly professed republican sentiments.[102] *Reynolds's Newspaper* (the title is now obscure, but at the time it sold about 350,000 copies per issue) was positively muscular about the whole royal expedition to Germany:

> Now, again, the Queen is off to Germany, where she is to remain for a month or six weeks – a much longer period than she has resided in London since the demise of her husband. While in Saxe-Coburg and Prussia, it has been shrewdly surmised that she will not be as distant and invisible to her German friends as she is to her English subjects. When she returns from the Continent she is to be immediately whisked off to Balmoral; and thus the English people, who pay for the whole thing, are, in reality, as destitute of the royal beneficence – whatever that may be – as if they were living under a Republican form of Government. We have a strong suspicion that if the King of Prussia, the Emperor of Russia, or any other sceptred and despotic monarch who has the honour of being related to our royal family, was to visit this country, a very different style of treatment would have been displayed towards him.[103]

Even *The Times*, ever loyal, felt obliged to note the large number of monuments to Albert already existing in Britain (so many that Charles Dickens talked of fleeing society to avoid the omnipresent statuary) and to warn Her Majesty against 'the danger of indulging in the luxury of sorrow ... The memory of the dead must not be allowed to withdraw us from communion with the living.'[104]

Victoria had been much criticised for helping to keep Britain out of the war of 1864, and the *Morning Post*, avowedly non-radical as it was, nevertheless fired a pretty open warning shot across Her Majesty's pro-German bow:

> The interview between the Queen of England and the King of Prussia, which was arranged to take place yesterday at Darmstadt, could only have been dictated by courtesy and etiquette, and by the family relationship of the two Sovereign Houses. It should be unnecessary to state that no political result could be contemplated, and that, consequently, no political result could be arrived at ... the foreign policy of England is prescribed by the interests of England, and can be in nowise subject to any influence save that which is expressed and exercised by English public opinion.

Already, the British press, at any rate, was clear: public opinion was to decide foreign policy, not the wishes of rulers, and there was no doubt what that public opinion thought of Germany after last year.

In fact, the public need not have worried, for Victoria had already begun to change her mind about the suitability of Prussia to lead Germany: even as she was packing for Coburg, she wrote to Albert of the Belgians that 'Prussia seems inclined to behave atrociously <u>as she had always done</u>. Odious people, the Prussians are, <u>that I must say</u>.'[105]

Still, Prussia was not Germany, of course, and the visit went ahead as planned. British readers were given blow-by-blow accounts of the trip. One patriot in Frankfort-on-the Maine managed, with the help of speedy footwork and a fat British wallet, to secure the ultimate Royal Visit to Germany souvenir:[106]

> The Prince of Wales, now a visitor to the old Landgrave of Hesse, comes almost daily to town, and was seen this week at one of our public gardens. A loyal Englishman is said to have bought the chair he sat on, and the glass he drank from.

At last came the day of the unveiling. The *Daily Graphic*, whose illustrations all still had to be hand-engraved for printing, awarded this event the ultimate honour of the proto-modern newspaper: a full two-page picture spread. The *Observer* still had only words, but used them to the full in a splendid account of the ceremony, a small portion of which must here suffice:

> The Queen stood up in her place while anthems were sung by the chorus, with an accompaniment by the band. She stood up while the Burgermeister of Coburg, from a very low platform in the middle of the square before the statue, delivered a long address, to which no answer was vouchsafed. Then there were more lofty strains from the band, more peals of the bells, more discharges of artillery, and at a given signal the linen wrappers of the statue fell, and the gilt-bronze of the hero's effigy stood out, all glittering in the flaming sun, with its countenance fixed upon the countenance of the royal lady by whose unwearied love it had been reared on its pedestal.[107]

The countenance of that royal lady was, however, about to be darkened, and her new opinion of Prussia drastically confirmed, by an event in Bonn which is now entirely forgotten, but which at the time rang in the entire British press for so many weeks that it made the *New York Times* and even the infant journals of Australasia: the murder of a cook.

The Prussian Bullingdon is angry

At or about half past one on the night of 4 August 1865, in Bonn – a Prussian city since 1815, thanks to Britain, and a famous university city since 1818, thanks to the Prussians – the young bloods of the most exclusive student society, the Corps Borussia, youthful Junkers to a man, downed their last drink (doubtless a ringing toast to the Hohenzollerns) left their flag-and-sword-bedecked fraternity house, and sallied forth into the unlit darkness.

Anyone who has read the immortal opening chapter of Evelyn Waugh's *Decline and Fall* will remember the consequences, in 1920s Britain, of running athwart the scarlet and baying Bollinger Club, a thinly disguised version of Oxford's Bullingdon. So let us think of the Corps Borussia as a nineteenth-century Prussian version of the Bullingdon. This should be easy, since both institutions still exist, the studied hauteur of gaze and dress having changed but little, deluges or no.

 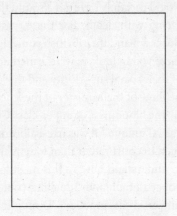

| The German Emperor as a member of Bonn's Borussia, *c.*1895. | A member of Oxford's Bullingdon, *c.*1985.* |

Britons of the sort invited to join the Bullingdon used famously to divide the world into 'U' and 'non-U'. Junkers eligible for the Borussia divided the world into 'von' and 'non-von' – at least, that is how it seemed to the Victorian polymath, Henry Vizetelly.[†]

> The Junker recognises but two classes of human beings, the Vons who alone enjoy the monopoly of living, and the non-Vons who only have their raison d'être in ministering to the requirements and

---

*Unfortunately we do not have permission to publish the photograph. But it is very easy to find on the web and *you know just who we mean.*
† His brother, Frank, was the great photographer of the American Civil War.

serving as foils to the ineffable qualities of the Vons. He is born "court-worthy" and by excluding the non-Vons from participation in this privilege, the Prussian court but confirms him in his belief that he belongs to a superior class of society.[108]

Even today, any pleb with the temerity not to heed the whims of a bunch of boozed-up young British military toffs in an ill-lit place might rapidly find himself without his trousers; a century and a half ago, he would certainly have got a sound thrashing; in Prussia, in 1865, he was dicing with death. For there was one great difference between the Borussen and their British equivalents, whether modern or Victorian: these young Junkers were armed not only with the ironclad conviction of their social superiority and the knowledge that one of them was the nephew of the Minister of the Interior, but also with cavalry sabres.

The bloodiness of upper-class German student life was (and indeed still is) unique.* It was irresistibly mysterious to Victorian Britons, who sued in court rather than fought at dawn and found it extremely hard to understand how, in this most famously law-abiding and efficiently policed of all lands, duelling could somehow be illegal in theory yet universal in practice. Throughout the nineteenth century, it is practically impossible to find a travel book on Germany which does not contain a suitably chilling account of student duels. ('"Lots of blood this morning," said a warlike Teuton, as he stuffed his mouth full of sausage. I shuddered, and took another sip of cognac.'[109]) This British lady reporter of 1866 was one of countless visitors to be amazed and horrified:

> Harry was right in saying that I should see plenty of gashes before I had been long in Heidelberg; they are evidently considered as trophies, and I have seen a young man *in a ball-room* with as many as three strips of plaister, each two or three inches long, adorning his cheek and brow! To say the least, it is singular taste on the part of those who are decidedly *not* indifferent to personal appearance.
>
> (I did *not* know at that time the fate of the student's nose, but I heard it afterwards,—a story too horrid for repetition.)

* The Borussia is still *pflichtschlagend*, i.e. membership is absolutely conditional upon duelling. Most modern Germans are deeply embarrassed when you ask about this.

The Corps Borussia was particularly hot on duelling, whether 'academic' (in which you were carefully armoured so as to produce only those much-prized facial scars) or actual (in which case you weren't, and could easily die), for many Borussen were sort-of army officers as well as students: to them, honour was a matter of social and professional life or death.

Prussia had a unique system which allowed certain young men to serve as quasi-cadets called One-Year Volunteers rather than as three-year conscripts. Provided that the officers' mess of their chosen regiment voted to accept them as gentlemen, and that they could pay for their own upkeep as well as translate Greek and Latin, these young men could live outside barracks, go to their university lectures and generally swank about the place in full uniform, even when not on duty, entitled, indeed required, to carry heavy swords whenever they did so to defend their honour if need be. The regiment of choice for the Borussen was the Bonn Royal Hussars, the one provincial regiment as smart as the Guards units of Berlin themselves; their commander was King William of Prussia in person.

Moneyed and militarist, the Borussen were the westernmost outpost and propagator of the Potsdam Tone, that nasal, clipped, parade-ground German which was the Prussian equivalent of the English public-school drawl. And on the night of 4 August they were angry young men.

A few days before, in these same streets, their conservative Prussia had seen its authority, even its legitimacy, publicly challenged by the Borussia's great rival, the liberal, middle-class Bonn student society, Franconia, who wanted a united Germany, run from Frankfurt by a British-style parliament.

Nietzsche's liberals

On 28–29 July the Prussian government had sanctioned, on strict conditions (all public meetings had to be government-sanctioned in

Prussia), an anodyne patriotic ceremony in Bonn – dancing, choirs, tableaux and the like – in memory of Ernst Moritz Arndt, writer of 'What is the German's Fatherland?', the unofficial anthem of German unity. Now that he was safely dead, the idea was that Arndt could be selectively honoured, rather than repeatedly imprisoned.

The Bonn Royal Hussars, though, took a tougher line than their own government. They refused the invitation to take part in the Arndt festival, in case this might involve the unbearable sight of 'so-called German flags' – that is, the black, red and gold ones of politically non-existent Greater Germany, as opposed to the white and black of their very real Prussia.[110] And their fears had been justified, for the festival had turned into a popular demonstration in favour of the Berlin regime's most-hated politician, Classen-Kappelmann, the liberal from neighbouring Cologne whose supporters had so recently been confronted by the bayonets (and indeed, the tusks) of Bismarck's authority.

The liberal students of the Franconia had not simply mentioned the forbidden name of Classen-Kappelmann. Fencing swords drawn, they had shouted it out, with what the *Heidelberger Zeitung* called 'a thunderous "Hoch!"', and escorted him to the railway station.

Below are the bold Franconians, photographed earlier that very year. One British visitor to Germany described such student clubs as 'a race

to be eschewed by all who have a wholesome reverence for soap and a horror of Kantian philosophy',[111] but this particular club is worth inspection by anyone with any interest at all in German history. For here, arranged in suitably thoughtful pose atop the club's beer barrel, already quite recognisable once you know, is none other than the young Friedrich Nietzsche.

Nietzsche was certainly in Bonn on 29 July. Whether he himself took part in the demonstration is probably impossible now to know.* At any rate, his club managed to seriously annoy their aristocratic rivals, for on 5 August the Borussia posted a letter to the press in Cologne, distancing their corporation strongly from the liberal, and socially inferior, students who had felt 'the need to celebrate Arndt with the *volk*' (by which, of course, the Borussia just meant the great unwashed). Here is the letter as it was printed:[112]

— Aus Bonn, 5. Aug., schreibt man uns: Gestatten Sie mir, die Mittheilungen Ihres geschätzten Blattes vom 31. Juli, ⚓ Bonn, 30. Juli, über die Betheiligung der Studentenschaft am Arndt-Feste zu berichtigen. Die Corps hatten sich gänzlich von der Arndt-Feier ausgeschlossen. Es kann also von „entsprechenden Farben der Corps" und später ausschließlich von „verschiedenen Corpsfarben" — worin die Senioren gekleidet gewesen wären — keine Rede sein. Nur die Burschenschaften und Verbindungen glaubten mit dem Volke Arndt feiern zu müssen.

Since it was dated 5 August, it seems reasonable to assume that the Borussians agreed this message on the evening of 4 August, and that when they left their frat house at about 1 a.m. that night, booted, bespurred and toasted-up, these young bloods were in the mood to rub the certainty of exactly who was boss round here into the nose of anyone who crossed their path.

Unfortunately for him, that man was one Daniel Eugene Ott.

---

* We do know that Nietzsche left Bonn forever on 9 August, the very day after the Franconians were arraigned at the court of Bonn University for their deeds on 29 July, and that he shortly afterwards resigned from the society, to which he would otherwise have been tied to for life. It is hard not to wonder whether there was some connection – if only Nietzsche's fear of his mother, who read the conservative *Kreuz-Zeitung* every day.

The unlucky cook

Ott was thirty-eight years of age, a native of Strasbourg and thus the-oretically a subject of Napoleon III, though he was assumed by most people, including his employer, to be a German of some kind or other (there were still so many different kinds of Germans in 1865). He had just thrown a dinner party for his friends at a restaurant near to the corner of the Court Gardens.* Ott was himself a *chef de cuisine* or *Küchenmeister*, and his party that night was to celebrate a new job which was going to set him up for life.

Chefs in 1865, however masterly, were rarely free. Composers, for example, had been liberated from patronage since Mozart's day, first by middle-class, paying audiences, then by the domestic pianoforte and the vast demand it generated for private lessons and printed music. But there was no mass-market for chefs yet: only hyper-modern Victorian Britain, the world's first industrialised society, had as yet found itself in need of, and hence prepared to pay for, a Mrs Beeton. Skilled chefs still needed places in the household of some grand personage or other.

Ott's employer was such a personage, a real prince-regent-to-be, and had just offered him an even greater post – the sort of job that would make you for life. Little wonder that the happy cook gave a dinner for his friends by way of celebration.

Well after midnight, they went home. Their way took them across the Hofgarten and through the gate in the old walls, the city proper being still locked up at night, as it had been for many dangerous cen-turies. It was here that this peaceable little group of jolly citizens drew the attention of the hearty pack who had just left the Borussia's frat house.

Across the mid-nineteenth-century world, the pavements were narrow, if existent at all, the streets muddy, dungy or worse. Demand-ing that someone coming the other way should 'cede the wall' (that is,

* The building, Adenauerallee 4–6, was destroyed by British bombers in October 1944. Its modern replacement now houses a car-rental business.

step aside and down into the dirt), or claiming that they would not, was one of the most familiar ways in which Victorian bullies insisted on public deference or picked a fight.

The *Standard* gives the most detailed account of what happened:

> A one-year volunteer and two students belonging to the Borussen Club left their tavern near the railway at one a.m., and had already entered the town by the little gate, when they heard loud voices in the Hofgarten. 'Stop!' said the volunteer, 'there's a row to be got up,' and the gate-keeper had to let them out again. They gave this man their purses and watches; two going on towards the speakers, and the third remaining behind in the town. The two repeatedly stepped in the way of the persons coming in, notwithstanding that the latter said to them—'If you want to quarrel go to healthy people. We are invalids.' For the party consisted, besides the cook Ott, who was unsteady on his legs, of a second man, having a broken arm but just healed, and a third, who had recently been laid up with a fractured leg. The cook had given a farewell supper at Kleins, upon the Coblenz-road, as he was to leave the following morning, and the three were going home peaceably through the Hofgarten. The volunteer, named Count Eulenburg, several times got in front of the cook to bar his progress; the cook as often begged the assailants to go home quietly and leave them in peace, till, finally losing patience, he said, 'What do you —— boys really want?'

With that, the young Count Eulenburg had successfully picked his fight. No one on Earth could call a young Prussian aristocrat, a nephew of the Minister of the Interior and a member of the Bonn Royal Hussars, a '— boy' and expect to get away with it. In fact, for an officer *not* to react properly to such an insult, given in front of witnesses, would be social death.

But Ott, a mere cook, however distinguished, was not *satisfaktionsfähig* (able to give satisfaction). That privilege was restricted and jealously guarded. You could not fight a duel with one of the *volk* – it was quite simply unthinkable. So what should a young Prussian quasi-officer do when such a non-von person gave him offence? The answer was clear, and Ott's fate was sealed:

> He immediately received a blow upon the head, sat down upon the ground, and remained sitting while the others tussled. One of the cook's friends got hold of the sabre and hid it under his coat; it was given up the next morning. One of Ott's friends was badly beaten, and, as the whole party of the Borussen came rushing out of the tavern to the spot, they would undoubtedly have been still worse treated if a certain Herr von Witzleben had not recognised the groom of the chambers of Prince Alfred in one of Ott's party who just came up. He called out, ' Why, these are Prince Alfred's people!' whereupon the whole band of some 20 Borussen took to their heels, and poor Ott was carried home, where he died a few days afterwards in most dreadful anguish."

One can imagine the consternation of young von Witzleben.* His friend, Count Eulenburg, had just half-beheaded not some mere papist Rhineland yokel or a damned middle-class liberal student with the temerity to answer back to his Prussian betters, but a senior household servant of a true-bred young fellow aristocrat who was heir to the throne of one of Prussia's few reliable allies in Greater Germany. Within the charmed circle of Bonn's gilded and spurred youth, the Borussen doubtless knew very well that this fellow student of theirs had, earlier that very year, been personally received, by King William, into Prussia's highest rank of chivalry, the Order of the Black Eagle – possibly because his royal mother had recently shown herself to be a good friend to Prussia, even at the risk of unpopularity among her own people.

The British people, that is.

---

* Von Witzleben is, of course, a name to conjure nobly with in more recent German history, and in the long story of Junkerdom's relationship to the alleged 'Will of the Nation'.

For Prince Alfred was, of course, the second son of Queen Victoria, and Her Majesty would now be seeking a replacement for the man who was due to be appointed her personal chef in Coburg tomorrow.

In which the Queen is not amused – and nor is Bismarck

The Queen, arrived at Coburg, was informed of the event and immediately made her feelings known in a letter sent from Lord Granville to Lord Napier, the British ambassador.

On 19 August, *The Times* gave British readers the first report of the event, expressing in different words the same hope as Her Majesty – that 'all will be done which is required by justice'.

> A sanguinary event is reported from the Rhine. One Herr Ott, a
> German cook in the service of the Queen, who had been long in
> Prince Alfred's establishment at Bonn, was killed a day or two ago in
> the streets of that city. It appears that on the point of starting for
> Coburg, whither he had been ordered during the stay of Her
> Majesty, he met some students in a public thoroughfare, and could
> not agree with them on the important question as to who was to get
> out of the way and allow the other to pass by. The difference led to
> a quarrel, in the course of which one of the students, being a vol-
> unteer in the Prussian army at the same time, and having his broad
> sword dangling by his side, struck the unfortunate man a blow on
> the head. Herr Ott expired a few hours after the blow, and an inquiry
> will doubtless be instituted by the military authorities.

No one in Britain (and only a handful in Germany) knew that this
news came at a very bad time indeed for Bismarck.

His closest and most important ally at this time, the man to whom
he wrote more letters than to anyone else in late July and early August
1865, was none other than the Minister of the Interior, Eulenburg,
uncle of the student who had just killed Ott. And this was no minor
alliance: Bismarck, Roon (the leader of the Prussian Army) and
Eulenburg were at this very moment hatching one of the most extraordinary and far-reaching plots in the story of modern Europe. For
Bismarck was aiming to Prussianise Germany by outflanking liberalism on the radical side. He planned to adopt, and actually deliver, the
great liberal causes of 1848: national unity, universal suffrage, free trade
and a navy.

The fact that we now know that he succeeded should not blind us
to just how unlikely Bismarck's plan was at the time. To read the
annals of the Prussian Crown Council in the summer of 1865 is to get
an unforgettable feeling of the steam-hammers of history at work.
While the liberal parliamentarians held festivals and talking-shops,
Bismarck spoke *in camera* of deliberately seeking war with Austria, of
a military coup, of dishing the liberals by introducing universal male
suffrage to enfranchise the loyal 'residuum' (Marx would have said,

the *Lumpenproleteriat*). He drove through his revolutionary plans despite the misgivings, even at times the clear opposition, of both the King and the Crown Prince. Only the rock-solid backing of War Minister Roon and Interior Minister Eulenburg (i.e. of the army and the police, if it came to it) let Bismarck get his way in these epochal meetings.

Bismarck's great trap was to be the Treaty of Bad Gastein, whereby Austria and Prussia would declare that the duchies which had been won from Denmark were not independent states of the German Confederacy, but the property of Prussia and Austria. By this, Austria and Prussia were both sure to be discredited among all the liberal Germans. But Bismarck did not care. As he explained to the Austrian Chancellor, Count Beust, with that openness which again and again confounded his political enemies: 'You would not know how to place yourself at the head of the revolutionary party in Germany. As for me, I could at any time become its chief.'

Bismarck was in the very act of negotiating this fatal treaty with the unwitting Austrians when news came of Ott's murder. The cook was, most inconveniently, both a British royal servant and a French citizen – and Bismarck needed to keep France and Britain neutral in his upcoming war with Austria. He corresponded urgently about the murder, and made sure that a witness was found who could place an alternative, spoiling story in the French and British press.

Of course, the British press did not know this. But the news of the murder, followed so soon by that of the Treaty of Gastein, meant that, at last, all the doubt and confusion which had plagued British minds over Denmark was ended. Here was the enemy, clear as day and clanking in his spurs: Prussian militarism!

The press finds its angle

There are scores of articles in the British press on the murder, and the following is just a small selection:

There are plenty of instances to be found, even within the last few years, in which Prussian officers guilty of offences quite as gross and grievous as that with which Count von Eulenburg stands charged, have either had their crime promptly condoned, or their escape from any possible consequences connived at. But in this case the Fates, it would seem, were rather against Count von Eulenburg, He "had the misfortune," as a Prussian official journal gracefully put it, to kill a man who turned out to be cook to Prince Alfred of England and at the same time a subject of the Emperor of the French. If the Count had only killed, say, any three or even more of German cooks, or waiters, or *kellner-mädchen*, or other fair and lawful game of that sort, the Prussian War Office would no doubt have arranged the matter quite to the satisfaction of the aristocratic slayer.[113]

It was hoped that Victoria herself would intervene – the language is much the same as that used today when a British leader is urged to use personal contacts to try to influence a foreign despot:

ARISTOCRATIC MURDERERS IN PRUSSIA

There is no other country in Europe where such a scandal would be countenanced by the Government or endured by the people as the immunity which Count Eulenburg enjoys in Prussia after having committed a flagrant murder ... It is to be hoped that her Majesty will find occasion to express the sentiments of herself and her subjects on this point during her interview with the King to-day at Darmstadt. Not that any personal explanations can do much to remove the cause of estrangement between ourselves and Prussia. What repels us and fills us with mistrust is the over-weening predominance of that temper which assures impunity to Count Eulenburg and makes M. Bismarck the foremost man in Prussia.[114]

What, in the name of Heaven, are the "duties" of a judge and public functionary in the degraded kingdom of Prussia? The young assassin, who in high-handed wantonness turned a man of inferior rank out of his path by cutting him down and killing him, is left untouched by judge or public functionary until an order arrives from his gracious father, the Minister of the Interior, or some brother of his in the band of political brigands who rule Prussia – and the young man is, by his father's wish, put for a few days in arrest. After a nominal inquiry he is liberated, and there ends the matter; even though the murdered man was a subject of France, and the servant of an English prince.[115]

The *Penny Illustrated Paper* – that revolutionarily cutting-edge journal which, for the first time in publishing history, made structural use of pictures to deliver news to its readership – openly joined up Denmark in 1864 and Bonn in 1865:

It would seem that Prussia is likely to become the *bête noire* of Europe, and that, singularly enough, not only in consequence of her faithless and unjustifiable conduct with regard to the duchies, but through a private case of assault, which in this country would probably have resulted in a charge of murder.[116]

Count Eulenburg has returned to his regiment, and we presume the next news will be that he has been honourably acquitted. His sword will be returned to him with a recommendation to use it against the enemies of Prussia as bravely as he has wielded it hitherto against her subjects.[117]

By September, the story made the *New York Times*:

The privileges of the military aristocracy in Prussia extend, it would seem, to murder. A Frenchman named OTT, chef de cuisine to Prince ALFRED, was passing, late in the evening, along the Poppelsdorfer Allee, in Bonn, when he was stopped by a soldier and

some students. He requested civilly permission to pass, when the
soldier, Count EULENBURG, a nephew of the Minister of the
Interior, drew his sabre, and with two blows on the head wounded
the cook so that he died. The murderer immediately went to Berlin,
and it is considered possible that he may suffer a few days' arrest. As
soldier and noble he had a right to cut down a citizen who wanted
leave to pass him. What hope of freedom for a people who, being all
soldiers, avenge a crime of this kind by sending their carriages to the
victim's funeral?

Forty-nine years before Sarajevo, the world's first recognisable, modern-
style mass media, the entirely free, newly cheap and truly national
British press, had found the catalyst, the personal tale, the angle which
the 'meeja' always needs to enshrine a greater story.

And by now, the British were beginning to doubt whether there was
really such a difference, after all, between the Bad Germans and the
Good Germans, if the Good Germans would not get rid of Bismarck:

We may wonder how a people could slavishly defer to the whims of
such a man. The humblest Prussian cannot keep clear of the police.
He must have police permission for every movement. He cannot
paint his name over his shop, or let his first floor, or have a meeting
of his friends, or set out on a journey, without having obtained the
grace of the police. He, then, is taught from his cradle to be the slave
of all the petty officials, or representatives of might, who surround
him. What kind of moral man can grow under such influences as
these? He becomes a tyrant in his turn. He cringes to the policeman,
and paints a sign over his shop; and his only comfort is that he, also,
has people under him. He can thrash his wife and children, and not
respect the back even of his handmaid.

Herr von Bismarck would seem to be a very natural leader in a
nation composed of men in police fetters. He is the mighty man
among millions who have no higher political creed than might.[118]

The *Guardian*, too, was preparing to write the lot of them off:

Is there any hope in the awakened conscience of the Prussian people? Is the nation of the Government exclusively to be held responsible for these offences and outrages? Gladly should we acquit the Prussian people, but to acquit them is impossible. A journal of the liberal opposition may here and there affect surprise and indignation ... but the melancholy fact remains that the general public in Prussia, to all appearances, accepts with indifference if not with approval these homicidal privileges of royal uniform and noble blood, this shameless defiance of all law and justice, these savage manners and barbarous usages. Prussian society is not the least surprised or scandalised. Perhaps, fortified by the example of the Crown Prince, it rather exults in the young Count Eulenburg's noble military exploit in cutting down an unarmed civilian in the street, and compares it complacently enough with the ever-memorable exploits of the royal Prussian army, aided by the forces of Austria, in overpowering by sheer weight of numbers two or three thousand brave Danes, badly armed.

Perhaps, indeed, in the secret souls of these sturdy Deputies and their patriotic constituents there may lurk a conscious admiration of Count Bismarck's brilliant foreign policy, his glorious deeds of violence, and his ravenous appetite for the territory of his neighbours. Perhaps that successful statesman knows instinctively that the Prussian people are more likely to be proud of seeing a poor defenceless Frenchman cut down by a gallant young Prussian noble and officer in their streets, than to feel degraded at the spectacle such an act presents to civilised Europe of Prussian law, Prussian justice, and Prussian humanity. Perhaps Count Bismarck is satisfied that if the Emperor Napoleon should demand satisfaction for the murder of a French subject, the whole people of Prussia would forget all questions of law, liberty, or justice at home, and rally as one man in defence of the national barbarism. [119]

Even the royal mind was radically changed in its view of Prussia as the future leader of a Good Germany. On 13 September 1865, Lord Palmerston, who had been ready for war in 1864, wrote to Lord Russell with undisguised gloating:

the fact is, as far as the Queen is concerned, that so long as the injustice committed appeared calculated to benefit Germany and the Germans, it was all right and proper: but now that an example is about to be set of extinguishing petty states like Coburg, her sense of right and wrong has become wonderfully keen.

By the spring of 1866, Russell was warning that Victoria 'proposes clearly an intervention by force against Prussian designs', and Lord Clarendon was obliged to inform the Queen that while 'he entirely concurs with her Majesty respecting the outrageous conduct of Prussia', war was out of the question.[120]

Meanwhile Lord Napier, the same ambassador who had communicated Her Majesty's outrage at Ott's death to Bismarck, was, by early 1866, in no doubt as to who in the overheating ferment of German politics now both envied and despised the British. It was, quite simply, everyone: 'Conservatives, Constitutionalists, Ultras, Liberals, Unionists, Separatists – all join in one way only – in repugnance to England, in noting her prosperity & in undervaluing her power.'[121]

Things had come a long way, and very fast. Yet if many Germans were by now losing their awe of England, and if British diplomacy was turning hard against Prussia, one vital thing was still missing from the fatal recipe. Most Britons, by the end of 1865, disliked the Prussians, and despised the Germans, with varying degrees of intensity, but absolutely none of them felt the single most important motivating factor in international relations: fear. The British were not remotely scared of Prussia or Germany. They considered rather that 'although the Prussian army has sufficient pluck to massacre an unarmed populace, it has an invincible repugnance to face an armed foe'.[122]

That was to change very soon – but not in 1866.*

---

* And what became of Ott's murderer? The fears of the British press about Prussian justice were all too well grounded (and the claims of the *Provincial Correspondence* that justice would be done all too transparent). The murder of Ott did so little harm to Eulenburg's career in the Prussian establishment that he later became engaged to no less than the daughter of Prince Bismarck himself, and only failed to become the great man's actual son-in-law thanks to dying suddenly of typhus in October 1875.

Prussia starts to work

As Bismarck lined Austria up in the summer of 1866, Britons saw it as a civil war with little between the two sides. After all, both had just stolen from brave little Denmark. If anything, most of the British press predicted a victory for Austria and the Federal States, the largest and best armed of which, Saxony, Bavaria, Hanover and Württemberg, all opposed Prussia:

> It is, however, difficult to believe that these two detested tyrannies can be so infatuated as to engage in a struggle which could hardly fail to prove fatal to both. For both the Austrian and Prussian Governments are universally hated by their own subjects most of all. The Prussian people, who have been goaded to the utmost verge of endurance by the systematic insults of Bismarck and their block-head of a King, would be almost certain to avail themselves of so favourable an opportunity to rid themselves of the Hohenzollern dynasty. We shall thus, in all probability, should this anticipated war really take place, be favoured with the presence of King William and his son – the husband of the Princess Royal of England. Claremont Palace is now vacant, in consequence of the death of Louis Philippe's widow; and as the English people have in some shape or other to support the exiled tyrants of the Continent, we shall not be in the least surprised or startled at having to make permanent provision for the son-in-law of Queen Victoria and his German relations.[123]

Then again, 1866 was not just a war between Prussia and Austria. Later German historians all but wrote out the vital part which the Italian front played in keeping Austria's forces divided, but Bismarck was well aware of this – and so were Britons, for they were the great historical sponsors of Italian national unity. Their marginal preference for Austria over Prussia was more than counterbalanced by their decided partiality for Italy over Austria.

In the event, no one's partiality counted for anything, because the Prussia General Staff managed to bring about an early and decisive battle at Königgrätz on 3 July. Whether or not the Austrian army was awfully arrayed that day has been debated ever since, but the central fact was simple: the Prussians had boldly embraced the latest step-change in military technology and their new breech-loading rifles, the 'needle-guns', simply mowed down the Habsburg infantry, who (like the British Army of the day) still only had muzzle-loaders. A technological edge like this would certainly have given Napoleon victory at Waterloo in 1815, and it made sure that German history was wrenched in a whole new direction on that single afternoon in 1866.

The dramatic smashing of Austria and her allies straight away resulted in a tectonic shift in politics. The liberals (the German Progress Party) who had fought Bismarck so hard for a more British-style constitution, and who had been the strongest party in the Prussian Parliament since 1861, now split on whether to indemnify Bismarck for his actions over the last four years. It was a very strange deal: if Bismarck admitted that he had acted unconstitutionally, Parliament would agree that he had done so out of a deeper necessity.

A majority of the liberals signed up to it, won over, like many people before and since, by the speed, gleam and sheer, undeniable fact of military victory. This faction re-christened itself the National Liberals. Bismarck embraced them with an alacrity which dismayed his old-fashioned conservative allies. Why bother with any of these despised urban liberals at all? Why not follow up the triumph against Austria with a decisive domestic strike – an 'internal Königgrätz', they called it – against the liberal enemy within? But Bismarck himself knew very well just how close Prussia had come to being completely ungovernable in 1865. He cared nothing for what his politics *looked* like to anyone, so long as it delivered what really mattered: power. He himself put it this way: 'The form in which the King exercises his authority has never been of any especial importance to me. I have devoted all the energies God gave me to strive for the substance of his rule.'[124]

It worked: the deal between Bismarck and the National Liberals lasted for a whole decade. The fact that the National Liberals continued to call themselves liberals confused many Britons for many years. The great British diplomat Sir Robert Morier, who knew Germany and the Germans and was a personal friend of the Crown Prince and Princess, was almost alone in divining the real post-1866 agenda which, for obvious reasons, Bismarck took great pains to keep secret:

> The Great Prussian idea not much given utterance to in the shape of programmes but living in the hearts of a very large and powerful party in Prussia and of many thousands of Prussians who would not openly confess it. Gradual absorption of Germany bit by bit and assimilation into the Prussian state by conquest or otherwise as long as each added bit was thoroughly Prussianised and disindividualised.[125]

You can hardly blame other British commentators for not seeing events with such clarity. After all, beating Austria was scarcely proof of irresistible power. Frederick the Great, Napoleon I and Napoleon III had all managed it repeatedly, and had not needed superior rifles. The lesson drawn by Britons was simply one of weapons technology, for there was no secret about the breech-loading rifle: 'we can quite well remember that its merits were discussed in this country many years ago'.[126] The Prussian victory merely demonstrated that other countries had better hurry up and get their own breech-loaders into service. 'When are we going to awaken ... breechloaders have been known to us for years,' cried the *Illustrated London News* of 21 July 1866.

And yet something profound *had* changed. In the wake of 1866, it was no longer possible to deny that Prussia was more than simply the backward, feudal jackal of Russia. There were obviously certain things about Prussia which quite simply *worked* spectacularly well – if only their efficiency in mobilisation and weapons procurement. When you see someone else doing something so well, the natural impulse is to suggest copying them. But there was a problem:

> Those who know anything about Prussia and England must at once see that the idea of organising our army after the model of the Prussian one is impracticable. To do this it would be necessary that we should revolutionise all our administrative arrangements and

ourselves into the bargain, that we should cast away all those habits which have been dear to us for centuries, and that we should freely sacrifice a great part of our individual liberty ... Will we allow ourselves to be moulded and drilled? Will we blindly and against our conviction always and under all circumstances be obedient to our government? Certainly not, and so long as we are incapable of such self-denial it is absurd to talk of our organising ourselves according to the Prussian model.[127]

In 1866 we find, for the very first time, Britons faced with the classic 'culture-clash' dilemma: they could see that Prussia did some things extremely well, but there was no point even trying to copy them, because that would require Britons to become, quite simply, un-British, to stop being everything that made us *us*. This dilemma would echo down the decades.*

Still, in 1866, it did not seem a very urgent one. Prussia might have a highly efficient army, but Austria remained a significant power; the smaller German states, most of them still independent, presumably hated Prussia more than ever after 1866; Napoleon III was making threatening sounds about compensation on the Rhine for Prussia's gains; and the Russians were making sure they kept plenty of men on Prussia's eastern frontier, just to remind King William who was the senior partner in Middle Europe.

There was little to persuade Britons, in 1866, that Prussia, however unpleasant and strange, was anything more than yet another example of Germany's backwardness: an inconvenient and troublesome stumbling block on the road of progress, but no more.

Then, of course, came the great shock that changed everything.

---

* It still does. BBC anchorman Evan Davis proposed, in 2012, that if Britain is to succeed, Britons need to find their 'inner German'.

PART THREE (1870—71): THE FRANCO-PRUSSIAN WAR

The first media war

In July 1870 Britons were pretty neutral about France and Prussia: no one liked Prussia, but Napoleon III had been so very, well, *Bonapartist* over the last few years that the Entente Cordiale of 1865 had faded. Any chance that Britain might actively support France was knocked out by Bismarck's genius for manipulating journalists.

His masterstroke came on 13 July, when he splashed the Ems Telegram to the world's press. By personally editing this otherwise relatively innocuous diplomatic report – in old age, he proudly described exactly how he had done so – Bismarck deliberately gave the French public the impression that their ambassador had been seriously insulted by Prussia. When France mobilised on 19 July, most Britons bought the story that this vainglorious, warmongering people and their restless Emperor had gratuitously chosen war. Bismarck followed up by releasing the draft Benedetti Treaty, in which Napoleon had been arrogant or stupid enough to put in writing his wish to acquire Luxembourg as compensation for Prussia's gains in 1866. On 25 July *The Times* published the document in full.

It was enough to make Britain's leaders think twice. Disraeli, for all his acuity, could see only that 'there are vast ambitions stirring in Europe and many subtle schemes devised', while he and Gladstone spent their parliamentary time in trying to score debating points off each other as to whether 'armed neutrality' or 'secure neutrality' was the best way to describe Britain's position. After all, who was Bismarck but the pupil of Napoleon III? What were his manipulations and suppressions of the press, his 'coquettings with the working classes' and his 'attempt to turn the attention of the nation, by a brilliant foreign policy, from internal affairs' if not 'various experiments in the noble science of Bonapartism on German soil'?[128]

The *Guardian* had John Bull conclude that 'there's been queer dealings between you two fellows which I don't half know yet. It seems to me that you're two big thieving blackguards; not a pin to choose between you, and that the best thing for me is to look after my own goods and chattels'. *Punch* agreed:

Bismarck against Napoleon! Who the odds will give or take,
   Which of the two more lightly his faith will bind or break?[129]

Moreover, most Britons assumed that although it might be a hard-fought, close-run thing, the war would be fought on German soil and France would win. France's army was comprised of battle-hardened professionals who (it seemed obvious) would be ready for battle far more quickly than Prussian conscripts, and more effective once they got there. Unlike the Austrians in 1866, they too were equipped with breech-loaders – indeed, theirs were known to be better than the Prussian version – and they also had the *mitrailleuse*, a primitive machine gun whose terrifying rate of fire was widely rumoured.

That Krupp's new generation of steel artillery totally outclassed the French bronze cannon was still unknown, and no one except Moltke and his general staff had worked out that Prussia's conscript army would be able to get there fastest with the mostest by using the railways with clockwork efficiency. Russia, her intentions vague, and Austria, assumed to be on the lookout for vengeance, were waiting on the borders of Prussia, while France had only one front to worry about.

All in all, most Britons, in July 1870, saw two deeply unattractive regimes about to fight it out, apparently at the instigation of the French, and with French victory the probable outcome. So there seemed little to worry about other than the loss of one's usual holiday via Paris to the Rhine – and even this sad possibility had a silver lining for a certain much-maligned class of Britons:

Mr Cook has given up the task of conducting his peaceful battalions
   of tourists through the intricacies of a continent disturbed by a war

of indefinite extent ... the suddenly awakened hopes of the English sea-side hotel and lodging-house keeper will probably prove to be well founded.[130]

Once the firing started, Bismarck's subtle understanding of the modern media came into play again. He had realised in his internal battles of the 1860s that if you woo, bribe and cajole the press skilfully enough, rather than trying to command it directly, you can get your message across while preserving for editors, and thus for their readers, the vital illusion of freedom. The *New York Times* noted with interest that the vast majority of British war reporters were welcomed by and flatteringly embedded (as we would now say) with the German armies, while the French tried to manage and guard the news.[131] This was deliberate policy: in meetings of the Prussian Crown Council that summer there are many gnomic references to the Guelph Fund, that vast and secret store of gold which Bismarck personally controlled and disbursed to bribe the German and blandish the foreign papers. The final straw in the early media war was that Napoleon's press loudly trumpeted French success at the first meaningless skirmish in Saarbrücken.

The result of all this was that, in Britain, people initially felt admiration and sympathy for the 'defending' German armies. Reports contrasted the 'tall, broad-chested, clean-limbed, fair-bearded Teuton'[132] with the incompetent, indisciplined (and, of course, Catholic) French soldiery. On 22 August *The Times* felt moved to publish the entire text of 'Die Wacht am Rhein', in order that its readers might have before them 'the original of this famous war song'.

The trouble with free trade

In fact, as the extraordinary series of German victories unfolded, it was not British views of Germany that soured first, but the other way around. This was caused by the gulf of incomprehension between

British and German views on the morality of state intervention in business.

Victorian Britons were obsessed with free trade to an extent which, even to the most sterling modern zealots of the market, must seem to border on madness. With war raging just across the Channel, they still refused point blank to embargo weapons exports to the belligerents. They had done exactly the same in the American Civil War: back then, the only customers, in practice, had been the Confederates, and the policy had deeply soured relations with the US; now, the only possible actual buyer was France – and the Germans were furious.

The Gladstone administration's high-minded, and loud-mouthed, style of making vague moral appeals to peace and humanity seemed to Germans the most atrocious hypocrisy, coming from a government which allowed the continued delivery of munitions to anyone who could pay for them, and knew very well that in the real world this meant supplying one side only.

Liberal Britain had contrived, in 1864, to seem inexplicably hostile to German ambitions, yet laughably powerless to stop them; liberal Britain contrived, in 1870, to seem almost diabolical to Germans, because having accepted that Napoleon was guilty of starting the war, she was now providing the means for him to continue it.

Even the Crown Prince of Prussia – married to Queen Victoria's daughter and supposedly very pro-British – complained to Britain's military attaché and threatened an American alliance.[133] The German Ambassador in London stated that 'even the most eloquent defender of the position taken by Her Britannic Majesty's Government will not succeed in the eyes of Germany'.[134] Sir Robert Morier tried to explain to his many liberal German friends that 'in a country in which Free Trade had become a cardinal point of faith, it was next to impossible for the executive to tamper with the unfettered circulation of commodities', but felt himself engulfed in a great wave of hatred.

Britain's selling of weapons to Napoleon III in 1870 was a disaster for Anglo-German relations, ramming home the fatal idea that, as shown in 1864, Britain was incurably, immorally and uniquely hostile to Germany.

Trapped by its own ideological shibboleths, just as it had been when faced with the disastrous Irish Famine of 1847–9, the British government simply had no idea what to do. Morier gave a memorable description of Gladstone desperately trying to assemble a sort of Victorian-style focus group to help him make up his mind:

> In the meantime the Ministry is going about asking here and there what public opinion wishes. I heard how Gladstone went about on the steamer of the Cobden Club, collecting opinions from individual members like a monkey asking for ha'pence.[135]

Soon Britons began to realise that they had managed to abandon an ally yet still make an enemy, as the German press went to town – led by Bismarck's own journals. The *Pall Mall Gazette* noted that 'the impulse was given from above. It was the inspired papers that started the agitation; and it was not only started with singular promptitude, but with exceeding energy.'[136] Surveying 'the most influential German newspapers', it made this sad report to its readers:

> The inaction of England under these circumstances is attributed to the fact that she is no longer a great Power in Europe. She is entirely given up, these journals say, to the pursuit of commercial interests. Her rulers belong to a middle class which has neither the courage nor the willingness to make the sacrifices which are demanded by a great policy, and they themselves have all the indecision which marks statesmen sprung from the bourgeoisie. The Hamburg *Börsenhalle*, itself a commercial organ of great weight, sets out this view with remarkable plainness and precision. The England we have hitherto believed in, it says, has been an ideal England, ruled by an intelligent and energetic aristocracy, which is in its turn supported by a vigorous and patriotic population of country gentlemen, sailors, and merchants. The German people have wilfully shut their eyes to the progress of that social decomposition which now threatens the existence of England. It needed their recent experiences to convince them how deeply the canker of "mercantilism" has eaten into the national character, and to how great an extent the "ferocious selfishness" of the shopkeeper incapacitates Englishmen from comprehending the policy which can alone secure the true and lasting interests of the British Empire.

It was a catastrophe for relations between the two countries. By the end of August 1870, one of the most persistent parts of the myth which led to 1914 was firmly in place: that British-style 'bourgeois' parliamentary rule made this nation of greedy, unprincipled shopkeepers now constitutionally incapable of making big decisions and great sacrifices.

The bogey born

Once again, Britain had handed the ideological battle to Bismarck. His personal hand in the campaign was immediately divined, and enjoyed, by the *New York Times:*

> M. Bismarck's official paper has been circulating throughout Germany all kinds of attacks upon England, well calculated to produce a vague but strong sentiment of popular indignation ... He does not, perhaps, intend to invade England, for that business would require a fleet, and thus far the Prussians have had their hands full in organizing an army. But Count Bismarck no doubt *does* intend to make England pay the penalty of "throwing over" France by practicing some humiliation upon her – and he is doubtless quite right in supposing that England will tamely submit to it.[137]

While Bismarck stoked the fires of Anglophobia in Germany for his own long-established domestic purposes, British public opinion began to turn rapidly against Germany. Though it was still to be many years before the revelation of exactly how Bismarck had personally spun events in order to produce war-fever in France, the suspicion was already widespread that 'The Chancellor published in his own organ and communicated to the governments of Europe, an incident which never took place, but which had the immediate effect of precipitating war.'[138]

> O Man of Iron, Man of Blood,
> Thy work is clearly pictured now,
> And perfidy well understood
> This age shall brand upon they brow![139]

Britons quite simply no longer believed a word Bismarck said, as this
widely syndicated piece suggests:

BISMARCK'S DIPLOMATIC REVELATIONS:

A Week from a Berlin Almanack.

August, 1870. *Monday.*—Count BISMARCK publishes a draft
treaty, in Count BENEDETTI's handwriting, proposing the annex-
ation of Belgium by France. [N.B.—BENEDETTI's penwiper
and pocket-handkerchief, marked with the Imperial arms, and
left behind by him, can be seen at the Berlin Foreign Office, as
evidence that BISMARCK was the lamb and BENEDETTI the wolf
in this transaction.]

Tuesday.—BISMARCK publishes another secret treaty, in which
France proposes to annex Austria, Russia, Spain, Portugal,
Italy, and a few other countries, and allows Russia to take the
coast of Greenland as an equivalent. [Rejected with virtuous
indignation.]

Wednesday.—A third document published at Berlin, showing
a proposal of France to annex the Atlantic and Pacific Oceans,
the Gulf Stream, and the Papal States; offering the Pope a
kiosque and the privilege of selling newspapers on the Paris
Boulevards. [Discouraged.]

Thursday.—BISMARCK prints another secret proposal, that
France should seize Europe, Asia, Africa, America, and Australia, and BISMARCK Great Britain (if he could persuade the
people there to let him have it). [Rejected, with disgust.]

Friday.—The German Official Gazette contains a further
secret treaty, under which the French agree to take Paris, and
the Prussians to march on Berlin. [Temporized with.]

Saturday.—Further revelation. French proposal to annex
the Eastern and Western Hemispheres, and allowing Prussia to
take the North and South Poles. [Refused immediately.]

Sunday.—Spent by BISMARCK at the Berlin Foreign Office,
rummaging up a lot more revelations for next week.

However much the British had come to distrust Napoleon III in his
final years, and however prone they were to think of the French as
excitable, unstable and always potential revolutionists, there was little
doubt in the public mind by now as to who was behind it all – not just
in the public mind either, for as Granville wrote to Gladstone on 15
October: 'it all looks much as if Bismarck wished to pick a quarrel with
us. He always hated the English.'

On 9 November, the war gained a potentially intercontinental dimension: with France on her knees, Russia took the chance to abrogate the Black Sea treaties which Paris and London had together forced on her after the Crimean War. It seemed to Britons that the old friendship between Russia and Prussia had been renewed, so that Prussia was not merely the great new power, but was ranged geopolitically with Britain's worldwide adversary: 'A secret treaty between Prussia and Russia is spoken of as a matter of certainty.'[140]

It began to look as though sitting on the sidelines had been very rash. The *New York Times* registered the new mood in Britain – and, for the first time, began itself to stop gloating at Britain's discomfiture and worry about the rise of Prussia:

> The working classes favor a determined effort to stop the war. While the moneyed men of "the city" are opposed to interference, all military and naval men concur in expressions of indignation that an effort is not made by England to save France from utter ruin.
>
> PRUSSIAN ARROGANCE.
>
> The insolence of Prussia is passing all bounds. Not content with menacing Belgium, its organ, for example, the semi-official *North German Gazette*, censures the United States fer recognizing the French Republic.   R.

The 'moneyed men of the city', of course, knew very well that Paris was London's sole competitor for the position of Europe's financial hub. As the *Gentleman's Magazine* of 1870 put it: 'with regard to money and capital it must be remembered that the plenteousness existing arises from London being again the great centre of finance of the world'.[141] In fact, from an economist's point of view, you could argue that the fall of France in 1870–71 – at the hands of a power whose stature in the world of money and trade was tiny compared to the might of its army – marks the start of Britain's absolute financial hegemony.

But for most people, any thought of gain by the fall of France was replaced by the new factor: actual *fear* of Germany.

The dawn of fear

British fears which we know from the final years before 1914 were in fact born the moment it became clear that the Franco-Prussian War was only going one way. Even before the conclusive German victory at Sedan on 1 September 1870, the *Daily Graphic* had hit upon one of the most basic images of British nightmares for the next seventy-five years: that of the German military as a force almost superhuman, or rather, virtually *in*human, in its combination of brutality and near-omniscience:

> Perhaps indeed, of all the features of the present war the marvellous secrecy and accuracy of the Prussian movements are the most remarkable . . . the invaders know everything: the resources of every town and village, the amount of stock possessed by the farmers, the nearest by-road from point to point . . . the terrible organisation of the German armies, the all-pervading intelligence which divined and frustrated the plans of its opponents even before they were matured.[142,143]

The shadows of *The War of the Worlds* are already visible. By November, the *Gentleman's Magazine* was airing the spectre of 'a German force being quietly transported to our shores' – exactly the scenario which, thirty-three years later, would make a bestseller out of Erskine Childers's *The Riddle of the Sands*.[144] Before the year was out, even the ever-careful and always non-belligerent *Times* was telling its opinion-forming readers that 'events may come to pass, with all our hopes and endeavours, which may bring us into an attitude of resistance to German aggression'.[145] No less a figure than the Undersecretary of State for India published a little book predicting that Germany, where 'worship of the idea of the state' rules, 'will never rest until she has squadrons in every sea and colonies all over the earth'.[146] A more radical voice, like that of the great historian Frederic Harrison, could demand immediate and outright intervention:[147]

> What should be our policy ? I do not hesitate to say—to check the progress of Prussian ambition. To check it by diplomacy if possible; but by arms if necessary. It is not in the name of France, nor of the French Republic; but in the highest interests of European peace and progress that it is the duty of England to with-stand the domination of a new empire of the sword. It is time to raise the retrograde and military weight of Prussia off Europe, and to force her back to her true place. How is this to be done, even if we wished it, men ask aghast, and what can resist Prussia ? As if statesmanship, energy, and power had left this country for ever. Is this nation Holland, Belgium, Denmark, that it is to count for nothing in European politics ?

In the first week of 1871, the report of a meeting at the Guildhall gives a flavour of this extraordinary sea-change in British views:

> Meetings had been announced with the avowed purpose of precip-itating this country into a war which should have for its object to sustain France in her unequal struggle against the barbarous treat-ment to which she was at present subjected. (The word "barbarous" seemed to strike a chord in the bosoms of the audience, being imme-diately productive of vociferous cheering on the part of the majority, who stood up and waived their hats, sticks, or umbrellas energeti-cally, a demonstration which was repeated at frequent intervals during the meeting when any particularly strong phrase was employed.) After the Emperor capitulated at Sedan and the Empress made her rapid flight, the war ceased to be a war of defence against the French Government, and became a war of aggression waged by the Prussians. (Cheers, and one cry of "No," followed by hooting, and voices – "He's a Prussian spy.")[148]

By now there was no doubt what Britons thought of Bismarck & Co.:[149]

OLD VON SLY BIS. AND PIOUS WILLIAM

A Little War Song.

THERE came three Mortals from the West,
   Three Mortals hale and strong,
And they all swore that fair Alsace
   Should unto them belong.

The first was very grey and wise,
   The second precious sly,
The third was always turning up
   To Heaven his sharp old eye.

The first built on his warlike craft,
   The second on his snares,
The third announced to Europe he
   Depended on his prayers.

VON BISMARCK donn'd his uniform,
   VON MOLTKE he drew his sword,
While Pious WILLIAM raised his orbs,
   And prayed unto the LORD!

They rain'd their shells on hospitals;
   They fired on flags of truce;
They taught the world that war may be
   One horrible abuse.

And then they sat, and reckon'd o'er
   The many fields they'd won;
BISMARCK and MOLTKE grew young again
   While thinking of the fun;

While WILLIAM traced the ruin'd towns
   His conquering foot had trod,
Counted the myriads he had slain,
   And offer'd thanks to GOD!

All this was even before the full horror of the siege of Paris was made manifest.

The siege of British hearts and minds

France in general, and Paris in particular, were foreign, of course – but they were quite simply no longer *strange*. The British *knew* Paris, and they knew at first hand just how close Paris is to London: by 1870, they were going there by the hundreds of thousands annually. The trip was by now well within reach of the British lower-middle classes, and to service their desires, Paris had developed the world's first ever short-stay, city-break, mass-market tourist industry. When the shells started falling, few middle-class Britons, even if they had not done Paris themselves, would have lacked a friend, a relative, or a colleague able to shake their head at the 'rain of fire and iron ... upon the fair sire of cities'[150] with the appalled self-importance of one who has actually been there.

The *Cornhill Magazine* assumes outright the essential familiarity of Paris to Britons: 'Everyone knows the Place by the bridge below: one of the brightest spots in the smiling environs of Paris. Every building around it is a roofless shell ...'[151]

The fact that this destruction was being wilfully visited on civilians was profoundly shocking, even from safely across the Atlantic:

Galleries, Museums, Hospitals, Residences, and Churches Struck.

Women and Children Killed at Night in Their Beds.

French Denunciation and Bismarck's Defense of the Fire.

With only the Channel between them and Bismarck, Britons were stunned. 'The most simple readers of Prussian manifestos', wrote the *Pall Mall Gazette*,[152] 'have now learned to estimate the true character of these "mild Germans"'. And with modern press methods at work, it was not just verbal reports which shocked Britons, but images too:

Bombardment of Paris: effects of a shell bursting in the third and fourth stories of a house.

This was the golden age of the middle-class Victorian house: a print-hung, furniture-stuffed repository of the first wave of consumer goods; a refuge from the boundless noise, smell and Malthusian threat of the big bad city without; a hygienically tile-floored miniature castle. Not for nothing did that matchless seismograph of contemporary feeling, Charles Dickens, give his very own organ a name which, to us, seems catatonically unpromising: *Household Words*. To the

Victorians, that cliché about people feeling raped when their houses are invaded was fresh and real: the Prussian shells which penetrated the homes of Paris smashed their way into the psyche of the British middle classes.

Freudian historians love this sort of thing, and here they surely have a point: the proof is in the pictures, for by the time Paris finally fell, *Punch*'s cartoons all showed France as a tousled, tattered, ruined female figure, being dragged about in chains by Bismarck or trampled upon by Wagnerian Teutons.

And now, there was a new medium to bring home to Britons the full shock of what was going on just across the channel:

> The science of photography, with its absolutely truthful delineations, has reproduced all the hideous features of the recent war and civil strife. Every revolting detail of human suffering, all the unlovely anguish which the most truthful artist would hesitate to portray, is registered by the unerring lens, and snatched from a too merciful oblivion. Pre-eminent among such masterpieces of horror are the photographs now in circulation taken of the dead victims of the recent struggle in Paris.[153]

We could go on and on piling up the evidence from the British press and Britons' recorded feelings, but there is simply no point. The facts are clear, and this is one of those moments when a couple of pictures really are worth thousands of words in trying to make clear just how radically British views of Germany – not just Prussia now, but *Germany* – changed between the summer of 1870 and the spring of 1871. Here are two, published alongside each other in the *Penny Illustrated Paper*.

The first German in Paris is the gay hussar, the gentlemanly warrior on his noble steed, *arme blanche* raised aloft in timeless flourish, entering a well-ordered and apparently undamaged city by the proper route, i.e. through the gate of the city walls. He is a figure who could have cantered straight off the battlefield of Waterloo, the very model of that conventional, aristocratically run, essentially limited warfare which the long eighteenth century had invented, and during whose campaigns, bizarre as it may seem to us now, people had come to expect, at least in theory, that much of normal civilian life – such as private trade even between belligerents, travel for pleasure between countries and learned exchanges between gentlemen – would continue for non-combatants.

The *last* German in Paris is a very different animal, and one which we recognise immediately as one of the dark icons of the twentieth century.

THE FIRST GERMAN IN PARIS

Here is the brute of 1914–18 propaganda, already seen quite fully formed in 1871, an entire generation and more beforehand. And the fears this Germany engendered were not vague, but already quite specific: 'the conviction has become general that England may not only have to fight, but to fight without much warning'.[154] *Blackwood's*, that favourite journal of the officers' mess, published this poem in February 1871:

THE LAST GERMAN IN PARIS

> The Prussian is at Paris's gates
> The Prussian dons the iron crown
> And marshalls all the vassal states
> That at his mailed foot bow down.
> Wake England, wake!

The ruthless treatment of France was enough to give one nightmares: 'If Prussia has the power to demand as war indemnity of the122 French people 200 million ... what be the amount of golden tribute which might be demanded and enforced from THIS country?'[155]

Of course, the Royal Navy was our safeguard. And yet, how long would that be so? The *Pall Mall Gazette* of 11 November printed a message from one of the most respected German liberal newspapers which must have sent a thrill of fear into British hearts:

> Those who believe with Mr. Gladstone that maritime supremacy has become "the indefectible inheritance of England," and that there is no thought abroad of disturbing us within our providential "streak of silver sea," will do well to ponder an article lately published in the *Zeitung für Nord-Deutschland*, the organ of Herr von Bennigsen, one of the leaders of the majority in the North German bund. "In England," says this article, "people look with philosophic calmness on the struggles of continental nations. They believe they are in no danger of invasion . . . Germany not being a naval Power. But let them not forget that we are well aware of our weakness on the sea, and that we are striving with the utmost eagerness to remedy this defect." The writer then argues that there is nothing to prevent Germany from making her fleet equal to that of any other Power in a few years, and proceeds as follows:— "In 1864 Alsen was no obstacle to the progress of our victorious army; and the time will come when neither the North Sea nor the British Channel will stop us.

As soon as this thought was born, the precise strategic blueprint for 1914 – England sending men across the Channel to confront Germany in northern France – arose, as if automatically, forty-three years before the event: 'an English army thrown into France might turn the German withdrawal from before Paris into a second retreat from Moscow'.[156]

It was all pretty drastic stuff. But there was a yet more pessimistic view of the future too: that the brutal despoilers of Paris might actually get to London . . .

The Battle of Dorking

Almost before the smoke had cleared, Prussia-Germany, as the new state was frequently called for the next few years, had become a power which Britons did not merely dislike, but mortally feared. The most extraordinary evidence of this was the rampant success of a magazine story in which Colonel – later General Sir – George

Chesney (1830–95) charted the invasion of Britain by a foreign power:[157]

> Would you like to peep into futurity? If so, read in *Black-wood* the story of the "Battle of Dorking." Upon the publication of a Secret Treaty arranging for the annexation of Holland and Denmark to Germany, England declares war, our fleet is sunk by torpedoes, the enemy lands in Sussex, and inflicts upon us a series of crushing defeats. | The result is terrible disaster.

The Battle of Dorking is still well worth reading, and not just because it is, by common consent, the direct ancestor of H. G. Wells's *The War of the Worlds*. For it shows that the precarious world of globalisation is nothing new to thinking men. In Colonel Chesney's story, Britain is invaded because it has been living in a fool's paradise, which may seem worryingly familiar to Britons today:

> But our people could not be got to see how artificial our prosperity was—that it all rested on foreign trade and financial credit; that the course of trade once turned away from us, even for a time, it might never return; and that our credit once shaken might never be restored. To hear men talk in those days, you would have thought that Providence had ordained that our Government should always borrow at 3 per cent., and that trade came to us because we lived in a foggy little island set in a boisterous sea. They could not be got to see that the wealth heaped up on every side was not created in the country, but in India and China, and other parts of the world; and that it would be quite possible for the people who made money by buying and selling the natural treasures of the earth, to go and live in other places, and take their profits with them.

This nation of deluded shopkeepers is easy prey for the 'North-landers' who have just defeated France and annexed Holland, wear spiked helmets, and happen to speak German. Their leaders are, of course, possessed of an unearthly ability to prepare and organise in secret:

> Everything had been arranged beforehand; nor ought we to have been surprised, for we had seen the same Power, only a few months before, move down half a million men on a few days' notice, to con-quer the greatest military nation in Europe, with no more fuss than our War Office used to make over the transport of a brigade from Aldershot to Brighton.

This is already war in the modern sense, no limited affair of honour and glory in the field, but the triumph of logistical mastery, of the ultra-modern forces which the British had watched shell Paris and shatter French society. The narrator of the book narrowly saves two comrades from being shot down in cold blood after surrendering, thanks only to his ability to appeal to a German officer in German. But this officer is no gentleman:

> The captain heard the tale, and then told the guard to let them go, and they slunk off at once into a by-road. He was a fine soldier-like man, but nothing could exceed the insolence of his manner, which was perhaps all the greater because it seemed not intentional, but to arise from a sense of immeasurable superiority. Between the lame *freiwilliger* pleading for his comrades, and the captain of the con-quering army, there was, in his view, an infinite gulf. Had the two men been dogs, their fate could not have been decided more con-temptuously. They were let go simply because they were not worth keeping as prisoners, and perhaps to kill any living thing without cause went against the *hauptmann*'s sense of justice. But why speak of this insult in particular? Had not every man who lived then his tale to tell of humiliation and degradation? For it was the same story everywhere.

The story ends with Britain hopelessly beaten and with emigration the one hope for its children: 'Happy those whose bones whitened the fields of Surrey; they at least were spared the disgrace we lived to endure.'

It was a sensational hit. Having appeared in *Blackwood's*, it quickly came out in book form and became a publishing phenomenon, selling 250,000 copies in its first year. This figure meant far more then than now: Colonel Chesney had achieved 'a success that has, we believe, been seldom attained by any publication'.[158] Such a stir was created, among professional military men, as well as the reading public, that Gladstone felt obliged to speak out against it publicly.[159] It came out in America too, within the month, and was a hit over there as well:

> Hardly since the time of Dean SWIFT has anything appeared in which imaginary events are portrayed with such startling vividness, and made to appear so real. The description of the battle itself, if it had been an account of a real occurrence in which the writer was himself an active participant, would have been regarded as a remarkable piece of work. As a fanciful representation of what never occurred it is wonderful. The anxiety and excitement at London are depicted with scarcely less power, and the whole piece is evidently the work of an able hand.[160]

Like all publishing sensations, then as now, it created its own market and spawned a legion of imitations. *The Times* quickly ran a serial called 'The Second Armada', in which the Royal Navy indeed saves Britain. By October, the list was substantial:

OCTOBER 1, 1871

LITERATURE.

PAMPHLETS.

We have before us several piles of pamphlets which we propose to look through. There considerable variety in the subjects treated, and also in the manner in which they are treated. We turn first, to those that refer to the possible invasion of England at some future time, to the downfall of our much-vaunted glory, to be effected by the conquerors of our gallant neighbours. There are several of these pamphlets. "The Siege of London," "The Battle of Berlin," "After the Battle of Dorking," "Revolutionary Shadows," "Our Present Crisis," "Probabilities of a Future Invasion," and "The Lull before Dorking," are the most notable. Sir Baldwyn Leighton, to whom we are indebted for the "Lull before Dorking" (publishers, Bentley and Son, New Burlington-street), is of opinion that the question that should occur to a practical mind, on reading the now famous "Battle of Dorking," is, whether our volunteer battalions, in their present unorganised and unprepared condition, would be able to make any stand at all against the Teuton forces.

By the end of 1871, then, Britons were only too well aware of how mighty was the new German Empire, and were only able to refrain from nightmares of invasion because of their confidence in their naval supremacy.

But how did things look from the other side?

The view from across the German Ocean

No nation can experience great victory without intoxication. A miniscule triumph of arms, against a second-rate enemy who never had been, and never could be, any kind of threat to Britain herself, was enough to transform British perceptions of Margaret Thatcher in 1982.

Germany, in the summer of 1870, had for generations been in awe or fear of France. Searing memories of cultural helplessness, physical occupation and widespread collaboration were as close to the Germans, then, and as defining of their attitudes as the Battle of Britain is to Britons now. When war came, almost everyone outside the innermost circles of Bismarck's regime believed that it had been forced upon Germany and would bring devastation yet again to German soil.

Within a single month, these long fears of national subjugation at the hands of France had been spectacularly lifted, and the great dream of national unity achieved. Little wonder it went to people's heads.

A simple comparison, a little 'before and after', can show how profound the change in German feelings was. In 1864 the old-fashioned liberal *Freiburger Zeitung* had called upon the Prussian *volk* to overrule Bismarck & Co. 'by any means possible' in order to deliver a democratic united Germany. But now Bismarck's Prussia had delivered on that dream. Six years later, the same newspaper – now in the National Liberal camp – cried down the notion that it might be best to hold plebiscites in Alsace and Lorraine before annexing them: such 'democratic-cosmopolitan ramblings' could only be 'born of idiocy or of blatant treason to the fatherland'. The 'decadent Alsatians' needed a spell of direct rule by Berlin to turn them back into Good Germans.[161] And in case there was any doubt in the matter – the Crown Prince had, after all, told the world in August that Germany was fighting a war of defence against Napoleon, not one against the French people – the paper then makes things clear:

> But we do not want to delude ourselves any longer about it: our enemy is France, is the French people, not Napoleon. We should be grateful to him inasmuch as he offered us, the most peaceable of all peoples, the chance to settle things with France earlier than we would ourselves have tried to create it. So let the French people devour itself – we want nothing less than to break its power and its arrogance, to force it at last to leave us in peace.
>
> And thanks be to God, Nemesis seems to be descending on this people.

The ancient threat from across the Rhine having been dealt with in such short order, and apparently for good, the Germans were in no mood to take any further lessons from across the North Sea. If the British thought the war had simply been about regime change in France, and that Germany was doing Britain's dirty work yet again (as in the Seven Years' War and at Waterloo), they had better think again:

In England, people seem to believe in all seriousness that the present German war is being waged to give the French a better system of government. As soon as Napoleon has gone, the Germans are supposed to retire from the great battle of the age with the uplifting consciousness of having done the right thing and with a "not negligible" financial compensation. The Moor has done his duty, he can go.[162]

If it's hard to exaggerate the enthusiasm which engulfed Germany after Sedan, it is very simple to explain how the Franco-Prussian War changed German views of Britain. It dealt a fatal blow to the most important of all liberal Britain's exports to Germany: her example.

The *Cologne Gazette* (one of Bismarck's principal mouthpieces) makes it plain that this is 1864 all over again, but in spades, and perfectly tells the tale of how Britain fatefully lost the hearts and minds of the German liberals. It's worth seeing this fatal story exactly as Britons at the time read it:

England of late has sometimes pursued a course which could not but blunt the feelings even of those of her numerous admirers in Germany who respected her as the prototype of a free commonwealth and a Power naturally friendly to ourselves. Her attitude in our national struggle against Denmark, which shook the sympathies formerly entertained for our English cousins, was just on the point of being forgotten when her policy in the French war wounded afresh the susceptibilities of Germany. It has been often explained why the American trade in arms did not irritate Germany to the extent the English trade did. The fact is, nobody expected anything better of the Americans; but that England, who seemed to have inscribed upon her escutcheon the ideal doctrines of peace and civilization, and who had so energetically stigmatized French wickedness at the beginning of the war, nevertheless permitted some sordid souls in her midst to prolong that war by supplying an exhausted enemy with arms; that England took no measures to amend her legislation so as to prevent this virtual interference in the campaign; that

English bullets were suffered to shed German blood, all this, it is but too true, has deeply disappointed Germany. What is the good, the Germans asked, of all that grand phraseology about the peace and progress of nations, if England is loth to take any active steps to secure the continuance of these blessings?

With Britain so clearly exposed, again, as a power who would neither stick by her friends nor stand up to her enemies if there were a fast buck to be made by 'sordid souls in her midst', and whose 'grand phraseology about the peace and progress of nations' was mere cant, why on earth would any German think of Britain as a political mentor now that a glittering counter-example – the Prussian state – had arisen at home?

A country which was united and was to have universal manhood suffrage was surely free? Bismarck had even embraced free trade. The only great liberal policy left unfulfilled was the German Navy, and with the bodies still unburied on the battlefield of Sedan, the *Freiburger Zeitung* already has its thoughts on that one, and drops a clunking great hint as to exactly who had better watch out when this German navy becomes a reality:

> The experience of this war will doubtless encourage Germans so that they do not shy away from any sacrifice to bring the German Navy up to par with the German Army – for only then will Germany be able to play a role thoroughly appropriate to her deserved status as a Power, and a people of millions will not allow nations who number about half as many to dictate laws to it, or allow itself to be shackled in its commercial policies, upon the sea any more than upon the land.[163]

The state of play, 1871

By 1871, Britons were well used to the idea that they might one day have to confront Germany in war, or even resist invasion by her. They were familiar already with the notion that this new Germany was not just another force in Europe, but one inimical to civilisation itself, a threat which *The Times* had described in terms of that great battle 'between East and West' against Attila and his Huns in 451AD. With the Siege of Paris the image had became general: 'Will the civilised world sit still and allow the history of the nineteenth century to be disgraced by deeds that would have shamed the Huns?'* The words 'Hun' and 'German' were not used as actual synonyms yet – no one did it until Kipling in 1903 (see p. 371) – but the mental seeds had clearly been sown. Meanwhile, many previously Anglophile, liberal Germans had become convinced, on the evidence of 1864 and 1870, that Britain was devilishly hypocritical as well as hopelessly corrupted by money-grubbing decadence, that the heroic Prussian way, not the shopkeeperly British one, was the future after all, and that the day would soon come when a united Germany would be able to stand up even to the vaunted Royal Navy.

The outlines of something far more than an ordinary national rivalry, of a full-blown clash of ideologies, were starting to emerge. But still nothing was set in stone. There was now to follow an extraordinary and confusing series of encounters, as the old hegemon and the vibrant new empire circled each other warily. The next decade would include vast boom and great bust, the open threat of Britain leading a grand European anti-German alliance, and the fatal solidification of the notion that the two countries represented fundamentally different paths for mankind. Yet despite all this, the 1870s would end with the great leaders of Britain and Germany on terms so warm that they seemed about to conclude a global alliance which would have radically altered the history of the world.

---

* *The Times*, 23 August 1870; *Standard*, 9 November 1870.

PART FOUR (THE 1870s): THE WARY DECADE

Bismarck turns liberal

After 1871, British fears about a possible German invasion disappeared almost overnight, and the reason is simple: Bismarck, who had seemed the quintessential Junker, now seemed, astonishingly, to have converted to liberalism.

The great American observer of politics, Herbert Tuttle, in the first comprehensive English-language guide to the politics of the new German Empire, explained to his readers just how radical the change was: 'This vast revolution in Bismarck's political opinions – and one more vast than from the old *Junker* reactionists to the Prussian Liberals can hardly be imagined – is one of the facts in his later career that have most invited the inquiry of critics.'[164]

At this stage, the fundamental difference between British-style liberals and German National Liberals was not yet clear to observers, or even to the German MPs themselves: after all, Bismarck really had broken with his old and natural supporters. The Junker estates relied on the Prussian equivalent of Britain's old Corn Law to keep up the price of their wheat in the face of increasing competition from Russia and the USA, so they loathed to the death the idea of anything like a free market in foodstuffs. Bismarck even began, at the direct behest of the National Liberals, to reform treasured and specifically Junker institutions, robbing his own caste of the ancient semi-feudal rights which they still enjoyed as de facto magistrates and police chiefs in the dreary flatlands of deepest Prussia.

The Junkers absolutely hated Bismarck for his treachery. Eulenburg, his closest ally in 1865–6, became a sworn enemy: they refused even to speak until reconciled by their shared grief at the death of Eulenburg's sabre-wielding nephew in 1875, which left Bismarck's daughter broken-hearted. The conservative *Kreuz-Zeitung* itself, though partly Bismarck's own creation and formerly his mouthpiece, turned against him and remained so for ever. It claimed that he would have done better to have died in the field in 1866 than to make his alliance with the liberals, and even accused him of being a stock-market speculator. On 9 February 1876, Bismarck told the Reichstag that 'One should have nothing to do with it. Anyone who reads it and buys it takes part indirectly in lies and defamation.' It was said that he would refuse to have anything to do with anyone whom he found to be a subscriber. A British observer noted how the Junkers in Berlin's equivalent of London's club-land now referred to 'thet [sic] fellow Bismarck, with the first syllable maliciously long'.[165] One member of the Prussian Herrenhaus (Berlin's House of Lords) went so far as to write to *The Times* to complain about the reckless modernity engulfing the new Germany.[166]

It was precisely this modernity that the liberals, all of them, adored. They saw the new Germany as *their* state. After all, it had been forged by the mightiest tools of a new age. Universal conscription, steel artillery and war-by-railways were not the products of a backward huntin' and shootin' feudal aristocracy, but of radical forces, of industrialisation, education, progress, hard work and merit – the very 'bourgeois' energies which, according to Marx, made all that was old and established melt into air. And to prove his allegiance, Bismarck, having embraced the great liberal shibboleths of national unity, a navy and manhood suffrage, now even prayed before the holy of holies, free trade.

To British liberals, nothing could have been more important. Marx was by no means the only Victorian to be convinced that the purely economic ordering of any society was What Really Matters. In fact, he was thoroughly conventional in this belief, for it was born and bred in all liberals, especially the British. They were certain that if only the economic building blocks were got right, the social and political ordering of any society would inevitably rearrange itself accordingly. If Bismarck had embraced free trade, that meant that his regime, however dubious it might otherwise appear at present, had implicitly signed up to progress and was thus, to liberal Britons, *prima facie* a Good Thing.

Like those fatuous modern cultural gurus who believe that any nation which embraces the internet will inevitably be transformed into part of the Free World, Victorian Britons were convinced that untrammelled commerce would, all by itself, convert every society into a version of themselves. They were so blinkered in this belief that it was even proposed to award Bismarck membership of that high church of free trade, the Cobden Club. Bismarck's most hated, and most insightful, British opponent, Sir Robert Morier, was appalled, for he realised that the Chancellor's apparent liberalism was merely a tactic. As a senior member of the Cobden, he blackballed the offer in these words:

> I am totally at a loss to understand on what principle of "unnatural selection" you prose to elect Bismarck, of all God's creatures under the sun, a member of the Cobden Club ... When our great-great-grand-children have to get up the history of the nineteenth century, they will to a certainty find Cobden labelled as the representative of one doctrine – exchange of cotton goods and Christian love internationalism – and Bismarck the representative of the opposite doctrine.[167]

If Britons fetishised free trade, the other great religious cause which united Bismarck and the German liberals went down nearly as well with them too, at first: the battle against the power of the Catholic Church, known to historians as the *Kulturkampf* – 'the cultural struggle'.

Liberal cultural warfare

Bismarck certainly wanted to make the whole new Germany toe the Prussian cultural line, but the liberals – not just the new National Liberals, but the old British-style liberals too – were his more than willing allies in the fight. In fact, the very word '*Kulturkampf*' seems to have been coined, as a positive expression, by the same heroic liberal, Doctor Virchow, who had in 1865 allegedly challenged Bismarck himself to that duel by poisoned sausage.

The Catholic Church seemed to German liberals to represent all the forces of regionalism, atavism and obscurantism against which they strove. The crusade was authorised by the shade of Hegel, to whom having nothing 'alien' in the body politic was a precondition of real liberty: no one in the shiny new empire was to have allegiance to anything outside it, and certainly not to anyone as anti-enlightenment as the Pope.

The British press saw clearly who was the leader here, and who merely the tactical follower: 'The creed of Germanism', said the *Economist*, 'is the mood of Germany and Prussia in the first instance, and of the vigorous but by no means either unobservant or compliant statesman who guides Germany, only in the second instance.'[168] Bismarck was even seen as a sane and moderating voice, reining in the dizzy ambitions of the liberal nationalists:

> Germany, according to the cry of those Germans whose heads were turned by glory of their victories, must receive into its bosom all kindred nations; it must become the first European power not only on land, but also at sea; it must possess colonies and make its power respected in distant parts of the world. The Chancellor of the German Empire seems to have laid all these desires down by his side.[169]

The *Kulturkampf* went down well in Britain at first because Victorian Britons, too, assumed that there was causal link between freedom and Protestantism. Whether they believed that religious modernity gave rise to social progress, or that it was the other way around, they were pretty sure that the two were somehow, if mysteriously, related. Vice versa, Britons also widely regarded popery as the sworn, global enemy of progress: they had daily evidence of this in the shape of Irish nationalism, which was by now thoroughly identified with Catholicism. Any politician who kept his tariff barriers down and stood against both papist 'ultramontanism' and Russophile Pan-Slavism was bound to be widely seen, in Britain, as admirably sound. Statements like these of Bismarck's in 1871 were geopolitical and ideological music to the ears of many Britons:

> The Slavs and Romans, in their alliance with Ultramontanism, try to preserve primitiveness and ignorance; all over Europe they are fighting Germanism, which seeks to spread enlightenment ... From

the Russian border to the Adriatic sea we are confronted with a Slavic agitation working hand in hand with the Ultramontanes and reactionaries.[170]

The *Times*, in 1873, was thus in no doubt that Bismarck was very much to be desired, and lists his foes (many of whom its readers would have recognised as the natural enemies of Britain):

> A great deal of curiosity has been excited by what is called the Ministerial Crisis in Germany – in other words, the communication by Prince BISMARCK to the Court of his desire to resign the Prussian Premiership. Vague hopes have been nourished in anti-Liberal breasts, and whispered congratulations have been exchanged. The "old parties" throughout Europe have been on the alert; the more retrograde of the Junkers, who ten years ago looked upon BISMARCK as their leader, or their instrument; the Romish priests, who have lately felt his hand heavy upon them; the sympathizers with the dispossessed or humbled Sovereigns; the friends of France, the friends of Austria, the friends of Russia; in a word, all who believe that the CHANCELLOR has given to Germany its latest influences, and who hate him accordingly.

But there was, above all, a very practical reason for Britons to feel that the new German Empire was a power with which they could do business: far from being a feared competitor in trade, it was a vast export market for British goods.

Good custom, cheap labour, deep fears

From 1871, the German economy boomed wildly, fuelled by a soon-to-be toxic mix of national overconfidence, half-understood reforms to company law and limitless credit underpinned by the vast French indemnity, which was shipped entirely as bullion, in lead-lined railway wagons under massive armed guard. The German authorities took what seemed to be the logical route and used the avalanche of free gold to straight away pay back all their debts, the vast majority of which were to their own citizens in the form of gilts and war bonds. At its birth, the new Empire was awash with hard cash.

As the world's greatest exporter, Britain was well positioned to supply the overnight spike in German demand. The balance of bilateral trade in Britain's favour between 1871 and 1873 was enormous: over £60m of capital was transferred from Germany to Britain.

It's always incredibly hard to translate such figures into modern equivalents, so perhaps the best way is to put Britain's 1871–3 trade surplus with Germany into a solid contemporary perspective. Bismarck, Roon and Moltke had imagined that an indemnity of £200m (F5bn) would be enough to paralyse France for an entire generation, and were amazed that she managed to repay this colossal sum by September 1873. In other words, the £60m that Britain gained from everyday trade with Germany between 1871 and 1873 was equal to 30 per cent of what Germany extorted from France over the same period by crushing her in a spectacular war and dictating a punitive settlement. Little wonder that, as nightmares about the German Army calmed down, Britons were very happy indeed with Germany's custom.

British businesses were also delighted to continue importing, by way of exchange, one of Germany's great exports: its people.

"A GERMAN PREFERRED."

THERE is an important grievance which the press has rarely dealt with, though it is nevertheless in part the cause of distress and pauperism. We allude to the fact that for work to be done in England and paid for by Englishmen, foreigners, for the most part Germans, are to a great extent employed. This naturally has the effect of throwing Englishmen out of work. Many families have claimed assistance from the parish, when, had it not been for the influx of Germans, they might have obtained work and wages sufficient to procure the necessities of life. In almost every department of commerce, not only clerkships in city firms, but trades such as those of the tailor, the fancy-bread maker, etc. etc., there is a glut of Germans ready to do anything almost at any price.

> These Germans have earned for themselves a good character.
> They are steady, regular, not so much given to drink as their
> English fellow workers; but, what is more important than all,
> they will be content with £60 per annum, where an Englishman
> would expect £100. These foreigners are also very often
> really superior men to the Englishmen who may apply for the
> same post. They are much better educated, more respectful,
> and, in a word, "do not give themselves such airs." No
> wonder, therefore, that the number of Germans in England is
> daily increasing, while Englishmen find no means of employ-
> ment. In fact, in our daily newspapers advertisements for
> clerks, assistants, etc., are sometimes coupled with the
> announcement: "A German preferred."

So, in 1874, a well-educated and respectful German would work for
only 60 per cent of what a half-educated and resentful Briton would
demand for the same job.

How did the Germans do it? Even at this relatively benign time in
Anglo-German relations, it was suspected that German workers had a
dark secret, an additional reason for their mysterious ability to so
undercut British labour:

> We should not omit another special advantage which, at least,
> many Germans enjoy when they live in a foreign country. It
> is a well-known fact that some of these apparently peaceful
> visitors are taking military surveys. In France this was prac-
> tised on a large scale, as was proved during the late war. The
> German maps of France were in several instances pronounced
> to be superior to the French; and there were men in every regi-
> ment personally acquainted with the localities they traversed.
> No doubt but that hundreds of Germans are at this moment
> taking notes even in England, however impossible and remote
> the prospect of an armed invasion may seem.

German spies were evidently invented many years before *The Riddle of
the Sands*. And British readers were left in no doubt of public feeling
across the North Sea. *The Times*'s long article of 4 February 1873 says
it all:

Germany looks with jealousy upon the growth of Russia, but she
hates England. Do not let us indulge in any illusion on this head.
Germany hates us with the intensity peculiar to a strong nature, and

there are few events which would be more cordially relished in the domestic circles of the Fatherland than a crushing defeat sustained by England. I do not presume to explain this feeling; I only record it as an indisputable fact. What is here set down by one correspondent has been frequently told the English by their journalists, not only during the French War, but also after and even before it. Most correspondents agree that England's indifference to recent continental events, her want of regard for ancient allies, and her pacific and conciliatory deportment towards adversaries, is the reasons why she is at once hated and despised.

When, a few months later, the *Kreuz-Zeitung* claimed that America, Russia and Germany were now the real 'three mightiest powers in the world', *The Times* waxed genuinely thunderous:

> if the German Empire will only avoid trenching upon our territory, or stopping any of our rights of way, it is perfectly at liberty to colonize to its heart's content, and to begin with any Bay, Delta, Island, or Peninsula it may choose. So long as it keeps clear of us, we shall neither be irritated nor scared by hearing of its achievements; if, on the contrary, it were to come perversely in our way, we might possibly try whether even in these days, when sailors have given place to stokers and artillerymen, we could not hold our own against one of " the three " mightiest Powers in the world."

So even now, despite brisk business and Bismarck's apparent liberalism, things were by no means all well in the Anglo-German garden.

They were about to get far worse. In 1874, decades of liberal hegemony in Britain came to end: the new Conservative government, headed by Benjamin Disraeli, immediately gave notice of a new and 'forward' foreign policy. Bismarck's personal propaganda organ, the *Provincial Correspondence*, described the surprise of Europe at

ENGLAND AND GERMANY.

British Nimrod (who has shot Tigers in India, and Lions in South Africa). "THE FACT IS, HERR MULLER, THAT I DON'T CARE MUCH FOR SPORT UNLESS IT CONTAINS THE ELEMENT OF DANGER."

German Nimrod. "ACH ZO? YOU ARE VONT OF *TAINCHER!* DEN YOU SHOULD GOM ANT SHOOD MIT *ME!* VY, ONLY DE ODER TAY I SHOODET MY BRODER-IN-LAW IN DE SHDÔMAG!"

By 1873, the once-despised German has crashed the Englishman's hallowed club itself – but he is still an object of ridicule, a combination of bespectacled bore and trigger-happy fool.

finding Britain 'devoting serious attention to events on the Continent'.[171]

That serious attention was soon to leave Bismarck himself spitting blood and iron, for the first unmistakable sign of this reactivated Tory Britain was nothing less than a full-scale bid to curb German ambitions.

Bismarck flies a kite, Disraeli cuts the string

The affair of 1875 is known as the 'War in Sight' crisis. It is almost entirely ignored by British historians, which is all the stranger since most German historians see it as a central event in the story of the young German Empire, the cold shower which made it clear to Bismarck that his new Germany was not, after all, the hegemon of Europe.

The cause of it all was that, by early 1875, Bismarck was in big trouble, and looking for a way out. He had imagined that the Prussian Catholics would behave much as the German liberals had done in 1866, and again in 1871, splitting handily into a 'state-supporting' faction and a rump which, however irreconcilable, would be small enough to ignore. Instead, they forgot their differences over whether or not to accept papal infallibility, and mobilised into an unbreakable unit. Their political movement, the Centre Party, became the most powerful single block in the Reichstag and, since it could count on instinctive backing in the south German states, became a far greater threat to imperial unity than Catholicism had been before.

Bismarck refused to see that he had called it wrongly. Instead, he ratcheted up the pressure to levels which no one had anticipated. As one contemporary British observer put it: 'Prince Bismarck has not only made mistakes, but has stuck to them with perverse obstinacy.'[172] The figures, given in Christopher Clark's wonderful *Iron Kingdom*, are extraordinary: in the first four months of 1875 alone, the Prussian state prosecuted 241 priests, 136 Catholic newspaper editors and 210 Catholic laymen, all of whom were fined or imprisoned. They also closed down 55 Catholic clubs or organisations.

These were merely the public and acknowledged faces of Bismarck's policy. In the secret meetings of the Prussian Crown Council, he even proposed taking the same steps as Henry VIII of England: the outright dissolution of the monasteries and the complete expropriation of all Church monies. Meanwhile, in those same meetings, away from the eyes and ears of MPs, the talk was of having to remind 'Reich-friendly' and 'Reich-loyal' groups of their duty against 'extremists' and 'state-inimical' groups, of dissolving parliament, of stripping MPs of legal immunity if they were held to have insulted the King or the Chancellor, of 'showing Parliament the limits to its powers'.[173]

With economic woes mounting and his parliament incendiary, there was one natural way out for Bismarck: a foreign policy triumph. 'It is obvious', as the *Examiner* put it, 'that the Prince relies on the national animosity of the Germans towards their French neighbours to enable him to carry through his home policy'.[174]

First, Bismarck publicly menaced Belgium, accusing its leaders of not doing enough to stop anti-Reich activity by asylum-seeking German Catholic priests. Tension in Europe rose so that even *The Times*, 'the sworn foe of alarmism', spoke of Germany in apocalyptic, not to say science-fiction, terms:

> Such is the description which the *Times* gives this morning of "the enormous, the preposterous armament" to which Germany now stands committed. The country is to be converted into one vast military machine, terrible alike in its aggregate dimensions and in the perfection of its minutest detail, in the overwhelming force which it is able to exercise, and in the complete subordination of that force to the direction of a single hand and the impulse of a single mind.[175]

On 9 April 1875 came what is perhaps the first example of a political leader deliberately flying a kite in the modern way. Bismarck used his tame but notionally independent press to test how national and international opinion might react if he chose the ultimate solution to internal German disorder: he arranged for an editorial to be published in which it was suggested that another war with France might be in sight.

What happened next made the crisis a milestone in Anglo-German relations, for Disraeli publicly faced Bismarck down.

The new PM had famously been treated to an advance preview of Bismarck's plans for Germany many years before, in London, and had memorably warned the world to 'beware of that fellow: he means what he says'. His view of the man in 1875 was simple: 'Bismarck is really another old Bonaparte again and he must be bridled.'[176] If not, 'we shall have no more quiet times in diplomacy, but shall be kept in a state of unrest for a long time: probably until the beginning of the next thirty years' war'.[177]

As well as possessing such almost prophetically clear sight, Disraeli was every inch as much of a gambler as Bismarck himself, and knew when it was time not to blink. To Derby, he stressed, 'We must not be afraid of saying Bo [sic] to a goose,' and then made an extraordinary suggestion which went against every assumption of his day: 'There might be an alliance between ourselves and Russia for this special purpose, and other powers, such as Austria and perhaps Italy, might be invited to accede.'[178]

It is hard to exaggerate just how radical this idea was. Britain and Russia *allies*? This was truly thinking the unthinkable to mid-Victorians. But Disraeli not only thought it, he and Lord Derby quickly took diplomatic steps to make it a real possibility. Bismarck immediately saw the danger: the British move was 'so serious a course of action, and one so hostile to us'.[179]

Bismarck's overconfident bellicosity had achieved the impossible: it had lined up against Germany even those arch-enemies, Britain and Russia, on the side of France. Faced with this mighty combination, Bismarck had no option but to hastily take the way out which his kite-flying had skilfully kept open, and he loudly denounced the article he himself had inspired.

There was no doubt whatever in Bismarck's mind as to who was the prime mover in his defeat. His foreign secretary roundly called the incident 'the English démarche'.[180] In a 'very confidential' letter to his ambassador in London, Count Münster, of 14 May, Bismarck said that it was now plain that 'England was prepared to raise Europe against us.' He blamed Queen Victoria herself for the British response: 'I think it not unlikely that the private correspondence between the Empress and Queen Victoria may have exercised some influence ... it would greatly relieve and assist my judgement, if I might accept this as accounting for the unexpected attitude on the part of Lord Derby.'

The episode is splendidly revealing about the paranoid self-delusion of which Bismarck was capable. A rational if cynical politician, a realpolitiker of the sort Bismarck is usually supposed to have been, would surely have drawn the obvious conclusion: that Germany was now capable of arousing such disquiet that if she did not watch her diplomatic step, she might even reconcile Britain and Russia. Instead, Bismarck's immediate reaction was to look out hopefully for some secret conspiracy against Germany, involving (of course) English influence at the German court. In a quite amazing letter to his sovereign, he implicitly requested that the Emperor William should interrogate his own household:

> I do not know whether your Majesty thinks it feasible to take Her Majesty [Victoria of Britain] at her word when she alleges that "it would be easy to prove that her fears were not exaggerated". In any case it might be important to discover from which quarter such "mighty errors" were forwarded to Windsor.[181]

There's no doubt how serious the War in Sight crisis was. Queen Victoria herself wrote to the German Emperor, firmly rebutting the suggestion that a chance remark had simply been misunderstood and stressing the unity of the British response: 'It was not an "occasional and lightly made remark", even coming from so eminent a person as Count Moltke, that caused the apprehension felt by my ministers, and which I personally shared.'[182]

The most popular British magazines shared her conviction. *Punch* gave half a page to a long and bleakly comic 'translation' of 'What is the German's Fatherland?', 'respectfully dedicated to Prince Bismarck'. The first and last of the ten stanzas will give the flavour clearly enough:

> What is the German Fatherland –
> As Bismarck seems to understand?
> The land that KAISER WILHELM schools
> In Blood and Iron's rigid rules?
> O, no! – O, no! – within that line
> Fatherland would be clipped too fine.

No doubt the world were Fatherland,
Its own good would it understand
Glad under *Faust-recht* [force majeure] to lie down,
And bow to Blood and Iron's crown –
O, yes! – O, yes! – when that's *my* line
Then Bismarck's Fatherland is mine!

Punch's less clubbable rival agreed completely, suggesting that British opinion was more or less unanimous:[183]

From "Fun."

NOT TO-DAY.

When through the land from lip to lip,
    The rumour rolls that German might
Still longs the dogs of war to slip
    On foes yet helpless from their bite,—
'Tis time for neighb'ring kings to pop
    Their noses in, and calmly say—
" Your little game we mean to stop;
    You had us once—but not to-day."

The truth, though forgotten in Britain today, is plain: less than four years after the end of the Franco-Prussian War, British leaders, with the backing of their public, were seriously considering a broad anti-German alliance in Europe, to include even Britain's arch-rival, Russia.

Nor did this go lost on the German public. When the immigrant ship the SS *Deutschland* was wrecked off Harwich on 5 December, Gerard Manley Hopkins could not resist making the event into one of the most famous religious allegories in British poetical history – and the German press could not resist making it into a political one. It was widely suggested that British ships and coastguards had been slow to aid the stricken vessel because of her nationality. The satirists of *Kladderadatsch* put the double meaning perfectly as the caption to a cartoon of the stricken ship: 'England would quite happily see *Deutschland* go under.'[184]

Already, the public mind in Germany was disposed to see an anti-German conspiracy wherever Britain was involved.

In 1875, then, there is really no sign of that mythical beast: a basically positive Anglo-German relationship. The events of that spring left Britons in little doubt that Germany was now the great potential source of European trouble. Yet again we find that image of Germany as a land almost inhuman in its methodical preparations for war: 'Germany is far better prepared for war than any other nation. The more we study her military institutions, the more we are amazed at their completeness. No knowledge seems beyond their grasp, no detail too trifling for their attention.'[185]

The *Fortnightly Review* reported that the Dutch were scared enough to be preparing to flood the dikes if attacked by 'gloomy, unquiet, agitated' Germany.[186] *Blackwood's Magazine*, reputedly to be found in every officers' mess in the British Empire, put it even more plainly, and was already quite specific about where the clash would (not *might*) take place. It is rather hard to remember that this article was published in September 1876, almost forty years before 1914:

A glance at the map of Europe at once reveals the importance of Holland and Belgium in the cast of the great drama that will have to be acted when Britain and Germany for the first time cross bayonets in a European and national war. We have often had to fight with Germans, but never when in the cause of Fatherland.

Distrust of German ambitions now went right to the top, to that very throne whose occupant had, in earlier years, regularly been accused of being too *pro*-German. Count Münster, the German ambassador, wrote to Bismarck that even Queen Victoria believed Germany was planning to incorporate Holland, and hence the Dutch Empire. He warned his chief that 'it is extraordinary how this latter idea finds credence amongst the English'.[187]

Still, Bismarck was allied to the liberals, and the liberals were convinced free traders. So long as that all-important factor remained, Britain could regard Germany with some hope.

By the mid-1870s, though, free trade itself was under siege in Germany, by the thing that always besieges free trade: economic crisis.

The first Great Depression

It's hard to exaggerate just how hard the Great Depression – as it was known at the time – hit the German psyche in the second half of the 1870s.

Stupendously victorious in war, and with their national money supply tripled in two years, the Germans had changed almost overnight from a poor, hard-working, hard-saving folk to a new-rich people who bought into the dream of endless fast bucks. Until June 1870, no one had been able to float a company in Prussia without a governmental concession: now anyone could float anything at all. Many Germans, accustomed since birth to paternal oversight in all things, failed to realise that this Big Bang, by removing all traditional barriers, had also removed all traditional safeguards. After all, the stock exchange building was the same as ever, the certificates looked the same, the language was the same ... Germany's biggest-selling magazine, *Die Gartenlaube*, explained to its readers, in 1872, how they could found a company themselves and thereby earn 'guaranteed dividends of 15%'.[188]

We have recently been reminded that when the popular media starts talking about guaranteed dividends of 15 per cent, it is time to sell whatever you can, as fast as you can.

The Berlin stock market began to tremble in early 1873, amid share-fixing scandals that came close to touching Bismarck himself, and when the empty train which had delivered the final load of unearned gold from France rolled homewards out of Berlin in September 1873, the crash proper hit almost immediately.

By the end of 1873, sixty-one German banks had simply gone bust. Over the following four years, the Berlin stock exchange just slid and slid, unstoppably. By July 1877 it had lost 60 per cent of its value and did not get back to its 1872 high for over forty years.[189] Prices of German pig iron and of coal – the Victorian equivalents of the oil price as an economic indicator – dropped by well over 50 per cent between 1873 and 1879. Bismarck's personal banker, Bleichröder, reckoned that the new German Empire lost one third of its entire national wealth.[190]

The belated insights of formerly proud and upstanding German industrialists will seem all too depressingly familiar to modern readers. The Society of Westphalian and Rhenish Ironmasters declared, in December 1875, that 'the operation of the laws as to banks and money had occasioned great commotion in the commercial affairs of Germany', while the Cologne Chamber of Commerce – the most important in German industry – bemoaned that 'old firms with good names, that had paid the highest dividends to shareholders for years previously, found themselves placed in a false position by increasing their capital to three times its original amount'.[191]

This first Great Depression affected every country to a greater or lesser degree. But the German experience, coming off the back of seeming invincibility, was uniquely harrowing. It is, in fact, inscribed in the German language to this day: the common term for the early 1870s is 'the Age of the Founders' (Gründerjahre), and we might naturally assume that, by this, Germans mean Bismarck, Moltke or Kaiser Wilhelm I, founders of the brave new empire. But they don't: they mean the founders of soon-to-be-bankrupt banks and limited companies. That is how deeply those mere two years, 1871–3, have been carved into the long German national consciousness.

The vastness of the blow was easily noted by visitors to Berlin. The

Colonial Service's favourite read, *Blackwood's*, dwelt rather gloatingly on the alleged reasons:

> Risky enterprise of any kind is an entire novelty to the German ... Panic masters them more absolutely, and its contagion spreads among them more with most demoralising rapidity. Overdone enterprise and unnatural inflation have sown and broadcast the seeds of mistrust, which may be forced to maturity at any moment.[192]

The German correspondent of the highbrow *Athenaeum* painted a picture just as gloomy:

> The five milliards have turned the heads even of sober people; they have brought in their train swindling, a foolish rage for wealth, credulity about values that never existed, overproduction, gambling on the Stock Exchange, exorbitant wages, high rents, the monstrous rise in prices – finally, the ruin of our ambitious dreams, the great "crash," and, as the necessary consequence of the material poverty, the moral depression, the sterility in the sacred realms of art and science ... The number of empty houses, the diminished attendance at the University, the failure of large banks, the fall, to a nominal value, even if they do not cease to be quoted at all, of shares which, a little while ago, represented hundreds.[193]

Britons knew what was wrong, of course: free trade had just not been tried *thoroughly enough* in Germany. The omniscient market would sort things out if its unseen hand were only permitted truly to work without let, hindrance or loss of nerve. No less an economic authority than the muscular author of 'Onward, Christian Soldiers' wrote that what Germany really needed was 'the throwing open of the ports to foreign competition, and the letting of labour loose to follow trade to its centres, and move with it as it migrates'.[194]

The idea of migrating to follow work was no more attractive to troubled Germans in 1876 than it is for people now. Then, as now, when a win-win bet turned out to be a busted flush, people who had been happily playing the international market looked hastily to the sheltering power of their national state. Another Victorian observer of Germany described things in a way we can hardly fail to recognise:

> Speculation on the Stock Exchange and elsewhere took dimensions and forms never heard of before or since. Those who had money squandered it with a prodigal hand, and those who had it not gambled with borrowed gold and doubtful credit. For a time all went well. It might have seemed that a commercial millennium had arrived. But the beautiful picture was soon found to have sad reverse ... the only people who had benefited were the wire-pullers ... all eyes turned to the State for succour. Self-help stood paralysed, unable to grapple with the terrible difficulties of the situation.[195]

Of course, anyone, then or now, who 'turns to the State for succour' has to have a pitch as to *why* they deserve help. This normally involves saying it was not your fault and claiming that you must now be protected for the general good against whoever or whatever was actually to blame.

This was certainly true in Germany after 1873. The reversal of fortune since the heady days of 1870–71 had been so sudden, and so unexpected, that it seemed almost a fracture in nature itself. How could the unbroken series of triumphs that had led so spectacularly to German unity have been stopped in its tracks like this? How could a country which had shown itself matchless in warfare now be brought low by the workings of mere financial markets?

Something was wrong, something was almost unnatural about it, and someone must be to blame.

But who?

Satan, located

If you are planning a bit of demagoguery, it always helps to find one simple and memorable term for whomever or whatever you say is to blame for everything. It should be a word that can seem vaguely to join up all sorts of things, one that can be chucked easily and damningly into any debate, or even shouted out in meetings, without too much examination of what it actually means.

During the five years of non-stop slide after the crash of 1873, many Germans came to believe that they had found a single word which summed up the cause of every wrong that had been done to them. It was a more or less exact synonym for what we today call 'globalisation' (and is, indeed, still used occasionally in Germany as an alternative to that dread word), but it had the advantage of being quite explicit about the geographical origin of the evil: Manchestertum ('Manchesterism').*

It was all the fault of the Englanders, then. As the crisis in Germany raged, the call from one of Bismarck's most favoured newspapers was to 'reject the egoistical theories of the English free-traders'.[196] The American observer Herbert Tuttle saw clearly that liberals who stuck to their guns were accused of being crypto-British: 'the Government naturally regards them as perverse fanatics, who wish to Anglicise the institutions of the Empire'.[197]

This obsessive identification of 'liberal' with 'pro-British', which had started with Bismarck's efforts to split the liberals in 1864, now became so strong that henceforth, those who continued to press for a freer political and economic regime were denounced as virtually a hostile, Brit-ish state-within-a-state. Bismarck accused Sir Robert Morier of being no less than the 'diplomatic adviser of the parliamentary opposition'.[198]

England was by now the power identified by many Germans with

---

* As a high-powered academic paper recently put it: the 'contrast between "Anglo-Saxon" and German capitalism begins in 1873. The distancing denigration of the "other" variety of capitalism, of the reviled 'Manchestertum' was a crucial part of German national identity formation.' (Jeffrey Fear and Christopher Kobrak, *Origins of German Corporate Governance and Accounting 1870–1914*, XV International Economic History Congress, Helsinki, 2006, p. 14.)

everything that was crossing Germany. When German politicians wished to denounce each other in public, they accused each other of being virtual Englishmen; when German diplomats sought to account for their reverses, they saw secret English machinations which even allegedly involved anglicised elements within the royal family; when German industrialists, having boomed madly and bust spectacularly, squealed for protection, their cry was specifically against allegedly unfair English competition.* All in all, the situation by the mid-1870s, was about as far from a default setting of some deep-rooted Anglo-German friendship as it is possible to imagine.

This sense of England as some kind of malign, underhand and specifically anti-German power was crystallised in the work of a man who was to be of fatal importance in the rising antagonism: Heinrich von Treitschke.

The voice of National Liberalism

Treitschke was the first great media professor in history.

He had it all: vast and unimpeachable research, a track record of speaking his mind even when it was unpopular (he was well known to be the son of a very anti-Prussian Saxon general), a prestigious university post, official status as Historiographer Royal to the Prussia State, a winning popular style derived consciously from Macaulay, a bear-like physical presence, unmistakable personal quirks (he was almost deaf and his voice was described as drum-like), a media presence which made him the gate-keeper for the careers of others, and a thesis that was splendidly timely.

---

* Big industrial employers did not want to abandon free trade entirely, because tariffs on imported foodstuffs would cause their workers to agitate for higher wages. So they argued that anti-British tariffs were not *actually* anti-free trade as such because Britain's industries had natural advantages – easy access to good coal, cheap water transport and low-interest capital – which amounted to an unfair subsidy and therefore distorted the market. For the specifically anti-British nature of the proposed import tariffs in Germany, see e.g. the *Guardian*, 5 August 1876; *The Times*, 2 December 1878 and 4 February 1879.

A contemporary American observer of the Reichstag described Treitschke's parliamentary speeches:

> I am compelled to say that Treitschke is one of the most outrageous speakers who ever addressed an audience. He has no control over his voice, his intonation, or his utterance. He mumbles, and roars, and shrieks; he brandishes his arms and shakes his fists; he pounds with hands and feet; and during all these physical contortions, never interrupts the foaming torrent of his words. His manner is more that of a fanatic, or a madman, than of a moderate and somewhat Conservative professor.[199]

It's hard to overstate Treitschke's status in the German Empire, his value to Bismarck in the 1870s, or his importance in the fateful souring of Anglo-German relations. Almost all the key figures of the Wilhelmian establishment in the thirty years before 1914 – men like Admiral Tirpitz and Chancellor von Bülow, not to mention, Kaiser Wilhelm II himself – cited Treitschke as a matter of course. It's also hard to exaggerate the almost demonic position which England more and more occupied in Treitschke's version of history. The distinguished Professor of Philosophy at Berlin University, Friedrich Paulsen, recalled attending Treitschke's lectures shortly after his own appointment in 1878: 'He was just speaking about England, and the invective he poured out in his blind hatred of English philosophy and the whole English mode of thinking became so intolerable to me that I walked out of the lecture room.'[200]

Precisely because his liberal bona fides in the years before 1870 were beyond reproach, Treitschke's drum-like shriek was assured the widest hearing in the Reichstag, where he sat as guru of the National Liberals. In his voluminous writings, he now preached, in jewelled, high-Victorian prose, a German version of the great sweep of history which Macaulay had held up to his grateful British readers.

Treitschke's vision revealed to entranced Germans that the hidden goal of things, traceable even in the most distant, obscure and apparently pedestrian minutiae of Prussian history, had always been national unity and that the Royal Prussian State, even in its most primitive forms, had always, even if unconsciously, been the fated vehicle of that consummation. He took Hegel's praise for the Prussian state as the vehicle of world history even further. The extension of Prussia, the unity of Germany, Germany's taking of her rightful place in the world and the triumph of Progress itself were, in practice, all one and the same magnificent story. Any augmentation to Prussian power was by definition good for Germany; any augmentation of German power was by definition good for the world.

But something was rotten in the state of things. The splendid and inevitable unfolding of world history was being blocked, as if in contravention of nature.

But who, or what, was the villain? Was it not obvious? There was one power on Earth which achieved its ends not in manly battle, but by the sneaky power of finance; one power on Earth which dominated things without a vast army; one power on Earth which denied the ultimate authority of the nation state to proclaim that 'modernity' and 'progress' consisted merely in men being allowed to seek private advantage and profit wherever it could be found, irrespective of morality or religion or community; one power on Earth to whom loud protestations of 'freedom' meant merely the freedom for itself to enslave the nations of the world by money. This power, though it worked ceaselessly to undermine all notions of independent nation-hood in others, remained in itself a potent and self-recognising political unit. Never prepared to stand openly, or to shed its own sons' blood, it was always on the lookout for satraps or hirelings to further its unsleeping pursuit of a vast, gold-driven hegemony. Germans, with their honest simplicity, had been the greatest dupes of this power. It was the presiding ideological deity of the market whose crash in 1873 had so soured the paradise of German unity, and it was well known to be especially inimical to Germany, which (as the great Hegel had often stressed) had a fundamentally different and far healthier, more organic, more rooted and communitarian definition of 'freedom'. This people judged things only on 'the basis of what is useful' and were unable to 'lovingly grasp the nobility of the soul of the German people'.

It was, of course, Britain.

According to Treitschke, Britons owed their world-bestriding empire to Frederick the Great (in the Seven Years' War) and Blücher (at Waterloo), but had so little intention of ever treating Germany as an equal – i.e. of sharing with her the hegemony of the world – that they even begrudged her that self-evidently beneficent triumph of 1870. By the mid-1870s, he wrote to a friend that 'through my historical stud-ies I am becoming ever clearer about England and about her permanently hostile policy towards Germany'. He now saw the enmity of England 'at every moment we were happy – in 1864, 1866 and 1870'.[201] His influence on other German historians was so widespread that by the end of the 1870s, the *Pall Mall Gazette* noted that 'Herr von Treitschke has assigned to England a very subordinate role in the wars which resulted from the French Revolution' and ironically praises a British historian who 'is old-fashioned enough to present the Battle of Waterloo as an English victory without alluding to the scoffs with which that claim is now received by German writers'.[202]

In particular, the triumph of Germandom would be good, said Treitschke, for the many countries at present under the sway of the hypocritically universalist Englanders who, driven purely by the desire for profit and having no truly, deeply folkish culture of their own left, valued no one else's. England might once have been an honest north German culture, but she now ran her affairs – and wished to run those of the world – simply 'after the fashion of the Manchester school, seeing in man a biped creature, whose destiny lies in buying cheap and selling dear'. The holy nature of the state was reduced to a 'priesthood of mammon'.[203]

Luckily, there was a global alternative for the world: Germany was now destined to supplant Britain, even on the seas.[204] A radical change of status in Anglo-German relations must come. It was time for the baton of world history to be passed on by the decadent English to a German empire which would be as a light to other nations: 'the day must finally come when the peoples of earth come to see that Kaiser Wilhelm I's battles did not merely create a fatherland for the Germans, but have also given a more just and rational order to the whole idea of the state and society'.*

In practice, this meant to Treitschke that Prince Bismarck was always right. The direct hotline between what Bismarck wanted and what Treitschke wrote was particularly obvious in 1876, when Treitschke's rabid anti-Britishness first began to be noticed across the North Sea.

Bismarck unleashes Anglophobia

Bismarck's policy towards Britain completely turned on its head and then back again in the years 1876–80, so the period can easily be confusing. The trick is to see what made him act in this way.

---

* The quotations in this section are from Heinrich von Treitschke, *Ausgewählte Schriften erster Band* (Leipzig, 1907), pp. 3, 22, 23, 321, 333.

In 1876, Serbia, by now independent in every definition of the word save that of international recognition, declared war on Turkey, starting that campaign to incorporate Bosnia which would rumble bloodily on through the next 120 years of European history. The powers now had to take positions as to who was going to inherit what from Turkey, the sick man of Europe. For some, the lines were clear: Russia would back Serbia, Austria would oppose her. The newly muscular Conservative Britain was not going to let Russia and her satellites dominate the Aegean and the western shores of the Black Sea, so Britain, under Disraeli, wanted to prop Turkey up, religious differences or no. This made Britain and Austria natural allies.

The great question – it was the same question as in July 1914, of course – was what Germany would do if the Balkans caught fire: 'Everybody is eager to know how Germany will act if Russia should pass the confines of diplomacy, for more easily than any other State could she hem in the contest or make it spread.'[205]

For a good Prussian Junker like Bismarck, an understanding with Russia was always second nature. But for all his apparent dominance, Bismarck's power at this time still depended on his alliance with the German liberals – and they were, by nature and historical experience, decidedly anti-Russian. They were also, however, deeply Anglophobic. So Bismarck wheeled out the very biggest of his still nominally liberal but in fact thoroughly biddable guns. Treitschke obliged by laying royally into England, informing his legions of followers that Britain was not only a Very Bad Thing, but also a complete has-been, and that the future lay in a Russian alliance after all. The press which backed his party joined in obediently.

Britons now learned that 'the *National Zeitung*, organ of the National Liberals, devours great Britain raw once a week' and that the whole press 'taunts the English nation with cowardice, impotence, perfidy and imbecility'.[206] They were introduced properly, for the first time, to Treitschke:*

---

* Treitschke had previously been known to Britons merely as a 'moderate liberal' who was considering a tactical alliance with Bismarck. See the *Standard*, 22 January 1867.

He is a Liberal Deputy in the Reichstag, a Professor of History at the Berlin University, and the most brilliant political essayist of Germany. It should seem that such a man would be drawn toward England by all the instincts of his nature, and that he would shrink with horror from the intolerable despotism of Russia. Such is not the case. In his essay which appears in the current number of the *Preussische Jahrbücher* he not only caresses the Russian bear with unmeasured affection, but he scolds the British Lion like a fish-woman. England, he says, is the representative of barbarism in international law. She not only refuses to surrender the advantage which her naval superiority gives her on the ocean, but she even refused to support the beneficent proposals of the Brussels Conference. She has been the defender of everything bad, and the open or secret foe of everything good. She was the friend of slave-holders in the United States as she is the champion of Turkish despotism in the East. These are mild statements of the ingenious publicist's position, although the habits of English composition require some reduction from the uncanonical vigour of his language.[207]

We are still, today, in thrall to Victorian notions of deep, if mysterious, 'forces of history', so it may seem to be stretching things to suggest that Bismarck's own hand is so tangible in these events. But that is exactly how British pressmen of the day saw it. *The Times* argued that it made no difference whether one was directly attributing statements to Bismarck himself or 'politely making a distinction between him and his journalistic staff', for 'the idea that the sensational articles of the *Nord Deutsche Allgemeine Zeitung* and its affiliated organs could have been penned without orders is, I find, regarded as simply preposterous'.[208] Bismarck 'does not disdain to dictate newspaper articles himself sometimes', and much of the German press was 'directed by a single hand'.[209] His changing policies and alliances would always be 'seconded by his journalists with a fierceness and an intense delight in extravagant verbiage which strikes one as almost incomprehensible'.[210] Looking at the German press of 1877, British newsmen were certain – and they should, after all, have known – that this was a deliberate media-political campaign:

> It is remarkable with what zeal the Government press has lately been inciting its readers against England. This can create no surprise in the *North German Gazette*, the Prussian *Moniteur*, as it is ironically called; but that a staunch Liberal like Professor von Treitschke should join in violent exclamations against England gives rise to serious concern. The embittered article published by Professor von Treitschke in the *Prussian Annals* is full of the most perfidious expressions … Treitschke, who is quite deaf, seems to have lost all comprehension of the present European policy, and yields to fantastic dreams having no real basis.[211]

LONDON, FRIDAY, DEC. 21, 1877.

Professor TREITSCHKE has often done yeoman's service for Prince BISMARCK in the pages of the *Preussische Jahrbücher*, and it is not impossible that his last performance is intended as a " feeler " for the German public on the subject of the Eastern policy of the CHANCELLOR. In spite of the confidence which the German nation are naturally disposed to put in the policy of their great MINISTER, it has been felt of late that the relations between Berlin and St. Petersburg have been too intimate for general approval.

The *Pall Mall Gazette* reminded readers that Treitschke was the chief propagandist of extreme nationalism in the Franco-Prussian War, and that he was paid by 'his official masters' to be so out of the 'reptile fund'. His opinions were known to be more than just private ones. Britons were told exactly what (according to Treitschke) the entire German nation now thought, or should think, of them:[212]

Despicable sloth and malignant activity can hardly be imputed with accuracy to one and the same offender, but Herr VON TREITSCHKE is much too angry to be logical. The first charge is used to persuade the German people that an alliance with this country would be worthless, the second to quicken their resentment against us for the wrong they suffered when we denied them "benevolent neutrality." At any rate the offences of which England is guilty justify not only her ostracism in the councils of Europe, but a retribution such as that which stripped France of Alsace-Lorraine. Herr VON TREITSCHKE warns us that "the time will and must arrive when Gibraltar will belong to Spain, Malta to Italy, Heligoland to Germany, and the Mediterranean Sea to the peoples of the surrounding countries."

The political cartoons of *Kladderadatsch*, Germany's *Punch*, in the years 1876–8 are peppered with this new importance of Britain for Germany. She is no longer shown as the moth-eaten, toothless old lion of the 1860s, but as a confident, arrogant power led by a cunning (and Jewish) leader.

Disraeli's Britain as the slippery, cunning, somehow inhuman Octopus Britanicus, embracing all Europe.

Disraeli promises Turkey that, if need be, the British Lion will devour Russia – with his big mouth.

Disraeli as shopkeeper (selling tea and opium) rebuffs Bismarck's offer of a conference at Berlin, since what really concerns him is India, not Europe.

'It is well known that the Englanders have a big mouth and small army.'
Disraeli desperately seeks someone (i.e. Germany) who will pull his chest-
nuts out of the fire for him.

But just as Bismarck's press tried to prepare liberal Germans for an
anti-British alliance with Russia, the wind changed. The real, and eventually deadly, horns of his dilemma took shape.

Bismarck's nightmare

The hero of German unification feared nothing on Earth so much as
its actual achievement. Russia could certainly menace the new German
Empire in battle. France was sure to try for revenge. Britain might cross
Bismarck's ambitions. But Austria was capable of destroying the new
Prussia-Germany without even firing a shot: the Habsburg Empire
could be revenged upon Prussia for 1866 at any time it liked, simply by
collapsing. If it did so, the pressure to admit the Austrian Germans into
the new empire, to let them leave 'the Monarchy' and enter 'the Reich',
as the Pan-Germans put it, would be simply overwhelming.

Bismarck had potently harnessed the logic of German unity for the enlargement of Prussia, but this was in the end a fudge, and he knew it well. He suffered actual nightmares, recorded in his letters, at the thought of what might happen to his Prussia-Germany if eight million southern Catholic Germans centred on Vienna entered the empire: their natural ties of religion, dynasty and custom with the big Catholic kingdoms south of the River Main would shift the balance fatally away from Berlin. But that is what it would come to if Austria-Hungary fell: the whole logic of German unity would demand it.

Bismarck's National Liberal allies remained Greater Germans, wedded to the law which said that all Germans ultimately belonged together. Their great eminence, Treitschke, had been declaring ever since 1871 that if anything happened to the old Habsburg Empire, it would be the national duty of the new German Empire to step in and 'save the Germans on the Danube from the ruins'.[213] Men like Treitschke certainly adored Bismarck, but their worship was still, in the final analysis, conditional. Bismarck was the man who had largely delivered, and was still completing delivery, on *their* great dream of national unity. Even Bismarck could hardly pose as the hero of German unification while at the same time openly blocking it.

No: if Germany was to stay safe for Prussia, Austria-Hungary had to keep on existing. The entire diplomatic history of Germany from 1877 to 1918 was determined by this single fact. It meant keeping the Balkan Slavs, in particular Serbia, from achieving their own ends. But that, in turn, would mean taking an open stand against Russia, who claimed increasingly to speak for all Slavs everywhere – and who believed that Bismarck owed her a massive debt for her neutrality in 1866 and 1870.

Stand against Russia with a vengeful France and a hostile Britain at Germany's back? Impossible. Allow Austria-Hungary to implode? Equally impossible.

There was only one way out of Bismarck's dilemma. Someone else would have to be found who was willing and able to take a stand against Russian ambition in the Balkans.

There was, of course, only one possible candidate.

The ships, the money, the men

In the spring of 1878, Britain was for once looking very un-decadent indeed. Disraeli knew exactly how to play to the gallery he himself had invited into the theatre of British politics: 'Raising his voice to its fullest compass, and uplifting his arms to add impressiveness to his concluding words, the noble Earl brought his well-sustained speech to an ultra-dramatic close by a piece of vigorous declamation which might have been inspired by the patriotic strains of "Rule Britannia".'

Britons were raring for a fight, loud in support of Disraeli's 'consistent and daring policy ... deliberately ostentatious preparations for possible war'.[214] London was alive with 'Jingos', who had made themselves and their mindset a name forever with their music-hall refrain: 'We don't want to fight but by Jingo if we do, we've got the men, we've got the ships, we've got the money too.'

But for all her ships, her money and her men, would Britain really have the guts? Count Münster, Bismarck's ambassador in Britain, reported closely on events in London to his master, and he thought Britain was serious. He believed Russia had underestimated Britain's military power, and he made sure that Bismarck knew Disraeli was merely channelling British public opinion: if Britain now backed down, Münster informed Bismarck, British ministers 'could not go through the streets in safety for fear of violence'. His report of the great pro- vs anti-war riot in Hyde Park in February 1878 is a reminder to us of just how splendidly muscular Victorian politics was: the battle was easily won by the Jingos, who then 'went to Mr Gladstone's house and broke his windows, whilst the larger number proceeded to Downing Street and cheered Mr Disraeli'.[215]

Was Britain, so long pusillanimous, truly ready for war with Russia? Bismarck had to know, and being Bismarck, the only way he could feel sure was to look Disraeli in the eyes. He summoned all the powers to a great conference in (or, as Victorians put it, *at*) Berlin, proclaiming that he would play the 'honest broker', secretly driven by his desperate wish to not be forced to choose between Austria and Russia.

Britons did not trust him an inch. Count Münster had tactfully failed to mention to Bismarck that as well as the Jingo song, there was another ditty, now long forgotten, doing the rounds about Bismarck himself:

> Vat is de German's vaterland?
> All dat Bismarck's hand can grasp
> Dat is de German's vaterland.

The *Graphic* told its many readers, with notable insight, that 'a war between England and Russia would suit Germany remarkably well',[216] and it seemed at first as though Disraeli might not even attend the conference. *The Times* reminded Britons of 'the support which Bismarck has given to Russia in the present war',[217] and the *Observer* warned that 'it seems to us doubtful how far England can take part with advantage in the deliberations of a court whose chief function will seemingly consist of sanctioning any arrangements Russia may think fit to propose'.[218]

By late April 1878 war seemed merely a matter of days away. Readers of the *Guardian* learned, on 27 April, that 'a powerful squadron of iron-clads and other steamers is to be immediately got ready for operations on the Baltic' and that merchants at Antwerp, Rotterdam, Hamburg and Bremen were 'refusing to consign their goods on board ships sailing under the British flag' for fear of them being taken by the Russians. The next day, the *Observer* reported that 'Advices from St Petersburg state that all negotiations between England and Russia have been finally broken off', and two days after that, the *Morning Post* voiced the British Empire's abiding nightmare of losing the Great Game itself: 'General Tchernayeff, who is the heart and soul of the panslavist party, has fully reingratiated himself with the Czar ... mainly by a plan for an invasion of India which he has worked out and submitted to the Czar. The Czar has laid the plan before a council of officers, and they have approved it.'

The *New York Times* reported that 'the Russians are preparing to attack the British on the seas',[219] and by the end of May, *The Times* declared that 'the culminating point of the crisis is now so near ... there will doubtless be many deeds of naval daring to add to the chronicles of the British Navy'.[220]

Which way would Germany jump? In May 1878 it looked to Britons as if Bismarck was going to side with Russia – which was no doubt exactly what Bismarck wanted everyone to think, as he tested the waters to see if Britain's apparent new resolve was real. As ever, his hyper-modern tactic was to use non-attributable, plausibly deniable articles in his pet newspapers to gauge possible reactions in advance. One of his best-known mouthpieces – his 'first fiddle', as *The Times* called it – the *North German General News*, was reported to be leading 'a cry of alarm against England ... that for years past England had sought to prevent the development of Germany and to thwart her policy'.[221] Britons were told exactly how Bismarck's press was portraying them: 'England, the champion of Mahomedanism; England, the advocate of Christian slavery in the East; England, the gasconading proprietor of a handful of tin soldiers – such were the style and title bestowed upon the British nation and Cabinet by the literary myrmidons of the German Chancellor.'

As Britain and Russia geared up for war in both the north and south of Europe, readers of *The Times* in May 1878 – and that, of course, meant everyone who mattered in Britain – were warned that Bismarck's first fiddle was talking of an active Russo-German military alliance not only in the Balkans, but in Britannia's own back yard:

> The attitude recently assumed by England has brought Berlin semi-officialism to a climax. It having been reported a few days ago that England might have occasion to send a fleet to the Baltic to blockade the northern shores of her possible adversary, the *Nord-Deutsche Allgemeine Zeitung* thought it appropriate to put the finishing touch to its many previous amenities and menace England with war.

It was amid these rumours of wars, on a fine May morning now long-forgotten but remembered for decades afterwards, that the new weapon in Prince Bismarck's military-diplomatic armoury, a totally unprecedented factor in the Great European Game, forged out of, and setting the seal on, his alliance with the German liberals, appeared quite literally out of the blue before the White Cliffs of Dover.

An ironclad in the shape of a gigantic fish

Thirty years later, the hyper-patriotic, and rabidly anti-English, *Marine Handbook for German Youth* of 1908 was to remember the day as a 'dreadful wound' and yet, as *Die Gartenlaube* was shortly to put it with melancholy irony, 'it can seldom have been that the sun has shone more happily down upon the coast of Old England'.

Victorian pathos aside, the last day of May 1878 really did dawn gloriously on the White Cliffs at Folkestone, dispelling the thick, stormy weather of the previous day. The *Observer*'s description did not omit the picturesque aspect, but added more prosaic, though more useful, information for its readers, who, Britons that they were, would be nautically literate to some degree. 'The morning was exceptionally fine and clear. Bright sunlight was streaming from a cloudless sky, and there was gentle breeze blowing from E. N. E.'

Mr W. J. Jeafyreson (as *The Times*'s compositors misnamed him in their haste to get his eye-witness account typeset that very night), 'hearing that some ironclads were in sight', went 'out upon the cliffs to watch them'.

And no wonder. In the war with Russia, which was widely seen as imminent and inevitable, everything rested on the ironclads, those vast, armour-plated, steam-driven warships which were the equivalent of today's aircraft-carriers: by far the greatest and most expensive pieces of mid-Victorian military hardware. To Britons in particular, they were objects of deep interest, national pride – and endless debate that often shaded into foreboding.

The mere sight of one of these metal-sheathed, piston-powered monsters flying anything but the homely ensign served notice that

British rule at sea, for decades assumed to lie secure in matchless seamanship, wooden walls and sheer Nelsonian pluck, was now at the mercy of technological change. Naval strategists were haunted by the possibility that a new step-change might at a stroke render all today's fleets redundant. As the nation which possessed and required the greatest fleet in the world, it was the British who always had the most to fear from such an event.

The great problem of the day was that there had been, as yet, so very few engagements between modern warships. The *Guardian* claimed that 'armour plated ships would always possess an advantage over guns', while the *Observer* argued that 'everything points to the final victory of the gun and to the time when ships, like men, will have discarded their mail as a useless incumbrance'.[222] Then, were the new turret guns or traditional broadside batteries more effective? The evidence from the American Civil War, and from the Italo-Austrian battle of Lissa in 1866, appeared to suggest that if ironclads were more or less invulnerable to cannon fire, there was another sure way of sinking them: by ramming. The destruction of the Italian flagship at Lissa by this ancient means had so impressed people that for the next twenty-five years every battleship in the world was conceived and built with an entirely useless ram.*

And there were new, hi-tech weapons to be considered. Whitehead's new torpedoes threatened to turn all ironclads into mere coffin-ships: in the spring of 1878 they were discussed, and even counted individually, in much the same way a later generation of British naval experts would fearfully track the supply of Exocet missiles. Count Münster's reports to Bismarck mention the feverish search, while *The Times* reassured readers that 'the Russians had only 50 Whitehead torpedoes at the commencement of the war with Turkey, and five of these we know to have been used'.†[223] As the crunch with Russia loomed ever closer, the AGM of the Institution of Naval

---

* Two decades hence, when he wrote *The War of the Worlds*, H. G. Wells would still call the doomed battleships of Earth simply 'rams'.

† Among the junior officers currently training with and developing this fearsome new weapon were both the future Admirals Fisher and Tirpitz.

Architects discussed a paper on 'Crude Petroleum Equipments for the Purposes of Naval Warfare' ('crude' referred to the state of the petroleum, not the apparatus). The Russians were stated to be actively interested in this terrible new weapon.[224] Another fearful possibility seemed to have sprung from the pages of 'one of the mildest of Jules Verne's wild romances':

> A vessel has been projected of which a model has actually been submitted to the Admiralty. It is an ironclad in the shape of a gigantic fish. In its forepart or head are large eyes through which is shot a strong electric light enabling its occupants to see their way before them beneath the surface. There are no masts, and the centre of the vessel is mainly taken up by large chambers, filled with compressed air. At the stern is a powerful screw and in the bows is a gun of more than usually complex character, and calculated to do considerable damage under water. It is claimed for this extraordinary vessel that she can remain beneath the surface for three to fifteen hours and can work at a speed of eighteen knots an hour.[225]

No wonder, then, that W. J. Jeffreyson hurried out to see these mysterious ironclads off Folkestone.

When they arrived at the cliffs, his wife 'immediately exclaimed "Why, it must be the *Great Eastern*!"' But her husband knew that it was not Brunel's leviathan, world-famous for having some ten years previously laid the transatlantic telegraph cable. It was 'obvious even to a landsman's eye' that this was not one gigantic ship but two large vessels in unusually close proximity.

Meanwhile another resident, who signed himself A. J. S., was also observing events nearby:

> I stepped into a balcony over the cliffs a few minutes before 9 to sweep the Channel with my glass. The most conspicuous objects were the three stately ironclads which had rounded the South Foreland and were moving slowly in line down the Channel. The foremost of them, at that particular moment seemed to be clearing

the heads of the Admiralty Pier at Dover. Two of them, single-funnelled, appeared to be almost sister ships; the motion of the squadron was as smooth as it was majestic and assuredly the monsters ought to have been under the most perfect command. After a leisurely inspection I went in for breakfast.

While A. J. S. breakfasted (on devilled kidneys and kedgeree, one imagines) and perhaps forgot the looming war by reading the lighter news in the papers – the preparations for erecting Cleopatra's Needle, or the latest triumphs of the first real, representative Australian XI on their progress towards the Oval next week – W. J. Jeffreyson's party stayed out on the cliffs, watching as the mighty ships 'glided with a rapid but stately motion a little to the westward of the spot where we were standing'.

The cut of these vessels' jibs – the phrase is literal here – was distinctly British. The flagship of the squadron, leading it past Folkestone at that moment, was a famous vessel: when launched ten years before from the Thames Iron Works at Poplar, she had been the most powerful single battleship in the world, and was still arguably so. Her consorts, though somewhat smaller, were more modern: turret ships, sisters, launched in 1874 and 1875, and easy to mistake for Britain's own state-of-the-art *Monarch* for the very good reason that they had been modelled exactly upon her.

But whose ships *were* they?

'At length,' wrote W. J. Jeffreyson later that day, when he sat down to describe the event for other readers of his favourite newspaper, 'a friend with a powerful glass succeeded in making out the German flag.'

Enter the forgotten German Navy

Now, according to all the standard modern works on the Anglo-German naval rivalry, W. J. Jeffreyson should have been perfectly astounded: everything to be found in any bookshop or public library will clearly suggest that until Wilhelm II and Tirpitz came along, there had essentially been no German Navy to speak of.*

Actually, any informed Briton would certainly *not* have been surprised at seeing the German flag flying over a squadron of the largest, most powerful ocean-going battleships on Earth back in 1878, for the simple reason that the British press had been following maritime developments across the German Ocean very closely, and with considerable misgiving, over the previous years.

Even in the 1860s, Britons had been well aware that Germany was a land 'whose long-cherished project was to become a great maritime power'.[226] Since the German Army's triumph in France, that prospect now became deeply worrying, for it was now only the Royal Navy's control of the Channel which kept at bay the bestselling terrors of *The Battle of Dorking*.

In 1871 it was already reported that 'a rumour is current in Berlin of Mr Reed's intention to accept an offer made to him by the German government to take an office in the Marine Department of the German service'.[227] Readers did not need any further clarification of 'Mr Reed', for he was a very well-known public figure indeed in mid-Victorian Britain: the Chief Constructor of the Royal Navy from 1863 until 1870, Reed had recently walked out of his post amid a great and public controversy over ironclad design.† The Germans, breathtakingly victorious over France on land, were, it seemed, immediately attempting to poach from England the world's greatest expert on modern warship construction.

As early as February 1871, readers of the *Fortnightly Review* were told that 'the one thing which is now the dream of every North German is a great navy and power at sea ... as to Holland, every step in affairs brings her nearer and nearer to the inevitable fate'. By 1872,

---

* Robert K. Massie makes no mention whatever of the German Navy before 1880, in either *Dreadnought* or *Castles of Steel*. Nor does Christopher Clark in *The Sleepwalkers*..

† He resigned when a rival's design, the *Captain*, was selected amid a great press campaign as the model for the new turret ships. The country was forced, in 1871, to eat humble, and horrified, pie when this ship went down with all hands (including its inventor). Reed thereafter became, in modern parlance, the chief private consultant for naval design and was later knighted.

rather unnerving notions were being voiced about Germany's world-political ambitions in connection with her fleet:

> public attention in Germany is again being drawn to that familiar object of patriotic aspirations in the Fatherland, the acquisition of a war-navy commensurate with the visions of world-wide influence and power which the policy of Bismarck and the strategy of Moltke have recently excited ... [our correspondent] does not fail to detect the popular German desire for naval stations, especially in the East; and the *Allgemeine Zeitung* does not hesitate to confirm the fact, adding that the rich and beautiful island of Formosa, half the size of Ireland, on the coast of China, would do very well as a commencement.[228]

Formosa was far away, but there was another island rather closer to home, and a British possession to boot, in which Germany appeared to take a worrying interest:[229]

THE ISLAND THAT GERMANY COVETS.

OUR German cousins, like those nearer to us across the Atlantic, have taken to their bosoms the creed which philosophic fatalism has symbolized as "manifest destiny." As our American brethren believe that they are destined to rule over the whole of the western continent—that, in fact, it has, in the order of things, been devised to them as an inheritance—so do the Germans maintain that every rood of ground which a Teuton has trod upon, and every people with Teuton blood in their veins, must sooner or later be absorbed within the huge body politic of the great Fatherland. Having whetted their appetites with the late Danish territories on German soil, and Alsace and Lorraine in France, they are casting hungry glances on the so-called German provinces bordering on the Baltic held by Russia; and while thus patriotically "prospecting," their attention has become fixed on the barren rock of Heligoland, which, like an advanced sentinel, stands shivering in the angry blasts of the North Sea.

But it so happens that Heligoland belongs to England,

In October, Mr Reed himself, in words which might fit seamlessly into the *Dreadnought* debate of three-decades-odd later, warned readers of *The Times* of 'the transformation of Prussia into a vast German empire with an extended Baltic seaboard and a huge naval arsenal rising in the North Sea ... the recent Prussia policy of building up a powerful navy of iron-clads is being pursued more vigorously than ever'.[230] It was clear that Germany was already becoming a naval force to be reckoned with.

By 1874, Britons were being informed that they could no longer rely on the monopoly of vital naval industrial technology, and that the German state itself was preparing to intervene in the holy free market: 'Messrs Krupp' were offering to produce the armour-plate for ironclads in Germany, rather than importing it from England, and the German government had declared that if private yards could not deliver a fully home-grown ironclad fleet, it would 'create factories of its own for that purpose'.[231] The *Cologne Gazette* boasted of Germanic efficiency when compared to unnamed possible adversaries. By 1875, the German Navy would be:

> a force that need fear no enemy. In the number of its vessels it will be inferior to some other navies, but its quality will be superb and moreover its component parts have been so carefully calculated and so nicely balanced that its efficiency may be estimated above its numerical force.[232]

The following month, the *Guardian* wrote in downright sombre mood of the growing power and confidence of the Germans at sea:

> Their progress has been remarkable, not to say alarming ... it is some comfort to learn that the Germans are still to some extent dependent on British aid in shipbuilding, and that their manufacturers are only beginning to turn out a creditable article in iron plates. But ... one of the German captains lately undertook in a most obliging manner to point out the shortcomings of our own fleet.[233]

The Times was concerned, by late 1874, at 'the tonnage of the German ships and the size of their guns',[234] and by January 1875, the *Pall Mall Gazette* sounded a real note of warning:

> It is no longer sufficient to take France and Russia into account. A new naval power has been born almost in a day. At least, when it is not yet three years old, it has shown its intention of ultimately measuring itself against the greatest maritime nations. Of the many facts suggesting matter for grave reflection since 1870 this is surely the most startling ... Englishmen may hereafter look back ... and wonder at their own blindness ... The great German river has only to be followed to the sea to give Germany the possession she needs ... extension of German territory in the direction of Holland forms one of the dreams of German statesmen ... [the German Navy] constitutes, by threatening our supremacy at sea, a new and formidable danger to the greatness and independence of England.

By this time, the idea of German naval power had filtered right through the national consciousness, for no less than *Punch* took up the theme. In a widely syndicated piece, it foreshadowed the battleship-building race of thirty years later:[235]

> RULE, GERMANIA!—The *Times* informs us that, of "iron-clad cruisers of the strongest type, Germany will, in the present year, have seven built against five of our own navy." The *Pall Mall Gazette* is of opinion that—"The Germans have too many irons in the political fire to give exclusive attention to any one of them." But very soon, unless we get beforehand with the Germans, will they not have too many irons in the water, too?

By 25 August 1875, *The Times* stated that the German Navy had now left the Russians behind: 'the claim of the German Navy to rank third among the navies of the world may be fairly allowed'. The article concluded – it must be remembered that *The Times* famously weighed its utterances with great care – that 'such energetic and extensive preparations are qualified to create alarm, and even now, considering the sensitivity of the political barometer, they may provide food to satisfy the unwholesome cravings of alarmists'.

Those 'alarmists' might have been fed even more by the *Guardian*'s report of 15 September, which seemed to indicate that the Germans were specifically testing their new muscle with a view to a future conflict with England:

> The Military Contributor of the *Cologne Gazette*, referring to the trials which have taken place this summer at Herr Krupp's shooting ground at Visbeck, near Dülman, observes that it has now been proved that even ironclads of the class of the *Devastation* would be powerless to force an entrance into a harbour guarded with the new heavy guns worked by the German navy ... the *Boersen Zeitung* [i.e. Germany's *Financial Times*] adds that the competition which has existed between the English and the German guns since 1868 may now be regarded as definitively closed in favour of the latter.

The *Pall Mall Gazette*, too, seemed to rank with the alarmists, for on 23 September 1875 it quoted the official *Allgemeine Zeitung* as saying that:

> The five new German ironclad frigates, with 10-inch plates and 26-centimetre guns are not as yet matched in England ... For the present, the English fleet as a whole must be regarded as far superior in the number of its ships to those of any other naval power; but a combination of the Russian fleet in the Baltic and the German ironclad fleet would, as regards fighting power, be able to furnish a complete equivalent for it.

The *Times* made plain the significance of all this on 12 June 1876, stressing that the German Navy, presently 'demonstrating' (as Victorians put it) in Turkish waters, was made up of

> powerful vessels, well armed and manned ... Indeed, were all the fighting ships under the German flag, which are already built and

finished put in commission, and reinforced by two or three others nearly finished, the whole force might be fairly termed formidable, and would probably suffice to turn the scale in favour of any one of two pretty evenly-matched powers.

Readers in 1876 would have known very well that the 'two pretty evenly-matched powers' in Turkish waters could only be Britain and Russia. Indeed, the fear of a Russo-German naval alliance was growing so fast that by June 1877, parliament was being urged by some MPs to consider this new reality and take up

the establishment of a harbour at Filey Bay as a naval station, in view of the contingency of a naval war with Russia or Germany ... between Sheerness and the Firth of Forth we had no station where a squadron cruising the North Sea could repair to coal or refit. In fact, the great German Arsenal of Wilhemshaven was very little further from the cruising ground.[236]

As readers of *The Times*, A. J. S. and W. J. Jeffreyson would no doubt have noted the two long articles devoted to the German Navy at the end of 1877:

Few achievements are more remarkable than that which has of late years been developing Germany into a Naval Power ... the systematic plan ... the energy shown in all these arrangements and the foresight of a good many of them ... we ought to derive not only a lesson, but a warning ... There is now a continental State which is bringing to bear upon naval warfare the same method, science, and patience which have late revolutionized the art of war on land. It is by no means inconceivable that a similar result is possible in respect to naval war.[237]

There really is not much doubt about it. W. J. Jeffreyson and A. J. S., atop the White Cliffs, watching those powerful ironclads steam by on the gorgeous morning of 31 May 1878, would not have been at all surprised to learn that they were German. On the contrary, assuming that they had been readers of any of the great national newspapers over the past few years, they would have been well aware that there was now a powerful Imperial German Navy to add to the invincible German land forces, all of them guided by that uniquely German capacity for 'method, science, and patience' and controlled by a man who was seen by most Englishmen as the natural ally of Russia.

What they would have wondered was what exactly those ships were doing *here*, at a time of such tension.

A threat or a promise: twenty years before Tirpitz

What was Bismarck's game in sending out the pride of his new navy to steam right past the White Cliffs, at this knife-edge in European diplomacy? That it was indeed *his* game, there can be no doubt. Bismarck liked to rule by broad hints, vague avowals and implicit threats given to people face-to-face, rather than by written orders.* So while there may be no documents which make explicit the political reasoning behind the cruise of the German ironclads, it is unthinkable that such a public move, at so white-hot a diplomatic juncture, could have taken place without the all-powerful Chancellor's knowledge and approval.

The *Standard* thought it knew exactly what the game was: 'the cruise of the German ironclads in the Channel' was designed as 'a little hint that Russia still has friends'.[238] *Blackwood's* described a whole complex plot between Germany and Russia, in which 'the Emperor William, to help his ally, was willing to let out his ironclads'.[239]

---

* Such meetings were generally conducted in the looming presence of Sultan, the 'Reich hound', his gigantic pet, which, on one famous occasion, bit the Russian Ambassador and, on another, 'maimed one of the Berlin Foreign Office officials for life because he sat down on the chair usually occupied by Prince Bismarck'. What Bismarck wanted, whether he actually said it or not, was clear enough to those who had the honour of these encounters. See the *New York Times*, 4 October 1879.

It seems very much as if, a full two decades before Tirpitz's first Navy Bill, Bismarck was flexing the new Imperial German Navy's muscles as part of his negotiating armoury. He was making Britain aware, at a time of high international tension, that Germany was no longer just a land power.

For almost 200 years, Britain had only ever had to worry about French naval power in the Channel. Was Bismarck now pointing out that those days were over? Was he demonstrating that Germany was now a foe to be feared, and hence placated, even at sea, or that she was now a worthwhile marine ally? Was the cruise of the German ironclads off Folkestone a threat or a promise? Or was it a curious mixture of both, which might serve as either on the chessboard of Bismarck's Great Game – that same strange blend of threat and promise to England which would become the vision of the Tirpitz Plan?

At any rate, on 31 May 1878, the seamanship of the Imperial German Navy was not yet up to the political machinations of the Chancellor, whatever they were.

Obsessed with aping the awesome close formations of the Prussian Guard, and perhaps keen to show their erstwhile mentor, the mighty Royal Navy, a thing or two, the German admirals had determined that their potent squadron should cruise past the White Cliffs in far closer order than British commanders thought safe for the unhandy new iron monsters. The result was that instead of impressing or scaring seafaring Britons, the German squadron ensured that it drove the Crisis, the tour of the Australian XI and Cleopatra's Needle off the front pages, and made itself remembered for decades afterwards, when, on a flat calm sea, with perfect visibility, and before the astonished eyes of W. J. Jeffreyson, A. J. S., the young composer Arthur Sullivan and hundreds of other witnesses, the men on the quarterdeck of the gigantic *König Wilhelm*, trying to avoid a fishing boat and 'terrified at the vessel not obeying the rudder with the requisite despatch',[240] lost their heads completely: somehow, they managed to strike their monstrous ram midships into the brand-new *Grosser Kurfürst*, sending her straight to the bottom, together with almost 300 of her crew.

The Last of the *Grosser Kurfürst* – sketched by an eye-witness at Folkstone.

Visiting Virchow

Not for the last time, British commentators were quite unable to work out what Germany's game really was, and in June 1878, *The Times* dispatched a journalist able to gain exclusive access to the great man of the age.

The Times's writer was, at first, as he frankly admitted, overwhelmed by Bismarck's sheer charm and power. Knowing that many before him had felt this way, he hurried to get a second opinion on 'this fascinator of the world' from one of the Chancellor's most resolute opponents, Dr Virchow, the founder of modern oncology, that same splendid liberal who had allegedly been ready to take a 50/50 chance of death by poisoned sausage if Bismarck would do the same. The article that came out of this visit reminds us, firstly, how fatuous it is to try to understand history without taking into account the aims of certain powerful individuals; and, secondly, how ridiculous or even terrifying will one day seem all the assumptions our most well-meaning progressive minds think self-evident.

Having been entranced by Bismarck, the man from *The Times* proceeded to clear his head in the study of Dr Virchow:

The second room was like a miniature Valley of Jehoshaphat at the moment of the first blast of the resurrection trumpet. There were skeletons erect, curved, seated, leaning, like men surprised in their sleep and stretching themselves before wholly waking. Bones of every kind covered tables, shelves, and chairs, and to find a seat chairs had to be cleared of the human remains which encumbered them. Numberless skulls crowned this charming collection, grinning at the shapeless fragments scattered over furniture and floor. On contemplating this spectacle and recalling Dr. Virchow's eloquent and incisive speeches, I expected to see a gigantic figure, strangely attired, with sparkling eyes and radiant countenance, personifying the double power of a man who penetrates the secrets of death and boasts of defending that life of the living, liberty. The door opened, and I saw nothing of all this. The man who advanced towards me was dressed like an antiquary busied in arranging his collections ; his head rather thin and bony ; hair and beard short and gray ; forehead bronzed, rather furrowed, projecting in front and slightly compressed at the sides ; veins visible in the temples ; eyes small and retreating, mouth resolute, nose sharp and restless ; hands bronzed, agile, and thin, denoting determination, energy, and dexterity.

The originality of the situation, however, soon displayed itself. The conversation turned immediately on the Congress then sitting. We discussed the rivalries of the small nationalities disputing supremacy in European Turkey. Dr. Virchow suddenly rose. "See," he said, "the really superior race in those countries. Look at these," and he put into my hands three skulls ; "one of your colleagues sent me the first, and I have since procured the other two. They are the craniums of Albanians murdered by Turks. Look at them. Are they not fine ? On receiving the first I thought it was an exceptional one, but they are all like that, these Albanian skulls. There is the race superior by far to all the others." Dr. Virchow, with enthusiastic tenderness and a countenance full of affection, caressed the cranium he held on his knees ; then, rising, carefully replaced it.

Dr Virchow's belief in comparative racial craniology may seem lunatic to us now (he himself used his studies to publicly dismiss all 'nonsense' about racial purity in Germany). But his political insight cuts through any number of modern arguments about what was really going on in Bismarck's Germany:

> Dr. Virchow abruptly rose, restored to their places first the three Albanian and then the other skulls, after which, as if freed from the occupations of the *savant*, he seated himself opposite me. He said: – 'What we reproach the Chancellor with is with wanting to impersonate all Germany, and to carry out, not a German policy, but a Bismarckian policy. The great object of all his endeavours is to remain at the head of affairs. He creates a policy of which he is the principal aim, and that is why we do not know whither he will lead us. Now, when a man pursues a goal beyond himself he has a farsighted policy; but when he pursues a personal policy he lives from hand to mouth and changes his projects according to his own convenience. Bismarck has given us glory, but he has deprived us of liberty without giving us prosperity. He is a man who knows Europe, but does not know Germany. He treats us as if he had conquered us. He does not consider our legitimate pride, or understand that we are as much interested as himself in our country's politics. He has coquetted (*gebühlt*) with all parties and deserted them all.' [241]

In other words, no one knew which way Bismarck was going to turn – for the very simple reason that he did not know it himself. The leader of Germany was by now simply a master opportunist with no ultimate strategy save that of preserving his own skin.

Having stared Disraeli in the eye at Berlin, Bismarck thought he saw his opportunity – and he swung the wheel of German history in a way so sudden and dramatic that it left contemporary observers gasping.

He chose to go with Austria – and, so he thought, with Tory Britain.

Bizzy and Dizzy: the greatest game of all

Events in Germany in 1878–9 were, with hindsight, so clearly pregnant with history that German scholars often refer to them as the 'second foundation' of the new empire. You could write, and many people have written, whole books on this subject. But in terms of Anglo-German relations, the vital fact is that, for a few months, Bismarck's turn held out the prospect of a completely new deal.

Bismarck had always disliked Britain – but then, for his entire political life, Britain had been governed by liberals. His hatred for her was simply as the great model for his own German liberal opponents. Disraeli's new Conservative Britain was a very different kettle of fish. She was no longer an example to liberal Germans. Disraeli had crowned Victoria Empress of India, he had sent forth armies to increase her domains and had displayed a positively Bismarckian scorn for ideological cant in his acquisition of Britain's vital stake in the Suez Canal.

In fact, true, old-fashioned German conservatism – from which Bismarck had sprung and to which he was about to return – always had a deep admiration for the way in which the British aristocracy and monarchy had come through the revolutionary storms of 1789, 1830 and 1848 completely intact. Bismarck's standard reply to the liberals in the mid-1860s can be found almost verbatim in von Bülow's retorts to Bebel forty years later:

> English examples were constantly cited, and to these Bismarck invariably replied: "Give us everything English that we have not got; give us the English fear of God, English respect for laws, the entire English constitution, but also the exact circumstances of the English land-owner – English riches, and English public spirit – then we shall be able to govern as they do.[242]

A good half of the German liberals definitively lost their deep but unrequited love for England in 1864 and 1870, and never again looked to her as an example of anything; but many German conservatives continued to have a vague but profound admiration for Old England.

So, really, it's no wonder that the prospect of a revitalised Tory England should have appealed deeply to Bismarck. But, of course, the most important thing to him was practical politics. Disraeli had shown himself to be a formidable opponent during the War in Sight crisis. And now here he was, apparently quite prepared to face down the Tsar, if need be alone. When, during the Berlin Conference, Disraeli theatrically ordered a private train and declared that he was walking away from the table, Germany's great chancellor was convinced that Britain really meant it for once – or, at least, that she now had a leader who could *persuade* people that he meant it, which, in Bismarck's lifelong Great European Game of threat, cajoling, alliance and deterrence, came to the same thing.

Bismarck famously declared that 'the old Jew' was the real man at the Congress. Disraeli returned the favour: his letters to Queen Victoria show him to have been quite star-struck at his unique invitation to dine with Bismarck *en famille*, and he 'gave the last blow to my shattered constitution' by staying up late and smoking cigars with Bismarck to seal their mutual respect.

These late-night talks between a British Jew and a Prussian Junker came within an ace of changing European history – world history – completely. We know that, in his letters to Queen Victoria, Disraeli spoke of throwing the Russians right back beyond the Caspian Sea. It seems hard to believe that he did not at least hint likewise in his private sessions with Bismarck.

Germany's leader must have had trouble controlling his excitement. At last, here was a British leader who saw things clearly. Russia, after all, was obviously the one power on Earth which could deal the British Empire a mortal blow without having first to do the impossible and defeat the Royal Navy: the land route to India was the Achilles' heel of Britain's entire world position. Any sane British PM would see that, and now Britain had one. With Britain truly alive, truly pulling its weight in the world, standing up properly for its own self-evident interests – taking the lead against Russia, in other words – Bismarck's Great Game was as good as won. Ever since the Eastern Question had raised its head again in 1876, relations between Tory London and Vienna had been so close that many people spoke of an unwritten 'understanding'. Surely there could be no doubt: an alliance between Germany and Austria would clearly imply a geopolitical league with Disraeli's Britain as well.

The vision was heady: British naval might would secure the Black Sea, as it had done in the Crimean War, keeping the Habsburg Empire afloat; France would never dare go for *revanche* with a potentially hostile Britain at her back; the presence of the mighty German Army on Russia's western border would mean that the Tsars could never again even think of menacing British India.

In the long view, Bismarck's scenario of 1879 was really just an anti-Russian re-run of the anti-French alliance in the Seven Years' War, which had been so decisively good for both Prussia and Britain: Prussia, concerned only to digest what she had just grabbed by force, in alliance with a transcontinentally militant Britain; the survival of an enlarged Prussia in Europe assured; the free hand of Britain in the empire enabled.

Bismarck, having done the diplomatic maths – and the all-important domestic maths, which said that an Austrian alliance would delight Pan-Germans, Conservatives and Catholics alike – now made his epochal *volte-face* towards his lifelong enemy number one.

Europe was amazed. *The Times* followed Bismarck's multiple visits to Vienna almost day by day, and soon divined exactly what was going on: 'Today Prussia [*sic*] confronts her colossal neighbour as the effective protector of the dual monarchy.'[243] The Russians, too, saw very clearly what had happened:

> Prince Gortschakoff, beaten by his hated rival, Prince Bismarck, is wrathfully recasting his policy; and the German and Hungarian peoples stand upon guard awaiting the issue, while their Governments are preparing to meet the storm of Panslavic power and Muscovite intrigue.[244]

No one grasped the significance of this grand New Deal in European diplomacy more swiftly, or with more enthusiasm, than Disraeli's de facto second in command and heir apparent, Lord Salisbury. On 18 October, he made his feelings plain to a large public meeting in Manchester:

> The newspapers say – I know not whether they say rightly – that a defensive alliance has been established between Germany and Austria (loud cheers). I will not pronounce any opinion as to the accuracy of that information, but I will only say this to you and all who value the peace of Europe and the independence of nations – I may say without profanity – that it is "good tidings of great joy" (loud cheers).

The speech zipped off along the telegraph wires of Europe, and made very agreeable reading in Berlin and Vienna:

ENGLAND, AUSTRIA, AND GERMANY.
(FROM OUR OWN CORRESPONDENT.)
VIENNA, OCT. 18 (8 P.M.).

Lord Salisbury's speech at Manchester on Friday has been received here with great satisfaction, as a guarantee of the complete understanding between England, Austria, and Germany.

It was all going perfectly for Bismarck. On 6 November 1879, Prince Henry of Reuss wrote from Vienna, reporting that Salisbury had 'expressed complete satisfaction' with the Austro-German alliance upon learning personally that it was indeed explicitly directed against Russia: the news was 'of the greatest importance to British policy'.

Bismarck now asked Salisbury outright whether England would support Germany against Russia if war came. The reply was evasive and yet extraordinarily telling: Salisbury promised only that, in that event, France would not attack Germany. This was quite amazing: the *British* Foreign Minister felt able to give the German Chancellor a guarantee against a *French* attack. The fact that Britain, by 1879, no longer felt the slightest real fear of France, and even regarded her foreign policy as essentially dependent on Britain's, could hardly be more clearly shown.*

It wasn't yet an alliance, but it was getting close, and Bismarck pushed to seal the deal. One of his main kite-flying outlets, the *Cologne Gazette*, openly spoke of 'a formal adhesion of England' to the new Austro-German alliance.[245] Britain's Tories were so enthusiastic at the prospect of this mighty new league against Russia that, on 19 November, the *Vossische Zeitung*, which was the closest thing in Bismarck's Germany to a genuinely national and independent newspaper of record, warned the British government against 'too much jubilation' too early.

Everything was set. There was just one little detail in the way of this tremendous, this logically perfect, alliance of the two great men whom *Punch* called Bizzy and Dizzy: the British electorate.

New politics

Mass politics was quite new in 1880, and no one really understood it yet.

Bismarck assumed – rather as all world leaders assumed about Churchill in 1945 – that no sane nation would eject a chief who had so clearly reclaimed its place at the Top Table. He built his grand new diplomatic edifice on this belief, which was, after all, backed by personal experience of how electorates can be won over by diplomatic

---

* Bismarck to Bülow, 10 November 1879. The Fashoda Incident is always cited as proof that Britain and France were still genuine imperial rivals, and possible belligerents, as late as 1898. The story, in fact, proves the opposite point: Salisbury was so clear about forcing France to stand down in 1898 precisely because he knew absolutely that after 1871 she could never again risk war with Britain.

triumphs. Disraeli backed his instincts and the encouraging results of a by-election.

The whole world realised perfectly well just what was at stake, and awaited the result of the British general election very much as it hangs today on the news from a pivotal, ideologically driven US presidential campaign:[246]

GERMANY.

BERLIN, APRIL 2.

With what degree of interest the German people are following the course of the elections in England may be partly judged from the tone and contents of the daily Press. Whether Whigs or Tories are likely to come into power at St. Stephen's is discussed with an eagerness which could scarcely be more ardent were the result being awaited of an appeal to the Imperial constituencies on some vital question affecting the public weal. Journals which from one year's end to the other never receive a single special telegram from England—or, indeed, from anywhere else for the matter of that—now seem to have become influenced by a spirit of rash and extravagant enterprise, and keep their readers posted up as to how the electoral wind in Great Britain and Ireland blows by reports of a dozen or 20 pithy lines wired direct from London. All other current events, declares the united Press, dwarf in importance before the choice of a new English Parliament. Nations and Cabinets, writes one ably-written journal, are waiting in suspense the result of the elections, while from India and Central Asia to the populations of the Balkan Peninsula, from Stamboul to Rome and St. Petersburg, all eyes are directed towards the great electoral battle now raging.

As that battle raged in Britain, Bismarck raised the domestic campaign against German liberalism to fever-pitch. He let slip, in a rare moment of unguarded public rage, that if his loyal allies since 1867, the National Liberals, did not abandon yet another plank of their alleged liberalism and go along with his anti-free-trade measures, he would 'crush them against the wall until they squealed'.[247]

The German conservatives, who had been smarting under the hated liberal alliance for over a decade, smelled blood: at last, their time had come again. Their in-house paper, the *Kreuz-Zeitung*, scented a 'vast turnaround in public opinion' and laid into the liberal 'Manchester men' in language which is curiously like that of the opponents of the free market today: 'Every "deal" in which the profit of one party necessarily derives from the loss which another party suffers is morally abominable'; riches gained from pure speculation in the rise and fall of shares should lead to 'well-deserved shame'. What was needed was a return to an organic society in which every member was a part of the whole: 'if the liberals want to call this "socialistic", so be it!'[248]

The most rabid version of this new and confident anti-liberalism came from a brand-new political party which did not shun 'socialistic' notions in the least: the Christian Social Party, led by the official Court Preacher, Adolf Stoecker.

Stoecker brought to the political table a fresh Big Idea which solved the problem faced by all radicals: who *is* to blame for the periodic disasters of capitalism?* He was ready to explain to the lower, and now voting, orders precisely who had visited the crash, and indeed modernity itself, on the innocent, loyal German people.

It was the Jews.

However, very few people, and almost no respectable people, took much note of Stoecker's ravings until, out of the blue, the most

---

* The correct answer is, of course, that no identifiable *group* is to blame. No one ever forced anyone to invest in an Icelandic bank or take out a mortgage. We all, as individuals, do what we do, and shit sometimes happens. This 'metaphysic of pure contingency', as the *Guardian*'s neo-Marxist philosopher Peter Thompson has memorably named it, is easy to mock but has the one very great advantage of not providing succour to murderous demagogues, for whom *groups to blame for everything*, whether they be classes or races, are bread and butter.

influential public intellectual in Germany published one of the most notorious documents in German history. By no coincidence at all, that man was also Germany's most famous Anglophobe.

The ultimate internal Englanders

In November 1879, Heinrich von Treitschke forever changed the political game for anti-Semitism in Germany.* In a single article, he both lent his vast intellectual weight to the anti-Semites and provided them, like the great media professor he was, with the fatally simple, hideously memorable and graffiti-friendly print-byte which would be used right up until 1945: 'Die Juden sind unser Unglück' ('The Jews are our misfortune').

Treitschke's infamous essay has entered the bleak annals of history in its 1880 version, 'A Word About Our Jews'. In fact, this keystone of modern anti-Semitism is only the final quarter of the far longer, and far less well-known, 1879 original. That article is rather less memorably entitled 'Our Prospects' and in its first fifteen pages, it contains not one single word about, let alone against, the Jews. However, it has plenty to say on the Englanders.

To Treitschke, Russia and Pan-Slavism were a menace, but German military power and skilful diplomacy could make sure the Russians left Austria be. The real trouble for Germany was not the visible battalions of the Tsar, but the secret hatred of the British. It was all Britain's fault that the Russians felt aggrieved at the Congress of Berlin and blamed the Germans; it was Britain which was now trying to inveigle Germany

---

* Henceforth, calling yourself an 'anti-Semite' became respectable. From 1893 (when they got organised) to 1907 (when they lost ground in what they afterwards called the 'Jews' election'), the Anti-Semites – meaning not politicians merely anti-Semitic in their views, but men who formally named themselves 'Anti-Semites' on the ballot slips – always polled between 2.6 and 3.7 per cent in Reichstag elections, giving them a solid handful of MPs, with all the headline-grabbing opportunities that delivered. This is remarkably similar to the percentage of votes cast for the NSDAP in 1928 and clearly suggests a small but tenacious hard core whose so-called 'world view' was *not* created by the Great War, the Bolshevik Revolution, or the 1929 crash, but well before any of these disasters.

and Austria into doing her dirty work against the Russians; and the reason, as ever in British politics, was to ensure financial gain while letting the naïve Germans foot the butcher's bill.

> ... the hollow phrases about national rights and European freedom with which the Britons' commercial politicians disguised their blatant lust for conquest ... the insatiable desire that English trading-politics has for other people's countries, which can never be enough to make markets for its mass-industries, and which has lately been powerfully spurred on by a series of cheap, undeserved victories ... Will Lord Beaconsfield's incessantly burrowing policies succeed in taking power over the starting-point of the world's most important future trading-route? ... Despite the speech of Lord Salisbury and the perfidious boastings of the English press, the Court in St Petersburg will know that neither Berlin nor Vienna are minded to do Britain's political bidding and to support Lord Beaconsfield's plans in Asia Minor.[249]

The very existence of Germany was endangered by the cunning, underhand, money-driven machinations of the Englanders and – now comes the fateful turn of the last five pages – by a dread internal enemy: the Jews. Who, of course, are 'heavily involved in the guilt for the lies and betrayals, the shameless greed of the disgusting Founders, for the base materialism of our age, which sees work merely as a business transaction'.

Lying, piggy-backing, money-driven, Manchesterist perfidity (English) outside; and base, materialist lies and greed (Jewish) within. These are the real threats to Germany, says Treitschke. They are very clearly one and the same thing.

It is no coincidence that it was Germany's most prestigious Anglophobe, of all people, who lent public authority, suddenly and decisively, to the attack on Germany's Jews. After all, what was Pastor Stoecker saying? That there was one power on Earth which achieved its ends not in manly battle, but by the sneaky power of finance; one power on Earth which denied the ultimate authority of the nation-state and proclaimed that 'modernity' and 'progress' consisted merely in men being allowed to seek private advantage and profit wherever it could be found, irrespective of morality or religion or community; one power on Earth to whom loud protestations of 'freedom' meant merely the freedom for itself to enslave the nations of the world by money. This power, though it worked ceaselessly to undermine all notions of independent nationhood in others, remained in itself a potent and self-recognising political unit. Never prepared to stand openly, or to shed its own sons' blood, it was always on the lookout for satraps or hirelings to further its unsleeping pursuit of a vast, gold-driven hegemony. Germans, with their honest simplicity, had been the greatest dupes of this power. It was the presiding ideological deity of the markets which had soured German unity, and it was well known to be especially inimical to Germany, which (as the great Hegel had often stressed) had a fundamentally different and far healthier, more organic, more rooted and communitarian definition of 'freedom'. Where Germans still knew true aristocratic honour, this other power knew only the love of commerce and money.

Stoecker meant the Jews. But this is, of course, exactly the same list of alleged sins which Treitschke and his followers had for years been setting at the door of the Englanders.

In fact, the idea that Jewishness and Englishness were somehow naturally related, perhaps even the same deep thing, had been bubbling under the murky surface of German nationalist thought for many years.

Take the case of Richard Wagner. The poisonous rantings of Wagner's *Jewishness in Music* (1850) are prepared for in his earliest full-blown piece of self-promotion, *A Pilgrimage to Beethoven* (1840). In this little book, our hero, a poor but honest German musician, is confronted at every turn by the villain, a spoiled, arrogant, rich young amateur musician who 'plays flute twice a week, blows the French horn on Thursdays and composes on Sundays' and blithely throws money about for poor but honest German musicians to pick up (proudly, they don't). This man's supposed love for Beethoven is just 'the foppish notion of a rich young man, not the deep inward need of a devoted soul'. Eventually, this foreigner becomes an almost satanic figure ('my nemesis!' cries the hero). Beethoven himself is so annoyed by the 'pushiness' of this man and his fellow nationals that he has shut himself up even from true German visitors. In the end, our hero triumphs, and is recognised as a fellow soul by Beethoven, while the ridiculous foreigner's superficial music is mocked.

All of this carries obvious pre-echoes of Wagner's loathsome sallies in *Jewishness in Music*. But, in 1840, the villain is not yet a Jew: he is that older enemy of true Germandom, an Englishman.

The alleged association between Jewishness and Englishness is quite overt in some writings of the 1870s. *Die Gartenlaube*, which sold more copies than any other periodical in Germany, began, soon after the great crash of 1873, to run implicitly anti-Semitic pieces. Here, for example, the blame for the economic disaster is placed on Jews like the fallen banker Strousberg – and on the Anglo-Saxon way of business:

> As a twelve year old Jewish youngster from Poland, Barusch Hirsch Straussberg emigrated to England and reappeared twenty years later in Berlin as Dr Bethel Henry Strousberg, a member of the Christian church ... No doubt he led a life full of changes and adventures, but it didn't work out for him: John Bull and Brother Jonathan were no more stupid than he was. And so he came back to Germany, where he could truly employ his genius ... Strousberg would never have been possible without modern economics, without those who back free trade and Manchesterism.[250]

The catechism of modern political anti-Semitism (and to an alarming extent that of some careless 'anti-globalisation' rhetoric) is right here, fully formed, in 1874: Britons and Americans, 'John Bull and Brother Jonathan', are said to be just as clever as the Jews, and to have provided the Manchesterism in which Jewishness thrives; less cunning nations, such as the honest but naïve Germans, are supposedly easy prey to this deadly cocktail of Anglo-Saxon liberalism/free trade/Jewishness/modernism/cleverness. The first classic of German anti-Semitic literature, Marr's *The Victory of Jewishness over Germandom* (1879), made the alleged deep connection between Jews and Englanders clear in the most lapidary way: 'Jewishness is the application of Manchesterism taken to the extreme.'

Anti-Semitism is a shape-shifter which the paranoid mould to fit the fears of each age.* In the first three-quarters of the nineteenth century, most critics had seen Judaism as a force hostile to the new creed of Progress, an inward-looking, superstitious, atavistic survival of the mediaeval world. This is certainly how the young Karl Marx, for example, saw things. But in the wake of the first Great Depression, Germany's Jews suddenly found themselves accused of Modernity itself. The hatred of England as the homeland of economic modernism, and of German liberals as internal Englanders, now became a new hatred of the Jews in which cutting-edge allegations of trans-national financial manipulation took main stage, with the old images of blood-sacrifice, secret rites and neighbourhood usury reduced to ghosts lurking in the wings.

This was something radically new.

The bizarre change was noted by Germany's Jews themselves right away. The *Allgemeine Zeitung des Judenthums,* the great voice of assimilationist German Jewry, immediately saw the political logic whereby Treitschke and his conservative allies had suddenly espoused anti-Semitism, and pointed out just how new were the charges against themselves:

> They want to make liberalism suspect to the people by calling it Jewish and at the same time, by calling the Jews the actual pillars of liberalism, make the Jews hated, isolated and perhaps even legally circumscribed and excluded again. Well, at any rate, there is *one* thing we can be glad of: that they are not crying down Judaism as a reactionary system, as a retrograde teaching, as a religion hostile to development and progress, but as the opposite.[251]

---

* Insane though it sounds today, as war with Germany grew all but inevitable, a few Edwardian Britons were even convinced that there was a worldwide Jewish conspiracy *in favour* of the Germans. The most famous believers in this theory were the future editor of *The Times,* Henry Wickham Steed, and Britain's calamitous Ambassador to the US, Sir Cecil Spring-Rice, author of 'I Vow to Thee My Country'.

Sometimes history moves in great, vague, slow-gathering shifts, but sometimes the tectonic slip is extraordinarily sharp and clear. In November 1879, Germany's Jews found themselves suddenly accused, by a grand cultural guru, of being the sponsors of a wicked modernity: they were accused of this in exactly the same terms which had for some years been flung against England, and by the very man who had been publicly leading that charge.

We are getting to the root of the mystery which, for obvious reasons, has been endlessly debated by historians: why was it Germany of all places which saw the birth of an entire and (in its own rank terms) cogent political programme centred on anti-Semitism? Germans, after all, did not invent modern, racial anti-Semitism, nor did any of their nineteenth-century rulers publicly espouse it. Those black honours go to a Frenchman and to Russia. The deadly pogroms of Tsarist Russia were entirely unknown in Imperial Germany; there was no parallel in Berlin, ever, to the manic parliamentary and public outrages set off in Paris by the Dreyfus Case.

The fatal difference was that, in Germany, the anti-Semites had a real, proper *theory*. One contemporary British observer noted that a man like Treitschke was only possible in an intellectual ambience accustomed to the idea of vast constructions built on little or no empirical evidence. Anyone who has had anything to do with British universities in recent decades will, sadly, recognise certain things:

A young teacher who has just taken his degree will start at once writing as many as two or three short works in the course of a *semester* – often of a kind which in England would be classed as magazine articles, frequently mere criticisms of the writings of others. The amount of theory, more or less supported by facts, which is thus produced, is almost incredible; and when we consider the immense encouragement afforded to unripe speculation by the requirement of a dissertation containing an original theory, for every doctor's diploma conferred in Germany, it is yet difficult to understand how such wild ideas as that lately put forward by Treitschke in Berlin can arise. In no country of Europe, probably, save Germany, could a public teacher be found to maintain, in the face of masses of historical evidence to the contrary, that non-performance of the duties of citizenship could be justly charged against the Jewish populations scattered over Europe.[252]

Uniquely, German thinkers, from Hegel to Treitschke, had by 1879 developed a thoroughgoing, widely disseminated, intellectually backed system of thought aimed against a liberal 'internal enemy'. The theory was originally created to discredit any German who looked to liberal Britain as a model. When it was suddenly turned against Germany's Jews, British pressmen had no doubt about who was really behind things, and what was the purpose of it all:

Opinion has been expressed in Parliament that the so-called "Reptile Fund" is being used for papers which have suddenly sprung up in the anti-Jewish interest. No open denial has been given to this charge. From such stray but significant facts the conclusion appears to be warranted that the reprehensible movement is really countenanced in "higher regions," and that the support given to it will perhaps some day be found to have been the precursor of a fresh reactionary move on the domain of political economy. Hence it well behoves the friends of German progress to be on the alert, and to stop the mischief by nipping it in the bud, lest a crusade apparently begun against the so-called Semites should suddenly develop into an attack upon all modern ideas of freedom.[253]

Those 'modern ideas of freedom' were, of course, British ones. The British press knew the enemy when it saw it and, within weeks, almost every paper in the country was carrying – and continued to carry, for many months – outraged articles on 'Jew-baiting in Germany' and suchlike. 'Ever since Professor Treitschke sounded that war-note ... nothing has been talked of or written about in Germany except the Jews.'[254]

This direct link between Anglophobia and the new anti-Semitism seems now to be forgotten.* It was intuited in the day. After the brief hiatus of the anti-Russian love affair between Bizzy and Dizzy, the Anglo-German diplomatic barometer swung quickly back to its post-1864 default setting of 'storms approaching', and *The Times* noted the uncanny way in which anti-Semitism and Anglophobia seemed almost directly interchangeable to Bismarck's press-pack: [255]

> One can scarcely take up any journal, no matter of what shade, without finding in it bitter and galling words about England and her Prime Minister. It almost seems, indeed, as if, tired of the profitless and ineffectual task of baiting the Jews, the Germans had sought recreation in the fresher pleasure of objurgating the English.

By 1892, Pan-Germans were using 'English' and 'Jewish' as more or less interchangeable insults:

> The whole state in Hamburg is these days in reality nothing more than a demesne for the cultivation of Jewish-patrician interest ... the patricians and their followers are kind of half-breed Englishmen in their lack of any understanding for the German national cause.[256]

The path which led to Kaiser Wilhelm II himself talking later of 'Judaengland' was set. But for now, the reason that Bismarck's press went back to objurgating the English was more immediate: in 1880, Britain betrayed him.

---

* A couple of important writers have noted in passing that Anglophobia and anti-Semitism in Imperial Germany seem to be curiously related. The leader of the Liberal Institute in Berlin sees that 'anti-British agitation was joined almost seamlessly by an anti-Semitic agitation' (Detmar Doering, *Mythos Manchesterthum*, Berlin, 2004, p. 22) and the great historian of Wilhelm's court writes that 'in the minds of German Anti-Semites there was an almost complete identification of the Jewish and the English menace' (John Röhl, *The Kaiser and His Court*). However, the vital fact is the *causal connection*.

Britain betrays Bismarck

Neither Bismarck nor Disraeli, those two great conservative enfranchisers and manipulators of the mid-Victorian masses, was the most modern force at work in 1880: it was W. E. Gladstone, and his victory made the British general election of that year into one of the great turning points in European political history.

The Midlothian Campaign is still a legend among political tacticians. At almost seventy years of age, Gladstone personally invented the idea of grandstand electioneering in swingable marginals identified by detailed local research. For the first time, a candidate's tour itself became The Story. His example has since been copied by, or forced upon, every politician who ever exhausted himself in a whistle-stop tour of anywhere.

Gladstone deliberately made foreign affairs – the alleged incompetence, profligacy and immorality of Disraeli's policies – central to this extraordinary new campaign. His lieutenants were not slow to seize on Salisbury's openly pro-German sentiments:

"Good tidings of great joy" are proclaimed to all people because Prince Bismarck and Germany are to be Austria's allies. Gentlemen, I marvel at the indiscretion of the Secretary of State who could apply such a phrase to such an event. Nearly 1900 years ago those solemn words were descriptive of an event in a humble Syrian village which was to bring "One earth peace, good will toward men." (Cheers.) And now they are to be applied to the union of one State which musters a million men in arms with another State which musters a second million against a third which musters a million and a half. (Hear, hear.)[257]

Gladstone himself was careful throughout the campaign not to be overtly anti-Bismarck. After all, his message was that Britain need not get involved in costly hostilities with anyone at all. But he laid into Austrian support for Disraeli in his splendidly inimitable, shamelessly self-enacting way:

Did you read in the London papers within the last few weeks an account of the energetic support they derived from the Emperor of Austria? Did you see that the Emperor of Austria sent for the British Ambassador, Sir Henry Elliot, and told him that a pestilent person, a certain individual, Mr. Gladstone, was a man who did not approve of the foreign policy of Austria, and how anxious he was that – so the Emperor of Austria was pleased complacently to say for the guidance of the British people and of the electors of Midlothian – how anxious he was, gentlemen, that you should all of you give your votes in a way to maintain the Ministry of Lord Beaconsfield? (Cheers and laughter.)[258]

The press left Britons in no doubt that if they voted for Disraeli, whom liberals accused of presenting himself as 'the Bismarck of England',[259] there was a real possibility of Britain actually joining the Austro-German alliance:[260]

ENGLAND AND GERMANY.

VIENNA, MARCH 16.

A possible meeting between the Queen of England and the Emperor of Germany is being talked of, opening out, of course, a fresh field of conjecture, the most daring seers already perceiving in this meeting the first step towards the expansion of the understanding between Germany and Austria into a triple alliance.

As the election neared, *The Times* set out exactly why Germany and Austria were so keen on a Tory victory:

The Cabinets of London, Berlin, and Vienna are since last October of the unanimous opinion that Austria must occupy Bosnia and Herzegovina for ever, and that she must be protected against a Slav eruption.[261]

The closer came the day, the greater grew the tension:

BERLIN, MARCH 17.

Prince Bismarck, backed by all his countrymen, would prefer to see the return of a Cabinet to Downing-street influenced by the same views on the foreign policy of Great Britain as the outgoing Ministry. Germany has, or believes she has, a latent foe in Russia, and an English Parliament, therefore, firmly resolved to curb and withstand the territorial ambition of that huge Slavonic Power would be hailed by both parties to the Austro-German under-standing as a strong and effective ally in maintaining peace. The German Press has by this time pretty well uttered the mind of the Empire upon the subject, and though I have searched far and ques-tioned freely, I have not yet encountered one expression which could not be constructed as a wish for the success of the Con-servative Government in England.

In Germany, this wished-for success was seen as a certainty, and the great and good were gearing up for it. Even Treitschke, who had so recently raged against both Englanders and Jews, was, in April 1880, ready to put his name to the brave new era of Tory Anglo-conservative German friendship. The unspoken implication is that such a new rela-tionship is badly needed:

ENGLAND AND GERMANY.—An Anglo-German or Germano-Anglian Society has been formed at Berlin, under the presidency of Prince Hohenlohe-Langeburg, with a view of making England better known in Germany and Germany in England, removing national prejudices, and preparing an *entente cordiale* between two nations which have the same blood and have hitherto never crossed swords or bayonets. There is to be as soon as sufficient sums have been subscribed an English reading-room at Berlin where travellers may receive information and intro-ductions into German society. We see among the names of the members those of Gneist, von Holzendorff, Hofmann, Pauli, Waitz, Joachim, W. Siemens, Van Sybel, Van Treitschke, Von Stockmar, Auerbach, and several Bunsens, all names that have a good ring in England as well as in Germany.

The trouble was that many people in Britain simply did not want an alliance with Germany and Austria:

> It is Prince BISMARCK'S method first to isolate an adversary and then to trample on him. He isolated Austria, and then won Sadowa; he isolated France, and made Paris capitulate. He is now engaged in isolating Russia. France is neither prepared nor inclined to make sacrifices for a merely possible ally with whom she has few present political sympathies. The Eastern question offers a fertile field for provoking issues on which, by skilful manoeuvring, Germany, Austria, and England might be got to combine against Russia. That Prince BISMARCK has now made up his mind to arrange for the breaking out of such a war no one has, as yet, a right to say; but it may be safely said that such a purpose would be altogether in his style.[262]

The question was plain, and it was exactly the same question which would rear its head in July 1914: 'What would we do in the event of an attack by France and Russia upon Austro-Hungary and Germany? This is the question eagerly debated at Berlin. The resolute action of England would turn the scale in favour of peace or war. It may now settle the destinies of nations.'[263]

Of course, it all depended on what one defined as aggression. The famous 'Scrutator' of the solemn *Contemporary Review* wrote that:

> Whenever I see Prince Bismarck accusing some other nation of warlike intentions, I feel tolerably certain that he is maturing some other scheme of his own of which war is the too probable outcome. I believe that Germany is much more likely than Russia to engage in a great war ... The support of England to an Austro-German alliance would be very convenient to Prince Bismarck as it would enable him to fight German battles with English blood and gold.[264]

The British people were fed up with giving blood and gold to anyone. True, they had seen their international status recover under Disraeli, had hailed their new Queen-Empress, had sung their Jingo songs. But since 1878 they had seen their imperial expenses rise dramatically, their unwary envoys slaughtered in Afghanistan, their incompetent soldiery massacred in Zululand. No politician before Gladstone had ever appealed so directly, so unreservedly, to them, nor so clearly told them that they could have things easier. He wooed them and confirmed them in a marathon tour of public speeches lit by his absolute certainty that he was doing God's very work:

> Tuesday March 30th 1880: The beginning of the Elections. May God from heaven guide every one of them: and prosper or abase and baffle us for His glory: lift us up, or trample us down, according as we are promoting or opposing what He knows to be the cause of Truth, Liberty, and Justice.

The message was rammed home in speech after multi-hour speech: Britain could rely on its limitless moral force rather than expensive imperial adventures; if treated with Christian brotherliness, all the Concert of Europe would naturally maintain peace; meanwhile, progress would take its appointed path towards a world of independent nations, all of whom would freely import what they needed from the Workshop of the World. As one of Gladstone's supporters told an 'immense meeting' at the very HQ of economic liberalism, the Manchester Free Trade Hall, the liberals would do away with 'the gunpowder and glory business' and have no more 'secret conventions'. Instead, they were going to 'maintain a policy of non-interference, of non-aggression, and to throw the influence of this great country, with all the power we are capable of wielding, upon the side of justice, of freedom, of progress and of nationalism'.

It was an irresistibly happy, and cheap, vista: the voters whom Disraeli had enfranchised, and before whom he had paraded the heady prospect of Empire, now went with God, Gladstone and their wallets, giving the Liberals a majority so large that their great leader did not as yet require the further revelation that the Lord also wanted him to embrace the scores of safe MPs who came with Irish Home Rule.

The result came as a complete shock to Disraeli, and to the Queen-

Empress, who loathed 'that half-mad fire-brand' Gladstone. It also stunned Bismarck and his new Austrian allies.

> The returns hitherto announced have caused surprise and a feeling, moreover, of apprehension for the final result not altogether unrelated to alarm. Political thinkers in Germany are equally astonished at and unable to explain the facts before them. They are utterly at a loss to understand the motives which might induce a majority of the English people now to withdraw their confidence from the statesman in whom they have so long confided, who, they assert, despite his shortcomings, has piloted them safely through a most perilous sea of foreign complications, and who has unquestionably recovered for England her former proud seat at the council-board of Continental nations.[265]

For Bismarck, the result was an unqualified disaster. He had only just tied himself to Austria, which meant defying Russia, in the confident expectation that this new alliance could rely at least on enough support from Britain to keep France from his back. Now he found himself faced with a liberal Britain which would most certainly not go to war against Russia, which would be instinctively pro-French, and which would look with favour on the emergence of independent Slav nations fatal to the Austro-Hungarian Empire.

Overnight, Britain and Germany once again became thoroughgoing ideological and geopolitical enemies.

This is no mere hindsight. The moment the election was safely in the bag, Gladstone's own son, Herbert, now a newly minted MP as well as his father's private secretary, and so hardly likely to be off-message, made no bones at all about how things had changed regarding Britain's relations with Bismarck: 'He next proceeded to state that he regarded the aspect of affairs on the Continent as very stormy. He himself very much distrusted the policy of Prince Bismarck.'*[266]

---

* In this same speech, Herbert Gladstone warned his electors that the exit strategy from Afghanistan might be a little more complex than the Liberals had suggested during the campaign: 'We owed the Afghans a debt. We bought chaos amongst them . . . we owed it to them to restore something like order.'

Within days of Gladstone's victorious entrance to No. 10, the *Guardian* happily told readers exactly how their liberal votes in Britain had ruined the grand strategy of the Austro-German militarists and saved Europe from war:

> Up to the very moment of the English elections everything seemed favourable to the dynastic and reactionary designs of the Cabinet within the Cabinet at Vienna. The Austro-German alliance, and the peculiarly intimate relations with the Cabinet of St. James's, which might at any moment be productive of the most practical results, seemed to make the moment an extraordinarily favourable one for that final advance to the Aegean which has long been the cherished dream of the military court of Vienna ... So favourable seemed the political constellation for the realisation of these ambitious schemes, which were ultimately to embrace Salonica as well as Dantzig in the protectionist area of a great Austro-German military confederation, that the war with Russia – sooner or later considered inevitable – was to be risked at a not distant date. And now the advent of Mr. Gladstone to power has postponed this favourable moment, perhaps for ever.[267, 268]

The *Guardian* also described how Bismarck reacted immediately to the wreckage of his plans:

> While all was confusion in the Austrian Foreign Office, there was a hand that did not waver – a hand of blood and iron. On the very day on which it first became certain that the Liberals would triumph at the polls Prince Bismarck sent off General Trescoff on an important mission to Vienna. The mission was ostensibly to obtain the co-operation of the Austrian ally in sending a joint deputation to congratulate the Czar on his birthday. But the attempt of the official press to restrict the meaning of the step to one of pure courtesy should deceive no one. I have good authority for stating that the Austrian General Ramberg ... was charged on the part of his Government with the delicate task of

smoothing the path for the return of Russia to the Triple Alliance.[269]

It was perhaps the most profound and sudden change in another great country's foreign policy ever effected by British voters: 'on the very day' the result of the British general election of 1880 became certain, Bismarck, the apparent arbiter of Europe, was forced to turn his whole new foreign policy on its head and scramble desperately to get Russia back onside.

The experience left Bismarck, perhaps unsurprisingly, with a lifelong loathing of Gladstone. More profoundly, that year gave him a studied opinion which he fatally bequeathed to his diplomatic successors: that treaties with Britain were worthless because she was not guided, like any normal power, by a rational grasp of her long-term interests, but by a fickle public opinion.

As for the triumphant British Liberals, they saw Germany as an unstable land defaced by 'the disgraceful anti-Semitic agitation', riven with social strife, led by a man who kept the ferment alive simply to keep himself irreplaceable:

Wherever we look in that country we discover a ferment of antagonistic principles and aims, and a conflict of interests, parties, and classes such as must before long issue in decisive changes for the better or the worse. Free trade and protection, agriculture and manufactures, militarism and retrenchment, religious liberty and ecclesiastical bigotry, Imperialism and Liberalism, personal and parliamentary government are engaged in a struggle of growing seriousness ... All these elements of strife and commotion, which go so much deeper down into the foundations of a nation's life than ordinary political motives, would of themselves create a condition of things beset with trouble and danger. But when found in Germany the trouble and danger become exceptionally great. For there the one great genius who it is sincerely to be hoped may help the country through her troubles and dangers is not inclined to end them even if he were able.[270]

It was very hard to see where the prospects for any sort of Anglo-German friendship might lie now. Very soon, great new bones of contention would arise, too. But for now, we must leave diplomacy and the daily press to take a look at how Britons and Germans were nowadays describing each other in more relaxed media.

Intermezzo I: visiting the new Germany

The British public had been interested in Germany as a holiday destination for many decades; in the 1870s they began to take an interest in the Germans. The first heavyweight guide books to what the Germans were actually like when in non-holiday Germany, written by people who claimed to really know them, now begin to appear.

The picture was not attractive. When you arrived at Berlin, the first thing you noticed was 'that empyreumatic odour for which Berlin is notorious, the rankest compound of villainous smells which ever assaulted nostril ... it accompanies you everywhere'. You hailed a cab to discover that 'in no other capital city of Europe are such rickety, dirty, tumble-down, rotten, broken-springed, flea-infested conveyances to be found'.[271] You got to your hotel and found that all the warnings of earlier decades still applied and you were about to be inflicted with the 'hateful bag of feathers' which Germans insisted on using instead of decent British sheets, blankets and bedspreads: 'The *plumeau* is what the German loves, and the Briton hates above all things; the mountain of down or feathers which tumbles off on cold nights and stays on hot ones. You hate it all year round.'[272]

Another writer warns of:

beds of Lilliputian dimensions – simple wooden boxes too short to allow of a tall man stretching himself out full length and too narrow for a fat man to turn around in, while in lieu of blankets and a counterpane, the bed is provided with a voluminous bag of feathers ... The wall-papers in many private houses and hotels are remarkable for their hideous patterns, which in the case of nervous individuals are sufficient to produce an attack of nightmare.[273]

That is, if you were not first choked to death by the fumes of the tiled, enclosed *Kachelofen* with which Germans heated their rooms (they can best be imagined as a sort of vertical Aga, embellished with cornices, cherubs and suchlike). Tales of death by ill-regulated *Kachelofen* were legion, and Britons longed in vain for the merrily blazing open hearths which Germans, in turn, found hideously draughty as well as insanely expensive.

But such concrete strangeness was nothing compared to the Germans themselves, for 'there is much in the institutions which surprise, something in the culture which shocks the foreigner'.[274] The first shock came to any British gentleman hoping for something easy on the eye as he left his hotel:

Berlin women as a rule lack the fatal gift of beauty, being neither handsome nor even pretty ... less graceful than the French, less handsome than the English, less clever than the Americans ... The worst feature of a Berlin belle is unquestionably her nose ... the face is usually fat and pasty-looking. The figure is generally good, although often diminutive, with a well developed bust, heavy loins, beautifully shaped arms, large hands and still larger feet[275] ... It is perhaps to the execrably paved roads and the equally abominable footways that one should attribute the extraordinary development of female feet in this part of Europe ... this remarkable development of the pedal extremities which characterises the Berlin belles.[276]

Having got over his erotic disappointment, the British visitor would now be faced with the complexities of the society into which he wished to gain entrance.

Language was not the barrier, for English was widely spoken: many

was the German who had been to London, 'willing to work for little or
nothing, considering his occupation in the light of an educational
course'.[277] The complication which most struck British visitors may
come as a surprise, so used are we to being told that Britain is a
uniquely 'class-ridden' society. Our ancestors found it the other way
around. When Germans, in the late 1870s, said 'class', they meant it in
a way which Britons simply no longer accepted:

> We lament, in England, the cleavage between the classes, but it is
> nothing to that which exists in Germany … in America, where there
> are no classes, the result is that every man or woman lives for, and
> thinks of, self only. In Germany the severance of classes produces a
> similar result, but in Germany it leads not to self-glorification but to
> class-glorification.[278]

And when people in Germany spoke of 'rank' they meant it quite literally: 'rank throughout Germany is military but certain civil offices are
reckoned as military offices. Thus a judge ranks as major-general and a
lord-in-waiting as a colonel.' These ranks were absolutely official, laid
down by law and treated as vitally important. Whether, for example,
senior school and university teachers should be awarded social class
five, rather than class four, was a question which might be debated by
Bismarck and his most senior colleagues in the same meetings where
they hammered out the greatest issues of domestic and foreign politics.[279]
Any freeborn Anglo-Saxon was naturally going to have trouble in such
a world, filled with 'the insane rage for titles of one kind or another':

> The exactions in this direction are almost sufficient to frighten a
> simple-minded person out of society. Have you given the right man
> the right title? Is he a *Geheimerath*, or a *wirklicher Geheimerath*? Was
> that prince who affably condescended to address you a Royal, or a
> Transparent, or a Serene Highness? You have just addressed a lady
> (who has no right to the title) as *Excellenz*, and made her your
> implacable enemy for life.[280]

Out and about, you would have to relearn something that Britons had by now forgotten: 'the fine art of bowing':

> In Germany you lift your hat to men as well as to women. If you meet General Schmoller, you raise your hat high and bring it down to your knees with a full sweep of the arm; if you meet Herr Schmidt, who is your social equal, you tip your hat as much as he does – and no more; whereas if you meet your tailor you respond to his low bow by the merest touch of recognition. To the initiated, every man proclaims his social position at every step.[281]

Such rigid stratification had highly undesirable results. None of the manners or taste of the upper classes ever trickled downwards in Germany, because there was virtually no contact between the upper classes and the rest:

> The aristocracy hold themselves as far aloof as possible from the untitled bureaucracy whose intrusion into administrative life have deprived them of salaries which, although framed on a scale to make a War Office or Foreign Office clerk shudder in horrified amazement, would still have served to re-gild their faded ancestral escutcheons. The military class keeps itself rigidly apart from the civilian element, eying such other un-uniformed mortals as it may temporarily be thrown into contact with, with an air which affects to mildly marvel as to what particular section of the *residuum* the interloper can belong.[282]

You could tell a member of this socially tone-setting caste at first glance by their duelling scars. That was the whole point of them, of course: 'the scars prove him a gentleman, i.e. a man apt to take offence'.[283] And anyone who gave such man cause for offence, even with a gentle joke, was as liable, in 1878, as Daniel Eugene Ott had been in 1865, to be 'cloven at once to the brisket'.[284] Charles Dickens's own organ, *All Round the World*, gives an idea of just how alarming the military aristocracy could be if – as the unfortunate Ott had done – you happened to get in their way:[285]

Only, as we are passing down a narrow street, madame's amiability receives a sudden check. There is a trottoir, about eighteen inches wide, the rest of the street is aggravated paving-stones. Well, on the narrow footway, comes clanking along the most superb specimen of a cavalry officer that eyes ever beheld, all green and gold and glittering steel, his head in the air, with a lofty far-away look in the steel-blue eyes; a fair-haired barbarian chief, terrible in war, no doubt, and even cranky in disposition in times of peace.

"Let us avoid this man of war," I cry, and we are on the farther side of the street before Madame Reimer knows what it is all about.

"I thought you English were pugnacious?" she said scornfully, when she saw the reason of the manœuvre.

But his highness the count is no better pleased either; he seems to detect a touch of sarcasm in the wide berth we have given him. The eye of steely blue is clouded with anger, his fair face is flushed, bringing out a terrible scar that stretches from brow to chin—a shrewd sabre-cut that must have brought that proud head to the dust. And yet to that face the scar was more an ornament than a disfigurement. Happily, a man can't well quarrel with you for getting out of his way, and the haughty warrior passed on, jingling his spurs furiously.

Such men cared nothing for art, learning or culture:

Berlin society is too absorbed in the worship of rank, the adulation of ancient descent, and decided reverence for the higher military element. Men who have made their mark in science, art, and literature, the luminaries of the bar, the great professors of medicine ... have no more part in it than the learned Baboo or reforming African potentate whom we English are so eager to welcome.[286]

The social magnetism of the military aristocracy was so profound that the well-off, middle-class German, instead of being a proud British-style citizen, 'apes the readiness to take offence of the unapproachable class above him in rank and below him in fortune'.[287] At the very top, and vouchsafing the whole order, was, of course, the Emperor William I, who dwelled in realms beyond all contact: 'in newspapers the Emperor is invariably styled the All-Highest in what sounds parlously like an infringement of Divine privilege'.[288]

Bereft of contact with their betters, the middle class seemed 'distinguished by their ill manners, their general coarseness of behaviour and deficiency of taste',[289] while 'the proletariat are more menacing and brutal than in any other chief city of Europe',[290] notable for their 'dastardly ruffianism'.[291]

The violence of German class conflict was mirrored in intellectual debate. Darwin himself tried very hard not to ruffle the feathers of the Church more than was absolutely unavoidable, but *The Times* described how differently his disciple in Germany carried on the fight in this 'land of strange contrasts':[292]

> Ernst Häckel, the learned and warlike Professor of Zoology at the University of Jena, and the ablest exponent of Darwinism in Germany, cannot refrain from appending to an exposition of the development theory a string of sneers, at best a little irrelevant, against the Church of Rome— complaints that the State allows the existence of monasteries and celibacy as an institution, and expressions of satisfaction that some bishops and Jesuits were in prison for disobedience to the law.

Everything in Germany just seemed so much less *civilised*. If this applied to social life, political debate and scientific controversy, it was most dismayingly clear to Britons at the dining tables of Germany. Even solidly bourgeois Berliners behaved, well, shockingly:

> They will blow clouds of cigar-smoke into ladies faces, and this not merely in the street but in railway carriages and even at dinner tables, and will roughly elbow their way through a crowd inside a theatre, regardless of women or children ... Still, what is to be expected of a people who think nothing of taking a comb out of their pockets and combing their hair in the midst of a conversation, or of standing before a looking-glass in a restaurant and performing the same operation, and who instead of reserving their tooth-picks for their teeth, clean their finger-nails with them in public and at times even thrust them into their ears ... their graceless habit of using their knife as a spoon, frequently thrusting three or four inches of the blade into their mouths.[293]

The writer of 'Onward, Christian Soldiers' tries hard to love the good Protestant Germans in his fat guide book of 1879, but even he finds his charity quite running dry when it comes to their table manners:

> With the kindest of hearts and the best of intentions, a German omits the little courtesies, and even decencies of life, without which civilized life as we understand it in England, is intolerable. His mode of eating, even in good society, is on a level with that of our agricultural labourers.[294]

As one Prussian professor himself admitted: 'It is not easy for well-bred foreigners to associate agreeably with people who mistake rudeness and bluntness for sincerity and frankness, who eat clumsily and wear unsightly signet rings on their forefingers, just as they find it difficult at first no doubt to accustom themselves to our execrable beds and bad cookery.'[295]

You had better not say anything about it, though, even as a joke. Britons, in 1879, had already decided that Germans were so touchy as to have no sense of humour, being distinguished by 'that utter want of command of temper and inability to pass over the slightest thing that touches self-esteem, even if uttered merely in jest, which distinguishes all Germans.'[296] It does not seem to have occurred to Britons that it may just have been the endless jokes made at their expense by arrogant Englanders which the Germans found hard to take.

But Victorian Britons (and, later, Americans) found something about Germany quite impossible to take, as well: 'the average German of every class is of the opinion that there is no difficulty with which the State is not fit to deal'.[297]

> The State looks after his mind, his bowels, and his soul. From birth he must be registered by State functionaries, educated by State functionaries, married by State functionaries and shovelled out of this world by State functionaries.[298]

Our own modern assumptions about the role of the state are far closer to nineteenth-century German ones than to those of our own great-great-grandparents. There is little in this catalogue of German strangeness which we, now, would find at all questionable, but it appeared completely bizarre to freedom-loving Victorians:

> If you would hear the best music, you must listen to musicians who are paid from the public treasury. A government minister preaches in the government-owned church that you attend on Sunday, and if you are a student in a university the professor who lectures you is a government official. Sometimes you can even trace the government inspector's stamp on the chop served at your restaurant.[299]

This state was served by legions of functionaries who seemed almost to worship it: 'No English Lord of the Treasury's private secretary ever identified himself more thoroughly with the government he served than the humblest Vice-Deputy Sub-Assistant Temporary Inspector or Supernumary Clerk in the Berlin Public Office.'[300]

The backbone of the German state, and the essential difference between that state and the high-liberal British way was, of course, the army. It was everywhere in Germany. Two British writers of the 1870s wrestled with trying to describe to mystified Britons the most striking visual feature of German militarism. *The Times* of 4 February 1875 describes the way the German infantry 'throw out their legs while passing line in a manner which may appear melodramatic but is certainly most striking', while the most compendious guide book of the late 1870s tries rather harder to explain what is going on:

> Imagine the upper part of the body kept bolt upright with one leg firmly placed in the same perpendicular position, while the other is spasmodically lifted up at an angle of forty-five degrees; imagine a hundred legs in a row simultaneously performing this exercise with the utmost regularity, moving with an identity of step, tread and intent as though they belonged to one immense multiple animal.[301]

Such displays of goose-stepping military power were no mere decoration. Britons, who had imbibed with their mothers' milk tales of bold parliamentarians standing up to Charles I and James II, were scandalised by the way things went on in the Reichstag of the mid-1870s:

> When the debate is over and the vote is about to be taken, the Prime Minister usually rises for a last word to the effect that the collective ministry have agreed to the measure, that the King approves of it, and that all that there now remains for the House to do is vote it in ... a door opens and in strides Prince Bismarck, in cuirassier uniform with huge jack-boots and an enormous sword which he clatters along the floor. The House is crushed and acts as though these military statesmen had behind them a regiment of the line ready to enforce obedience at the point of a bayonet.[302]

The liberals who might properly be expected to stand up for parliament against such outrages did not. By now, it was very obvious that the people who *called* themselves National Liberals were scarcely liberals at all in the British sense:

> *Liberal* is a word having a somewhat different significance with regard to matters parliamentary in Germany ... [the National Liberals] to whom the complete unification of Germany, by any possible means, appears to be the acme of Liberalism ... the love of liberty expressed by this party is for the most part rather platonic.[303]

It was all deeply confusing, but anyone who hoped to better understand the currents of German parliamentary doings by sitting down in a café and reading the papers was in for a disappointment:

> As the leading organs are in great measure either under the influence of the Press Bureau or the thumb of the police authorities, the expression of independent views on political matters is reduced to a minimum ... The German government has an even more effective method of dealing with newspapers than proscribing them, namely by taking them into its pay ... after 1866 came a golden dawn to the literary agents of Prince Bismarck ... to such perfection has the system been brought of late that all traces of a suspicious unanimity have been carefully and systematically eliminated.[304]

Even the less informed visitor would be struck by the tone of the press:

> On the language of German journalism we can barely touch at this moment. It more nearly approaches the American model in style than that of any other country. To say that it is 'tall' is to say nothing; it is always on the high-horse; it is pompous, prancing, and aggressive; there is a gush and garrulity about it that is infinitely vapid and fatiguing. It twirls its moustache and clanks its spurs, and stalks.[305]

For all the swagger, though, there was a curious but palpable sense of national fragility:

> The habitual timidity of the Germans makes them very much afraid of anything of which they are afraid at all. They live in an atmosphere of panic as to what the Court will do, as to when Prince BISMARCK will retire from the scene, as to what the POPE will order, as to what France or Russia may be plotting. It is extraordinary how the faintest adverse rumour will flutter a people which ten years ago performed some of the greatest military feats recorded in history, which is armed to the teeth, and is supposed to be without a rival in the arts of war.[306]

A strange and febrile place, then, governed by bureaucrats, policed by *gendarmerie* and cowed by the army to an extent which Britons could hardly credit – and yet, one where things were allowed, in public and even in the presence of apparently respectable folk, which would not be tolerated for an instant in Victoria's London. The largest guide book of the day waxes lengthily about such places (several of whose exact addresses it helpfully gives for any visiting Briton wishing to be appalled):

> No European city, large or small, has so many dissolute dancing-places on a grand scale, "where the half-drunk lean over the half-dressed" ... it is not pleasure that is waltzing but depravity which is flinging itself about ... vice performing its libidinous contortions ... These nymphs showed themselves to be under no kind of restraint ... erotic frescoes on which Germans gaze through their spectacles without the slightest appearance of being shocked ... one impresario complains that "we can never go far enough for these Germans, no matter how low we cut the bodices of our ballet-girls or how high we cut their skirts" ... the walls are hung with very coarse pictures, conspicuous for their too lavish display of the female form divine ... if you visit the place with a female companion, you are allowed all the privacy you could possibly desire ... disgusting scenes are far too common – scenes which would not be tolerated in the lowest sailors' "dancing shop" in Shadwell or Wapping.[307]

The society which permitted such abominations had no place for one of the most characteristic institutions of late-Victorian Britain:[308]

GERMANY AND THE SALVATIONISTS.

BERLIN, JAN. 3.

The German Empire, it seems, is about to be invaded, not by the French or the Russians, or the Danes, or the Dutch, or any other of its malignant neighbours, but by the Salvationist Army of "General" Booth. How the commander and captains of this incursive host will fare it is not difficult to predict. They will most assuredly be laughed out of the country, and in all probability laid by the heels. "General" Booth could not possibly have selected a more unfavourable field of operations than Germany. The Germans, on the whole, being pretty much devoid of individuality themselves, are too intolerant of eccentricity of conduct in others to endure unusual behaviour of any kind off the stage. In countries like England and America the military nature of "General" Booth's Evangelical system has no doubt had a certain charm for minds to whom rank and degree are always imposing and alluring things, but the Germans are too intimately acquainted with the grim and grinding realities of army life to entertain the slightest weakness for its sham and sentimental aspects, and "General" Booth might as well carry coals to Newcastle or owls to Athens, as try to convert the souls of German men by the rolling of drums and a show of text-embroidered banners.

Amid all this thoroughly alien life, there was one thing – one thing alone, really – which Britons, by 1878, were thinking, and would keep on thinking, that they really ought to copy about Germany: education.

German schools were the marvel of the age, German illiteracy rates astonishingly low. Thanks to their education, and their readiness to take low wages, 'already in London and Manchester and Liverpool

Germans have dethroned English clerks from their stools'.[309] Should not Britain, too, create such a class of educated lower orders?

The most amazing thing was that these excellent schools, even the ones frequented by aristocrats, were practically free. There was simply no equivalent whatever in Germany of the public school system which loomed so large in the life-plans (and, often, in the family budgets) of middle-class Britons. Some of them were even emigrating to Germany simply because by doing so, they would save a small fortune in school fees.[310] Even the youngest child could enjoy the kindergarten which were 'full of attractions to the pupils'.[311]

However, even in this one area of German life which Britons seemed ready to admit was obviously better, there was a warning attached. British schools liked to claim they inculcated 'character'. German schools actually *taught*, and German schoolchildren faced levels of exam stress utterly unknown in Britain. The daunting examination taken at eighteen or nineteen years of age, the famous *Abitur*, was (and still is) known to cause suicide among young Germans.[312] It was 'the day of judgement looming before the child's eyes, and their childish life is a solemn march to that *Dies irae* ... unless they issue from that examination with a certificate of "ripeness", every learned profession is closed to them and three years' military drill instead of one is their doom'.[313]

In the age of *Tom Brown's School Days*, visitors from Britain were amazed that 'German boys have no public games, their school-work is exhausting and it takes all their energies out of them,'[314] or that 'German schools have no playgrounds, German boys no games. They never obtain a practical knowledge of life ... they grow up to live in worlds of their own creation, in ideas and theories.'[315]

With all that hard work and no play, a boy might even end up *wearing glasses*: the sorry sight of bespectacled youths was 'one of the first things that strikes a stranger' about the country.[316] All Britons agreed on 'the short-sightedness so prevalent in Germany' and blamed the 'physical depletion caused by close and constant brain-work'.[317]

This applied just as much to the universities. British students were obsessed with sport but 'such a thing as single manly sport of any kind is utterly unknown to the Berlin students'. Where Oxford or Cambridge varsity men aimed to win Blues or Half Blues, German students were only concerned with examinations – and with getting the scars that would proclaim, for life, at fifty paces, that they belonged to the elite of people able to give satisfaction: 'the nearest approach to anything resembling sport are the duelling encounters which disgrace Berlin almost as much as other German universities'.[318]

This bizarre German mixture of overdone brain-work, heady theories, a biddable press, state worship and brutal militarism could only lead to one, dread thing: *socialism*.

The lines are drawn

Whatever we nowadays may think the word 'socialism' means, our forefathers were quite certain of it.

Two generations later, the first guru of neo-liberalism, Friedrich August (born von) Hayek, was to make his epochal claim that despite their apparent deadly rivalry, National Socialism and Soviet communism both sprang from exactly the same roots in Bismarckian anti-liberalism.[319] But Victorian Britons did not need another seventy years of thinking time, or the personal experience of the Great War and its ghastly aftermaths, to come to the same conclusion. To them, the Bismarckian state and 'socialism' were in practice, quite simply, one and the same thing.

> Socialist ideas are by no means confined to the lower stratum in society. The whole professional class is more or less infected with them. This class, living in a world of dreams, delighting in destructive criticism, utterly unacquainted with the practical aspect of such questions, has been captivated by the specious promises of Socialism. This is especially the case with the professors of political economy in the German universities. The chief professor of political economy at the Berlin University is a rank, an undisguised Socialist.[320]

The *Guardian* warned that these German professors of economics are 'a class of thinkers whose views frequently differ essentially from those usually adopted in this country'. For 'though holding most of the doctrines of Adam Smith' (as well they might!), they 'take certain peculiar views', namely 'the policy of State intervention, which the socialistic professors are continually advocating in regard to all kinds of questions'.[321]

From the Great Crash of 1873 onwards, article after article on 'the German Socialists', 'Bismarck's State Socialism' and suchlike makes the same point:

> Like PRINCE BISMARCK, the Socialists – whose popularity among the working classes is evidently growing – aspire to give the central Government authority over every sort of national institution and industrial enterprise.[322]

> [Socialism and Communism]: In both bases their acceptance is facilitated by the position of the State in Germany. For the State in the concrete form of its officials is traditionally a much more familiar power than with ourselves in England. And hence the idea either of regulation of all property in the interests of labour, or a community of property administered by State officers, is not so hard to grasp as it would be for us.[323]

> The journal that advocates the re-imposition of the duties on iron in Germany might be described, without much straining of criticism, as a Socialist publication.[324]

> The habit of initiative, without which Englishmen could not live and which in Germany had certainly made some progress, is fast disappearing before an omnipresent State power. The millennium of every Socialist dream, viz, a condition where all work is fixed, ordered and requited by Government, has more than dawned in Germany.[325]

So, at the end of the 1870s, Germany was a very strange place indeed to Britons. It was a world at once far more controlled and far less safely respectable than home. Going there, you would find a land plagued by striking class divisions, where a 'toad-eating titular mania' confronted an equally foreign, assassination-attempting social democracy. Even well-bred people had awful manners. There were soldiers, and penniless but dangerously touchy aristocrats, everywhere you went. The politics of the country appeared to be a quasi-military, one-chancellor arrangement comprising bitterly opposed parties, none of whom exercised any real power over the executive arm of government. Precisely because they knew that in the end nothing they did or said would change anything, these parties allowed themselves 'to play at opposition and fronde' with a level of public invective unknown in real British politics.[326] 'We talk of class hatred; but it is in Germany that true class hatred exists ... the daily increasing hate and estrangement between the different political parties.'[327] These parties seemed able to agree on one thing and one thing only: the bizarre German doctrine that the more powerful the State, the better.

Perhaps most strikingly, going to Germany in the later 1870s, you would no longer find the obsequiousness which earlier British holidaymakers had mocked or enjoyed. You might expect instead to encounter, if not outright hostility, then 'this settled antipathy which seems to animate all classes when they write and speak of England'. At times it seemed to 'rankle into absolute hatred', and visitors in 1878 were given an up-to-date warning that with Disraeli's more bellicose policies, 'whilst forced to respect us more, they do not hate us less'.[328]

By why did so many Germans seem, to British visitors of the 1870s, to hate them so? Nothing – absolutely *nothing* – had as yet physically occurred between Britain and Germany which would have accounted for such deep-set feelings. No war, no trade war, no colonial entanglements or inimical alliances. The worst things had ever got had been during the War in Sight crisis of 1875, and because he had been beaten, Bismarck had made sure that the significance of that was publicly downplayed, so this could hardly account for it. One puzzled German colleague of Treitschke asked himself 'how England had really managed to incur his undying hatred, a hatred that knew no bounds'.[329]

Whatever the reasons for such Anglophobia, it was by now part of German public life.

It was not – at least, not yet – the whole story, of course. If the British were now interested in the Germans, the Germans had long been fascinated by the British. The age of unconditional admiration was now gone forever – one German guide book to Britain from 1869 opens with the note that 'in recent years it has become the fashion in Germany to greet everything that comes from England with a gesture of rejection just as in earlier times everything was excessively praised',[330] but there were still people who thought Britain had something to offer.

It is to them we now turn, to see how things looked from the other side.

Intermezzo II: the mysteries of Britain

The great British offer was still quite simple: freedom and wealth.

To poor Germans, little had changed since the 1860s. Britain, and more especially London, was still an almost mythical place. Dangerous political refugees or hopelessly starving people took ship into the fogs of the Channel, from which many of them never returned, but where a few made their fortunes and came back in glory. The sight of the place had led Marshal Blücher, the co-victor of Waterloo, to exclaim in 1815: 'What a city to plunder!' and, in 1882, Baron von Ompteda, whose ancestor had died leading the King's Fifth German Legion of the British Army to virtual annihilation on that same field, was still possessed by 'the highly-charged consciousness of approaching the greatest emporium of all the treasures of the Earth'.[331]

Here, you would see things almost unimaginable in Germany: you might gape at the legendary Ten Thousand who ruled the British Empire gathered at Rotten Row in the season; it was, said one entranced German visitor, 'a sight like nothing else on earth'.[332] Or you might tremble at the thought of the terrible docks, where 'white, yellow and black men, the freshly paid-off crews from countless ships, appear on the banks of the Thames like wild animals freed from their cages' and would proceed to drink in bleak establishments with none of the comfort and homeliness of German inns – no newspapers, tables, dominos – until the 'ruinous, American' way of drinking in such bars turned them into beasts and the knives came out. After all, 'everything is gigantic here, so vice is naturally gigantic too'.[333] You might even see women agitating for the vote, though the reporter who described this unheard-of fact to his Berlin readers calmed them by adding that 'in Britain the old Germanic family-life is still too strong, and the Englishwoman too charming, to allow herself to be Americanized in this way'.[334]

Utterly modern, incredibly wealthy, incalculably dangerous: there was something almost literally otherwordly about London to Germans: 'in Germany, we are used to surrounding the world-city of London with thoughts that have more to do with some foggy Hades than with reality'.[335]

The essential magic of London, then as now, dark and light, was that it was a place where *anything* could happen. In this, it was completely unlike class-ridden, policed, conscripting Germany, where the chances of one's life were laid down very much at birth and ruled thereafter by the state. Compared to this, the sheer freedom of London was irresistible – to some, fatally:[336]

> The German passion for wandering, the longing for a wider range of view, the hope of improving their personal condition or of some lucky stroke of fortune, the mere love of adventure or swindling propensities, or other frivolous or sordid motives, induce annually many thousands of Germans to wend their way to London without introductions and scantily provided with money.

If they were lucky, these hopeful immigrants might 'serve apprenticeships in English business-houses, barber-shops, restaurants, hotels and the like, gaining a knowledge of the language and of the weights and measures, and at the same time studying business methods generally'.[337] They were, therefore, often prepared to work for far less than the British: in 1887, just as in earlier years, this made them naturally 'preferred not only by their own countrymen, but frequently also by English employers, with the equally natural consequence that it made 'the intruders unpopular in many circles'.[338]

And that was if they were lucky enough to find work. If not, the boundless freedom of London could turn into hopeless free-fall. 'Unacquainted with the language of the country, without money, without acquaintances, and without the smallest conception of the prevailing circumstances, the new-comer would soon fall into misery'.[339, 340]

> among the numerous homeless Germans in London there are always to be found persons of culture and education, who have seen better days, and now would be thankful to be sure of a bed, a crust of bread or a cup of tea. It is frequently matter of astonishment on the Continent that men willing and able to work should be left to starve in rich London, and the question is asked whether they cannot find employment. To this we answer decisively : No, in innumerable cases they cannot. Competition is so fierce in all departments of labour, in all branches of business, that there are constantly many thousands of natives, as well as foreigners, who can find no opportunity of utilising their stalwart arms or their acquired skill.

Quickly, those who had been poor but respectable in Germany could go to the dogs:

> What then? Then sorrows and troubles come in like a flood. Those who do not prefer to return to the Fatherland richer in experience, or who do not succumb to despair and go to the bad altogether, have recourse to charitable societies and, later on, to individual countrymen blessed with means. Persons who at home could never have conceived the possibility of begging for anything become professional beggars. Bitter necessity forces them to apply for assistance, and the long want of occupation co-operates with the habit of allowing themselves to be supported by others, and reduces many to the condition of lazy dependents, shameless beggars, and depraved characters.

Such people would be easy prey for the German political refugees already operating in London, shielded by the inexplicable British obsession with freedom. These men were turning the capital of Britain into the centre of international terrorism.[341]

> London has become, especially during these last years, the headquarters of the German Nihilists. It is the central point of that anti-social movement, the high school in which the disciples are trained, who, having served their apprenticeship, return to Germany as apostles of the new gospel, for the purpose of recruiting new disciples, and keeping up communication with the central post. . . . In the present condition of things, the chances are that most working-men who arrive in London will in a very short time be found in the bosom of the Communistic party.

It sounds like modern 'Londonisthan': poor Germans arriving in London were offered aid by 'their Communistic brethren' and thereby fell into 'the ranks of Red Republicanism'. Safely beyond the reach of the German law, they could then develop their 'diabolical plots', such as that to assassinate Bismarck and the Prince Wilhelm, involving the most modern terroristic devices, 'infernal machines which are partly electrical'.[342]

As for women, the situation will again seem sadly familiar: enticed to London by newspaper adverts offering apparently respectable jobs (and perhaps by the well-known fact that women were much freer in Britain), poor German girls discovered too late that they were in fact to be forced into prostitution in and around Leicester Square.[343]

Such were the dangers awaiting the rash and penniless immigrant to Britain. But there was, of course, another kind of visitor from Germany: the self-conscious observers who had come, well intentioned, especially to report on the mysteries of the most powerful society on Earth. They found that they had to coin a brand-new word to describe their general experience: 'Londonmüdichkeit' – 'London-tiredness'.[344]

What tired Germans so much about London was partly the sheer pace, noise and wealth, the 'deafening hubbub of the City, the black labyrinth of the underground railways'.[345] But there was something else which amazed them even more: 'The most remarkable sight in England, however, is without doubt – the Englanders themselves!'[346]

Like British visitors to Berlin, Germans in London checked out the local beauties and found them wanting. German girls might have those big feet, but Baron Ompteda struck back: 'I have made a special study of this matter and have in England never been able to find a small, fine, delicate hand.'[347] It was not much fun watching English girls dance, for the waltz and the polka seemed to be something 'foreign and learned with great effort' to them. No, young Englishwomen 'appeared to their best advantage in such motions as require bodily grace as well as a certain degree of effort – in the saddle, ice-skating, or at lawn-tennis'. Best of all was to watch them on horseback, for 'here, as if the saddle were her natural element, the young Englishwoman unfolds, all unaware, aye, unconsciously, her sure, strong, flexible grace'.[348]

So much for the outer person. What was truly strange and fascinating about the English was 'their complete, compact, homogenous and insularly cloistered way of living, of acting, of feeling and of thinking'.[349]

The Englanders all prayed to one God: propriety. Their greatest fear was of doing anything 'unprecedentet' [sic]. Of course, this had one very obvious good side. It meant, as Baron Ompteda put it with waspish tact (unconsciously backing up what Britons said about manners in Germany), that 'decent, cleanly table-manners reach far deeper down into the middle-classes in England than in – certain places I could name. The hateful use of the knife in place of the fork is absolutely looked down upon, and at table bread is always broken, never cut up.' But it was about far more than just table manners, and the Baron was forced to make a striking comparison in order to give his countrymen any real idea of just how strictly conformist the society of 'our English cousins' was: 'We do, in fact, have one similar phenomenon, though it is more limited in extent: I mean, the uniformity in outward appearance, mode of speech and way of thinking of our own officer-corps.'[350]

Here was the great chasm. In Germany, social intercourse, like every aspect of national life, followed strict rules – even the drinking bouts of German university students were carried on in accordance with printed handbooks. Britons found such things absurd or impossible.

But at least these rules were *knowable*. If social class in Germany was set in iron, you could look it up and thus avoid calamity. In Britain, everything from law-making to dinner parties was governed by unpublished precedents completely incomprehensible to anyone other than the British themselves. It was this, above all, which exhausted German visitors to London. British social life was a minefield without maps.

The noble Ompteda, who was very close to the Crown Princess of Germany (and hence a liberal Anglophile), went out for a walk in Piccadilly one sunny July morning in 1881, dressed, as he thought, quite properly in frock coat, silk hat and umbrella. He found himself so blatantly mustered from head to toe by every British gentleman he passed that he was at last forced to retreat back indoors and check himself out:

> That was it! I was wearing a *white* waistcoat, modestly but fatally visible under my frock-coat. And lo! It was the only white waistcoat in Piccadilly, for on this particular day in the Season, this handy item was not yet worn, and every eye in Piccadilly was drawn to the "incorrect thing."[351]

The same writer was also faced with the mysteries of British 'At Home' cards:

> These cards state nothing further than that Mrs X. or Lady Y. will be "at home" today. The only indication that this interesting fact is in any way concerned with you – your own name is nowhere on the card, nor is there any suggestion that you should appear – is that your address stands below the mysterious communication.

After a few weeks of this, he ends up sympathising with Dr Livingstone,

> of whom it is said that he more than once found the test of a dinner in the London Season too hard, and left for Africa mid-meal, in

order that he might, by bivouacing in the fever-infested Tropics, gather his strength to resist the hospitality of civilisation.

Precedent versus book-law, the social tyranny of mysterious propriety versus the strict and public ranking of persons: here was the contrast between the whole British way and the whole German way. One sympathetic British writer described how the visiting German 'honestly feels checked at every turn by our unwritten laws, while when you go to Germany you wonder how he can submit so patiently to the pettiness and multiplicity of written ones ... suddenly you see one of the great everyday differences between your countryfolk and his'.[352]

The British could not see how Germany functioned with so many laws, while the Germans could not see how Britain worked at all, since 'what we call "the State" simply does not exist ... in the twenty years I have spent in England I have not to my knowledge a single time experienced a train arriving on time'.[353]

And yet, the British way clearly *did* work – look at her empire. So might this forbidding British monoculture not be a *good* thing? Was it not 'a stark contrast to our own fragmented individualism' and the sign of a more advanced, united country? Yes, the British were egoistical and self-obsessed, despising anything that was '*unenglisch*' or 'foreign-looking', but at least they were free from 'our national sin of admiring and preferring all that is foreign'. The British had no 'cosmopolitan fantasies or unpatriotic religiosity – both the marks of an immature nation'.[354]

Well-off, well-disposed German observers thought that the great secret was Britain's ability to absorb and incorporate progress without sacrificing what was good about the old ways. It was such a contrast to Germany, that fractured, fractious land with its 'doctrinaire obsession with systems'.[355] Here, one found:

A relaxed way of life, which on the surface may seem anarchic, but which exists at the same time as the rule of old laws and customs; a conservative insistence on the creations of earlier generations coexists with a powerfully advancing sense of common national interests.[356]

The sight of 'the past and the present living together so peacefully' might make the German traveller melancholy when he considered the 'alas! very different fate of our own Fatherland'.[357]

When Germans sought for an image that would sum up for their readers all that was utterly strange and yet admirable about England, one thing sprang always to mind: that unique, incomprehensible institution which was truly national, truly rooted in the people, yet beloved by all classes, that concern which 'has spread over the entire Anglo-Saxon Earth, into Europe, Asia, Africa and Australia, and which embraces and binds together the entire Anglo-Saxon family of peoples'.[358] It was, of course, cricket.

> There is perhaps no popular game which is in a better sense and a higher meaning democratic. Every degree of age and every social class encounters each other in easy sociability on the green sward of the cricket-field. The social differences of everyday life are here levelled out. There is no question here of privilege for wealth and class. The peer submits himself to the same rules as the common worker; power, skill, sharpness of eye and steadiness alone take the prize.[359]

Perhaps this was the secret of British success, for here was the 'national' and unifying element of a people which 'is ahead of all of Europe in this respect'. The sight of a foreign *volk* so united in the pursuit of a national – an imperial! – pastime which overrode all class differences was little short of a beatific vision to German visitors, who looked in vain to their own country for any sign of such unity. This, surely, was the deep strength of the Englanders: 'Simply to re-tell the tale of the English eleven's tour to Australia is enough to make any objective beholder doubt the prophecy that England is doomed to swift decline.'[360]

A real, living national unity and an empire: the old liberal dreams still haunted German visitors to Britain. These were what made Britain mighty, despite all her drawbacks; these were what German visitors still admired and envied.

That admiration and envy was about to turn to outright emulation –

and outright confrontation – for the first time, and the playing field on which this new game was to take place announced itself just before the old decade ended.

On 20 September 1879, six weeks after having been posted, a remarkable and plaintive letter was received by the staff of the Queen-Empress Victoria:

Dearest Madam,   *Cameroons River, Acqua Town, August* 7, 1879.
WE your *servants* have *join* together and thoughts its better to write you a nice *loving* letter which will tell you about all our *wishes*. We *wish* to have your laws in our towns. We want to have every *fashion* altered, also we will do according to your Consul's *word*. Plenty wars here in our country. Plenty murder and plenty idol worshipers. Perhaps these *lines* of our writing will *look* to you as an *idle* tale.
We have *spoken* to the English Consul plenty times about having an English *Government* here. We never have answer from you, so we wish to write you *ourselves.*
When we heard about Calabar River, how they have all English *laws* in their towns, and how they have put away all their *superstitions*, oh, we shall be very glad to be like Calabar now.

We are, &c.
(Signed)   KING ACQUA.
PRINCE DIDO ACQUA.
PRINCE BLACK.
PRINCE JOE GARNER.
PRINCE LAWTON.

The writers of this unusual plea were indeed soon to sign away their burdensome independence – but not to Queen Victoria.

PART FIVE (THE 1880s):
BISMARCK vs THE BRITISH

Mr Gladstone has his hands full

Gladstone's 1880 government had a huge majority but was in trouble almost from the start. He quickly found that getting out of Afghanistan (alive, if you are lucky) is rather more difficult than going in; that running Egypt together with France was always going to cause problems; and that before he could defuse the troubles in Ireland with benevolent and Christian legislation, he would somehow have to restore something like law and order by almost any means.

Lord Roberts's touch-and-go victories in Afghanistan saved the day there, enabling Britain to escape without her tail too obviously between her legs, but the Transvaal War was a catastrophe: the Boer marksmen picked off entire platoons of brightly dressed British soldiers, officers and all, culminating in the epochal humiliation of Majuba Hill on 27 February 1881.

Gladstone was now desperate for a top-speed exit strategy from southern Africa, so it is perhaps not surprising that when the King of Bell Town again sat down, scarcely a week after that historic disaster to British arms, his second plea to be annexed fell on deaf ears. Nothing daunted, the King tried again in November, this time writing to Mr Gladstone in person.

Dear Sir,   *Cameroons River, West Africa, November 6, 1881.*
  WE both your servants have met this afternoon to write to you these few lines of writing trusting it may find you in a good state of life as it leaves us at present. As we heard here that you are a the chief man in the House of Commons, so we write to you to tell you that we want to be under Her Majesty's control. We want our country to be governed by British Government. We are tired of governing this country ourselves; every dispute leads to war, and often to a great loss of lives, so we think it is the best thing to give up the country to you British men who no doubt will bring peace, civilization, and Christianity in the country. Do for mercy sake please to lay our request before the Queen and to the rulers of the British Government. Do, Sir, for mercy sake, please to assist us in this important undertaking. We heard that you are a good Christian man, so we hope you may do all you can in your power to see that our request is granted. We are quite willing to abolish all our heathen customs. I hope you may take this matter into a deep consideration, and do all you can, for the sake of God, to see that our request is granted. No doubt God will bless you for putting a light in our country. Please to send us an answer as quick as you can.
                    With kind regards, we are, &c.
                              (Signed)   KING BELL AND
                                              KING ACQUA.

This letter at least got a civil reply:

Sir,   *Foreign Office, March* 1, 1882.
    MR. GLADSTONE referred to Earl Granville, Her Majesty's Secretary of State
for Foreign Affairs, the letter of the 6th November last, signed by yourself and King
Acqua, begging that your country may be taken under the protection of Her Majesty's
Government. I am now directed to convey to you the thanks of Her Majesty's
Government for the friendly expressions made use of by you towards them, and to state
that although they are not prepared as at present advised to undertake the Protectorate
of your country, they will further examine the matter and write to you again.
    A similar letter has been addressed to King Acqua.

                                                    I am, &c.
                                    (Signed)   T. V. LISTER.

But if Britain could afford to fob off pesky applicants to her vast empire,
it seemed to a growing number of Germans that they had left it too late
to get any colonies at all.

The old dream stirs

The German liberals-cum-nationalists had for decades wanted an
empire like Britain's. Now it was getting urgent. Why should Germany,
now the most powerful country in Europe, be the only one not to have
any colonies? Even Austria-Hungary had one.* The movement had
already been growing in 1878, when Europe and Asia Minor were
carved up at the Congress of Berlin. By 1883, it seemed that Germany
was in grave danger of missing out completely.†

---

* In Austria-Hungary, after 1878, it was universal to refer to Bosnia-Herzegovina as 'our
colonies'. Even someone as aware of language as Franz Kafka did so without thinking twice.
† Colonial mania was perhaps related to the dawn of what we would now call 'celebrity culture'.
By the turn of the 1870s, the popular press was regularly printing actual photographs of individual officers, sometimes even of Other Ranks. When a British lieutenant, finding himself alive
and victorious amid the dead on some distant imperial hilltop now asked, 'What will they think
of this, in England?' he no longer meant 'What will the War Office or the *Gazette* think of this?'
but 'Will the *Penny Illustrated Paper* run our portraits?' The newly urban mass populations of
the Western world were entranced by the way that a miniscule shoot-out in Texas or a colonial
skirmish might make you *someone* overnight. This was *The X-Factor* or the National Lottery of
the day: it might only happen to a very, very few people – but it *did* happen and there, in the
papers, were the names and faces to prove it. It could, in your dreams, be you.

Zeus asks Germania: 'Where were you when the world was divided up?'
Even Austria-Hungary is walking off with colonies in the shape of Bosnia.

The spirit of *Kladderadatsch* (the German equivalent of Mr Punch) asks the
belated German idealists, 'Where were you when the world was divided?'

The curious thing was that whenever the question was raised of where exactly those German colonies might be founded, the answer always seemed to involve places where Britain was already established. Of course, the sheer size of the British Empire made this a statistical probability, but if you look at the original documents, it does seem to have been almost a deliberate aim of Germany's first would-be colonisers. The central document in the 1870s revival of the liberal imperialist dream, Friedrich Fabri's *Does Germany Need Colonies?* (1879) specifically declares that Germany must "learn from the skilful colonialism of our Anglo-Saxon cousins and begin striving in peaceful competition to catch up with them.'[361]

Such competitions, however, rarely stay peaceful. The very first concrete foray of the German colonialists was the Samoa Bill. This asked the German Empire to nationalise the famous Hamburg firm of Godeffroy & Co., which had gone bankrupt in late 1879. According to the *Vossische Zeitung* of 11 December 1879, the reason a national response was demanded was because this good German firm had not gone bust naturally. The bankruptcy had, it was said, been caused by 'English machinations' in which Baring Brothers had been the financial 'tool'. This first public and formal demand for the imperial government to take German overseas interests under its stately wing was framed as a specific response to alleged Anglo-Saxon financial chicanery. The bill narrowly failed in the Reichstag, by 112 votes to 128, the resistance of the Catholic Centre being vital. But Bismarck himself actually supported it, so it should rank as his first testing of the colonial waters.

In 1880, an article so worried Sir Bartle Frere, the great high commissioner for South Africa, that he thought it worth sending to the Secretary of State for Foreign Affairs. Frere wanted London to know that the Germans had, for many years, been casting their eyes on South Africa:

GOVERNOR the RIGHT HON. SIR H. B. E. FRERE, BART., G.C.B., G.C.S.I., to the RIGHT HON. the EARL OF KIMBERLEY. (Received August 9, 1880.)

Government House, Cape Town,
MY LORD,   July 19, 1880.

I HAVE the honour to forward a translation of a remarkable article by Ernst von Weber, published in the Berlin "Geographische Nachrichten" for November last, which has attracted much attention among persons interested in South Africa.

It contains a clear and well argued statement in favour of the plan for a German Colony in South Africa, which was much discussed in German commercial and political circles even before the Franco-German War, and which was said to have been one of the immediate motives of the German mission of scientific inquiry which visited Southern and Eastern Africa in 1870–71.

In the long article, von Weber argued that 'Germany ought not to resign all this immense spoil to England' and that the Boers were natural allies of the Germans, being 'of the right Teutonic blood, for our Dutch neighbours, too, are really German'. The Boers were desperate to exchange the 'negrophilist English administration for a simple and just national government, and good sensible laws for protection against the barbarous black population'. All in all, 'this splendid country, taken possession of and cultivated by a German race, ought to have been entirely won for Germany'.

It was worrying enough a thought for Britain's greatest expert on Germany, Odo Russell, Lord Ampthill, 'Bismarck's favourite Englishman', to be consulted. He was quick to reassure his colleagues:

Herr Von Weber's plan will not meet with any support either at the hands of the German Government or on the part of the German parliament, while German emigrants feel more attracted by a republican form of Government than by that of a Crown Colony.

The German Government feel more the want of soldiers than of colonies, and consequently discourage emigration.

The German parliament has marked its disinclination to acquire distant dependencies however advantageous to German enterprise, by the rejection of the Samoa Bill.

Under present circumstances therefore the plan for a German Colony in South Africa has no prospect of success.

I have, &c.
The Earl Granville, K.G.,   (Signed)   ODO RUSSELL.
    &c.   &c.   &c.

The government gratefully took his word for it. And you can hardly blame Russell for getting it wrong, because it was certainly true that, up until now, the block on the German liberals' long-standing colonial ambitions had been none other than Bismarck himself.

But that was about to change.

First contact

On 8 September 1883, Lieutenant J. W. Sanders, proud commander of the highest-tech piece of hardware to be found on one of the most inhospitable and least-known coasts outside Australasia, the brand-new, iron-framed, oak-planked, copper-sheathed, screw-powered gunboat HMS *Starling*, arrived at Robert Harbour, Angra Pequena, in what is now Namibia, to see if the rumours were true.

Reports had spoken of a German trading station there, offshoot of a tobacco firm from Bremen, which had purchased land for guns and had given 'a considerable quantity of ammunition gratis' to the local Hottentots. Guns and ammunition were the jealously guarded guarantors of European supremacy. A British firm, which claimed it owned the land by lease from Cape Colony, had complained of gunshots disturbing the birds which nested on the nearby islands: these birds provided, in the course of nature, if undisturbed, valuable guano deposits which British traders exploited. 'Taking into consideration', wrote Lt Sanders, 'that the Germans are a shrewd and pushing race', it seemed that the rumours should be checked up on.

Guano diggers against tobacco merchants: such were the uninspiring minutiae of Royal Naval duty in the more distant parts of the empire. But this time there was a truly disturbing rumour: 'that the Germans had hauled down the British flag in Angra Pequena, and hoisted the German flag in its place'.

What made the report mystifying was that there should have been no British flag flying there in the first place, since the area was not officially British. On the other hand, this was southern Africa, where Britain had for decades exercised an unofficial and unchallenged local

·version of the Monroe Doctrine by proxy, via the Cape Colony. This was an age when merely to hoist the flag of a European power in Africa was to lay claim to that territory in its name. To actually *take down* the flag of another power, under whatever circumstances, was a serious business. This might now be more than a mere question of a legal dispute between a British guano merchant and German tobacco dealer.

When Sanders arrived, he indeed 'found the German flag flying over the company's store'. Worried, he went ashore and found that the manager, a Mr Vogelsang, was away with the wagons in the interior. An intelligent young man called Wagner informed him that the land for five miles in every direction had been purchased from the natives by the German firm of Adolf Lüderitz, a tobacco merchant and general trader from Bremen.*

Lt Sanders immediately saw the problem:

"I then pointed out to him the anomalous position that now existed (he had previously informed me that the harbour had been placed under German protection), namely, the coast line belonging to Germany and the islands in the bay, forming a great part of the harbour, belonging to England, as part of the Cape Colony, when he at once stated that the islands in the bay were included by the chief in the sale, and that they intended to claim them.

"I pointed out to him, in my 'sailing orders,' the paragraph which refers to 'the islands in the Bay belong to the Cape Colony,' but he seemed not at all inclined to forego what he appears to think is their just claim by purchase from the Chief.

"I told him that the Chief had only power to sell what belonged to him and as these islands were annexed by the 'Valorous' in 1867 or 1868, in the name of Her most Gracious Majesty, the Chief could not sell them in 1883.

The intelligent young Wagner was not at all willing to waive the point and informed Lt Sanders that a German man-of-war was due there in a week or ten days. Sanders then made contact with a local, landless Briton who had lived there for many years and was 'anything but an

* It turned out later that, in fact, the natives had signed away 'the country up to 20 geographical miles inland' and that the Germans intended to define 'mile' in this document not as the well-known British geographical mile (only slightly over a normal mile), but as the obscure yet undoubtedly existent German geographical mile (about 7.5km), about which the natives were, of course, completely ignorant. As with the case of Fiji land claims, the British authorities often complained of the Germans deliberately cheating the native populations.

intelligent man and who may be classed among the lower class of traders'. It appeared that it was on this unimpressive citizen's self-built 'store' that the British flag had been hoisted, without his knowledge, by a merchant captain: when he returned, the Germans told him to take it down, and when he refused, they did it for him.

Standing amid these little wooden shacks, pin-pricks on the vastness of the African coast, Lt Sanders must have felt dismay. The sacred British flag, banner of the greatest empire the world had ever known, the emblem for which men had died all over the planet, had, it seemed certain, been hoisted by someone – though 'on what grounds I cannot see' – but taken down by the Germans. And a German warship was apparently on its way. Sanders was several days' steaming away from any possible contact with his superiors, but as a good British officer, he knew what to do on his own initiative:

Under the circumstances, and in view of possible contingencies, I deemed it advisable to give an English Ensign to the Caretaker on Penguin Island, and gave him instructions to hoist it, should a German man-of-war arrive, that there might be no mistake as to the Island being British Possession.

The situation was serious. If the British government did not do something, someone else might: no sooner had Sanders's report arrived at the Foreign Office in London than a plaintive telegram followed, from the Officer Administering the Government of the Cape of Good Hope: 'Party English traders start tomorrow morning for Angra Pequena: it is said with the intention of expelling Germans recently established there. Please instruct me.'

For once, London reacted with reasonable speed. The Foreign Office wrote to the Colonial Office (they were not at all the same thing) and within three days telegraphic orders had been sent: 'Gunboat should proceed to prevent collision, and report.'

But what was going on? After all, it was only on 31 August that the Foreign Secretary had been reassured by a dispatch from the British Chargé d'Affaires in Berlin: despite the excitement in the German press at the thought of a German owning land in Africa, Bismarck had no intention of creating a crown colony, dependency or protectorate: 'the amount of protection afforded is to be precisely what would be granted to any other subject of the Empire who had settled abroad and acquired property'.

So was this merely a commercial trading post – or more than that? What was the line between a 'commercial dependency' and an official colony? Between 'protection of citizens' and a 'protectorate'?

The British themselves had been happily blurring this line in southern Africa for decades, but now someone else was on the scene and asking the question straight. On 17 November the German Ambassador called in person at the Foreign Office to enquire if the British claimed any rights of sovereignty there, and if so, on what basis. The British prevaricated, and on New Year's Eve 1883, the Ambassador demanded in writing to know if the British claimed the place, and if so, 'upon what title this claim is based and what institutions England there possesses which would secure such legal protection for German subjects in their commercial enterprises and justly won acquisitions as would relieve the [German] Empire of providing itself directly for its subjects'.

But what exactly did 'providing itself directly for its subjects' mean? It meant, in fact, the start of the German Colonial Empire, and it had caught the British completely off guard.

Bismarck's grand change of mind

The sudden German drive for colonies, and for colonies in direct competition with the British Empire, has been written endlessly about as a baffling and almost overnight change in Bismarck's policy. There is actually nothing at all mysterious about it.

Bismarck knew very well that colonies on the British model were a national-liberal obsession, but he also knew – he repeatedly said it – that going for colonies (as demanded in von Weber's 1880 article) would inevitably create diplomatic fallout which would hamper his European chess game. He famously dismissed one enthusiast for colonisation by pointing to the map of Europe on his office wall and declaring that *this* was his map of Africa. His conversion to colonialism thus stunned contemporaries.

However, if they had read Dr Virchow's explanation to *The Times*'s interviewer in 1878, people would have recalled that the only policy which now really guided Bismarck was the maintenance of Bismarck himself in power by any means possible. By late 1883, his very political survival was at stake.

His lifelong liberal opponents were preparing to unite at last into a single bloc, the German Free-Thinking Party, under names to conjure with: Virchow, Richter and Stauffenberg. They formally agreed the merger in January 1884. Now they outnumbered the National Liberals and Conservatives. Like all near-dictators, Bismarck feared such solid, genuinely liberal parliamentary opponents far more than he dreaded the loud but unrealistic clamour of socialist extremists. Wild reds, as he explained to his trusted circle in the Staatsministerium, might in fact be useful as bogeys to 'teach some of the opposition to moderate their views'.[362] But the hated liberals were unlikely to back down: not only were they now united, they knew that within the lifetime of the next parliament, they would probably have the ultimate, all-highest backing.

Kaiser Wilhelm I really couldn't live for ever (he was now eighty-seven). The Crown Prince Friedrich was so well known or, at any rate, so firmly believed, to be planning a more British-style regime that the newly combined liberals were popularly known as 'the Crown Prince's party'.*

Bismarck had written of his dread at the prospect of having *that* Englishwoman as the Prussian queen as far back as 1856; now, after almost thirty years of manoeuvring against the Anglophile liberals, he was faced with the prospect of soon having an empress who was so unapologetically British that after almost thirty years in Germany, she

---

* How liberal (in the accepted sense) the Crown Prince actually was is open to some doubt. In the Prussian Crown Council meeting of 1 August 1866, his was the voice loudest in favour of unconditionally annexing to Prussia several of the minor states which had supported Austria in the recent war, while his old-fashioned father was concerned about the rights of his fellow sovereigns. In August 1870, Bismarck had to deter him from threatening the south German states with force if they would not accept Prussian hegemony. But that Friedrich was a moderniser who liked Britain and detested Bismarck, there can be no doubt.

still insisted on remaining a member of, and publicly sponsoring, the Anglican Community in Berlin. If both Reichstag and throne were to be occupied by people who loathed him and looked openly to Britain as their model, even Bismarck would be hard-pressed to survive.

This all meant that, in 1884, diplomatic spats with Britain were positively desirable for Bismarck – and the obvious way to create them was for him to embrace, at last, the loud demands of Hamburg traders and national-liberal professors for German colonisation. It's vital to get this cause and effect right: Bismarck did not *engender* the idea of a colonial drive in competition with England, he merely decided to *use* it.

If he chose to sanction advances in the right areas of the world, avoiding trouble with France and Russia, Bismarck would be able to manufacture any number of small and far-off quarrels with the Englanders, which, with some judicious use of the reptile fund, would enable him to inflame national passions while falling well short of actual occasions for war. Come those vital Reichstag elections, this would help the notoriously Anglophobic National Liberals, who always voted with him, against the allegedly 'anglicised' free-thinking liberals, who were his sworn foes. It would also make an openly Anglophile policy impossible for the Crown Prince and his English wife.

Now, this may all sound improbably neat. But sometimes history is not as complicated as historians make out, for this is exactly how the calculation was described at the time both by Bismarck and by his son Herbert.

The younger Bismarck wrote to a friend that the whole point of suddenly going for colonies was 'the creation of artificial points of friction' with Britain, while his mighty father left the Tsar open-mouthed in admiration when he explained how his Machiavellian policy was designed precisely 'to drive a wedge between the Crown Prince and England': 'Voilà que est intelligent!' exclaimed the Russian monarch.[363] Most famously of all, Bismarck said to his closest colleague, in September 1884, that 'this whole colonial business is a lot of tosh, but we need it for the elections'.

What made this grand Bismarckian electoral plot feasible was that it was now *safe* to plague England. She would be sure to react, but

Bismarck gambled – carefully at first – on her unreadiness. For, as he well knew, the British Empire in 1884 was at overstretch already and in no position to make a stand.

Bismarck knew this better than anyone for the simple reason that he himself had been the grand and conscious agent of Britain's isolation.

Gladstone besieged

To isolate Britain was the central plank of Bismarck's foreign policy from the moment he was cheated of his world-historical anti-Russian alliance with Disraeli. After 1880, he re-set that policy with masterful speed, restoring the League of the Three Emperors on his eastern borders and making huge efforts to defuse the French will for *revanche* in the west.

The vast plan had, in fact, been outlined in Bismarck's famous Kissinger Diktat of 1877, and he simply went back to it once the hated Gladstone took over: France would be persuaded *force majeure* to forget about Alsace-Lorraine, but offered a free hand to seek compensation in the wider world, naturally bringing her into potential conflicts with Britain. The unbreakable Austro-German alliance would deflect Russian ambition away from the Balkans and towards India, with the same result.

Britain, in other words, was now to serve as the general Aunt Sally. The other powers would focus their expansionist urges (Russia) and desires to rebuild their status (France) against Britain, rather than against the new pairing of Germany and Austria.

It was a truly gigantic master plan: one German scholar has called it nothing less than 'the outlines of a political system which would have completely turned the constellation of the Powers on its head. It would have excluded Britain and, had it been fated to last, might have become a mortal danger to her.'[364]

Half the scheme motored along nicely by itself. Russia did indeed find Central Asia a far easier nut to crack than the Black Sea. In the early 1880s a heady series of victories took the Tsar's armies to within striking distance of British India. To the other half of the plan, the Rhine-ward side, Bismarck devoted all his energy. His diplomats went so far as to talk with the French of a genuine alliance, even a customs union, with Germany. To proud French navalists in particular, it was suggested that since Germany had no ambitions in a westerly direction, France, if only she could reconcile herself to the events of 1871, could concentrate on regaining the overseas position which the Royal Navy had wrested from her in the long eighteenth century.

Why French politicians fell for this has baffled historians ever since, but they did so, if only for a couple of years. The British were well aware of it, though in no doubt as to who had the toy sword and who the real power.

A FRIEND IN UNLIKELY QUARTERS.

OF this we're certain one and all, a mighty man is BIS-MARCK ; Great Chancellor, he's sure to make where-e'er he goeth *his* mark. He well-nigh snuffed out *La Belle France;* but now the little Frenchman Expects to find his former foe a loyal friend and henchman ;
And BISMARCK winks with roguish eye, and looking sapient—very—
Declares he'll ferry Monsieur FERRY across th' Egyptian ferry,
While bluff John Bull now sighs in vain for England's faded glories,
And says, " I'm one too many here—*O Tempora ! O Mores !*"

There could be no better way of proving Germany's bona fides to France in this scheme than by having Germany herself pick spots to colonise which were far away from French possessions – and right next door to, if not actually in, areas claimed by Britain.

The aim of making Britain the general bogey of Europe was openly acknowledged in some respectable German quarters. It was certainly plain in the Berlin political cartoons of the years 1880–85. The result was extraordinarily like some modern British patriots' nightmares.

> It is not so very long ago since the *Kreuz Zeitung* suggested that all the nations of the Continent should band themselves together, under the hegemony of Germany, to combat the growing predominance of Great Britain all over the world, and thus to confer on the unified of the Fatherland the crowning glory of also being the unified of Europe.

Gladstone presents a fairground attraction: 'John Bull, the Fat Child'.

Bismarck's plan to focus all Europe's energies on an anti-British drive is here perfectly illustrated: Germany (with her new colonies) rushes to join France and Russia in prodding the British Lion (pictured with Gladstone's head).

John Bull nets colony after colony as Europe wrangles.

Bismarck's timing was perfect, his game-play brilliant. When Count Münster knocked at the Foreign Office in November 1883 with his careful question as to whether or not Britain actually owned Angra Pequena and could 'protect' German businesses there, the Sudan was in meltdown and British rule in Egypt, along with the huge investments of British bondholders (one of whom was W. E. Gladstone), was itself at stake. The British Lion was looking more moth-eaten than ever.

The Germans become the British

With their eyes on Khartoum and Kabul, it's easy enough to imagine how highly the F.O. officials in London would have valued the arguments of a couple of 'the lower sort of traders' in a scarcely charted region of Africa. Their first reaction was to telegraph the Cape Colony, asking if *it* thought it owned Angra Pequena – or, if not, would it take over there?

Gladstone's government itself was far too busy trying to avoid doing anything about the Sudan to do anything about Angra Pequena. While it was desperately doing nothing, the German diplomats came in from another angle. In April 1884, they ingenuously informed the British that one Dr Nachtigall, who would be making himself known to the British authorities on the west African coast shortly, would be doing so in an official capacity, in order to ascertain 'the state of German commerce' there, and would also be empowered 'to conduct, on behalf of the Imperial Government, negotiations connected with certain questions'.

Bismarck later openly admitted that this information had been deliberately misleading, and that even his own diplomats were not fully informed, but the Foreign Office did not smell a rat, even when the Secretary of State for War forwarded the precis of an article from the *Cologne Gazette* (a paper well known to be 'inspired' by Bismarck) saying that the real object was to establish a German coaling station. The War Office official, a certain Lt Colonel Bell, also pointed out that the Germans had declared that Africa was 'a large pudding which the

English had prepared for themselves at other people's expense, and the crust of which was already fit for eating. Let us hope that our blue-jackets will put a few peppercorns into it on the Guinea Coast, so that our friends on the Thames may not digest it too rapidly.'[365]

The 'blue-jackets' meant the German Navy, and in retrospect the implication is clear, but still London did nothing. Then, on 11 July, Commander Moore, RN, reported that 'Mr Schmidt and the other Germans in the river had commenced holding night meetings of the natives, at which they told them that the German Government wish to annex the territory.' The hapless King Bell, having pleaded so often to be annexed by Britain, now said that unless his request was accepted 'within one week', he would sell out to the Germans instead.

At last the British Consul was ordered to race to the scene and annex it for Britain – but he came too late. At midnight on Saturday, 12 July 1884, King Bell and his fellow chiefs had signed their land over to the German Empire. However much the chiefs said they now regretted it, it was too late: since all European countries proceeded on the same basis with colonisation, there was no legal question that the Germans had won the race.

Bismarck did not take kindly to signs of a belated British resistance. In the Reichstag, he pointedly said that his 'confidence had been shaken, not perhaps, as far as regarded the British government, but by the attitude of the English Colonial Governments'. He added that 'If the question were asked what means the Empire had to afford effective protection to German enterprises in distant parts, the first considera-tion would be the influence of the Empire, and the wish and interests of other Powers to remain in friendly relations with it.' In other words, anyone who crossed Germany in Africa would have to reckon with German retaliation nearer to home.[366]

The general threat implicit in this was made quite concrete when Britain, belatedly realising what was going on, started to show signs of resistance. Count Münster and Herbert Bismarck both told the Foreign Secretary, Lord Granville, 'that the German Government could not maintain a friendly attitude on Egyptian matters if we continued to be unfriendly on Colonial questions'.[367]

On 26 June, Bismarck made another grand speech in the Reichstag which would not have been misunderstood. His policy was to 'leave the development of these Colonies to the energy of the merchants who had undertaken them ... to follow the example of England, and to grant these merchants something similar to the Royal Charters granted to the East India Company'.

This may sound, today, like a disavowal of any national strategic purpose, but to anyone schooled by Treitschke, the message in 1884 was plain: the golden age of British expansion, the era in which pre-decadent Britons had been worthy, freebooting conquistadors of half the world (even if they had only really managed it thanks to Prussia), was to be the guide. Germany was now to 'follow the example of England' in a trade-driven bid for colonies. This was, as Bismarck well knew, the great national-liberal dream coming true at last.

Sometimes the little details of history are the most telling, and in this case a tiny black-comic one says it all. The native chiefs of King William Town, Bimbia (who could all more or less speak English) complained to Commander Craigie, RN, that as far as they were concerned, despite having signed their town over to the Germans, 'they, as did their grandfathers, live under the Queen'. The recent treaty did not count, they said, because they had been cheated.

And how had they been cheated? They had told the Germans they were too late, and that their town belonged to the Queen of England. But the Germans had promised them – in English, of course – that 'Germans be all the same for English, they be one.'[368]

The very first German colonisers were not only consciously emulating the trade-driven modus operandi of the British Empire, and not merely choosing to claim land that everyone knew would be disputed by the British – they were actually pretending to *be* British.

Bismarck hits a seam

Gladstone, with splendidly bad timing, had just told readers of the *Fortnightly Review* that although Bismarck was unprincipled, having been 'deferential to this country exactly in proportion as he saw he could manipulate our simplicity and respect for international ethics to his own advantage', England did not have to worry, because 'Germany and Russia are natural enemies', and we had no 'close and critical contact' with German diplomacy. Predictably, the article had outraged Germany.

Gladstone tries to persuade France and Russia that Bismarck is the devil.

More to the point, the happy vision was starting to look somewhat premature.

For the anti-British colonial card was proving a trump. As the Reichstag elections neared, the British desperately prevaricated, Bismarck acted – and Germany applauded.

Meanwhile the colonial policy of Germany continues to engage the attention of the Chancellor, and meets apparently with the approval of the whole German nation. The addresses of Opposition candidates have contained strictures on almost every item of PRINCE BISMARCK'S policy except those touching on foreign affairs and on colonial establishments. Even the Socialists have in a reluctant fashion been obliged to admit that it might be for the interests of Germany to have colonies.[369]

The Reichstag elections indeed delivered all that Bismarck can have hoped: there were drastic losses for the opposition liberals, holds for the National Liberals, substantial gains for the Conservatives. Once the results were in, *The Times* analysed them. It found that the voters loved Bismarck's foreign policy: his alliance with Austria, his maintenance of peace with Russia, his causing of the French to 'forswear, or profess to forswear, their vow of revenge'. But, above all, the Germans were delighted at the specifically anti-English drive of Bismarck's policy. They liked colonies per se, but they liked them even more when they were taken in the face of England:

> They are exultant at the fact that their great Chancellor, yielding at last to the importunity of Chauvinistic dreamers, has now elevated Germany to the rank of a colonial Power and paved the way to a new Fatherland beyond the sea; and, above all, it rejoices them in their secret hearts to think that their undaunted statesman has shown distinct signs of an ambition to mould the will of haughty England.[370]

Bismarck had hit a seam deeper than even he had expected. The 'settled dislike' of Britain which British writers of the late 1870s had felt was clearly a solid, electoral fact.

The right way to deal with John Bull on colonial questions.

'England is afraid that Germany might one day discover Heligoland too.'

John Bull is fat enough already – but Germany is not.

John Bull watches the first German colonists and curses: 'Goddam, what about all my flags? Where should I hoist them now?'

The sense of Anglophobic gloating which *The Times* had detected as a factor in the elections was not imagined, as this widely syndicated translation from the *Cologne Gazette*, one of Bismarck's most favoured organs, made clear to Britons:

> In Cameroon, as well as in the Togo region, the English employ the same tactics to stir up the natives against the merchants, and the whole of the population against the Germans. But if John Bull thinks he can thwart our colonial policy in this manner he had better be told that he is giving himself bootless pains. Germany is resolved to keep a hold of what she has got, and she knows the vulnerable points in the colonial empire of England well enough to pay the Britons back in their own coin.[371]

Meanwhile, of course, Treitschke, Germany's most respected public intellectual, rejoiced openly at every setback to the hated 'Bifs':

> I can still hear his voice in the professor's room in Berlin, when, on hearing of the fall of Khartoum and Gordon's death, he gave vent to his feelings in loud jubilation. "Just what ought to have happened!" he exclaimed. "Every one of them ought to meet with the same fate!"[372]

But now feelings in Britain were beginning to run high too. The British press raged at the 'insult to the British flag' and briefly exulted when a Polish adventurer, Rogoziński, who hated the Germans, 'saved the Cameroon mountains for England'.[373] It was all to no avail: the 'supineness of the home government' seemed to know no limits.

THE GERMAN ANNEXATIONS.

SEIZURE IN THE CAMEROONS.

INSULT TO THE BRITISH FLAG.

THE WEST COAST OF AFRICA.

EXTRAORDINARY CONDUCT OF THE GERMANS.

The *Pall Mall Gazette* spoke baldly of the German annexations as 'an act of war',[374] but is *The Times*'s account of the whole business which is most remarkable. Yet again, here is that spectre of a Germany almost unearthly in its planning and cunning: [375]

> A survey of the negotiations reveals strategy as deliberate and prophetic as that by which COUNT MOLTKE gained the most complete of his victories in arms. PRINCE BISMARCK understood from the first what he wanted, and the means by which he was to attain it. He was aware of the inherent weaknesses of his antagonists. Probably he anticipated at some point or other the occurrence of a blunder which would give him a short cut to his destination. Good luck contributed to the absoluteness of his triumph, inasmuch as errors in his opponents, on which, in their actual shape and degree, he could hardly have calculated, conducted them into a diplomatic Sedan.

If even *The Times* chose to speak now in terms of 'Moltke' and 'Sedan', there can have been little doubt in Britons' minds as to the real magnitude of the defeat they had just suffered. And, in fact, much the same language was being used in Bismarck's own official press:

> Die Nation, das Gemüth der Nation — so behaupten wir — hat volles Verständniß für diese Aufgabe. Es verfolgt die Fortschritte unserer Colonialpolitik mit steigendem Interesse, es beobachtet mit Spannung die verschiedenen Phasen des diplomatischen Feldzuges, welcher in Folge dessen zwischen Deutschland und England entstanden ist, und sieht mit Genugthuung, wie alle die von England aufgeworfenen Hindernisse aus dem Wege geräumt werden.

The Nation – the spirit of the nation – so we maintain – perfectly comprehends this mission. It follows the progress of our colonial policy with growing interest, it tensely observes the phases of the diplomatic campaign [the word used, '*Feldzug*', is a military term] which has, in consequence, arisen between Germany and England, and it notes with satisfaction the way in which all the hindrances which England has thrown up have been swept out of the way.[376]

However, Britain was about to have its spine stiffened – whether it wanted it or not.

Enter the colonies

The colonies now became the theatre where Britons and Germans re-enacted and magnified that sense that they were not simply ordinary rival powers; that despite superficial resemblances so strong that the colonists of Germany might successfully pretend to be British in order to fool the natives, they actually represented fundamentally different cultures.

Almost as soon as the Germans were established, violence began. By the end of 1884, they were already using naval shell-fire and marines, without warning or declaration, against the recalcitrant villagers of the Cameroons, who, in revenge, beheaded a German firm's agent and paraded his head on a pole. Nothing like this had ever been seen here under the informal British rule – though of course plenty of it had been seen in Zululand and the Transvaal.

Germans, both diplomats and the press, blamed Britain for setting the natives against them. Bismarck himself spoke at length of this in the Reichstag on 10 January 1885, even naming the British officials and merchants who were allegedly to blame. Within weeks of the start of the German Colonial Empire, a cycle had begun which was to be repeated again and again over the following twenty years and which would become almost a pathological reaction among German colonialists.* The Germans deliberately went into areas where British influence and the English language had been paramount for decades, if need be pretending that the British and the Germans were one and the same thing. The natives simply did not want the Germans there, and openly preferred the British. To the Germans, as a British consul put it in 1884, 'the undeniable and increasing preference' of the natives was 'a source of great personal annoyance'.[377] Having no idea of flexible response to perceived acts of rebellion – this was, after all, the same state which had semi-criminalised its domestic socialists and Catholics – the Germans always took route one to military force. Since they were unable to conceive that their own methods were failing, they blamed it all on the British for, as Bismarck himself put it, 'exciting the natives against us'.

This built into the strange conviction among German colonialists that the *real* 'otherness' in the colonies, the true polar opposite of German values, was not actually the natives, with whom the Germans, in their own mythology, had a deep and natural empathy, but the British. As the agents of worldwide Manchesterism, the British were somehow equipped with limitless powers of manipulating primitive cultures and thus opposing the progress which German thoroughness offered to one and all. The British were equally convinced that there was a vast conceptual difference between them and the Germans – that the Germans were simply not cut out for the delicate business of colonisation: 'The English are popular, whereas the Germans frighten the Africans, displease the Europeans and terrorize the Arabs.'[378]

Whatever equivocations we may now make, German methods were at the time quite distinctive enough to make even the Americans, who had no interests in Africa, many old reasons to be suspicious of the British Empire and no *a priori* grounds whatever to dislike the Germans, sit up and stare:[379]

---

* See the illustrations from 1905–7 on pp. 376–7.

HOW GERMANY SEIZES COLONIES.
HER DESPOTIC CONDUCT IN TAKING POSSES-
SION OF THE CAMEROONS.

This turned out to be lucky for some. For now the Germans pushed further, clearly convinced that the pusillanimity of liberal England was limitless. But when they moved on New Guinea (they did so while the British were under the impression that it had been agreed to discuss things there), the limit of British – or rather, Australasian – patience was reached.

It's one of the great founding myths of modern Australia that she entered the Great War out of a blind and foolish loyalty to the unde-serving mother country. The truth is that the Australians and the New Zealanders joined in so keenly in 1914 – they didn't even wait to be asked – because they had a thirty-year-old itch to kick the Germans out of what they saw as their own private backyard. As indeed they swiftly did, when at last given the green light by Britain.

In 1883–5 Britain was desperately trying to *hold back* Australia and New Zealand from an aggressive and specifically anti-German policy of pre-emptive annexations. The Antipodeans were raring to have a crack at the Germans then and there, and were outraged at the inaction of the mother country.

GOVERNMENT OF VICTORIA to AGENT-GENERAL, December 20, 1884.

(Telegraphic Despatch.)

" AT last the end has come. Information received reliable source that Germany has hoisted flag on New Britain, New Ireland, and north coast New Guinea. The ex-asperation here is boundless. We protest in the name of the present and the future of Australia if England does not yet save us from the danger and disgrace, as far at least as New Guinea is concerned, the bitterness of feeling towards her will not die out with this generation. We now appeal in terms Lord Derby's Despatch, 11th January 1883, second paragraph."

GOVERNMENT OF VICTORIA to AGENT-GENERAL, December 21, 1884.

Telegraphic Despatch.

" WE have reason to expect that Samoa and Tonga will follow next."

The Samoans, who earnestly wanted to be annexed by either Britain or New Zealand, rather than Germany, were now saying that if the British Empire would not let them in, they would unilaterally enter it anyway, by doing 'what they have threatened to do before, viz. hoist the British flag and proclaim themselves British'.[380] The shade of the hapless King Bell flits once more into view:

To their Excellencies the GOVERNOR and CHIEF ASSISTANT RULERS of NEW ZEALAND.

YOUR EXCELLENCIES,   Mulinuu, Samoa, November 5, 1884.

WE are the King and rulers of Samoa. We write to you to make known our prayer and entreaty to Her Highness the Queen of England in order that there may be set up the sovereignty of the Government of Her Majesty the Queen of England in our islands, and that it should be entirely at the disposal of Her Majesty's Government as to whether they should be formed into an English colony or be connected with your Government in New Zealand.

Our King wrote nearly a year ago giving over the sovereignty of these islands to Her Majesty the Queen and the Government of England. We have also been very anxious for an answer, but no answer has yet reached us.

We, therefore, send this entreaty to you in order that you may forward it to Her Majesty and the Government of England.

We earnestly entreat you to assist us by praying Her Majesty the Queen of England to accept our request.

We earnestly beg that you will listen to our prayer, and will render us all possible assistance, for our fear is great on account of the information we have received that our islands are about to be seized by Germany.

We love much and respect the Government of England, because we know the Government of England acts justly and protects well the people who are under its rule. We do not want any other government to take possession of our government.

We earnestly entreat and beg your Excellencies to make known our prayer to the Queen and the Government of England by means of a telegram.

We rely on Her Majesty the Queen of England to devise some means to prevent Germany from taking possession of our islands, which is not according to our desire.

We trust that your Excellencies, by your aid and by your entreaty to Her Majesty the Queen, will bring to pass the setting up of Her sovereignty in Samoa.

May your Excellencies live.

It was not just terrified local kings and colonial diplomats who were begging or demanding anti-German action from London. The citizens of Melbourne voted, on 7 January 1885, that if Samoa was lost, it would 'endanger public faith in the wisdom, firmness and patriotism of the Home Government', and the next day the more rural folk of Warrnambool declared the need to 'combine the whole of the English-speaking race under the British Government into one grand concentrated mighty nation. Australian outrage was made plain to the British public in letters which *The Times* printed over Christmas 1884.

GERMAN ANNEXATIONS IN THE PACIFIC.

TO THE EDITOR OF THE TIMES.

Sir,—Your correspondents, Messrs. Baden Powell, Thomas Russell, and " An Australian Pioneer," evidently do not look at the above question from a Queenslander's point of view. If their lot were cast in a colony within easy striking distance of " a strong man armed," and if they had to pay a part of the heavy outlay that will necessarily be incurred in preparing to give the " strong man " a suitable reception should he come that way, they might not look with such philosophy on the subject. It should be borne in mind that the mother country may not always be in a position to assist her distant offspring in time of need, and they must, therefore, be ready to resist the sudden onset of so formidable a neighbour as a German colony would certainly become in a few years.

The government in London was now petrified lest some unofficial action in the colonies should spark a shooting war with Germany. Bismarck had made it perfectly plain, with reasonable logic but a complete misunderstanding of the way the British Empire actually ran itself, that he simply did not believe the colonies could act without at least tacit sanction from London. The Acting Colonial Secretary for New South Wales put the unpalatable facts on the table to a banquet in Maitland on 18 January 1885. If the colonies did not take care, they might enrage 'that personification of absolutism in European statesmanship, the Prince Von Bismarck' and cause a breach with

a nation that, on the weightiest grounds of national policy, it would be a perilous thing for any European Power to provoke: a nation of which it is said, without drawing on its last reserves, it can place in the field at any time two millions and a half of men in the most perfect state of military discipline ... this colossal power which, if it did

not regard us with a mingling of amusement and contempt, would
hold the Mother Country responsible for our silly impudence.

The truth was that the British were in a blue funk. Half their army was
in the Sudan, belatedly trying to save Gordon from the Mahdi (assuming that they could save themselves en route); the other half was
preparing to defend Herat against the Russians. The colonies were up
in arms, the Germans in Samoa were 'talking in a very loud and
decided manner' and the chances of an accidental clash, of someone,
somewhere, as Bismarck himself put it in the Reichstag, 'attacking and
firing on us in a most reckless manner' were looking frighteningly
high.

Having been so carefully isolated by Bismarck, Britain was now desperate to appease him. And yet, harried by the bellicose colonies,
London showed enough spine in December 1884 to authorise a regular little race and scramble that was successful enough to secure at least
part of New Guinea – and to seriously annoy Bismarck.

Bismarck reads the riot act

In the Reichstag, on 10 January 1885, the Catholic Centre leader
openly feared war with Britain, but Bismarck was pointedly confident
that 'the British government will disapprove and condemn' the attitude
of the colonies. His great speech of that day is one of the most fascinating he ever made. Here, the grand themes and images of the whole
story came together plainly.

Bismarck said that the British were naturally surprised to see 'their
land-rats of cousins' taking to the sea, but that the 'highest and leading circles in England' did not share this popular view.
Unfortunately, the British leaders were having 'a degree of trouble
moderating the outrage of their subjects in good time'. Despite this,
he said, Germany and England still had good relations – and 'both
countries would be well advised to maintain these friendly relations'.

For if the British government were to come to share such views of Germany's colonial policy, it 'would be impossible to support British policies without incurring the disapproval of the German people. In which case we might find ourselves compelled to support those who are, without wishing it, antagonistic to England.'

In other words, popular opinion on both sides was by now very edgy and needed careful management by the leaders of Britain and Germany: responsible statesmen in Britain would do well to disavow their own colonials in favour of German claims, or face the consequences. Already, the clamourings of the new mass voterships on both sides were becoming hard to control.

Two weeks afterwards, on 24 January 1885, the British Ambassador in Berlin was summoned to Bismarck. It must have been one of the most uncomfortable interviews of Sir Edward Malet's career for, in the context of studious Victorian diplomatic *politesse*, he was read the riot act.

The Chancellor refused to accept that he had done anything underhand – though, of course, he knew very well that he had, for he later boasted of it – and blamed Britain for not accepting that if she wanted Germany's friendship, she must help with German colonisation, even if this meant ignoring her own colonists' wishes. He complained of 'the successive annoyances to which Germany had been exposed' and read Sir Edward a long dispatch in German. This was a psychological ploy he had used against the French in 1871, to stress who was in the driving seat of negotiations. The gist was that he had now successfully obtained a French alliance and that the British had missed their chance to do a good deal with Germany. He then raised the question of British rule in Zululand itself, clearly suggesting that he might support the Boers and cutting short Sir Edward's historical point about Britain's rights there with the curt statement that 'it was not a question which a lawsuit would settle'.

Sir Edward must have wondered exactly what this meant. If international disputes were not to be settled by lawyers, what *was* going to settle them? It seems that he could see nothing more to lose, for he now laid his own cards on the table, asking to know what Bismarck's full demands actually were, never mind the consequences: 'whatever they might be, was better than that we should go mutually acting in the dark, and consequently running against each other'. Did Bismarck, for example, actually want Zululand for Germany?

At this point, Bismarck, who was far too clever to make the same mistake into which he had led Napoleon III and actually name his price, abruptly ended the conversation by repeating that he now had a French alliance and regretting the 'phase of the political relations between the two countries'.

This was all extremely close to the edge of what the Victorians called a diplomatic 'breach'. And the brink was being reached not just in the secret halls of diplomacy. In the same week that Sir Edward was being roasted in private by Bismarck, the *New York Times* of 18 January 1885 explained how ordinary Britons – and the whole British press – felt about things:

> The average Englishman firmly believes that a grand conspiracy is on foot to humiliate and despoil Great Britain. This Englishman believes it has been invented and that it is sustained by Prince Bismarck. The hatred here against him and his has probably had no parallel since the days of the Czar Nicholas. There is also seen contemptuous wrath for France, who allows herself to become the cheap cat's paw of the Chancellor, and an ugly dislike for Russia, who is fortifying Batoum in defiance of treaty promises, and insultingly bestriding the Afghan frontier. But neither the feeling against France nor that against Russia compares in intensity with the bitter wrath expressed against Germany. Much of this has really been of long standing, having grown in fervor each time a Duke of Teck, or Prince Christian, or Prince of Leiningen, or Prince of Battenberg is turned loose inside the Treasury to fatten on English earnings. Much more has been due to the great influx of German waiters, barbers, tailors, and

other craftsmen during the past 10 years, who work longer hours and for less pay than the English of the same classes, who accuse them of an undue share in creating the present depression. It is a common experience to hear it said that all these immigrants are really German soldiers who have come over to look at England as countrymen of theirs looked at France just before the Franco-German war. It would not be difficult, if a sudden crisis came, to provoke a serious anti-Teuton riot. Even the most temperate papers insensibly reflect this feeling in the hostile tone of their leaders. Bismarck's great speech, in which he so obviously went out of his way to declare his love for England, is read between the lines as a most ominous menace by the entire press.

The *NYT* did not get the mood in Britain wrong:

FUN.—January 21, 1885.

BISMARCK'S "HAPPY FAMILY."

"THE BRITISH LION WILL NOW, BY KEYIND PERMISSION, RULE THE WAVES WITH THE PRUSSIAN BEAGLE A-SITTING ON HIS TAIL, EMBLEMATIC OF PEACE AND 'APPINESS."

But, by one of those superb coincidences of history, something now happened on the far side of the world which was to change the whole game – and make the German Chancellor think twice about pushing any further.

Enter the cavalry

On the very day Bismarck, confident that he held all the good cards, was dressing down Sir Edward Malet in Berlin, a short, locally printed proclamation was affixed to the doorway of the municipal court house in Apia, Samoa, modest power-base of the beleaguered King Malietoa, whose urgent requests to become British rather than be taken over by Germany had so far fallen on such deaf ears.

We should take a moment to envisage this innocuous-looking little document, and the obscure Pacific island court-house door, belonging to a still-independent native king, to which it was affixed: a small message knocked up in a hurry by two men representing, part-time, two different governments, each many thousands of miles away and many thousands of miles apart, with which neither had any means of swift communication and which had within recent memory been at bitter loggerheads. The note deserves framing with massy oak in the Library of Congress and the Houses of Parliament, for it is the very first concrete marker of a factor which would decide the fate of the world in the following century:

PROCLAMATION posted upon the MUNICIPAL COURT HOUSE, APIA.

Apia, January 24, 1885.

IT having been made public that the German Consul has assumed the right of rule in the municipality in contravention of the Convention of 1879 and renewed by the three Powers,

We, the Consuls of the United States and Great Britain, do hereby make known that they will insist upon the rights of the Convention being observed, and deprecate force consummating the assumption.

(Signed)   T. CANISIUS,
United States Consul.
W. B. CHURCHWARD,
Acting British Consul.

The cavalry had arrived. Notice had been given that, in the Pacific, Britons, New Zealanders and Australians were not the only 'Anglo-Saxons' to be reckoned with.

Over the next fifteen years, it was to be German expansion in the Pacific, more than anything else, which unwittingly contrived to patch up the old wounds between the British Empire and its mighty former colony. By 1898, it was (as we shall discover) plain for anyone with eyes to see that the one certain way to make Britain and America forget their differences was for the Germans to steam into view.

It's strange that more German nationalists did not see the way the wind was blowing, since their whole 'world view' was based on the idea that the most important common factor between people was a shared language. Bismarck, though, was a man of hair-raising insight, and recognised the danger. It was, after all, he who famously declared towards the end of his life that the simple but essential bond between the USA and Britain – the fact that they both spoke English – would be the decisive factor in the coming century.

Quickly, he stopped the advance on Samoa, realising that his best hope was now to negotiate bilaterally with the haggard British rather than allow events to draw in this new and hungry power. He was genuinely furious when, in a graphic demonstration that even he could not fully control the national drive for colonies, the Germans on the ground went too far. He ordered a hasty retreat – not because of Britain, but out of fear of unilateral action by the United States.[381]

Samoa was let be, at least for now: it was time for a good gambler to cash in his chips and take his profit.

Bismarck revenged

And what profit it was.

An overseas empire had been founded in the teeth of British opposition, to the evident delight of German voters from across all parties; the Reichstag election had been thoroughly won, the liberals dished;

and the Crown Prince would now never dare openly say anything which could be construed as pro-English.

To set the seal on Bismarck's triumph, the hated Gladstone publicly threw in the towel. Only his superhuman ability to reinterpret every tactical squirm as a strategic and moral choice could ever have enabled Gladstone to rise in the House and give his famous 'God speed her' speech about German colonisation. The Grand Old Man of British liberalism (who was by now widely known in Britain not as the G.O.M. but as the M.O.G. – the Murderer of Gordon) had been beaten hollow and was soon out of power.

Bismarck was amply revenged for 1880. British diplomacy was a laughing stock and Germany was the unchallenged arbiter of a Europe which seemed ready to accept her leadership. The *Provincial Correspondence* gloated over the success of the 'diplomatic campaign waged by Prince Bismarck against England'. It also voiced yet again the conviction which would prove fatal to Anglo-German relations in the coming years: that England had only abandoned her position of 'envy and jealousy', had only stopped her consular officials deliberately inciting native rebellions in the Cameroons, and had only come to terms because Bismarck had fought Germany's corner so hard.[382]

The disastrous myth was by now fully established: the way to deal with the cynical but cowardly Englanders was not with the carrot, but the stick.

Then, suddenly, the bets were off and a brand new game was afoot.

Bismarck backtracks

The change in Anglo-German relations which now took place was remarkable. From the nadir of January 1885, when a breach seemed a genuine possibility, things grew so much warmer that within a couple of years Bismarck was – just as in 1879 – seriously hoping to win Britain formally over to the Austro-German alliance.

The reason was classically simple: in the second half of 1885, the diplomatic balance of power swung suddenly, radically and permanently away from Germany. Never again would Bismarck himself, or the Second German Empire under anyone, bestride Europe as in late 1884.

By the summer of 1885, it was becoming clear that all the energy Bismarck had spent in trying to persuade France to become a sea-going empire inevitably ranged against Britain, rather than a European land power with its eye inescapably on Alsace and Lorraine, had been wasted. The Sino-French War was not quite a disaster for France, but it came very close: the politicians who had spent French gold and blood in the failed drive for distant *gloire* rather than local *revanche* were discredited and driven from office, while General Boulanger himself came back a military hero – and promptly made it abundantly clear who he thought was France's *real* enemy. What truly spooked Germany, though, was, as ever, Russia.

In the autumn of 1885, the Three Emperors' League was blown apart once again as Bulgaria went into crisis. Russian ambitions to make Bulgaria a puppet state ran head-on into Austria-Hungary's existential need to control the Balkan Slavs. Bismarck needed urgently to rethink his foreign policy.

It's simple to compare the tone of German diplomacy in January 1886 with the glowering reproaches and implicit threats which Sir Edward Malet had endured in Bismarck's office exactly a year earlier. Then, the ambassador of a liberal Britain stretched to breaking point by the Mahdi and the Russians had been forced to stand and listen to Bismarck's tirade of accusations. Now everything was reversed: Tory Britain was blithely annexing Burma, while Bismarck was sending his underlings to apologise hastily and officially to London, when his own inadequately supervised colonial agents went too far:

> Count Hatzfeldt, German Ambassador, called upon Lord Salisbury at the Foreign Office yesterday afternoon. The visit was paid in accordance with the express instructions of Prince Bismarck, and for the purpose of informing the British Government that the action of the Commander of the *Albatross* at Samoa was taken without the previous knowledge or sanction of the Imperial German Government.[383]

Much seemed to be in favour of co-operation. The Tories were back in power, under the very man, Lord Salisbury, who had been so openly keen on the Dual Alliance in 1879. Bismarck no longer needed to tweak the tail of the British Lion for domestic consumption because his liberal enemies, seriously hurt by the colonial elections of 1884, were well and truly routed in 1887: for the first time since 1866, Bismarck simply did not have to worry a jot about what they thought.

So, for once, there was no tactical benefit to be gained by policies designed to split them by pandering to their naval and colonial ambitions. Bismarck's new allies, the good old, bad old German conservatives, wanted a big army run by their own sort, not a big navy run by unreliable liberals like Admiral Stosch, who had been thick with the Crown Prince until Bismarck engineered his downfall in 1883. Military budgets apart, the conservatives were concerned with persuading parliament to subsidise and protect their rural estates, which were, they claimed, the true, profound heart of Prussia. They cared not a jot for the colonies so longed for by National Liberal professors and those notoriously anti-Prussian, famously anglicised, non-von Hamburg traders.*

With battleships and colonies no longer needed as an electoral card, Bismarck could return to his real Great Game: to deflect Russia away from Austria-Hungary while somehow maintaining friendly relations with the Tsars. As ever, the only practical way to achieve this was for Bismarck to get Britain into bed with Austria-Hungary, so that Germany could stay on the sidelines.

But the age of 'cabinet politics' had gone forever. Salisbury knew – he had learned the hard way in 1880 – that whatever he agreed to had to stick at the next polls. It was not so bad for Bismarck, since only the Emperor could sack him, but a bad election result could make life very difficult even for him. The British and German *people*, in other words, had to want, or at least accept, an Anglo-German alliance. And the trouble was that, by now, the prejudices of each side were already becoming all too solid.

---

* The most splendid clothes shop in Hamburg, Ladage & Oelke, founded in 1845, still proclaims that it purveys English 'country life' style. Yet emulation always suggested the wish to compete and even overtake: the *Vossische Zeitung* of 25 October 1899, right at the star of the Boer War, condemns 'the Anglophobia in which the Hamburg meeting waded'.

Bismarck had for many years used the lurking Anglophobia of his countrymen to good electoral effect, and especially so in 1884, but it was no invention of his, and he certainly could not turn it off at will. Even when Britain was no longer being deliberately cast as the Great Satan, she remained the object of widespread popular dislike. One British guide book of 1888 was so very positive about German state-run efficiency that Bismarck's own official paper, the *Neueste Mittheilungen* (successor to the *Provincial Correspondence*), twice gloatingly cited it against German Anglophiles. But even this very pro-German author, whose avowed aim was 'to depict the best attributes of a foreign nation', has to confess to his British readers that 'of late there has grown a distinctive political dislike for us. It began with our attitude towards Germany before the '64 Danish war; it has increased since, through a variety of causes.' Your boastful German 'talks of his countrymen ousting the English from South Africa'; he will 'meet his companions in the beer-house, and will enlarge on the enormous strides German commerce has made of late, being able to laugh at English competition & c'.[384]

In Britain, an opposing myth was beginning to take firm shape: that Germany was not only growing stronger, but was doing so in ways that made her more and more different from Britain. This was clear when, for the first time, that dreaded mark appeared: 'Made in Germany'.

Made in Germany: cheap, nasty – and state-backed

The Merchandise Marks Act of 1887 was not aimed at protecting British industry from more efficient German competition, simply because, in 1887, no one in Britain was yet ready to accept that German industry might actually *be* more efficient. Like all people everywhere, Britons found it easier to deny the plain evidence of their senses than to throw off long-held opinions.

Britain remained wedded, in an almost religious way, to the notion of free trade. The same convictions which had forbidden British governments to intervene decisively in the Irish Famine, or to prevent the export of arms to France in 1870, still declared that the British state could not lobby foreign governments on behalf of British firms, since this would logically involve it in *choosing between* British firms, thus interfering unforgivably in the holy market. Most British economists still believed that it was just not really possible to be prosperous and efficient without embracing free trade. That by no means anti-German guide book from 1888 was still able blithely to assert that 'we in England make the best articles', while Germany was 'the home of the cheap and nasty'.[385]

However, it was becoming apparent that the shoppers of Britain, the Victorian world's consumers of last (and indeed first) resort, were starting to buy German in serious amounts. Since no one would rationally prefer cheap and nasty German products to quality British-made goods, the conclusion was obvious: the Germans must be deforming the market by cheating the British consumer.

This was the point of the 1887 act: to enable Britain's shoppers to distinguish for themselves between British items and inferior foreign ones. Protection was bad, but information for the consumer was good. After all, 'It is not that the Germans are alone in producing rubbish – every commercial nation does the same; but the Germans have a special faculty for copying the rubbish of other nations, beside producing their own.'[386] Now that British consumers *knew* that a product was from the 'home of the cheap and nasty', they would obviously not choose it.

The Germans were largely untroubled by the act. For they knew the fact: that 'Made in Germany' was already a recommendation, not an accusation:

Inasmuch as the English law demands that German wares be marked Made in Germany, it will scarcely attain its aim of harming German exports; for our products have gradually found the highest regard in the world and it can only increase their success if the simple label "foreignness" be shaken off so that they are immediately recognisable as German.[387]

Now, what exactly made it possible for Germany to overtake Britain has always been, and still is, the object of passionate debate. But what economists or sociologists today think is neither here nor there for us now. The point is what Britons at the time thought gave Germany an unfair edge, and what they thought was very clear and simple: the Germans were cheating.

One way of cheating the market was by fraudulent marking. Another was by having impossibly low wages:

> The industrial and commercial progress Germany has made in the past 15 or 20 years is attributed here to so many causes, and so frequently to any but the true ones, that it is desirable people should clearly understand how largely the low rates of wages prevailing in every part of the Empire have contributed to the development of the export trade of the Fatherland.[388]

The 1880s were a time of industrialisation without mechanisation: steam-power could haul or lift vast loads in straight lines, but every rivet in a mighty ship was still hammered into place by hand, every seam of coal still worked by hand-pick and sheer muscle-power, every legal or commercial document still written out in gorgeous copperplate by countless ink-stained fingers. Wage costs were thus a hugely more significant factor in every business than they are today. The maverick Edwardian economist Thorstein Veblen (father of the theory of 'conspicuous consumption') certainly thought that low wages had been a decisive factor in Germany's success, and might almost have been lecturing a modern audience on the advantages possessed today by China when he wrote of

> the disposable labor supply, which was of abundant quality and good quality, both physically and intellectually, and which had moreover the merit of a ready pliability under authority and was well trained to an impecuniously frugal standard of living.[389]

Another American writer also sounded very like someone trying to explain why China can wipe the floor with Western producers today:

It is probable that no civilised workman in the world would change places with the German. Few indeed work longer hours for smaller pay, eat coarser and cheaper food, live in more crowded homes, and none gives more time and substance to the government which in return hems him in with an infinite multiplicity of rules and regulations, and curtails right of free speech, none has less control over that which is his own, for even the spending of part of his meagre wages is ordered by law, and few there are who possess less influence in making the laws which regulate their conduct ... a carpenter in the ship yards will receive about 90 cents per day for 11 hours' work. In America, a carpenter commonly expects $2.50 to $3 for 8 hours' work ... the staples of food actually cost more in Germany than they do in America though wages generally will average hardly more than one third as much.

What made it possible for Germans to live on so little? The answer was plain: it was that utterly alien, military culture they lived in. Three years of brutal, Prussian, parade-ground discipline 'trained the German to obedience, methods of order, hard work, plain living, and frugality'. But it seemed impossible that the German worker would put up with this forever: 'If he does begin to consider his condition, he does one of two things – he either becomes a socialist or he commits suicide.'[390]

'Anglo-Saxon' observers of Germany, like some China-watchers today, thus took a sort of dubious comfort from the idea that this rival form of social organisation could not last for very long without generating uncontrollable social unrest.

Until that time, though, this mighty commercial rival was cheating in one final, and perhaps decisive, way: by direct state help for business.

The House of Commons was informed that while the British Foreign Office rejected with fastidious horror the idea that its consuls should become mere 'commercial touters', the Germans 'gave all the assistance in the power of the State to assist the progress of her commerce'. This 'mode of working the interests of German manufacturers had now become a regular system', and in China and Japan, 'the building of the iron-clads had gone to Germany, procured beyond a shadow of doubt, for Germany by the Berlin Foreign Office'.[391]

By 1887, then, the German nationalist story of having been duped by Britain into winning an empire for her had a British counterpart: that the Germans were somehow not competing on a level playing field, but were cheating their way into Britain's markets by short-term and underhand means which could not last and merely distorted, by political agencies direct or indirect, that naturally perfect mechanism, free trade.

Just how deep-set the antagonism already was became crystal clear in 1887–8, when all great questions of colonies, trade and diplomacy took a back seat to the question of one man's throat and who should treat it.

The Crown Prince's throat

By early 1887, Friedrich, Crown Prince of Prussia, was at last about to ascend the imperial German throne. His father was now ninety, and failing visibly. For seventeen years, the Iron Chancellor had made sure that Friedrich, together with his unapologetically English wife, daughter of Queen Victoria and Prince Albert, was kept out of political affairs and relegated to the unimportant role of running art and culture. But even Bismarck could not hold back the grim reaper forever.

The grim reaper, however, was not aiming only at the ancient William I. In early January, a persistent huskiness developed in the voice of the prince who had been denied for so long a real voice in Germany. In March the leading German doctors were summoned en masse and found a small growth in Friedrich's throat. For weeks they tried almost daily to burn it out with a terrifying machine known as the galvanocauter, which used electricity to raise a platinum wire to white heat. The agonies of this procedure, like those of much Victorian medicine and dentistry, are scarcely conceivable to us today.

It did not work, and on 16 May the German doctors – led by

Bergmann, the first surgeon to insist on modern-style sterilisation of instruments – diagnosed cancer of the throat and recommended an immediate operation.

Friedrich did not want to go under the knife. Kaiser Wilhelm refused to order his son to be operated on. He was outraged when it was suggested that Friedrich might be tricked into accepting one of these new-fangled anaesthetics and then be operated on without his prior knowledge. The German doctors were desperate. In 1887, medical men still had to bow to royalty, figuratively as well as literally. They were certain of their diagnosis, and knew that if the operation did not go ahead, they might be blamed for the death of the heir to the German Empire. Yet if they did insist point blank on an operation, it might kill him.

The entire country was now in an extraordinary state of tension. Bismarck had deliberately hiked up war-fear to win the 1887 election, and Germany was filled with rumours whose bizarre or even magical nature seemed no bar to their circulation. It was widely, though wrongly, believed that there was a secret clause in the Hohenzollern law of succession which meant that if Friedrich lost his voice during the operation, he would be forced to yield in favour of his son. *The Times* of 4 June 1887 reported that the whole nation was troubled by a strange prophecy from the monastery at Lehning:

> This prophecy, discovered a few years since, says that the time will come when a Sovereign will create a great German Empire, which will be the most powerful among the nations. That the Emperor will live for over a century, and, his eldest son having died, will be succeeded by his grandson, who will be paralysed.

A more scurrilous rumour – started by a senior doctor friendly with Bismarck and loathed by the Crown Princess – suggested that Friedrich's illness had somehow been caused by a visit to a brothel during the festivities for the opening of the Suez Canal.[392]

In this atmosphere, the German doctors understandably felt that they needed to cover their backs beyond all doubt before insisting on the operation. They agreed to bolster their position by sending for the most eminent throat specialist available, in order publicly to confirm their diagnosis. The name of Dr Morell Mackenzie from London came up among the German doctors – one of whom happened to be translating Mackenzie's seminal *Diseases of the Nose and Throat* at that very moment – and was enthusiastically accepted by the Crown Princess, who telegraphed Queen Victoria asking her to expedite his journey.

So confident were the German doctors that Mackenzie would merely provide the backing they wanted that they had already scheduled surgery for 21 May. The Crown Princess herself supervised the scrubbing down of the room where it was to take place. Mackenzie arrived – and ordered the German team to drop their scalpels, declaring that they must not think of proceeding to the life-threatening operation without what we would now call a biopsy.

Instead of the German doctors carrying out the full and terrifying operation, Mackenzie used a cocaine anaesthetic to remove a small piece of tissue from Friedrich's throat and send it off for analysis.[393]

By a coincidence which no mere dramatist could hope to get away with, the man to whom Mackenzie sent his bloody piece of tissue was not only, by general consent, Europe's pre-eminent exponent of pathological microscopy, but had also been, for over two decades, Bismarck's most-hated liberal political opponent: it was none other than the splendid Dr Rudolph Virchow.

The British press followed the progress of the treatment with great care, and after Mackenzie removed another portion of tissue on 8 June, all seemed miraculously well. There no longer seemed to be any reason to doubt that the decrepit old German Emperor would be succeeded by his famously liberal son.[394]

> The Emperor rose to-day about noon, and received a visit from the Crown Prince, who came into town from Potsdam to acquaint his father with the success of the operation performed yesterday by Dr. Morell Mackenzie. The portion of the growth which was removed from the throat of his Imperial Highness has been submitted to the famous anatomist, Professor Virchow, for

minute microscopic examination, and to-morrow
the professor will communicate the result of his
inquiry at a general consultation of all the doctors
who have been in attendance on the Crown Prince.
This ailment of the Prince, it must be admitted,
continues to form an engrossing subject of rather
nervous conversation in Berlin, all the more le-
cause it is known that the doctors themselves are
not exactly unanimous as to the real nature of the
growth. But if the result of Professor Virchow's
second examination with the microscope agrees
with his previously expressed opinion, which is
understood to have been most clear and decided,
then there ought to be no longer any reasonable
cause for apprehension on the subject. Meanwhile
Dr. Morell Mackenzie means to return to London
on Saturday, and the Crown Prince with his
family will start for England on Monday.

The Crown Princess and Friedrich, being human, clung desperately to
any diagnosis which was not that of a malignant tumour. Mackenzie
was the bringer of good news, and they gratefully accepted his opinion
that a simple rest and a change of air was the best treatment. Fatefully –
it was later suggested, out of a desire to ensure that he himself was
lucratively retained – Mackenzie recommended that this change of air
should take place in Britain.

There's no doubt of the Crown Princess's desperate state of mind. It's
said she actually screamed into her son Wilhelm's face that he only
wanted the German doctors to stay in charge to make sure his father
died more quickly.[395] Many people saw her as mainly concerned, quite
understandably, if rather unattractively, with her own financial, social
and even personal fate if Friedrich died before he made her empress.
Extraordinarily, she so dreaded being thrown on her own son's mercy
that she used the trip to England secretly to bring entire trunks of her
personal papers safely home to Mama.

Whatever her motives, though, taking Friedrich to Britain on 12 June
to attend Victoria's Jubilee, against the explicit and public advice of
the German doctors, was a dreadful tactical error. By doing so, 'die
Engländerin', as she was widely called behind her royal back, fuelled
dark suspicions, especially when it became known that only one

German doctor was to be allowed to observe and report on Mackenzie's treatment.

What had begun as a mere question of national honour concerning the relative trustworthiness and skill of German and British doctors now became something far bigger, and is extraordinary testament to the deep-seated Anglophobia which was, by 1887, already embedded in Germany.

To many Germans, it was irresistible to imagine that there was some kind of dark conspiracy going on. It was believed that the English-born Crown Princess and her mother had insisted upon an English doctor who was now in cahoots with the arch-liberal, and hence of course congenitally Anglophile, Dr Virchow.

For a time, these voices had to remain soft, for it seemed at first that Mackenzie and Virchow were triumphantly vindicated. Whether it was relief at having avoided the knife, respite from being cauterised in the throat almost daily with white-hot platinum, escape from the ever-watchful eye of Bismarck, or the simple delusion of hope when voiced by an eminent doctor, the Crown Prince really did seem to get better. The change seemed so profound that Friedrich considered Mackenzie to have saved his life. Not content with awarding Mackenzie a high decoration in the Hohenzollern Order, he moved his mother-in-law to give him a knighthood. She was delighted to do so, since, as she wrote to her 'beloved Fritz', she regarded a long life for him as the best hope for the 'happiness and well-being of your country and Europe'.[396]

The liberal newspapers of Germany agreed that Friedrich had been saved by Virchow and Mackenzie, causing a press war there between liberal and 'patriotic' newsmen which *The Times* followed in considerable detail.[397]

By November 1887, however, it was clear that the disease was indeed cancer. Supporters of the Crown Prince clung to the hope that he might yet survive for some years, and Friedrich himself continued to refuse the drastic operation now diagnosed as inescapable. Feelings ran even higher in Germany. The stock market slid at the news (though Herbert Bismarck brazenly said that if he were a stock, he would be going up).[398] People cast around for someone to blame, and the culprits were obvious:

the Briton Mackenzie and the liberal Virchow had doomed the patient.

Only days after the cancer was confirmed, one Berlin arch-insider wrote that 'worrying currents of feeling against the Crown Princess are making themselves felt amongst the *volk*'.[399] Such feelings were not confined to the superstitious or troubled hoi polloi: the Prussian Envoy to Munich wrote, 'what misery we owe to these damned Englishmen. First Prince Wilhelm's crippled arm, and now the Crown Prince's life is endangered'.[400]

Of course, it would have been patently absurd to claim that the English and the German liberals *wanted* the Crown Prince dead, so a complex and nefarious conspiracy theory built up: if Friedrich were unambiguously diagnosed as suffering from an incurable cancer, or if he lost the use of his voice after a life-saving operation, he would not be allowed to succeed to the throne, and his son, Prince Wilhelm, darling of the conservatives, would leap-frog him. So the Crown Princess, in league with the notoriously liberal Virchow and with doctors sent over by her English mother, had *deliberately* risked the life of her husband, first by concealing the true nature of the disease, and then by forbidding the operation that would save him. She had done all this to ensure that Friedrich had at least *some* time on the throne to force through her liberal and Anglophile notions, such as getting rid of Bismarck.

The Chancellor's official state press stoked the fires by making, yet again, that old and so endlessly useful insinuation that there was some kind of subterranean link between external English plotting and internal German liberalism:

> The tissue of lies and deceit of the English doctor Mackenzie, who was entrusted with the care of the Emperor Friedrich, and who has been supported by all the liberal press as if they were thereby defending their political ideals, has been uncovered even for those who did not wish to admit his questionable behaviour.[401]

Whatever the medical truth – it's blurred by the fact that the great German surgeon Bergmann himself seems to have made a gross and horribly painful error at one stage – only the atmosphere of a general Anglophobia could ever have allowed this medical and dynastic tragedy to become widely seen as a full-blown English and/or liberal plot to destroy the Hohenzollern monarchy and remake Germany in England's image.

Friedrich did at last become Kaiser, but only as a doomed and dumb man. His supporters tried desperately to believe that he might live and reign for some time yet. *The Times* gave readers bulletins on a daily basis:[402]

STATE OF THE EMPEROR FREDERICK.

BERLIN, March 15.

We are still without any official bulletin this evening as to the health of the Emperor Frederick, and this morning the Bourse was depressed by dis-quieting rumours on the subject ; but from all I can gather there does not seem to be any doubt that His Majesty has been free from pain, has preserved a firm carriage, a clear eye, and a good appetite, and has shown a capacity for work and a freshness of intellect which are astonishing.

In truth, Friedrich's ninety-nine pain-wracked days on the throne were spent largely fighting his wife's wearying and hopeless battle with Bismarck as to whether their daughter might become queen of Bulgaria.

By the end, the Chancellor's supporters barely even troubled to conceal their relief at the turn of events. It was, inevitably, Heinrich von Treitschke who summed it up. Friedrich's short reign was made a sad one 'by the mendacious plotting of the English doctors and their dirty journalistic gang, by the impudence of the free liberal party who greedily crowded around the Kaiser as if he belonged to them'.[403]

Bismarck's own son, Herbert, whom Bismarck seemed to be grooming for a hereditary chancellorship, went beyond all taste and tact. To the outrage of the dynastically minded Russians, he publicly went and got 'beastly drunk' in St Petersburg during the diplomatic mourning period for Friedrich:

his theme was all that wd. have befallen Germany and how the flood gates of democracy & Jews & God knew what more besides wd. have been opened if the reign of the Emperor Frederick & the Empress Victoria had been prolonged. But, he added, *un bon petit cancre nous a suavé!* [404]

A pig-headed young German

In Britain, Friedrich's demise was recognised as a 'matter of direct concern to England', since good relations – even a full alliance – with Germany had been thought possible under 'him who was buried on Waterloo Day in this present week'. [405]

The figure looming over Anglo-German dealings was, as it had been for twenty-five years, that of Bismarck, who now seemed even more omnipotent. Britons knew that Friedrich had clearly 'severed himself from that absolutist and repressive policy to which Prince Bismarck was attached', but that his son, now ascending the throne, had been 'placed under the political guidance of Prince Bismarck'. On the very day it announced Friedrich's death, *The Times*, its columns thick-bordered with funereal black, pointed out that Bismarck was now more firmly than ever in the saddle: 'in circles where politics are the chief topic, some think that Prince Bismarck, owing to the deep and almost passionate admiration professed for him by the new Emperor, will be at least for a good while the uncontrolled master'.

There was nothing good to be heard about the new Emperor-to-be:

Of Prince William's opinions and tendencies there is one further piece of evidence. In the autumn of last year he attended a meeting held under the auspices of Count Waldersee in favour of a Berlin society of Christian Socialists. A typical figure at this meeting was Pastor Stoecker, the author of the disgraceful Jew-baiting movement which disturbed Berlin society a few years ago, and a clergyman whose principal merit in the eyes of his admirers is that he has opposed to the utmost of his abilities the liberal and tolerant ideas of which the Court of the Emperor Frederick and the Empress Victoria was always the centre.

It has for some time been the fashion with the military party in Berlin to describe Prince William as promising to be a second Frederick the Great.[406]

Less tactful analysts went further:

This Prince, who is only eight-and-twenty, is a spiteful, obstinate and really pig-headed young German with the worst national characteristics of his race, and but few of its better qualities. He has an insane love for a drum and a sword, and fancies that the bloody business of war is the noblest profession on earth. This category of defects is broad enough, but the temperament of the Prince, so far as we ourselves are concerned, is more dangerous because he is bitten by a perfectly insane Anglophobia. Notwithstanding that his mother is an English woman and that his nation is permitted to come over to our shores and compete with English artisans and English workers in the labour market, the Prince detests the English people, English customs, and English ways with an intensity of feeling which is all but ferocious.[407]

British journalists could not have known, as modern historians do, that Wilhelm had already managed to outrage his grandmother during her Jubilee celebrations, or that he had recently told his new best friend that 'it is high time the Old Woman died ... Well, England should look out when I have something to say about things ... One cannot have enough hatred for England.'[408] Then again, they did not *need* to know such things in order to realise, even before his accession, that the new Kaiser 'does not inherit his father's broad views, nor his regard for England'[409] and that Britain was now unexpectedly going to have to live with 'the most bellicose, impetuous, and impatient of princes'.[410]

His first public statements did little to calm nerves:[*]

> It is true that such words as "war-lord" have a much more formidable and a much more awkward appearance and sound in English than in German; and it is true, also, that a certain disposition to exaggerate the bellicose note, if in the circumstances of questionable taste, was also in the circumstances far from unnatural. But there were certainly some unpleasant things about these documents. The reference to the dead Emperor stood out, it might be urged, with surely unnecessary sharpness against that to his father, and supplied an unlucky, and almost painful, parallel to the huddling up of the interment of the one as compared with the stately functions attending the interment of the other. The whole of the document or documents, too, had, very perceptibly to a Devil's advocate, a flavour of brag and of flourish which might advantageously have been dispensed with in the case of a young man who has never drawn the sword, and who, in the present ostensible circumstances of his affairs, has no decent pretext for assuming that he will draw it. There might be said to be, in short—for we have little desire to dwell on this part of the matter—a sort of sham Spartan air, according too well with the disreputable sentiment of the clique who, as is well known, wished to exclude the Emperor FREDERICK from the throne altogether, as not being in health to play the swashbuckler, and who vented their rage upon Sir MORELL MACKENZIE for not lending himself to their cabal.

British fears about the tone of the new Kaiser seemed all too justified. In the first months of his rule, he appeared to be entirely the creature of the Bismarcks, father and son. Russia was demonstratively courted by the new regime and Albert Edward, the Prince of Wales, was mortally offended by being informed that he must clear out of Vienna before Wilhelm arrived. No sooner this, than Bismarck's press roundly accused Sir Robert Morier, by now Britain's most senior diplomat, of having betrayed the Crown Prince's military confidences to France during the Franco-Prussian War.

[*] Modern British revisionists have argued that the term 'All-Highest War-Lord' (*Allerhöchster Kriegsherr*) simply meant 'Supreme Commander'. That is nonsense. The German Army had, and used, a perfectly serviceable term for that – *Oberster Befehlshaber*. The title All-Highest was uniquely that of a kaiser (in fact, it had been first used by Franz Josef II) and appeared in many other forms as well: a minister wanting to pursue a certain policy or an officer wanting to dance the tango might learn that his wish had been vetoed '*an Allerhöchster Stelle*' ('at the All-Highest level').

Within six months of Wilhelm's accession, the Anglo-German atmosphere was so poisonous, and the Bismarckian tactics so familiar, that the founder of the *Pall Mall Gazette* wrote in *The Times* of the 'Cultivation of Hostility to England':

Carefully to reserve this or that "revelation," for publication in the newspapers at the right moment, is a habit with Prince Bismarck, and one of his best known methods of working. But so far it has never been employed for a trivial purpose or without serious intention. In this case, what is the purpose and intention? All the answer I have yet seen is that the present Emperor or his Chancellor wishes to convince Germany that the Emperor Frederick was in the habit of blabbing to the English (having been unfortunately Anglicized himself), and that the English turned his confidences to a treacherous and malevolent use. And that, I think, is the true explanation, rightly understood. For we have now to ask ourselves whether the main purpose of these so-called "revelations" is to discredit the late Emperor, or still further to deepen the popular hatred of England.[411]

The letter – not by some crackpot in an obscure pamphlet, but in the greatest organ of the British Empire and signed by one of London's most powerful newsmen – ends by warning that the

country may as well prepare for the sort of provocations which the French had to endure so long after they were conquered. We have not been conquered (though in the eyes of most Germans nowadays that is a mere matter of detail), and yet it behoves us to be prudent too, remembering that tameness is not always prudent by any means.

Your obedient servant,

January 4.   F. GREENWOOD.

By April 1889, Greenwood's own paper was reporting that the Royal Navy in Samoa, already operating as a de facto ally of the USN there, had come close to actually opening up on the German Navy:*

> The situation is very strained; on one occasion, it is reported, a British man-of-war was going to fire into the German ships owing to their having laid lawless hands on a British-subject. [412]

The new reign truly had not begun well for Anglo-German relations.

Intermezzo III: stock-taking, 1889

We've now arrived at the time when, according to our popular historians, all was still well between Britain and Germany, so perhaps we should pause here to look at how things really stood.

For twenty-five years, Britons and Germans had been imbibing more or less unchanging pictures of one another, and to say that those pictures were hardly good ones would be to put it very mildly indeed. Germans and Britons in the prime of life at the accession of Wilhelm II, men in, or coming into, positions of power and influence, had known the same things about each other ever since their university days: Britons, in 1889, knew that the Germans were poor, backward, conformist, happy to be hyper-governed by a Junkerised state, ill-mannered, mystical, boastful, obsessed with rank and title, humourless, unpleasantly pushing or even fraudulent in business and an inveterate military danger to their neighbours. And they were still poor, diseased, low-wage immigrants, thanks to whom London was 'day by day becoming more like the Tower of Babel': it was estimated that fully six-sevenths of all immigrants came from Germany.[413]

---

* According to the US Department of the Navy's Historical Center in Washington, there was a 'serious risk of war' between the US and Germany at this time.

The images simply did not change over the decades. Here are two, from 1840 and from 1892:

THE ALIEN PAUPER QUESTION.
FOREIGN PRODUCE—"MADE IN GERMANY."

Meanwhile the Germans, in 1889, had known since 1864 that the British were rich, spoiled, lazy, arrogant, selfishly individualistic, hypocritical, militarily hopeless when confronted by any halfway well-armed foe and able to keep their undeserved empire (which had really been won for them by Frederick the Great and Blücher) only by their sneaky Jew-ish financial might coupled with the abuse of a naval supremacy which allowed them safely to foment the troubles of Europe.

By a fatal coincidence, the genuine Anglo-German conflicts which arose in the 1890s followed decades of this popular stereotyping – and coincided with the very first age of modern mass electorates.

We, now, are so used to the spectacle of politicians scrabbling desperately for the votes they imagine can be delivered by the media that it is hard for us to remember just how brand-new this political territory was. For all of history, European governments – like the Chinese government today – had simply been obliged to make sure that the masses did not get so angry as to actually start burning buildings and making barricades. It takes a truly outraged citizen to face a whiff of grapeshot, but any voter merely irritated or spooked by a timely editorial in his newspaper can muster the guts to mark his ballot paper.

The opinion of mass voterships on both sides was now becoming the unique, historically unprecedented element in the growing Anglo-German antagonism.

There are two vital things about these new electorates which are easy to forget, but which would loom vast in the number-crunching of any modern campaign guru. The voters were exclusively *male*, and a very large proportion of them were *young*. In 1911, over half of all British voters were men under forty: the figure today, even with our lower voting age, is not even one in five.

British electors, who had been informed all their lives that Britain was the natural and proper ruler over large parts of the world, and German electors, who had been told since youth that Britain was selfishly barring Germany's destined way, thus had more in common demographically with the electorates of Iran or Pakistan today than with modern European voterships.

Constituencies dominated by young males rarely make for reasonable politics, and the leaders of the 1890s, all of whom had cut their political teeth in the age before mass voting, had very little idea how to manage them. Politicians unused to playing to the gallery were now tempted or obliged to do so with little conception of how powerful were the genies they might unleash.

And yet, in the simple mathematical world of diplomatic-military game-play theory, Britain and Germany had so little to lose and so much to gain by an alliance that it would have been the most obvious thing in the world.

The question for the reign of Wilhelm II was whether the lack of real and present conflicts, and the presence of potential mutual enemies, would be enough to bridge that long-nurtured sense of a fundamental clash of cultures before it got out of all control in this first age of the new mass politics.

PART SIX (THE 1890s):
THE ONLY FRIEND
OF ENGLAND

An unexpected admirer

The entirely unexpected feature of Anglo-German relations between 1889 and 1894 was Wilhelm II's love-affair with Englishness.

In the first year of Wilhelm's reign, he appeared thoroughly under the control of Bismarck. The needle of German diplomacy seemed to be swinging very much back towards Russia, and Salisbury decided to fight back. Helped by medical warnings from years before and delicate hints, unusually enough, from the German Foreign Office itself, he had early concluded that Wilhelm was 'a little off his head' and needed treating with the full soft soap.[414] He therefore asked Victoria and Albert Edward to forget their huffs, pull out all the stops and invite Wilhelm to England in 1889. It was no secret in Britain that the Prince of Wales, for one, was anything but keen.

Nor was Bismarck. When his official press announced the visit, the tone was hardly ecstatic. Readers were pointedly reminded that Wilhelm had already been to all the other major courts of Europe in 1888 and that the belated visit to Britain, which was to be only a couple of days long, would simply be one of 'princely politesse'. They were also told that the squadron escorting him would be 'the first foreign, let alone German, fleet to appear in such strength off Osborne House'. The sight of such a German fleet might serve to

remind the Englanders that Germany has become their neighbour on the sea just as in distant regions of the world. Their insular seclusion having given them the experience of being untouchable by any foe, the vulnerable points of Great Britain are in their world-strewn colonial possessions ... Germany certainly does not want to increase the number of its opponents, but just as little can England wish that Germany's rightful, though only so late-initiated, ambition to assure itself of its share of colonies should lead it into the ranks of England's opponents ... the impression of this visit, and the sight of German sea-power will move England to everywhere show a friendly attitude to Germany.[415]

It was hardly the announcement of a friendly state visit. In fact, it looks very like another instance where we can see the fatal thinking behind the Tirpitz Plan well before Tirpitz himself took the reins: the sight of German sea-power was to *persuade* England into being friendly to Germany by reminding her of the consequences of doing otherwise.

Unfortunately for Bismarck, it was not the British who were most liable to be impressed by demonstrations of sea-power. Lord Salisbury had cunningly made sure that the greatest fleet the world had ever seen in one place was waiting off the Isle of Wight to greet Wilhelm, so that 'he will not misunderstand the nature of the welcome which he is receiving here or the strength of the nation from which he receives it'.[416] Moreover, he had played a massive psychological trump card. Shortly before the visit, he had prevailed upon Queen Victoria to award Wilhelm a very unusual distinction. As a result, the first German emperor to visit Britain came in to dock, past mile upon serried mile of Royal Navy ships, resplendent in the full-dress uniform of a British admiral of the fleet.

The thought that these mighty squadrons were in some sense *his* worked on the young Kaiser more effectively than even Salisbury could have possibly hoped. Wilhelm's delight was quite unbounded and, some thought, almost unhinged. It astonished and dismayed his own courtiers. The letter Wilhelm wrote to the British Ambassador in Berlin, Sir Edward Malet, was indeed extraordinary in its implications:

I feel like Macbeth must have felt when he was suddenly received by the witches with the cry "All Hail who art Thane of Glamis and of Cawdor too." I shall of course gladly accept the kindness Her Majesty so graciously has preferred with all my heart.[417]

History can show few more perfect Freudian slips: Wilhelm was casting himself unconsciously as the future king of Scotland by deluded usurpation and murder – and for a few bizarre months it seemed that he was indeed rapt.

He certainly loved his first visit to Britain. To a young monarch from the Continent, where German, Russian and Austrian emperors went about with clattering escorts for very good reasons (Alexander II had been assassinated in 1881 and Wilhelm's own revered grandfather had twice narrowly escaped attempts on his life), the wealth, security and ease of the British royal family, his *own* family, must have seemed magical. To Britons, ruled for decades by an ageing queen in widow's weeds, Wilhelm seemed like a real king as he strode about in various gorgeous uniforms, giving impromptu speeches in English.

The visit was a huge success. Britain welcomed Wilhelm as one of the family in a very real way: 'not only as the kinsman of our own royal house but as the ruler of the most powerful of continental Empires, and the head of a kindred race'.[418] Wilhelm clearly felt the warmth: he suddenly and personally decided to put off his return to Germany, turning a short call 'at the fag-end of the season' (as *The Times* had rather sniffily called it on 3 August) into a national progress. The culminating moment came at Cowes, when a grand dinner was held to celebrate Wilhelm's election to the Royal Yacht Squadron.

The magic of British royal pomp worked, and it did not wear off. For several months, Wilhelm behaved as though he actually was, and should be treated as, co-commander of the Royal Navy. He flew the Union Jack at his topmast, together with the German Imperial Ensign – on one occasion, when entering Corfu, he even insisted on flying it *instead of* the German flag, to the horror of his own captain. He demanded that ships of all nations salute his British rank, inspected British squadrons as if they were his own and advised his grandmother on the disposition of her fleets.[419] It sounded as though his dearest wish on Earth was to be an obedient ally of the British; his anti-Russian utterances at this time were so uncontrolled and damaging that 'his advisers were horrified and sometimes even doubted his sanity'.[420]

The most extraordinary thing about it all – there can be few parallels in history – is that, from now on, Wilhelm repeatedly warned the British about *his own people*.

One of his first letters as kaiser to Queen Victoria informs his grandmother that 'I am a friend of England. The prevailing sentiment among large sections of the middle and lower classes of my own people is not friendly to England. I am, therefore, so to speak, in a minority in my own land.' His position would be exactly the same, almost to the word, twenty years later, in the *Daily Telegraph* interview which led to so extraordinary a wave of outrage against him in Germany that some felt it even threatened the Hohenzollern monarchy itself. Often, he seems genuinely to have thought of himself as the one friend of England in Germany.

How Britons had misjudged the Kaiser! Here at last was a German ruler, and one with a royal English mother and grandmother, openly doing what the Germans had always been supposed to do: adoring and admiring Britain. He declared publicly, in 1891, that 'I have always felt at home in this lovely country,'[421] and *The Times* gushed back:

> He has disarmed any prejudice which may have existed by many acts, and not least by his frankly expressed, ungrudging admiration of the two distinctively British institutions, our navy and our colonies; and it is his most evident ambition to teach his countrymen how to emulate both.

Their national vanity thus tickled, some Britons briefly managed to reset to that old default, according to which, when Germans professed admiration for Britain, the Royal Navy and the colonies, and declared their wish to copy them, this simply meant that they loved the British Empire (why on Earth would they not?) and were respectfully applying to become its junior partner.

After all, Prince Bismarck and the young Emperor were still clearly in no doubt as to the rational limits of German ambitions. When Dr Carl Peters, the German Stanley, tried to go a-colonising for Germany on a freelance basis, he was slapped down, together with his 'extravagant invective against everything English', by the Kaiser and his chancellor, both of whom 'understand the danger of colonial entanglements to a country which does not possess a first-class navy' and who had just been shown that they could not prevail in Samoa against 'the superior naval force of the United States'. With such eminently sensible men in charge, the 'entente cordiale between Lord Salisbury and Prince Bismarck' was looking good.[422]

In 1890, though, the man who had since 1871 been the grand master of European diplomacy was finally defeated by the power which had kept him immune for so long: the will of his own emperor.

After a series of disputes about who ran Germany, Wilhelm pushed his former teacher into resignation. Salisbury was deeply concerned, preferring the devil he knew, and whom he at least considered sane. But, at first, all seemed well: no sooner had Bismarck gone than Britain and Germany signed the Heligoland and Zanzibar treaties. In these, Germany agreed that it did not have worthless and unenforceable rights in Zanzibar; Britain agreed that Heligoland should be German.

There was, in fact, no direct linkage, for neither treaty mentions the other, but it seemed a splendid example of how festering little issues could now be solved, almost overnight, by the new Kaiser and Salisbury. After all, had not Bismarck been the great driver of Anglophobia? He was gone, and with the Kaiser – Victoria's grandson! – now truly in charge and so clearly in love with Englishness, there had been nothing so good in Anglo-German relations since the brief romance of Bizzy and Dizzy in 1879.

The timing of the great 1891 German Exhibition in London, the excuse for yet another visit by the Kaiser, could scarcely have been better: it was happy indeed that the exhibits included 'an old fashioned Schleswig-Holstein house built to typify the cradle of the Anglo-Saxon race'.[423]

LONDON'S
GERMAN EXHIBITION.

On a balmy August evening, it is really delightful to stroll amid the enchanting illuminated gardens of the German Exhibition at West Brompton, and be cheered by the excellent music discoursed by the fine military bands of Germany. The gay scene can only be regarded as

Fairyland Realised.

Londoners promenade to the infectious tune of a pulsing waltz of Strauss, and are inspirited by the kaleidoscopic beauty of the coloured lamps festooning the trees of the cosy Welcome Club. Among the fresh attractions, very dear to the Germans in London, is the large and bright

Kaiserhalle,

wherein, to the strains of the Duke of Ratibor's band; comely and plump Munich waitresses in their native costumes serve cold collations and the most deliciously cool lager beer in capacious tankards. In this comfortable refreshment-room, the walls of which are enlivened with vivacious pictures of Teuton bacchantes, Londoners may obtain a fair notion of the rational way in which our German friends take their pleasure. The beer is light and good, the smart waitresses form a picturesque sight of themselves, and good cheer predominates.

The good cheer ends

So why didn't this holiday atmosphere of family harmony lead to anything concrete? The answer is simple: Salisbury refused to be inveigled by Wilhelm's passionate Anglophilia, which, since he had helped create it himself, he well knew might simply be a passing fad. He would not commit to the Triple Alliance, even though – or perhaps, because – Wilhelm had so comprehensively alienated the Russians.

Meanwhile, the public on both sides was becoming less and less willing to be impressed. In Britain, the law of diminishing returns meant that Wilhelm's decisions 'to honour ourselves with one of his not wholly rare appearances, to review at Wimbledon, to race at Cowes, to make excursions to the Hebrid Isles'[424] made less and less actual impact. And like any showman's act, the moment the Kaiser's grandstanding stopped being impressive, it began to seem bizarre. In *Punch*'s cartoons, he began to appear as a jack-in-the box or 'fidgety William'. The *Contemporary Review* described him as a mere 'modern man' in the very *bad* sense of a man craving media attention, busyness and praise, whose 'latest admiration for England and English things' is only 'a capricious reaction against former undisguised dislike and vilification'.[425] 'The Man of the Moment' started to mutate into the comic 'Greatest Man of the Age':

> Proudly he strides in manner grand,
> Across our Lilliputian land
> So now the German Gulliver comes
> Bang the trumpets and blow the drums[426]

Wilhelm was not yet disliked in Britain, but by the time of the German Exhibition, even as 'uniforms were being exchanged and deputations received, and gala performances were in full swing', observers had begun to say, publicly, in the respectable press, that Wilhelm was 'an over-rated article, and certainly not well-balanced'.[427]

Across in Germany, how people felt was even plainer, and was graphically shown by the reaction to the Heligoland–Zanzibar treaties.

Getting Heligoland, which had never been German, was in fact a major coup, as Wilhelm's advisers well knew. During the final run-up, his diplomats were specifically and urgently instructed not to let the British know how important the island was to the German Navy. Many people in Britain, including Victoria, did not like the idea much, but reaction was muted simply because, not being privy to the discussions of the Kaiser's newly formed Imperial Naval Cabinet, the British could not put their finger on exactly what was wrong with the deal. The German diplomats thus won the day hands down, and had every right to brag.

But that was not how it played to the gallery in Germany. Vengefully, the newly dropped Bismarck, who had in truth himself sanctioned the sort-of-deal before his fall, told the press that had he still been in charge, he would have stuck to his guns, got Heligoland for nothing and avoided the loss of Zanzibar. His weak-willed successors had, he snorted, 'swapped the trousers for a button'.

The outrage in Germany at this supposed betrayal of her colonial dreams was so profound that it led directly to the formation of the Pan-German League, one of the great drivers of Anglophobia and anti-Semitism over the following years.*

For the remainder of his reign, Wilhelm consistently found himself outflanked by the Anglophobia and Bismarck-worship of his own people, many of whom seem already to have become incapable of accepting any deal at all that was done with the Englanders.

Worse, popular German myths about the alleged nature of the Englanders were by now so widely accepted that they did not just affect the views of the masses. German diplomats seem to have bought into them as well.

Rough wooing

Since most German diplomats, including Bismarck and Wilhelm himself, clearly saw how advantageous and logical it would be to have Britain on their side against Russia, and since most British leaders were very anti-Russian indeed, you might imagine that the obvious course for Germany would have been to demonstrate very clearly the advantages of her friendship to Britain. Instead, the policy, as Hatzfeldt, ambassador in London, put it himself, was once again to 'demonstrate the disadvantages of our hostility'.[428]

---

* One of its early luminaries was the young Max Weber, father of modern sociology, who, in 1895, demanded of the Poles in Germany exactly what Treitschke had demanded of the Jews: that they give up their culture entirely and become real Germans. This theory is not much cited today by sociologists.

The central plank of this bizarre diplomacy was the idea that Britain would only become Germany's friend if she were shown the dangers of being Germany's enemy. The more you think about this, the stranger it becomes.

Of course, all diplomacy between countries as yet unaligned with one another involves a degree of both the carrot and the stick. But since national leaders have more pride than donkeys, not to mention those new and excitable electorates to keep happy, the generally successful practice is to display the carrot as enticingly as possible while admitting only in the most delicate terms to the very existence of the stick. German diplomacy with Britain in the 1890s – following Bismarck's of the early 1880s – did things exactly the other way around.

It is extremely hard to think of another example in history of one major power seriously believing that another major power might best be wooed so roughly into a full-blown, functioning military alliance. Perhaps Napoleon I and Russia was a similar case, but Napoleon was the all but unchallenged master of Europe in 1807: a touch of megalomania in him at that time, though eventually fatal, was at least comprehensible. Germany, in the 1890s, was already faced with a solid and potent Franco-Russian combination: no sane statesmen in this position would have conducted relations with the British Empire on the basis of implied threats unless he genuinely believed that Britain quite simply would not react to such menaces as other major powers would.

It seems that the generation-old myth of Britain's alleged decadence, shopkeeperliness, unheroicness, hapless parliamentary government, money-driven Jew-ish policy-making and so on genuinely affected the capacity of German decision-makers in the 1890s to rationally appraise the choices before them. Unlike any other power, the British would supposedly be guided not by national pride, or honour, or even treaty obligations, but by a simple calculation of where they might find their best short-term profit – which meant, their least immediate danger.

The British, who still regarded themselves as militarily equal, and morally superior, to any other power, did not remotely intuit the unusual logic of the German advances. The diplomats in London were distinctly more positive about the Germans than their voters and pressmen were,

1894   und   1899.

How to treat the British Lion: tread on his tail and he will come to you.
Right to the end, this remained a fixation of German political-strategic
thought.

but even they were baffled and ultimately repulsed by a policy which flip-
flopped from theatrical invitations to rule the world hand-in-hand with
Germany to barely concealed threats about what would happen if they
turned the suitor down.

One plain example of this came in 1894, when France and Russia
officially published their well-known relationship. For decades, Russia
had been the great threat to the British Empire, and the Franco-
Russian treaty was blatantly anti-German: there was now the very best
of all possible reasons for things between Britain and Germany to get
warm, and fast. The Kaiser and his diplomats now indeed made
another big push to get the British to join the Dual Alliance – but at
exactly the same time, they whipped up international opposition to
Britain over the Congo Treaty. Lord Rosebery's reaction was to throw
up his hands and ask Sir Edward Malet if he could understand what
was going on in Berlin's corridors of power, since 'I can't pretend to
read the riddle.'[429]

The chance was soon gone.

Wilhelm, baffled

In 1893, the workers of Germany showed how grateful they were for Wilhelm's paternalistic reforms by voting in even larger numbers for the Social Democrats, while the big Prussian landowners demonstrated their loyalty to the throne by excoriating the commercial treaty with Russia. At times, members of the two extremes even spoke of uniting to end the regime of the hapless Chancellor Caprivi, who had always known that the massy chair carved by Bismarck himself, for himself, could only be a siege perilous for his successor.

And, indeed, many Germans were already making less and less flattering comparisons between the state of things now and the golden age of the great chancellor, who had made sure that when he left office, he physically took with him enough of the Guelph Fund to continue spiking at least part of the press. By now, a mock version of the German national anthem was being widely sung in public places, in protest at Wilhelm's geographical and political aimlessness (the tune was the same as 'God Save the Queen'):

> God save Thy royal train
> Rush back and forth again
> Keep up the speed
> When Thou com'st off the track
> Call Bismarck, bring him back
> He's who we need*

Meanwhile the Staatsministerium seriously discussed whether to arrest the entire Social Democratic Party in the Reichstag for not standing during the singing of the genuine imperial national anthem.

Wilhelm knew very well how badly he stood among his people, for he was the most media-sensitive ruler in history, famous for reading the daily press 'to which he attaches abnormal importance' with 'a

---

* Author's translation. 'Heil Dir im Sonderzug/Reisest noch nicht genug/Reis' immer mehr/ Wenn Du dann bald entgleist/Rasch Du zu Bismarck eilst/Holst ihn uns her.'

hyper-sensitiveness quite unique in a monarch'.[430] He began to feel that he had simply been played along by his English family, who had cunningly induced him to fling away, by 1894, the earlier acclaim of his own subjects and the friendship of his fellow autocrat, the Tsar.

For Wilhelm was now bent on a truly 'personal regime' and was even considering a military coup to alter the constitution. Around him gathered a strange circle of toadies, headed by the mystically inclined Count (later Prince) Philip Eulenburg, who had been an intimate friend of the notorious anti-Semite, the late Count Arthur Gobineau. Among themselves, the Liebenberg Circle, as they became known, referred to Wilhelm as '*das Liebchen*' ('the little darling') and encouraged him to believe that what the German *volk* really wanted was a genuinely ruling sovereign on the Russian model.[431]

By the summer of 1894, Wilhelm could no longer restrain himself. He was entertaining his relations, the Prince of Wales and the Duke of Cambridge, aboard his yacht off the Isle of Wight when the news came that France and England were in serious dispute in Siam. He leapt on to the table, waving his napkin and crying, 'Hurrah, at last you are in trouble!'[432]

An irresistible chance to show the British a thing or two about how much they needed German friendship – i.e. about what trouble Germany could cause Britain – now came in Africa.

The Boers, the Germans and the fleet

German colonialists had been taking a distinctly paternal interest in the Transvaal ever since von Weber had suggested, in 1880, that it was somehow naturally German.

This was the one place in the world as yet unclaimed by Britain or the United States where a white *volk* closely related to the Germans (simply part *of* the Germans, according to more advanced thinkers) could evidently thrive and lord it over the local helot races. Here, if anywhere, was where Germany could realise a British-style settler empire.

In the German nationalist book, the Dutch and the Germans shared not just a language, if you looked at it the right way, but also certain racial virtues which were in direct and specific contrast to the English. Germans and Dutch were honest, hard-working people, farmers and engineers, who would exercise a strict but beneficial rule over the natives; the English were mere speculators and adventurers who used 'negrophile' laws (as Weber had called them) to manipulate the natives for their own ends. If Germany was ever going to be a true colonial empire, this was where it had to be centred. The Boers were to be Germandom's advance guard.

For some time, Sir Charles Dilke, the prominent, indeed notorious, Liberal MP, had been warning that the Boer leaders were inviting Germany to consider declaring her nominal suzerainty over the Transvaal. As relations between Kruger's regime and the Cape Colony got more and more heated, Germany sent two warships as a gesture of support for the Boers. Even ten years earlier, in the days of Bismarck's iron rule, a deputation from the Transvaal had been received in Berlin with an enthusiasm which was 'a significant illustration of German feeling towards England'.[433] Now, in the more fevered days of restless Wilhelm, sending a couple of German warships there could generate real excitement:

> the German Press reproduces with great satisfaction a letter published by the *Volkstem*, in Pretoria, thanking Germany in the name of the people of the Transvaal for having despatched two ships of war to Lorenzo Marquez to counteract the evil designs of the British Foreign Office upon Delagoa Bay, and assuring Germany that her flag can always reckon upon the good will of the South African Republic.

Wilhelm was almost beside himself with excitement at the thought of such transoceanic naval reach, and of having his people behind him at last. Then it became plain that his own fleet off the coast of West Africa would easily be trumped, if need be, by the Royal Navy's newly formed Flying Squadron.

The situation was clear enough on both sides: Germany and Britain were anything but friends, but the Royal Navy made Britain, and her Empire, untouchable:[434]

> THE Berlin *Echo*, in a recent edition, throws out some queer lights upon English history. Having begun by casting on the English all the guilt of the German blood spilt in the Loire campaign—M. Gambetta having received arms and money from—where do you think? You will *never* guess!—perfidious Albion!—it pitches into our army and navy. Our soldiers, we are told, have never done anything worthy of mention. We would have been annihilated at Waterloo but for Blücher! The French saved us from total destruction at the Alma! The Balaclava Charge was due to the general in command indulging too freely in port! The French took Sebastopol—not we! We had nothing to do with it!
>
> Well, we don't know. We always held it rather lucky for Prussia that Wellington did take the field at Waterloo—at least, if one can judge by the brilliant results achieved, before that battle, by the Prussian army against Napoleon. The French even say that, but for *ce maudit Vilain-ton*, Germany would now be a nice little French province—but, of course, the French are prejudiced. We have never been to war with Germany—luckily for the land of cheap beer and scurrilous newspapers. Not but that they have some advantages over us; for instance, our Queen does not play tin soldiers in the nursery, nor cry "Hoch! hoch! hoch!" about fifteen times a day, nor send her photograph to the Sultan. But we *have* a trifling Empire here and there, a few goodish men to guard it, and—what Germany will never have—a Flying Squadron!

Wilhelm was furious and demanded vast numbers of new cruisers immediately. His public agreed. The Chancellor, Prince Hohenlohe, appealed to recalcitrant free liberals by reminding them that a big fleet had been their own policy in their grand old revolutionary days of 1848. The main reason for wanting to increase the German Navy was to 'uphold and protect our relations with the South African Republic' – an area where Britain was the only possible adversary.[435] It was indeed a vision straight out of the old liberal-nationalist dream: German warships halfway around the world, helping out a fellow Germanic people, and securing an important trading bay, in the teeth of the selfish, plotting Englanders. If Britain wanted peace, that was fine, said the *Cologne Gazette*, and *The Times* gave Britons the full wording:

"But," it continues, "as surely as Germany will never cross England's path when it leads to the maintenance of peace, so surely will the two Powers come into collision if in the future as in the past, England is the Power which we find ever ready to throw hindrances in the way of German colonial undertakings. From the very beginning of the German colonial policy England has employed the most contemptible means to hinder the progress of Germany – *e.g.*, in the Cameroons, in Togo, in Samoa, and at Delagoa Bay. Germany has put up with this opposition for years with the greatest patience. But her long-suffering has reached its limits, and the English Government must be aware that Germany has both the power and the will to prevent a continuance of this antagonism."[436]

It was now that the fateful decision came. Admiral Tirpitz argued that Wilhelm's cruisers, however numerous, would be useless in browbeating the British into an alliance. The iron facts of geography dictated that all Germany's sea routes were controlled by the invincible Royal Navy. Unless England permitted it, no German cruiser would ever make it into the North Atlantic, let alone into the Indian Ocean or the Pacific. If the Kaiser was ever to get genuine freedom of action for world politics – be accorded genuine equality with the English – he must create a real battle fleet. Then, and only then, would Germany be, like America, a power which Britain feared, and with which she would therefore ally, Q.E.D.

There's no doubt that Tirpitz actually believed this strange theory himself. In a letter of this time to his mentor, Admiral Stosch, he indulged in a fantasy of the German fleet hurrying out to bombard London before the main force of the Royal Navy could arrive, in order to win 'a compromise peace with which both sides can be satisfied'.[437] Sneaking a march on them while their navies, far-flung, were not on the home station, bombarding London itself: now *that* was the way the English would come to see Germany as a friend and equal!

Unfortunately this was not the daydream of some armchair fantasist, but of the Imperial Germany Navy's new chief. It was more than this, though, which is the only reason it won the day. Tirpitz's bizarre view of how England worked chimed not only with the Kaiser's own split feelings, but with the whole Treistchkean, national-liberal view of the Englanders as somehow both mighty (and enviable) yet decadent (and bully-able). This unique logic won the day: England was going to be *made* to ally with Germany at last.

On 16 December 1895, Wilhelm sent an official All-Highest Cabinet Order to the Reichskanzler from Kiel to order a grand new fleet of ships, not to cruise the blue oceans, but to do full-on battle in home waters. Tirpitz immediately suggested that they appeal to the country on the issue of a great German fleet. This would, he said, publicly sort the truly *German* MPs out from the mere crypto-Englanders: it would be a great tool against 'misguided parliamentarians' and the 'Anglo-mania in certain circles'.[438]

At that very moment, the Cape Colonists acted and invaded the Transvaal in what history knows as the Jameson Raid. All Germany was livid. When the raid was easily and ignominiously quashed by the Boers, all Germany rejoiced – and, on 3 January, Wilhelm himself fired off the single most popular communication of his entire reign, which has gone down in history as the Kruger Telegram:

> Berlin, 3rd January 1896
>
> I express my sincere congratulations that you, together with your people and without appealing to friendly powers for help, have, through your own vigour in the face of the armed hordes which have invaded your country as disturbers of the peace, succeeded in restoring peace and preserving the independence of the country against outside attacks.
>
> Wilhelm I. R.[439]

A bad year to go to Cowes

The British had been confused by German diplomacy, and by Wilhelm's erratic displays of bumptious friendship, but they knew a public slap in the face when they got one.

British popular opinion was willing to blame an easily identifiable individual:

> Let Pinchbeck Caesar strut and crow ...
> Hands off, Germany! Hands off, all!
> Kruger boasts and Kaiser brags, Britons hear the call!
> Back to back the world around, answer with a will –
> It's England for her own, boys! It's rule Britannia still![440]

Even across the Atlantic, 'the turbulent echoes of music-hall patriotism' on both sides were clearly audible:[441]

LONDON AND THE KAISER

Fanning the Flame of Antipathy Which Burns in Great Britain.

"Whatever may have been the Kaiser's sentiments, the whole of Germany was glad to see the English get a lesson from the Boers."

The *New York Times* saw clearly the domestic political gain for Wilhelm and his courtiers. At last, they had re-found that great seam of popular approval, and it was deep enough to outgun even the former chancellor, who was at this stage posing as the voice of reason:

> Prince Bismarck's personal organ, the *Hamburger Nachrichten*, prints articles almost daily making pointed criticism of the Kaiser ... These sentiments, however, find small sympathy in the press as a whole, official and unofficial. The tide of popular feeling continues to run strongly in the direction of Anglophobia. Anything the Kaiser could do or say to satisfy this feeling would receive the hearty acclamation of all classes.[442]

Wilhelm was again beloved by his people, and as the first modern media monarch, he knew it. The political truth was becoming more and more obvious: in divided, fractious Imperial Germany, the greatest single sure-fire, across-the-board vote-winner was Anglophobia.

More informed Britons were not blind to this. They knew that it was not just the wild action of one unstable man that was to blame for a message which was, as *The Times* said, 'perilously close to a threat'. If anything, the reverse was true. It was well known that the message had been agreed in cabinet, and the motives of those who had sent it were all too obvious: 'the desire to gratify public opinion in Germany'. For 'to question the fact that German historical and political literature is saturated with a feeling of hostility to Great Britain is like denying that a statue of Nelson stands on a tall column in Trafalgar-Square'.[443] The *Pall Mall Gazette* even claimed that the German government had known of the Jameson Raid in advance and had helped prepare the successful Boer response.[444]

Unlike many people since, thoughtful British observers could see the deeply uncomfortable fact that you could not blame the Kaiser personally, or even any single group of people, for what was by now something approaching a universal feeling. When Wilhelm decided it would be best not to come to Cowes in 1896, given the feelings of his own countrymen, *The Times* did not blame him in the least:

> Unfortunately upon this occasion the EMPEROR cannot act solely in accordance with what we may hope are his own feelings and desires. He is obliged to pay attention to the feelings and the desires of others who look upon England and Englishmen with eyes very different from his. There exist, unhappily, men and circles in Germany who regard our Constitution, our habits of thought, our commercial and industrial greatness, and our success as a colonizing Empire with a bitter detestation incomprehensible

to us. They are not all of the same classes,
social or political. They do not all hate us
for the same reasons. Indeed, the reasons why
some of them hate us have little or no relation
with the reasons why others cherish towards us
the same amiable sentiment. But whatever their
differences and their mutual animosities even,
they do agree in cultivating a hearty dislike and
distrust of the English race and name.

The unlikely and thoroughly unexpected honeymoon of half-English Wilhelm and England was well and truly over – and Wilhelm's subjects were heartily glad of it. So were the British: Salisbury himself later told the Kaiser that if a single German soldier had landed in the Transvaal (this had been seriously mooted in Germany) no British government could have survived without an immediate declaration of war on Germany herself.

By another fateful coupling of events, the Transvaal Crisis ushered in the very year when Britons at last realised that Germany was a truly mortal competitor in the business of business.

Made in Germany (or on Mars)

The Kruger Telegram was not the only thing marked 'Made in Germany' which outraged the British in 1896: the other one was a book of that name.

As with Japanese penetration of America and Europe in the 1970s, and as with China in recent years, Germany's initial way of 'securing a foothold in the greatest market in the world' was not with heavy metal, but by supplying, at prices with which domestic manufacturers could not possibly compete, what we would now call accessories and gadgets: 'small articles which excite the interest of ladies and of those traders who are constantly in search of novelties'.[445]

By the mid-1890s, the world's first modern consumer society was finding that 'since the Merchandise Marks Act has made us familiar with the label "manufactured in Germany" we have many of us been surprised to find that so many things we thought made here were imported'.[446] It was slowly dawning on Britons that simply marking goods 'Made in Germany' was not stopping rational British consumers from buying shoddy tat – because German products were no longer shoddy tat at all. The mark had become 'the reverse of injurious'.[447]

E. E. Williams's 1896 *Made in Germany* was a vast and instant best-seller, thanks to its simple and timely thesis: Britain was living in a fool's paradise if she thought German industry was so competitive just for passing reasons of sneaky tricks or low wages. The hallowed free market would *not* put things right of its own accord. It was time for Britain to awaken.

> For Germany has entered into a deliberate and deadly rivalry with her, and is battling with might and main for the extinction of her supremacy.

The trouble, said Williams, was that the average Briton clove to his national myths about Germany:

> Germany has not the capital, he will tell you; her workmen are no workmen at all; her capitalists and her managers are poor bureaucratic plodders; the world will soon find out that her products are not of English make, and so forth. And he goes on vocalising 'Rule Britannia' in his best commercial prose.[448]

Such deadly smugness had to be abandoned. Low wages were not enough to explain the way Germany was overtaking Britain.

> I do feel it important to beg my readers not to lay too great a stress on the point. No one is likely to minimise its effects; but there is great danger of making too much of it, and neglecting other causes, the

wholesome contemplation of which is likely to have more fruitful results than can accrue from a continued appeal to English workers to work longer and ask less wages.[449]

Having dispensed with the myth of low German wages, thus rendering his argument safe for the working and clerking classes, Williams listed many rational reasons for Germany's export success, most of which will be familiar to modern readers: the Germans were better educated, technically and in foreign languages; the state subsidised German industries, protected them with tariffs and encouraged them with active support from commercial attachés and the like; the Germans went for long-term market share, even if it meant selling below cost at first; their business leaders lived modestly, not like some new class of nabobs and – still more shocking to the English commercial mind – they even sometimes *deliberately* limited their dividends to shareholders in favour of reinvestment in, and securing of, the business.

---

[1] For example, one Rhenish ironworks makes it a rule, whatever its profits, not to pay a higher dividend than 5 per cent. The rest goes into a reserve fund, and a fund for the purchase of fresh and improved plant and machinery.

But when all was said and done, this was all mere statistical window-dressing. The real reason for German success was profounder and more mysterious: 'Lastly,' Williams concluded, 'let me reiterate that the great cause of German success is an alert progressiveness, contrasting brilliantly with the conservative stupor of ourselves.'[450]

The only way for Britain to save at least *some* of what she still had left – that was the best prospect that Williams could hold out to his readers – was nothing short of a radical national awakening.

Made in Germany was not a rational programme for improving Britain's economic survivability in the face of Germany, but a gloom-ridden tract disguised by professional jargon and well-researched 'colour'. It makes a fascinating pair with *The War of the Worlds* – which

H. G. Wells was writing just as *Made in Germany* broke like a freezing wave on the mesmerised British reading public.

Famously, Wells's invading Martians (who bear a distinct resemblance, in their patience, planning, coldness and near-omniscience, to the Prussian general staff of the invasion scares of the 1870s) are defeated not by modern power, or even by British pluck, but by a simple, biological factor – an essential, timeless force which no one could have foreseen. The feeling is exactly the same in *Made in Germany*: there, just as in *The War of the Worlds*, logic proclaims inevitable demise; hope is only to be found in some kind of completely indescribable turnaround in things.

In the end, after all his reams of statistics and claims about research, Williams's plea was simply for Britons to be 'ever alert and watchful', which sounds curiously like the admonition in the Gospel According to Mark (13:37). In the face of impossibly advanced Germans and Martians, the only thing that could save Britain was a miracle.

Made in Germany is thus a relic not of economic history, but of a profound existential fear in the face of Germany – and *only* in the face of Germany.

Williams clearly suggested that German competition was uniquely malevolent. He several times admitted that the USA was also successfully competing with Britain, and at one point evidently felt that his readers might want to know why he wasn't prophesying about this threat as well:

> As for the United States, in some departments it seems to be knocking English goods clean out of the market, even in England. It is not for me to discuss the question in this place. But I note it in passing, for the purpose of reminding my readers how vital is the necessity of a stand against the still more insidious and deadly practice of the German.[451]

But isn't a lost market a lost market whomever you lose it to? So why was *German* competition 'more insidious and deadly' to Britain than

American competition? Williams does not say. But the answer is surely clear: to rage against American competition didn't sell books, because the British quite simply did not – do not – regard being overtaken, or even assimilated, by America as a terrifying national catastrophe.

Theoretically, Britain and America actually came closer to war in 1895 over Venezuela than Britain had ever done with Germany, yet there was so little sense of abiding dislike that, within three years, the two were clearly acting for all practical purposes as one in the Pacific – against Germany. There might well seem to be logical reasons for Britain and America to fight it out (Leon Trotsky was still famously sure it was bound to happen as late as 1927), but when it actually came to it, the idea was simply a non-starter. If America beat us at business or colonisation ... well, after all, they were not really so different to us.

But Germany was a different matter. If Germany overtook and humiliated Britain, that would mean the victory of something 'insidious and deadly', of a power so foreign as to be almost alien. America's triumph could be wishfully seen as a baton-pass; Germany's triumph would mean the end of the world as Britons knew it.

Williams must have guessed that this irrational level was his USP, for he chose to place right at the start of his book a very striking quotation from the newly ex-PM Lord Rosebery himself:

" MADE IN GERMANY "

LORD ROSEBERY (at Colchester):—" Germany has long been—20, 30, or 40 years—ahead of us in technical education. I am afraid of Germany. Why am I afraid of the Germans? Because I admire and esteem them so much. They are an industrious nation ; they are, above all, a systematic nation they are a scientific nation, and whatever they take up, whether it be the arts of peace or the arts of war, they push them forward to the utmost possible perfection with that industry, that system, that science which is part of their character.

Rosebery was *afraid* of things in the Germans which you could not blame them for. These things were simply in the German nature, in themselves admirable. Just like Wells's Martians, who (says the book) couldn't be morally blamed for treating us as we treated the natives in our colonies, Germany was not our deadly rival because of the things she *did* – but simply because of what she *was*.

The premier partner in Prussia & Co.

By 1896, there was no doubt what Germany was to Britons. She was a 'socialistically' organised state which had an agenda (i.e. to outdo Britain) that was being consciously pursued all the way to the very, All-Highest top.

When Wilhelm went to Arabia in 1898, he went, Britons were certain, not simply as a monarch, but as part of a corporate state:

> The modern Crusader is no dreaded foe,
> But the premier partner in Prussia and
>   Co. !
>   He has personal charms,
>   But his mightiest arms
> Are his price-lists, and, say, a yard
>   measure or so ;
> So the Caliph is happy to have such a
>   guest,
> For German-made trifles are much in
>   request,
>
>   And the infidel horde,
>   We are told, can't afford
> To go to Great Britain, and purchase the
>   best.

It was by now clear that despite having broken all the basic, and supposedly universal, rules of British-style progress – free trade, political liberalism and a non-interfering state – Germany was actually working *better* than Britain in almost every meaning of the word. Most graphically terrifying of all, Germany was forging ahead of Britain in spectacularly modern fields, as the brother of a man who was about to immortalise himself pointed out:

AN AERIAL STEAMSHIP.

TO THE EDITOR OF THE TIMES.

Sir,—Having lately had the opportunity of inspecting the vast contrivance now being " made in Germany " which is expected shortly to plough its way through the realms of the air even as the Atlantic liner glides over the waters, I may perhaps be allowed once more to call attention to the great importance of the advent of such an innovation.

It was time for Britons to realise, wrote Major Baden Baden-Powell (for he it was) from the Guards Club, London, on 17 October 1896, that 'wars in the future will without doubt be decided in the air' and that they had better follow the lead of 'our energetic cousins' with all speed, though such technology had 'hitherto baffled our ingenuity'.

By now, Germany was, beyond doubt, the main potential enemy in the eyes of most Britons. *The Times* was, after all, informing them straight out that 'the paramount necessity of the moment is to bring home to the German mind the fact that England will concede nothing to menaces'.[452] No wonder that less careful, and more populist, newsmen quickly hit on the obvious but radical solution which Britain's diplomats would take another decade to make reality. It was, in fact, nothing new, being exactly the same constellation of powers to tame Germany of which Disraeli had spoken in both 1864 and 1875: Germany's open hostility, said the *Pall Mall Gazette*, had gratuitously brought Britain 'within measurable distance of an agreement with France and Russia'.[453]

> Nor need France be forsaken,
>   Proud, generous, mighty France,
> The paths that she has taken
>   Have always meant advance.
> No retrogressive German
>   Whose " friendship" seems to be
>   A fruitless weed,
>   A broken reed,
>   Stamped " made in Germany !"
> Great Britain, France, and Russia,
>   What might is in those names !
> Pretence, your name is Prussia,
>   With all your futile claims.
> France, Russia, and Great Britain,
>   Who can withstand their might,
>   If they lift high
>   The noble cry,
> For God and for the Right ?

The full constellation of 1914 was in the British mind – once again – by 1897. On 11 September of that year, the *Saturday Review* made it plain just how bad things had become between the two supposed relations:

> Prince Bismarck has long recognised what at length the people of England are beginning to understand—that in Europe there are two great, irreconcilable, opposing forces, two great nations who would make the whole world their province, and who would levy from it the tribute of commerce. England, with her long history of successful aggression, with her marvellous conviction that in pursuing her own interests she is spreading light among nations dwelling in darkness, and Germany, bone of the same bone, blood of the same blood, with a lesser will-force, but, perhaps, with a keener intelligence, compete in every corner of the globe. In the Transvaal, at the Cape, in Central Africa, in India and the East, in the islands of the

> Southern sea, and in the far North-West, wherever—and where has it not?—the flag has followed the Bible and trade has followed the flag, there the German bagman is struggling with the English pedlar. Is there a mine to exploit, a railway to build, a native to convert from breadfruit to tinned meat, from temperance to trade gin, the German and the Englishman are struggling to be first. A million petty disputes build up the greatest cause of war the world has ever seen. If Germany were extinguished to-morrow, the day after to-morrow there is not an Englishman in the world who would not be the richer. Nations have fought for years over a city or a right of succession ; must they not fight for two hundred million pounds of commerce?

The Marxist idea of capitalist rivalry really was true by 1897, but it had such power over the British imagination for reasons that were far older, and nothing to do with economics. America was a rival in trade; France, in Africa; Russia, in Asia. But only Germany was all these things. And only Germany seemed to represent an entirely different, corporate way of ordering society that actually, scarily, *worked*.

In 1897, Britons still had no rational grounds to fear the Germans militarily. France and Russia were balefully united against Germany, and the Imperial German Navy was not remotely a threat to Britain – it had been allowed to decay so far from its high point in 1878 that the *König Wilhelm*, the same ship which had rammed the *Grosser Kurfürst* off Folkestone, was still on active service.[454]

But that is, of course, the whole point: by 1897, there was already no need for normal diplomatic-military grounds to the Anglo-German hostility.

Still, Admiral Tirpitz was about to put that one right.

The Tirpitz Plan: class warfare (but not as we know it)

Historians still argue in entire books about what the Tirpitz Plan *really* was, the problem being that Tirpitz not only very obviously lied about his plans to the Reichstag, but seems also to have been unable to say exactly what he was aiming at to his closest circle – even to himself. The best guess is that his ambitions grew each time they succeeded in clearing a hurdle, so that what was originally meant simply to force the mighty Royal Navy (under whose wing the young Tirpitz had trained) into treating Germany as a desirable naval ally, eventually turned into a heady dream of actually defeating it in a one-to-one war.*

The British were well aware, by late 1896, that something big was going on in Germany and that Wilhelm 'has been fired with the idea of a fleet and an empire like our own'.[455] But events which, in retrospect, seem to be utterly clear have a habit of not appearing so at the time. Britons simply had no conception of just how greatly, and how quickly, things were about to change: they no more expected Germany to declare a real move to contest the Channel than the USN now expects China to announce that it is flooding the Pacific with brand-new submarines and aircraft carriers.[†]

It was a shock when the 'gigantic scheme' was sprung upon the world – and, indeed, upon the Reichstag. However, The Times was convinced that 'the whole matter is in truth somewhat of a mystery'[456] and remained confident that the wild plan had no chance of passing 'unless recourse be had to a *coup d'etat*'.[457] Any sane professional would be sure to realise this, and 'the appointment of Admiral Tirpitz to the Secretaryship of the Marine is a guarantee that the extreme projects which may have found advocates in naval circles will in no case be countenanced by the Emperor's responsible advisers'.[458] By

---

* On 29 January 1900, Tirpitz told the Staatsministerium that one of the advantages of his enhanced plan was that the army could now 'be as economical as possible'. This was because '*Weltpolitik* implies making our defences strong in such a way as to secure our borders and avoid the need for immediate mobilization of the whole German army.' Since it was quite impossible, in the constellation of 1900, that Germany would ever fight Russia without mobilising on the French border, or vice versa, the implication was clear: Tirpitz had in mind a war in which other powers would merely be deterred by the German Army standing on the defensive, while the German Navy fought Britain alone.

† As she is now perfectly capable of doing. At present, China – just like Germany up to 1900 – claims that her vast shipbuilding capability is merely employed in modernising and replacing existing vessels.

'extreme projects', *The Times*, at this stage, could imagine nothing more incredible than 'a fleet equal to that of France'.

The mantra was repeatedly mouthed that no country could possibly afford a great navy as well as a great army. The idea that anyone in Germany was thinking of going *mano a mano* with the Royal Navy was too fantastic even to occur to Britons.

What they did not realise – or had forgotten – was that the idea of a mighty fleet was not just a pet of militarist German 'naval circles', but an old and popular obsession. Tirpitz's vital supporters were *not* the traditional 'right wing'. On the contrary, as one German historian puts it, 'to the Prussian conservatives and landowners, everything to do with the fleet was suspect', and it was only the appalling thought of going into the lobbies alongside the Socialists which stopped them from actually voting against Tirpitz.[459]

Tirpitz's vital backers were the National Liberals, the voice of Protestant state-centralisation, industry and technocracy. The media programme launched by his propaganda bureau in 1897 was headed by a phalanx of tame media professors, each desperate to become the new Treitschke, and was decades ahead of its time. It made many of the earliest cinema films in Germany for its national road-shows, and this is no coincidence: the people who wanted to arm up against England and go full steam ahead for 'world politics' were not the scar-faced aristocrats but the early adopters of a shiny, technocratic modernity. The Imperial German Navy, conceptually non-Junker, quintessentially mechanised, tied to age-old Greater German dreams of winning a British-style empire, was to become their great cause.

This is strikingly clear in one of the most famous German fantasies ignited by the Tirpitz Plan. *The Coming Conquest of England* (1904) ends with the Kaiser about to enter London, following a grand naval victory. But the author is not dreaming of a triumph for a reactionary aristocracy. The heroic German Chancellor explains that, in her victory, Germany must not embrace 'a false agrarian policy', but help the merchant and industrial classes:

Your Royal Highness! The bargain which gave up Zanzibar to get Heligoland would never have been possible if our diplomacy had shown the same far-sightedness and intelligence as the English in economic questions, which I can only designate by the honourable title of a 'business-like spirit.' This business-like spirit is the mainspring of industry and agriculture, of trade and handicrafts, as of all industrial life generally, and it is necessary that this business-like spirit should also be recognised in our ministries as the necessary condition for the qualification to judge of the economic interests of the people. In this respect our statesmen and officials and our industrial classes can learn more from our vanquished enemy than in anything else. England owes her greatness to being 'a nation of shopkeepers,' while our economic development and our external influence has been hindered more than anything else by the contempt with which the industrial classes have been treated amongst us up to the most recent times. In England the merchant has always stood higher in the social scale than the officer and official. Amongst us he is looked upon almost as a second-class citizen compared with the other two.

Part of the fantasy of defeating England militarily was for Germany to become more like England socially.

The navy was the ideal vehicle for such radical feelings. Tirpitz's office became a state-run conduit of gigantic cost-plus contracts for burgeoning industries, and a vista of endless career-cum-social prospects for men on the make who had nothing whatever to do with, and nothing whatever to expect from, the caste-ridden, landowning Junkers.

The architects of the Navy Laws knew all this perfectly well, and they sometimes sound bizarrely like outright class warriors themselves. It's hard to recall that the man here consigning the backward, agrarian Junkers to the dustbin of history by sheer necessity is not some Red professor, but a senior officer of the Imperial German Navy:

Sea-interests and Agrarian ambitions will be brought again into opposition with one another [by a renewed drive for the navy] and the belief in the fleet will not win ground on Agrarian soil … The contradiction between Industry and the Agrarian lobby will be ever sharper … ultimately, in response to the pressure of conditions, the industrial direction will be victorious.*[460]

The drive for a big new German navy was not a 'right wing' policy, if by that we mean a conservative one. It was a *socially radical* movement which appealed to the dreams of the non-Junker classes. Of course, Wilhelm personally wanted a big fleet to force England into loving him (just as he wanted a special yacht to beat Edward). But Wilhelm wanted an awful lot of things personally from 1888–1914 which he never came close to getting. His fleet, he did get – and he knew very well why. He himself said, in 1896, that he wanted to *exploit* anti-English feeling in order to press for it.[461] To Wilhelm, the true cause and effect was perfectly clear: the reason he was going to get his fantasy navy was that so many of his people shared the dream.

In March 1898, the bill passed the Reichstag and Britons blinked: 'Germany has now definitely embarked on a policy of large naval expansion.'[462] And yet they still did not want to believe the evidence of their eyes. After all, the figures showed that the Navy Law of 1898 would still leave the German Navy (just) inferior to the French or Russian. You could hardly argue with that, really, and Tirpitz assured the Reichstag itself, on the anniversary of the passing of the law, that he wanted no more.

He was lying, of course, and merely awaiting the moment when the Reichstag, in which conservatives and Catholics had so nearly scuppered his law in 1898, would be more malleable.

It was not long in coming.

Meanwhile, though, the Kaiser's navy was about to create, witlessly, something that would ultimately doom all its ambitions.

---

* This is a good reminder that the notions, and the very language, of Marxism are simply those of the German culture from which they sprang – a culture in which almost everybody who believed in progress, whether they were of 'the left' or 'the right', believed that it took place as a series of more or less literal battles between implacably opposed groups.

Germany creates the special relationship

Manila Bay, in July 1898, presented a curious spectacle. Admiral Dewey had just annihilated the Spanish fleet there in short order, but his was not the most powerful unit now present. A strangely large German squadron had gathered, commanded by a full admiral, easily outgunning all the other visiting navies and even the victorious USN itself. The Kaiser's force was blatantly in excess of any legitimate 'observation unit'.

Admiral Diederichs hung around inexplicably, week after week, giving vague but implicit hope to the defeated Spanish, with whom he seemed to have notably good relations: not only that, he somehow contrived to order his ships about, day by day, in such a way as to gratuitously enrage the bellicose Dewey.

No one, in 1898, could fathom what the Germans were actually up to and no one since has really explained it either. One way or another, it's hard to resist the idea that the Kaiserliche Marine, which had just won a highly political battle in its homeland for a gigantic increase in funding and knew itself the darling of its emperor, was simply feeling too big for its boots.

Whatever Diederichs intended by his bumptious manoeuvrings, he certainly drew the fire of the American press:[463]

> The performances of Admiral DIEDER-
> ICH at Manila continue to excite the at-
> tention of all beholders. The latest of
> them is perhaps the most extraordinary.

Dewey not only worked out plans to fight, if need be, the more powerful Germans, but even spoke of this to American journalists. At the height of the tension, a German officer came aboard his flagship to demand the respect due to ships flying the Imperial German Ensign. Dewey replied that such flags 'could be bought for half a dollar a yard anywhere' and added that 'if your people are ready for war with the United States, they can have it at any time'.[464]

The Royal Navy, as befitted the greatest marine and colonial power on Earth, had a couple of what we would now call 'significant assets' at Manila as well. What precisely, if anything, was discussed by the Americans and British, and how far, if at all, their officials were involved as well as the seamen on the spot, is still debated by naval historians. Some versions of the story have the Royal Navy actually sailing in to block the German line of fire at a vital moment, others limit British intervention to having the Royal Marines Band pointedly strike up 'The Stars and Stripes' as the German and American ironclads passed close by them.

At any rate, Diederichs felt obliged to call personally on the RN commander, Captain Edward Chichester, in order to find out what he would do in the event of a battle between the USN and the Imperial German Navy. Chichester's memorable reply did so much to improve Anglo-American relations that it is engraved to this day on a wall of the US Naval School at Annapolis: 'That is a matter known only to Dewey and me.'

Whatever the facts and details, the general impression was clear as day: when it came to the Germans, the British were, by 1898, ready to place themselves, in effect, under the command of the Americans at a moment's notice and without waiting for orders from London. They were even happy to help celebrate the greatest day in the calendar of the ex-colony whose capital city they had burned less than ninety years before, a gesture not lost on the *New York Times*:[465]

THANKSGIVING DAY AT MANILA.

Observed by British as Well as Americans—Banquet to Officers.

The sudden new warmth between two powers who had, theoretically at least, come close to blows over Venezuela in 1895 was shown in spades at Samoa a year later. The island was notionally under tripartite governance, but the Germans complained that majority voting was a sham, since the British and Americans always voted together. The two camps backed rival contenders for the throne, and in early 1899 full-scale local war broke out. King Mataafa won 'by the help of violence, treachery, German arms and German leadership'.[466] In the chaos, it very nearly came to a shooting fight between the Anglo-Americans and the Germans.

The American Chief Justice of Samoa was in no doubt as to the great (Hegel would have said, the world-historical) significance of what happened:[467]

> " Here was a mixture of English and American feeling which, though developed in this far-away little island in the Pacific, means more than a Faneuil Hall or Cooper Union oratorical discussion —an American citizen occupying an official position under a treaty between England, Germany, and the United States flagrantly broken by Germany's representatives and defended by the two Anglo-Saxon peoples ; the British and the United States Consuls acting in perfect accord.; American and British subjects on shore ready to mingle their blood in defence of their rights ; a British man-of-war protecting Americans, as thoroughly as Britishers, guarding the women and children of both nationalities with its guns ready to do service as well and as sincerely in behalf of the American as the British flag."

The special relationship, though as yet unchristened, was already a diplomatic fact in the Western Pacific – and Chancellor von Bülow, for one, knew it. Had his insight been taken seriously by German diplomacy, things might have turned out very differently for the whole world:

> The question of good relations with the British fleet and authorities becomes of considerably higher importance on account of the undoubted rapprochement which has taken place between England and the United States, even if it has not yet reached the stage of a binding alliance. Every disturbance of our relations with these two States would be succeeded unfailingly by a rapprochement between them, in spite of any differences.[468]

Unfortunately for all of us, Tirpitz and his legions of professorial tub-thumpers came to a different conclusion: Britain was only friendly with America, and hostile to Germany, because the Americans played hard-ball, while the Germans were too accommodating.

By now, it was almost impossible for wiser diplomatic counsel to prevail anyway. How *could* Germany have 'good relations with the British fleet and authorities'? Whatever her diplomats might want, they nowadays had to clear agreements with the German electorate, who, spurred on by Tirpitz's formidable, cutting-edge publicity machine, were on the lookout for any sign of Anglophile weakness overseas. On 25 March 1899 the German Ambassador in London sent a coded message describing how he had warned Joseph Chamberlain that if Britain and America continued to gang up on Germany in Samoa,

> it would be quite useless for me to continue my former efforts for an Anglo-German rapprochement, and that, even if it desired it, my Government, when faced with the inevitable irritation of our public opinion, would be unable to continue its hitherto friendly attitude towards England.

By 1899, dealings between the two most powerful empires, and the largest bi-lateral traders, in the world could be determined by 'the inevitable irritation of public opinion' over something as insignificant as whether a tiny island on the far side of the world would be ruled by the local king the Germans wanted or the local king the Anglo-Americans wanted.

This super-heated feeling exploded that very year over something that was, at first sight, nothing whatever to do with Germany: the Boer War.

PART SEVEN:
FEAR AND LOATHING

The hate grows hot

Here, pictures really are worth far more than words. In 1899, there was no sane way in which isolated England could have been seen as any kind of real and present threat to Germany. And yet little, if anything, in all the life-and-death propaganda of 1914–18 exceeds the visceral, at times almost pornographic, modernity with which mainstream German satirists attacked Britain in the biggest-selling magazines during the Boer War. The sheer hatred in these pictures makes it plain that, as far as many Germans were concerned, the Boer War was not just about the Boers.

'From an English despatch: two more victories like this and we will have reached Cape Town.'

'English Concentration Camps'. Edward VII worries that the blood might spatter his crown.

Edward's nightmare: he is carried off to hell for the Boer War.

'In dangling pain'. The mockery is all the more visceral because the title of the grotesque picture is taken from one of Goethe's most famous love poems.

John Bull dances as death cries, 'All Right!'

A hapless British soldier declares: 'Oh, if only it had been "made in Germany" it would surely have lasted better!'

The pictures were no secret to Britons:[469]

> " These papers are not gutter-sheets, but
> are sold everywhere at the stations of the
> State railroads, even at Potsdam Station,
> where the Emperor is constantly traveling.
> He was finally obliged to personally order
> their removal. Neither are these papers
> anonymous. One of the most infamous of
> all, entitled ' The Boer War,' bears on the
> title pages the names of persons dis-
> tinguished in the literary and artistic world
> of Germany. From a purely technical
> standpoint the paper is an art production,
> but it is difficult to find words to convey
> a notion of the filth which its cultured
> artists and writers venture to lay before its
> cultured German readers. British soldiers
> are represented as robbing the dead, Mr.
> Chamberlain's state coach is depicted as a
> cart laden with skeletons, and King Ed-
> ward is shown dead drunk in his bedroom,

This Anglophobia in Germany was not invented, or controlled, by anyone, or by any clique. It was by now a fact, as the *New York Times* repeatedly noted, whether the government or the businessmen of Germany found it convenient or not:[470]

> BERLIN, March 26.—Considerable dis-
> quietude is being felt in Government circles
> regarding the manifestations of anti-Brit-
> ish feeling which have occurred recently,

DEFEAT GLADDENS THE GERMANS.
Berlin Crowds Rejoice Over the News of Gatacre's Reverse.

VON BUELOW REBUKES GERMAN ANGLOPHOBIA

OPPOSE GERMAN ANGLOPHOBIA.
Bremen Chamber of Commerce and the Frankfurter Zeitung Deprecate It.

The *Pall Mall Gazette* suggested that the only reason individual Britons could (usually) go unmolested amid the seething hatred in Germany was Wilhelm II himself: 'The known partiality of the Emperor for things English keeps them in countenance. But the Emperor has suffered because of his so-styled English tendencies.'[471] It was clear to *The Times* as well that 'the passionate enmity of the German people' threatened to become 'a more powerful and permanent factor in moulding the relations of the two countries than the wise and friendly statesmanship of German rulers'.[472]

The *New York Times* wrote of a popular Anglophobia which 'verged on the hysterical', and *The Times* thought German minds utterly poisoned:[473]

> This is only one out of scores of similar falsehoods disseminated every day amongst the German people in newspaper articles, in caricatures, in doggerel rhymes, in novelettes, in music-hall songs, in public meetings—in fact, through every channel by which the eye and the ear can be reached. That our soldiers are bloodthirsty ruffians, that our officers are cruel, licentious brutes, that they outrage women, torture children, and murder prisoners, that the whole policy of the concentration camps has been deliberately conceived with the purpose of killing off the Boer women and children has been dinned so continuously into German ears that the vast majority of the Germans actually believe these things.

As the war went on, German rejoicing in the defeats of the laughably incompetent hirelings in the British Army gave way to the realisation that the decadent British were in fact going to go the whole, brutal way – and that, even without an ally in the world, the power of the Royal Navy meant that there was simply nothing anyone could do to stop them.

More and more, the German press began to take aim at their own government, and even at the Kaiser himself, for being too pro-British. The cartoonists had to be careful, of course, for disrespectful pictures of His Majesty could, and often did, land people in jail, but it was perfectly clear what they meant:

The German Great Dane defers blatantly to the savage English bulldog – i.e. German policy is in thrall to England.

The Boer deputation – poor but honest folk – arrive in Germany only to be told by the Kaiser's official: 'My dear sirs, if your only letter of recommendation is the sympathy of the entire German people, you might as well go straight home.'

'The banning of the torchlight parade which was to have taken place in Cologne in honour of President Kruger has had a positive effect in the place where German policy is determined.'

Victoria tells Joseph Chamberlain not to worry about robbing and murdering Kruger because the Tsar and the Kaiser 'won't disturb us – after all, they are part of the family'.

The cartoons so far have been from Berlin's *Kladderadatsch* and Munich's *Simplicissimus* – but the pictures from the socialist magazine *Der Wahre Jacob* are no less hostile:

Edward sweats as hell beckons for Britain's deeds in 1901.

Nr. 426²⁴   Stuttgart den 18. November   1902

DER WAHRE JACOB

Der Flug des deutschen Imperialismus.

German imperialism is in thrall to the aristocratic British Lion. 'Left' German Anglophobia theorised that the triumph of German state organisation over Britain's ruthless 'Manchester' capitalism would preface the inevitable dawn of world socialism, which everyone (including Lenin, right up until 1917) assumed would be led by the German socialists: in practice, Karl Liebknecht even made cause with the anti-Semites in the Reichstag to attack Wilhelm as too Anglophile.

In these pictures from the socialists' own great satirical magazine, the John Bull who is getting a well-deserved black eye from Kruger has the unmistakable features of anti-Semitic caricature, while the British imperialist money-makers, stoking war in pursuit of profit, are in league with Rothschild.

≫ John Bull am Anfang des neunzehnten Jahrhunderts. ≪

Englische Köche mästen den Ewig-Unzufriedenen mit Liebesgaben. (Nach einem engl. Zeitbild.)

≫ John Bull am Anfang des zwanzigsten Jahrhunderts. ≪

Der Ewig-Unzufriedene ist wüthend, daß diesmal die Liebesgaben ausbleiben.

Socialist gloating about Britain's evident decline was indistinguishable from any other version: the infamous 'donkeys' of the British Army were evidently well known in Germany many years before the Great War.

Nr. 416¼   Stuttgart den 1. Juli   1902

DER WAHRE JACOB

Das südafrikanische Kontingent bei der Krönungsparade in London.

By the end of the Boer War, England had no friends left in Germany.
Well, almost none. The National Liberals saw England as the decadent
old power that needed sweeping from the seas and the colonies so
that the bright new German century could dawn; the Socialists saw
England as the great redoubt of robber capitalism, which needed to
be swept off the Earth so that the bright new socialist millennium –

it would naturally be led from Germany – could dawn; the Catholics were instinctively anti-British for obvious historical reasons; the old Anglophile liberals were a fast-fading rump, their free trade economics baffled by the unstoppable rise of protectionist Germany, their politics mocked as that of mere English dupes, their own convictions understandably shaken by the British use of concentration camps in the war.

The great liberal, Mommsen, is mocked as a mere tool of John Bull, Joseph Chamberlain and the 'meat-eating' British Lion, who secretly laugh at his 'milk of pious thought'.

Which left only those notorious aristocrats – and the Kaiser himself.

Trouble in the crowd

Of all Germans, the least likely to hate Britain were the upper classes.

This is not really surprising. England was just so much safer for aristocracy. There was no equivalent of the blood-and-thunder social democrats of Germany. But that was not all: no one in Britain proclaimed, like the National Liberals, that the modernising, centralising state was the be-all and end-all of national life. German conservatives feared that the logic of excessive state-worship would, as Chancellor von Bülow himself put it, 'pave the way for a republic'.[474] They looked wistfully across the German Ocean at England, that instinctively conservative country which still loved a lord, never mind a monarch, and where no one preached either the workers' revolution or the technocratic state.

The image of England which well-bred Germans, and Wilhelm himself, so loved was exactly the same one which is today still so successful in attracting tax-sheltered international wealth to London's shops. Like Arab princes, Russian oligarchs and African dictators today, the Kaiser and his aristocrats were entranced by the vision of a ruling elite which could go about its pleasures without having to trouble itself in the slightest about revolutionaries or even radicals:

The Aquascutum Coat
FÜR JEDEN ZWECK

Bester und zuverlässiger Regenmantel / Kein Gummi / Für jedes Wetter geeignet, genügt allen hygienischen Ansprüchen / Original Etiquette „Aquascutum Ltd. Regstd." London

In den feinsten Herrenmode- und Sportgeschäften eingeführt. Eventuelle Bezugsquelle durch
RALPH OPPENHEIMER, CHARLOTTENBURG
18 Kaiserdamm :: :: Generalvertreter für den Kontinent

Many German conservatives thus 'spoke English and copied English manners, sports and dress, in a strenuous endeavour to become the very pattern of an English gentleman'.[475] They were led from the top, for Wilhelm himself raced at Cowes, owned the first indoor tennis hall in Germany and for years sent congratulatory telegrams to Oxford whenever they won the Boat Race. When he finally beat Albert Edward at Cowes, his delight was unbounded, if not entirely graceful:

> The Emperor wired to the Sailing Committee at Cowes the following reply to the congratulations on the Meteor's victory in the race for the Queen's Cup:
>
> "Sincerest thanks for kind wishes. So sorry the Empress's mishap forbade my being present. Am overjoyed at winning my grandmother's trophy. The handicap time allowance to the Britannia was simply appalling.   WILHELM. Kiel."

Though Wilhelm and Albert Edward increasingly loathed one another, they were alike in one notable way: both were happy to be seen in non-U or non-von company, so long as it was very, very rich. Both even consorted openly with *Jews*, which was fine in Britain by now, but anathema to Wilhelm's own Prussian aristocracy.

This gives a clue about one of the unspoken attractions of English sport to the rapidly increasing group of rich but sadly untitled, or insufficiently titled, Germans: it offered a social bridge for new wealth in a society obsessed by formal rank. Guides to etiquette made the connection plain: 'der Gentleman' will naturally be kitted out in the latest English innovations:

Die Breeches.[476]

It's no accident that 'der Gentleman' and 'der Sportsman' were not translated into German but imported straight, and even turned into rather bizarre-sounding adjectives.* For it was not just a question of language: the very *ideas* of the gentleman and the sportsman cut across the rigid distinctions of German social rank. At the court of Wilhelm II, there were, among those deemed eligible to get in the doors in the first place, no less than *fifty-one* official, book-noted gradations of persons, each of which decided where you would be sat, to whom you could talk first, whose daughter you could marry, and so on. This almost impossible complexity was aped further down the social classes of Germany. But the British sporting-social tournament was an open one. Provided, naturally, that you could afford to join the club, to take the time off, to kit yourself out with the correct imported English clothing and to learn the correct English expressions, you could hang out with, compete against and maybe even physically up-end chaps who, in everyday life, would feel obliged not to register your social existence.

Sport showed the central difference between porous English *class* and rigid German *caste*.† Mass-market consumer goods might be increasingly 'Made in Germany', but the wherewithal for social climbing was, like the Kaiser's own yacht, his racquets and his tweeds (not to mention his beloved admiral's uniform), most definitely 'Made in England'.

With such instant upward mobility on offer, it's no wonder that wealthy but non-von German men queued up to buy English sporting togs and to learn the arcane secrets of cricket and football:

---

* 'Je unauffälliger der Gentleman von heute reist, desto gentlemanliker ist er.' ('The more unobtrusively today's gentleman travels, the more gentlemanliker he is.') (Franz Koebner, *Der Gentleman*, Berlin, 1913, p. 20.)

† Tirpitz's Navy League also – quite deliberately – offered a forum where people could mix with and even talk over their social betters in a way which traditional conservative politics had never permitted. Since everyone there was there because they wanted a mighty fleet and hated England, the bigger you wanted that fleet and the more you hated England, the more right you had to speak: a radicalisation of the demands was thus built in, and was powered by a subterranean revolt against the existing social order.

Football.

eingebürgert und dürfte das von allen Jugendspielen am meisten bei uns ge-
triebene sein. Z. B. spielen es an meinem jetzigen Gymnasium die Schüler
der beiden oberen Klassen fast das ganze Jahr hindurch mit großem Eifer.

Statt der Wickets haben wir beim Fußball zwei übermannshohe Thore
(goals), über welche der große Ball mit dem Fuße hinübergetrieben
werden muß. Dieselben bestehen aus je zwei etwa zwei bis drei Fuß

Fußball.   Fußball (andere Form).

Tennis was perhaps the most perfect example of why English sport was
so attractive to the newly rich. In normal life, the daily social round of
a young German lady of splendid, part-royal pedigree, like Countess
Clara von der Schulenburg, comprised a series of obsessive decisions
about who was, or was not, fit even to be acknowledged in the street
by her, never mind who might escort her to a dance or be sat next to

Ausführung des Dropstoßes
(aus: F. Heineken, Fußball, Stuttgart 1896, S. 176)

her at table. Yet she was perfectly able to play serious mixed doubles
with Reggie Doherty, four times Wimbledon singles champion but
otherwise a man without a title to his name.[*]

Graced with All-Highest approval, and as yet demanding little in the
way of undignified sweat, *das Lawn-Tennis* was the perfect theatre of
dress, manners, health, leisure and income for New Money: still blackballed from the royal court, it could hit with aristocracy on the grass
court. This advertisement for the *Official Journal of the German
Football and Cricket Union as Well as of All Major Lawn-Tennis and
Other Sporting Clubs* shows the direct connection between wanting to
do English sport and wanting to *sound like* moneyed Englishmen:

[*] Together, they beat the Comte and Mlle de Robiglio at Monte Carlo in 1902.

The first German handbook of tennis, published in 1887 by Robert Freiherr (that is, old-nobility baron) von Fichard, is indeed much concerned with the issue of which language to chat in while on court. Like the Kaiser, Fichard had English blood and he was proud to state that the *Pall Mall Gazette* called him 'the amiable baron'. By the time of the 1895 edition, the Anglophile author was evidently aware that some people in Germany considered tennis politically dubious. Still, he insisted that 'it would be a complete misunderstanding of our mission if we were to rob the game of its English name and expressions'. He also provided a helpful guide to pronunciation, so that even Germans who did not actually speak English could sound the thing at fashionable places like Bad Homburg, where, by 1896, 'not only the red-locked English Miss but the blue-eyed daughter of the Teuton smacks the tiny ball about'.[477]

Das Lawn Tennis. 31

Englisch	Aussprache	Übersetzung
bye	bai	Rast (Aussetzen in der ersten Runde eines Tourniers)
court	kohrt	Spielplatz
cut	katt	Drehung des Balles
cross drive	krossdreiw	Schlag quer über den Spielplatz
deuce	djus	Einstand, gleich, (40 : 40)
deuce game (auch deuce games all)	djus gähm	Partieeinstand
double	dobbel	Spiel zu 3 oder 4
double faults	dobbel fohlts	2 Aufschlagfehler (= 15 oder 1 Punkt)
drive stroke	dreiwstrohk	Treibschlag
drive down the side line	dreiw daun de seidlein	Flankenschlag
drive volley	dreiwwollä	Treibflugschlag
dropstroke	droppstrohk	Fallschlag (kurzer Hochschlag)
fife all	feif öhl	5 Spiele gleich (auf)
fault	fohlt	Fehler, Verstoß (= 15)
footfault	futtfohlt	Fußfehler
forty	fohrti	40 (40 : 40 = deuce)
forehand (stroke)	fohrhänd	Vorhand(schlag)
four games all	fohr gähms öhl	4 Partien gleich
four handed game	fohr händ'd gähm	Spiel zu vier Personen
game	gähm	Spiel, Partie
games all	gähms öhl	Partie gleich
gravel courts	gräwwel kohrts	Harte Spielplätze
ground	graund	Boden, Spielplatz
half court line	hahlf kohrt lein	Mittellinie
half volley	half wöllä	Sprungschlag
handicap	händicäpp	Spiel mit Vorgaben
handicapper	händicäpper	derjenige, welcher die Vorgaben verteilt
in play	in plai	im Spiel
lawn tennis	laun tenniss	Rasenballspiel
left	lefft	links
let	lett	Versuchsball
line	lein	Linie
line umpire	lein ampeir	Linienrichter
lob	lohb	Hochflugball

But the atmosphere of the off-field Anglo-German game was becoming hard to ignore, however much one enjoyed playing *der Gentleman*. The amiable Baron fell foul of the editors of the *Zeitschrift des Allgemeinen Deutschen Sprachvereins* (*Journal of the All-German Language Association*) in 1897, for writing that the All-England Club had authorised his suggestions for translating certain basic tennis terms: it was not, the outraged linguists declared, up to any English body to authorise anything in the German language!

The different editions of Fichard's book provide some of those little social details which say so much about the general state of Anglo-German play. In 1895, he could still confidently proclaim the essential Englishness of tennis as part of its charm, advise his readers to buy British tennis balls rather than German ones and suggest consulting *The Gentlewoman* of 24 March 1892 to source the proper attire. But rival tennis guides began to warn their readers to be careful with their on-court chat since 'many people complain of the players' love for English expressions and accuse them of Anglomania', [478] or to suggest that players should translate phrases so that 'the masses' would not see playing tennis as 'objectionable foreignness'. [479]

The picture is clear: as the sport trickled slowly downward, posh German tennis players were coming under fire *from below* for being too Anglophile. With such pressure from off-court, by 1911, Fichard felt obliged to tell his readers that it was 'a matter of honour' to use German terms and thus 'nationalise' tennis. The adverts say the same thing, now admonishing patriotic Germans to play with German balls:

Deutsche, spielt mit deutschen Tennisbällen!

Standard Harburg-Wien ist der einzige vom Deutschen Lawn-Tennis-Bunde anerkannte deutsche Turnierball

One classic British sporting occasion sums it all up. In 1896, Wilhelm decided that it would be best not to go to Cowes Week that year, so bad were feelings between the two countries after the Kruger Telegram. He did send his yacht, though, which had been especially designed and built at no expense spared, in Britain, to beat that of the Prince of Wales. When she indeed won, *The Times* made the mistake of mentioning Wilhelm's English blood and boatyard in praising his victory. The outrage in Germany at this dreadful insult was audible right across the Atlantic:

It would, indeed, be difficult to imagine anything more at variance with the sportsmanlike spirit of the Emperor William than the attitude adopted with regard to this incident by the German press, which alludes to the contents of your article as "monstrous," "impertinent imputations," "insolent presumption," "an incomparable piece of impudence," and so on. Instead of taking advantage of a favorable opportunity for a mutual exchange of congratulations on events far removed from the sphere of politics, the German press has once more burst out into senseless invective rivaling its language in the early months of the present year because, forsooth, the yacht was English, the waters were English, and The Times suggested that there was some English blood in the veins of the German Emperor.

For there were many Germans who did not want to play tennis and sound like Englishmen – and did not want their emperor to do so either. At the revived 1896 Olympics (which were a huge triumph for the USA):

the Germans wisely confined themselves for the most part to those gymnastic exercises at which they are so extraordinarily proficient ... the German high jumper stood to attention for half a minute after each jump, apparently supposing that it was more important to appear to be undisturbed after a jump than to clear a respectable height.[*][480]

---

* Hardly any British athletes competed, apparently because they assumed, until too late, that any chap with a Blue would naturally be *invited* to Athens rather than have to *apply*.

To many people in Germany, English sports were just another example
of the dreaded process whereby Germandom was yielding ground, even
at home, to cultural Englishness. How could true Germans give themselves names like Berlin Britannia or Viktoria (two of the earliest football
clubs)? You do not have to read German to grasp the frothing outrage
in the pages of *Fusslümmelei: Stauchballspiel und englische Krankheit*
(*Foot-Boorishness: Ball-Crushing and the English Disease*), written by a
patriotically Germanic teacher of gymnastics in 1898. He simply cannot
abide the sight of a German fool, suffering from an adoration for all that
is foreign, 'putting on colourful rags got fresh from Albion and a big,
broad, English bulldog-face' to take part in these decadent sports:

> Oder ist etwa die verfluchte deutsche Fremdsucht dabei nicht im
> Spiel? Ei, so sieh ihn doch an, den feuchtohrigen Laffen, wie er mit
> seinen bunten, frisch aus Albion geholten Flicken und dem breitesten
> englischen Bulldoggengesicht dem erstaunten Repsbauern sein „half-time"
> „Full-backs" „scrummage" entgegenfletscht! Wer das mit ansehen muß,
> dessen Geduld ist „out", er macht einen wütenden „try", den ganzen Fuß-
> ball- „match" und „matsch" mit einem „Kick" in die Luft zu sprengen.

> schönsten Schnitzbuckel der Welt dem Teufel zugeritten! Wer wird heut-
> zutag noch gehen oder laufen!*) Wie unmodern! How little zeit-
> gemäß! How unfashionable! Cricket matches! Tennis tournaments!
> And oh! last not least: Rowing, Rowing! Juniors! Seniors! We
> must have challenge cups, first prizes and so on! Also setzte er
> sich — welches Glück! — abermals auf seine lieben vier Buchstaben,
> gampte in Gondeln, tollte in Dollenbooten, verschaffte sich gigs und
> allerlei Gigerlzeug, hip, hip, hurrah!

Making it abundantly clear that he is not really talking about sport at all,
the author finishes his book-length rant by saying that Germans should
by now have outgrown the need to take lessons from their 'loving neighbour' and should 'leave it to Rhodes to dedicate football-pitches, and to
Jameson to trample the clear rights of other peoples underfoot!'*

---

* It is perhaps no wonder that the athletic but apoplectic author died of a heart-attack, aged only
forty-eight, shortly after publishing his little book.

True German athletics was all about teamwork, discipline, work-rate and grace, whereas 'Anglo-Saxon' sports were simply an enactment of the ruthless, prize-oriented individualism which their cultures pursued at all costs – even to the participants themselves. General von Bernhardi, one of the most open prophets of war against Britain, blamed their addiction to sports for the fact that the English were now decadent: organised games had 'usurped the place of serious work … England has more and more become a nation of gentlemen at ease and sportsmen', no longer spiritually fit for the 'great duties' of a world power.[481] This cartoon from the programme of the Ninth German Gymnastics Festival of 1898 leaves little doubt as to whether the bizarrely developed, if not crocked, pursuers of British sports or the classically perfect German athlete is going to be the more useful citizen to his nation:

But *why* did the question of which kind of sport to play generate such hysteria? Surely a country so obviously powerful, and growing in power, could be sure of itself?

The fear of assimilation

The curiously intense battle over sport in Germany reveals one of the most mysterious and fatal aspects of the new empire: that for all their new might – industrial, military and cultural – many Germans were haunted by the fear of being somehow completely overwhelmed by foreignness. In the eighteenth century, the nemesis had been France; in the twentieth, it would be America; in the nineteenth, it was England.

The root of this fear was that Englishness was so fatally attractive. Men like the notorious German colonialist Karl Peters, whose Heart-of-Darkness behaviour was so blatant as to make him officially unacceptable even then, and who repaired his fortunes by retiring to Britain and writing the bestseller *England und die Engländer*, saw no reason whatever to hide from their readers that they openly admired the British Empire. This, after all, was the story at the old core of all German imperial dreams.

How could one *not* want to be like a race which ruled most of the world, 'irrespective of whether it is under the Union Jack or the Stars and Stripes' and yet 'sticks fast to its own national character wherever it goes'? How could you not wish that your own culture promised a 'grand citizenly polity' of men who strove as free individuals, yet worked together as one, 'dragging their tea-pots and marmalade with them wherever they go, erecting their football-fields, cricket-pitches and lawn tennis-nets'.[482] This was nothing bad – it was 'the most glittering revelation of the state-building genius of the European race'.[483]

The trouble was simply that Englishness was bound, by the Darwinian rules of nature herself, to throttle the rest of the world – not by military victories, of course, for that was not the way Englishness worked, but by the disease-like 'spread of Anglo-Saxon *Kultur* over our whole planet'. The unstoppable advance of this vast monoculture and the English language was, to Peters, a vision 'simply terrifying'.[484] Only a European Union carried through by Germany had any chance of standing up to Anglo-Saxony: this must be the 'practical goal of all German policy'.[485]

Even while preaching Tirpitz's ever-growing Plan *à l'outrance*, the most extreme German pamphleteers were, right to the end, still frankly in awe of Britain. The ecstatic writer of *England's World Rule and the German 'Luxury Fleet'* (1912) looks forward to the day when some 'bank, or trench, or sandspit in the North Sea, as yet unknown to all but seamen, will be toasted along with the names of Fehrbellin and Sedan', but even he can't deny his admiration: 'There is something that carries you away in such a grandiose sense of self, something so innately royal, that smaller nations instinctively whip their caps from their heads. The Englishman is at home wherever he goes.'[486]

Just as back in 1864, what the Germans envied was this sheer, arrogant sense of themselves which made the British act as if they owned even Germany:

> If you meet someone on the train who seems to hold it against everyone else for not staying at home, it will be a so-called son of Albion. This Albion has brought up her sons in a curious manner and has convinced them that since the world belongs to them, they have the right to treat inhabitants of other countries as interlopers ... It is proof of how little the railway companies care for the traveller that having provided special compartments for smokers and ladies, and special carriages for horses, dogs, geese and other classes of the agricultural population, they have not also got going special compartments for Englishmen ... if an Englishman speaks German, he is not a real Englishman: he is only real if he refuses to answer anyone who doesn't speak English.[487]

At the height of Boer War fever in Germany, which hit white-hot when Joseph Chamberlain dared to point out that the German Army, during the Franco-Prussian War, had regularly executed combatants not in proper uniform and burned the villages which allegedly sheltered them, the diamond magnate, banker and philanthropist Carl (the future *Sir* Carl) Meyer, wrote to *The Times* enclosing a letter from a concerned German friend:

> " Chamberlain's speech is only a pretext used by my worthy countrymen so as to give them an opportunity of abusing England. The hatred of England is undoubtedly very intense, and even the Emperor is powerless to stop it. What has produced the hatred is not easy to say. I personally am convinced that envy is at the bottom of it, just the same as in the case of German anti-Semitism. For some time the Germans have been longing to own colonies, and, finding that everywhere England possesses already the most desirable parts, they look upon this as a personal injury. On the top of this feeling came the Transvaal war; rightly or wrongly, the conviction has gained ground that by this war German interests in South-West Africa suffer; and that, while England becomes more and more powerful in Africa, Germany is pushed into the background. That is how our beerhouse politicians argue."

Meyer's German friend surely had it right. Envy was at the base of it: envy of two peoples who seemed, above all, to know exactly who they were.

In the mindscape of German nationalism, the Germans had not yet attained even their own whole Fatherland, but the English and the Jews were everywhere at home in the world. When Germans emigrated, they simply assimilated to their Anglo-Saxon hosts and were lost, but the English and the Jews always remained their own, true, ruthless, national-racial selves wherever they settled; Germany was always being duped or misled, but the English and the Jews somehow always knew where their best advantage lay; Germany only survived in Europe by arming itself to the teeth against its neighbours, but England-and-the-Jews ran a quarter of the world without breaking sweat.

Of course, all such fantasies actually tell us about is what the fantasist truly thinks of himself, and the truth seems to be that many Germans lived in a state of psychic siege. German Anglophobia and German anti-Semitism were linked like Siamese twins by this profound, irrational fear of being infiltrated and ultimately overcome by a power which – unlike Germany – was *absolutely sure of itself*. It was exactly this 'supreme national self-confidence' which General von Bernhardi so envied in England, and so recommended to Germany, in his infamous bestseller *Germany and the Next War*.[488]

Again, a picture says it all. In this before-and-after cover from Germany's most-respected satirical magazine in 1902, Herr and Frau Schmidt, evidently a jolly, affectionate and unselfconsciously parvenu middle-class German couple (Herr Schmidt complete with power-shoulders and kaiserly moustache), make the fatal error of going on holiday to England to see Edward VII crowned. In eight days, they are completely metamorphosed by the joyless cultural radiation of Britishness:

The notion of being anglicised was as terrifying to many Germans in 1900 as being americanised is to some people today. It was especially terrifying to a certain kind of German – the kind who were actually a majority but felt, and voted, as though they were a threatened minority.

German socialists, German Catholics, German vons and German Jews all had their own mighty fortresses of tradition and self-belief. They were all Germans, but they were something else as well: they knew exactly who they *were*. The many, many Germans who were none of these things, the Protestant Germans who had believed national unity to be the millennium, and who had come to worship Bismarck above all men, seem, after his fall, to have known only what they were *not*: not socialists, not Catholics, not aristocrats, not Jews. They were ... just *Germans*.

Since their only distinct quality was Being German, they elevated that into something approaching a religion: a notion of Germandom (*Deutschtum*) developed which was, in varying degrees, anti-Catholic, anti-Semitic, colonial, naval and, above all, defined itself as the *opposite of Englishness*. Germany was a massive power, yet many of its people felt as though they were a small nation, permanently threatened with cultural extinction at the hands of a hegemonic neighbour; like some gigantic version of a Welsh or Scots rugby crowd, the louder they shouted against England, the more truly German they felt.

The Boer War gave them something to really shout about, and shout they did. The *Morning Post* told Britons the story not in its own words, but in those of Dr von Stradonitz, rektor of Berlin University:

> hatred against Great Britain, or more correctly expressed, against the British people, is undoubtedly prevalent in the widest circles in Germany – not amongst the intellectual aristocracy, not in the select rank of the really and scientifically educated, not among those who, as they say, occupy a leading position in the nation, but most certainly among the great masses of the population ... if you only knew in what a shameful manner the German Emperor has been slandered ... Go into the small towns of Germany, sit in the public

houses and listen to the pothouse politicians. It is everywhere the same. It is a most fatal infatuation. "The Boer War", Mommsen has written, "has accentuated the antagonism but did not produce it". The great historian is right.[489]

It was a perfect time – as Tirpitz saw, and said – to ask the German people if they wanted an even bigger fleet.

The beginning of the end: the Second Navy Law

The near-universal Anglophobia of 1900 having provided the perfect opportunity for Tirpitz to introduce his Second Navy Law, his tame media professors again toured the country with their hi-tech presentations, making full linkage between the need for an even bigger fleet and the Boer War.

> I have met with the same sequence of thought recently in very many German provincial newspapers. It was to be found in their reports of the addresses of peripatetic lecturers in support of the German Navy Bill. In many instances the lecture, illustrated by magic-lantern slides, was divided into two portions. The first dealt with the navies of Germany, Great Britain, and other Powers, the second was devoted entirely to the Boers, whom the pictures showed defending kopjes against the British.

Britons did not need to have seen these roadshows to know the plain drive of the Second Navy Law: 'The two arguments which have been used with most effect have been the security which a large fleet would afford for the further development of trade and industry and the prospect of being able to "settle accounts with England".'[490]

Within weeks of the bill being presented to the Reichstag, a warning was given in the House of Commons:

It is impossible to shut our eyes to the fact that there have been distinctly proposed to the German Houses, by Admiral Tirpitz, Estimates which are based on the possibility of an outbreak of war with England. Von der Golz, who is the highest literary authority on this subject, has said the same thing.[491]

Readers of *The Times* were informed roundly that Germany was now possessed by an 'almost national blindness and infatuation' against Britain.[492]

From the day the Second Navy Law was passed, in June 1900, the only real question was whether Britain would react as the German myth predicted to this obvious challenge. If she did as was to be expected from her history (according to Treitschke), and chose to keep her ill-gotten money bags when bullied, the world could steam forward in peace and progress into the new, German century.

If not, if Britain chose, against all reason and expectation, to defend her morally and physically indefensible position in the world, it could only mean war.

The choice, as it had been since 1879, was Britain's, but this time it was being posed in the shape of a direct challenge, and there was now no way to evade it: with Germany, or against her?

PART EIGHT:
THE LAST DECADE OF THE OLD WORLD

The kings and the commoners

Britain reacted to the challenge of the Second Navy Law with a speed which has few parallels in diplomatic history and which is itself the best proof that a move to oppose Germany had been long in mental preparation.

In November 1901 Britons were treated to the ABC Memorandum, which historians often cite as the first real sign of the new alliances to come. It went further, and into greater detail, than anything yet in saying that Britain should ally with both France and Russia to deter an incurably bellicose Germany. No one at the time knew that one of the authors was Sir Edward Grey, but its impact was enormous, for it was clearly written by persons in the know. And, of course, it was really saying nothing new, since Disraeli had said exactly as much in both 1864 and 1875: the Memorandum had such an effect precisely because it merely stated at last what had long been hovering on many tongues.

The official advocates of the Naval Bills which have been introduced into the Reichstag during the last three years have made no concealment as to the objective of the modern German navy, and that portion of the German press which takes its cue from the Government has told us in language impossible to misunderstand that Germany aspires to deprive us of our position on the ocean ... the people of this country will no longer tolerate a policy of "graceful concessions," and will not permit any Ministry or any personage however exalted to adopt towards any Power the attitude which has been too long followed as regards Germany.[493]

In fact, Britain's reaction between 1900 and 1908 was so radical and so clear that the real question is why on earth the German leadership did not see that they had so obviously got things wrong?

The answer to this is simple and deeply troubling: it was not about the leaders any more.

Of all the forgotten truths about the final run-up to Armageddon, the most striking is that, from the Boer War onwards, Wilhelm II and his governmental elite were incessantly accused of not being anti-English *enough*. Wilhelm might be officially called the All-Highest in Germany, but he was certainly not in control. Before his appointment in October 1900, Bernhard von Bülow had grovellingly promised that, as chancellor, he would be a mere 'tool for the carrying out of His Majesty's wishes'. The political reality in Germany was very different.

After Victoria died in January 1901 – in his very arms – Wilhelm lingered long in Britain. Worse, he conferred the treasured Order of the Black Eagle upon Lord Roberts, who had finally defeated the Boer field armies so widely adored in Germany, and who now proceeded to rebuild the British Army in the image – what else? – of the German Army.

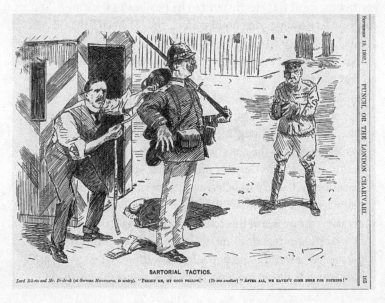

SARTORIAL TACTICS.

Lord R-b-rts and Mr. Br-dr-ck (at German Manœuvres, to sentry). "PERMIT ME, MY GOOD FELLOW." (To one another) "AFTER ALL, WE HAVEN'T COME HERE FOR NOTHING!"

In a remarkable session of the Reichstag, on 5 March 1901, Bülow had to defend his emperor against repeated attacks from right across the political spectrum. Suspicion of the Kaiser's motives was almost openly voiced. Was he making a personal attempt to forge an actual alliance with his relations there? Was he not breaking Germany's neutrality in the Boer War by decorating Lord Roberts? Was the extended visit not the sign of some secret 'hyper-friendly' policy towards England that was 'against the interests of the country'?

To quell the house, Bülow repeated a mantra which might have sounded like a harmlessly evasive formula, but which was, in effect, a blanket assurance that he and Wilhelm would never truckle to Britain: he assured the restless MPs that Germany continued to demand 'full and lasting equality of rights with Britain' – 'absolute parity with Britain'. What exactly that meant was fatally vague. How exactly did you demand 'absolute parity' with Britain? By insisting on a fleet and an empire as great as hers? By forcing her to clear her foreign policy with Germany? It amounted to a blank cheque to the Anglophobes.

And the trouble was, that meant, by now, almost everyone. Anglophobia was such a catch-all that, extraordinarily enough, it produced a tactical alliance in the Reichstag between one of the iconic figures of German socialism and the leader of the anti-Semites, each of whom claimed, in his own way, to speak for 'the people' against the Kaiser and his elite government:

> Liebknecht, the well-known Socialist, attacked the Emperor for his attitude towards England. He regretted that the German people, whose sympathies were almost without an exception on the side of the Boers, should be officially represented by telegrams saying the opposite of what the people desired that they should. Herr Liebknecht, whose remarks assumed a very personal form, was repeatedly called to order. He found an ally, however, in the notorious Anglophobe and Anti-Semite Herr Liebermann von Sonnenberg, who begged that the blood of the

> German people, who were so closely related to
> the Boers, might not be made to boil with reports
> of telegrams of congratulation to England. On
> being requested by the President not to pursue
> the subject any further, Herr Liebermann von
> Sonnenberg concluded by expressing the hope
> that " the English fog which has interposed itself
> between the German Throne and the German
> people " might soon disappear.

With even Socialists and anti-Semites publicly joining forces in parliament to attack the Kaiser as too pro-British, it's perhaps not surprising that an American travel writer, in 1902, talked to ordinary Germans and decided that 'they cannot forget that their sovereign is by birth half an Englishman; and many there are who look with only half-concealed suspicion on the cordial relations that existed for so many years between the Kaiser and his grandmother'.[494]

In 1901 the Kaiser made yet another of his personal hints at an alliance, but the Foreign Secretary, Lord Lansdowne, reacted in a 'very secret' memorandum of 11 November 1901: 'it is out of the question that we should entertain the German ouverture'. The Prime Minister, Arthur Balfour, agreed and explained exactly why this was impossible: 'the sentiments of the German and English peoples are at present so hostile as to make negotiations undesirable'.

The 'sentiments of the German and English peoples' could by now veto the best efforts of politicians, and even kings. The Kaiser, and the governing elite of Britain, had not given up, but they were rowing against the tide.

At the tail end of 1902 the Royal Navy helped the Imperial German Navy enforce debt collection in Venezuela. It seemed to be a good reminder that, even now, there really was no reason that the world's greatest trading partners could not find plenty of little things in common, and that if they could only work together, even America's backyard would be within their grand joint reach.

The trouble was that their voters did not see things that way. British opinion was appalled at the idea of annoying the Americans just to help the Germans. The Poet of Empire knew exactly what his vast public wanted, and his fame, in 1903, was so great that his reaction made the front page of the *New York Times* the same day:[495]

KIPLING DENOUNCES THE ANGLO-GERMAN ALLIANCE.

Neath all the flags of all mankind
That use upon the seas,
Was there no other fleet to find
That you strike bands with these?

Of evil times that men can choose
On evil fate to fall,
What brooding Judgment let you loose
To pick the worst of all?

In sight of peace – from the Narrow Seas
O'er half the world to run –
With a cheated crew, to league anew
With the Goth and the shameless Hun!

In Germany, the Reichstag also took note, and seethed with rage. On 20 January 1903, Chancellor Bülow denounced Kipling as a 'feral poet' and blamed the British press for stirring things up – but also pointed out that German Anglophobes made life difficult too. For perhaps the last time in European history, a leader stated openly that he was proud *not* to conduct diplomacy in the alleged 'spirit of popular feeling': diplomacy had to be done with the head, not the heart, said Bülow. The governments and monarchs of Great Britain were perfectly able to get along with each other; it was the *people* who were the problem. Horace had famously said that 'when kings lose their heads, the common people pay the price'; now, Bülow declared, to catcalls from the left, it was more often the other way around.

A couple of months after Bülow's speech, *The Times* announced two new books which made it clear just how far the voting people on both sides were now beyond reach of rational argument.

Smuggled in between volumes of fact, and for all the world sounding like fact itself, was the original of an entirely new genre in modern literature: Erskine Childers's *The Riddle of the Sands*. Here, for the first time, one of most profitable templates of modern publishing was set: a somewhat lonely, rather ordinary, yet manly hero accidentally uncovers a vast geo-political conspiracy against his country, in which the reader is persuaded to believe by the authenticity of the detail – and by the way the author plays to the fears of the day.

THE TIMES COLUMN OF
NEW BOOKS and NEW EDITIONS.
*₊*This column is restricted to books published during the last six months.

SMITH, ELDER, and CO.'S NEW BOOKS.

Ready This Day.   With an Introduction by J. St. Loe Strachey.
Crown 8vo., 2s. 6d., net.

GERMAN AMBITIONS AS THEY AFFECT BRITAIN AND THE UNITED STATES.
Reprinted with additions and Notes from the "Spectator." By VIGILANS sed ÆQUUS.

A RECORD OF SECRET SERVICE RECENTLY ACHIEVED.
On May 27th.   With two Maps and Two Charts.   Crown 8vo., 6s.

THE RIDDLE OF THE SANDS. Edited by ERSKINE CHILDERS, Author of "In the Ranks of the C.I.V."

An account of the Cruise of the Yacht Dulcibella, being a page hitherto unwritten, but of vital interest to all Englishmen, in the recent history of our relations with Germany.

Just like *Made in Germany*, Childers's genre-founding bestseller didn't say that the Germans were threatening Britain by choice, or that they were morally bad. The coming war was just the inevitable way of things:

> Here's this huge empire, stretching half over central Europe – an empire growing like wildfire, I believe, in people, and wealth, and everything. They've licked the French, and the Austrians, and are the

greatest military power in Europe. I wish I knew more about all that, but what I'm concerned with is their sea-power. It's a new thing with them, but it's going strong, and that Emperor of theirs is running it for all it's worth. He's a splendid chap, and anyone can see he's right. They've got no colonies to speak of, and *must* have them, like us. They can't get them and keep them, and they can't protect their huge commerce without naval strength. The command of the sea is *the* thing nowadays, isn't it?

The novel pretended so successfully to be based on a real plan for a German invasion, and hit the zeitgeist in Britain so squarely on the nose, that it altered reality in its own image, helping to inspire the founding of the Secret Intelligence Service, parent of both MI5 and MI6.

The first book announced that same day by Smith, Elder & Co. makes a fascinating pair with *The Riddle of the Sands*, for it was a survey of extreme German nationalism by John St Loe Strachey, editor of the *Spectator*. Strachey blamed the followers of Treitschke for Germany's rampant Anglophobia. But he was rebuked in the *New York Times* for confusing cause and effect:[496]

> The author misconceives. therefore, the facts as to the Pan-German movement. He confounds cause and effect. That keen aspirations of a greater Germany are so widespread; that the conviction is held by millions of the younger Germans that the German-speaking part of Austria-Hungary, of Switzerland, that Holland and the Flemish part of Belgium must inevitably fall to the share of this greater Germany at the next general upheaval—that is what makes this Pan-German movement a formidable one, and that at the same time causes professors and writers to discuss these topics.

The American reviewer – he was himself a German von – realised that blaming a clique and their cunning manipulation of the press was far easier for all concerned than facing the deeply unpalatable fact that 'millions of younger Germans' supported policies which could only result in confrontation with Britain.

With many Britons prepared to believe, in the face of all sane reckoning, that Germany might seriously be planning a surprise invasion in flat-bottom boats across the North Sea, with millions of Germans ready to see Britain as their nemesis, and with each seeing the other as representing a fundamentally different view of the world, there was by now little hope.

Britain saw that she needed allies. But who? To Strachey, there was an obvious answer:

> One last word. Two of the Pan-German prophets of the future, 'Germania Triumphans' and Dr. Eisenhart, represent Germany as fighting against both Britain and the United States, but fighting against them separately. In 'Germania Triumphans' the United States are first attacked and defeated by both sea and land and Britain is represented as chuckle-headed enough and base enough to look on and do nothing. Then comes Britain's turn. The only difference in Dr. Eisenhart's vaticination of the future is that Germany takes Britain first, and the United States look on. Britain is disposed of, 'and now,' says the prophet, 'it was time to reckon with America.' Not even these half-sane Pan-Germans contemplate the possibility of dealing with Britain and the United States *together*.

The moral, Britain and the United States should hold together.

The time, unfortunately for the world, was not yet ripe for such an alliance. So Britain looked elsewhere: to her own resources, and to her ancient foes.

Germany undeterred

The reborn Entente Cordiale with France in 1904 had no deterrent effect whatever on Germany. This may seem extraordinary, but there were two simple and (it seemed) perfectly sensible reasons for this: German experts did not believe a Franco-British league could possibly last; and they thought that the attempt to create one would merely ruin the very dangerous Franco-Russian alliance, since England and Russia could self-evidently never be on the same side. Thus the Entente was considered by many German diplomats to have actually strengthened the Triple Alliance.

To the German public, all it did was confirm that Treitschke had been right: Britain would do anything to stop the rise of Germany, even ally with her oldest enemy.

This sense of Britain as uniquely inimical to Germany – indeed, to nature itself – grew in 1905: Britons were accused of racial treachery in inciting the rebellious Herero tribe of south-west Africa, which inflicted considerable losses on German forces before being wiped out. It perhaps hardly needs saying by now that there is not a whit of evidence that Britain did anything of the kind. In fact, from our modern point of view, most of the British press was sadly untroubled by the sight of the Hereros being utterly and deliberately annihilated: the Germans were simply making the region safe for whites, if rather heavy-handedly. But in Germany, it was taken as read that the agents of international Manchesterism – who, of course, cared nothing for true racial unity, hated Germany and had a unique ability to manipulate inferior peoples – were behind it all. These are not obscure cartoons, but full-page plates from the most prestigious magazine in Germany:

'Negrophile' British policy (as von Weber had called it in 1880) showed a unique ability to use inferior races: 'Come with us to London, Jim,' says the British Tommy. 'You'll have more luck with our ladies than with those picky Boer women.'

Made in England

'In the Cameroons, unrest against the Germans has been noted.'

The brutal Hereros, armed with modern weapons, declare, 'We've killed thirty Germans, now we'll get free beer from the English again.'

'Our English friends' are ready, in the eternal pursuit of profit, to commit that ultimate sin in colonial Africa: the arming of natives with modern European weapons to use against other whites.

Then came *Dreadnought*. By building her, Britain deliberately chose to make every battleship on Earth, including her own vast squadrons, redundant. She took Tirpitz by surprise and threw his Plan into chaos.

Logically, the launch of this one ship should have been enough to dispel at last the myth of British pusillanimity and decadence. It wasn't. Tirpitz still clove to the theory that the only reason Britain had not responded as she ought to have done to Germany's naval challenge was that she had not yet been challenged *enough*. One eminent German historian has described it as a 'miscalculation verging on the insane'.[497]

Verging on the insane, perhaps, but if so, the insanity was not just Tirpitz's. By 1905, the Tirpitz Plan itself no longer belonged to him, for the German Navy League, a million paying members strong, now regarded its own founder as a mere moderate. Tirpitz himself found the Navy League's undisguised clamour for '*der Tag*', the day of reckoning with England, so politically embarrassing that he severed the official link with the popular movement he had himself purposely called into being. Anglophobia had been easy enough to find, but was impossible to control.[498]

From now on, Germanophobia was as central to British political debate as Anglophobia had long been in Germany. That debate was carried out in shrill new voices like those which had, during the Boer War, greeted the relief of a previously obscure railway junction by going hysterically 'mafficking' around the streets of central London. In 1906, this feverish public bought one million copies of William le Queux's *The Invasion of 1910*, created by the *Daily Mail* and sold complete with dummy maps and proclamations:

ENGLISHMEN !
Your Homes are Desecrated !
Your Children are Starving !
Your Loved Ones are Dead !
WILL YOU REMAIN IN COWARDLY INACTIVITY?
The German Eagle flies over London. Hull, Newcastle and Birmingham are in ruins. Manchester is a German City. Norfolk, Essex, and Suffolk form a German colony. The Kaiser's troops have brought death, ruin, and starvation upon you.

> **WILL YOU BECOME GERMANS?**
>
> # NO!
>
> Join THE DEFENDERS and fight for England.
> You have England's Millions beside you.
>
> # LET US RISE!
>
> Let us drive back the Kaiser's men.
> Let us shoot them at sight.
> Let us exterminate every single man who has desecrated
>   English soil.
> Join the New League of Defenders.
> Fight for your homes. Fight for your wives. Fight for
>   England.
>
> ### FIGHT FOR YOUR KING!
>
> The National League of Defenders' Head Offices.
>   Bristol, September 21st, 1910.

Newspaper readers above being swayed by Lord Northcliffe's favourite populist hack might pay more attention to the editor of his eminently respectable *Observer*, Austin Harrison, who informed them, in 1907, that 'instead of decreasing since the Boer War, Anglophobia has increased in scope and intensity ... all Germany believes that England is bent on her destruction ... the entire German press is consciously permeated with Anglophobic sentiment.' Like the good journalist he was, Harrison brought his message home to his readers with a memorable personal anecdote:

> Some years ago after a bathe I was lying naked on the Dune of Heligoland, rejoicing in the warmth of the sun, according to good German custom. Presently a burly Teuton, emerging from the sea, sat on the sand beside me. Discovering my nationality, this apparently good-natured man grew almost delirious. For two hours we shouted politics at each other with expletives as naked and unashamed as was our condition. The bareness of the outward man seemed to unbare the

> inner.   He told me that Germany was in-
> evitably the future Power of Europe, must
> inevitably crush and ruin England.   " It is our
> hope," he said, " our destiny.   These seas," he
> exclaimed, " will some day be strewn with the
> relics of proud England's fleets ; your doom is
> our victory, your fate our apotheosis !   It is
> the decree of history.   It cannot be averted."

Harrison's burly, naked Teuton was merely the all too corporeal representative of his corporate state, for 'Germany's whole scheme of government is one of scientific politico-economic propulsion, co-ordinated and applied.'[499] Awesomely scientific, terrifically organised, frighteningly applied – yet still appallingly backward: 'No Englishman can live long in Germany', stated a popular encyclopaedia from 1909, 'without feeling that he has come to a country where material and social refinement, manners, customs, and all the other graces of civilised life are at a decidedly lower level than in his own, and that the Germans of today are only at about the same stage of development as were the English of Queen Elizabeth.'[500]

Nothing could be more alien to all that Britain stood for than this nightmarish mix of modernity and primitivism. By now, anyone was better than the Germans – even the Russians. And so, in 1907, the impossible happened.

1908: world's end set

In August 1907, Britain and Russia, global enemies for almost a century, came to terms. At first it was merely a tentative settlement of their joint influence in Persia, but it right away made Britain beyond any doubt the most hated country in Germany. Not the most *feared* – that was always Russia – but the most *hated*. England was loathed because her evident mortal enmity seemed, to Germans, to have such base motives.

For rich, safe, aristocratic England to make up with her oldest enemies, to join first with the republic which was the womb of all revolutionary excess, and now with the semi-Asiatic despotism which had always menaced civilisation in Europe – that was against nature. And to make that league against a nation with whom England had never gone to war, a cultural first cousin, simply because England would not acknowledge that Germany was now her full equal in the world? That was something close to sheer evil. As the Pan-German Congress declared, such an alliance was 'unnatural and designed merely to serve the selfish interests of Great Britain'.[501] If the French and Russians could not see that, it was testament, yet again, to the matchless duplicity of the British and their king, who was by now widely seen in Germany not as the rather louche yet loveable monarch known to British history, but as the fiendishly cunning Edward the Encircler ('a real Satan', Wilhelm II himself called him):

The simple German policeman is told (by John Bull, the leader of the conspiracy) that Britain, France and Russia are merely trying to unite Europe – not surround Berlin.

And now it all fell into deadly place. Austria-Hungary formally annexed Bosnia-Herzegovina, bringing Europe to within an ace of war. Edward VII met Nicholas II at Reval and sealed the understanding of 1907, over-turning the most basic assumption of German diplomacy. Wilhelm II's *éminence grise* and best friend, Prince Philip von und zu Eulenburg, was publicly accused of something so appalling that the respectable British press dared not even speak its name (not that it had to, after Wilde), leav-ing Wilhelm aghast and now with none around him but military men.

In personal crisis, Wilhelm opened his heart – it was almost inevitable, knowing Wilhelm – to a decent English country gentleman, Colonel Edward James Stuart-Wortley, whose fine English country house he was renting. Stuart-Wortley thought the British people should know how the Kaiser felt, and Wilhelm agreed: he truly wanted the British to know that they were mad – 'as mad as March hares!' – if they could not see that he was their real friend, a friend who had secretly helped out in the Boer War and was, almost single-handedly, holding back the Anglophobia of his own lower orders. The result is known to historians simply as 'the *Daily Telegraph* Interview', and, in October 1908, it went off under Wilhelm's throne like a mine.[502]

> **Millions of Germans, apart from their disapproval of these outpourings, resent bitterly the Kaiser's allegation that the lower middle classes of the German Nation are so Anglophobe at heart that he feels himself isolated**

In the Reichstag, the Socialists, the National Liberals and the Pan-Germans alike raged that the Kaiser and his elite were simply not competent to safeguard Germany's future; in the magazines which almost all middle-class Germans read, satirists again and again depicted Wilhelm's regime as hoodwinked by, or crawling to, England.*

---

* It's striking that the same satirists who accused Wilhelm of being too English also disliked the corseted, costumed Prussian officer caste: it sometimes feels as if the wonderful cover pages of *Simplicissimus* are almost equally divided between jibes at England and at the Prussian Junkers.

Nr. 18
Erstes Beiblatt   Beiblatt zum Kladderadatsch   Berlin,
den 3. Mai 1908

Verschiedene Tätigkeit
oder
der ideale Neffe und der praktische Onkel

„Onkel, willst du nicht auch die schöne Luft im Süden genießen?" —
„Nein, danke! Ich speise so langsam „à la Carte" weiter, das bekommt mir auch recht schön!" —

'The ideal nephew' has no chance against the appetite and cunning of his 'practical uncle'.

'What have you got in your pocket, dear Uncle,' asks the hapless Wilhelm II. 'Europe, dear Nephew,' replies the hooded-eyed Edward VII. Critics of Wilhelm's regime claimed that even when he tried to stand up to Edward, such old-fashioned monarchical ways – typified here by Wilhelm's theatrical military dress – were simply not *modern and efficient* enough to safeguard Germany against the cunning of the Englanders. It was this feeling which led Maximilian Harden, editor of the cutting-edge cultural journal *Die Zukunft* (*The Future*) to publish throne-shaking revelations of 'perversions' among Wilhelm's aristocratic coterie in 1907.

The demand that the Kaiser be more *German* grew louder and louder.

Nr. 12
Erstes Beiblatt **Beiblatt zum Kladderadatsch** Berlin,
den 22. März 1908

Gerechte Entrüstung

"Wenn Ich Großadmiral der englischen Flotte bin,

Oberst der Royal-Dragoons

und Ehrendoktor der Universität Oxford —
so werde ich auch das Recht haben, einen englischen
Brief zu schreiben,

sonst werfe Ich euch auf gut deutsch den ganzen
Plunder vor die Füße!"

Wilhelm is advised to throw off all his Englishness – in his uncle's face.

Edward VII, the good uncle, personally attends to Kaiser Wilhelm II when the latter catches cold on yet another visit to England – i.e. he makes sure that Wilhelm is well and truly 'wrapped up'.

In 1909 Wilhelm is still ready to forgive his uncle everything and to kill the fatted calf for him.

The final straw of the fatal year 1908 was the tenth anniversary of Bismarck's death. A raging cult swept Germany. Spontaneously, and with no official encouragement whatever, frowning monuments to the Iron Chancellor went up all over the country.

This was indeed a mass-protest movement against Wilhelm's 'personal regime', but it was not one that called for democracy, or liberty, or defusing of the arms race with England. Bismarck's graven image, suddenly rearing up in hundreds of towns and villages across Germany, spoke of a non-royal yet majestical figure, somehow chosen by the people, yet also their undoubted ruler, working within semi-parliamentary forms and yet fundamentally above all party politics. A leader who was essentially always right about everything – and had, above all, been the one German who had ever shown the Englanders who was boss.

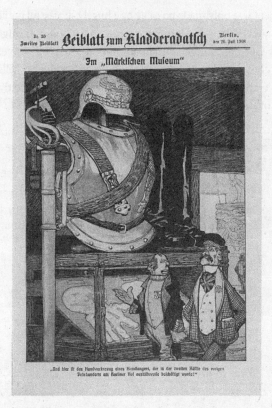

The smug British tourist is shown colossal relics of Bismarck, now merely called 'a servant who was employed now and then at court in Berlin in the second half of the last century'.

Amid all this excitement, mighty new evidence of Germany's technological leadership enthralled the country: the Zeppelin was at last a truly viable machine. Here was modernity for you!

Contrary to the British legend of limitless German state sponsorship guided by matchless cunning, Count Zeppelin's great invention was a purely private affair, carried on by simple trial and error over many years, which had by now bankrupted him. The Balloon Division of the army had looked at the plans in 1907 and thought them possibly worth looking at again, but no more. The Marine Office contributed a modest sum in case the craft proved useful for naval reconnaissance, but further development was only made possible by a hugely successful public lottery.

For whatever the slow-moving army or navy bosses thought of air-ships, the German public was ahead of them. In 1908 – a year *before* the army committed to its first vessel – both of the biggest-selling magazines in Germany were absolutely clear as to the best use that might be made of the Zeppelins:

A year before the German Army actually bought a Zeppelin, the public mind had little doubt as to their best use. In this cartoon, Count Zeppelin throws dynamite upon the Royal Navy during manoeuvres: 'The success is wonderful' and war is abolished thanks to this new German weaponry.

Edward VII tosses and turns in the nightmare of 'Zeppelin's shadow'.

Edward as Belshazzar at his feast (with a battleship as the pièce de résistance). The moving finger writes, and has writ: Zeppelin.

The amateur partisans of Zeppelin warfare against Britain in 1908 thought in exactly the same bizarre way as Tirpitz had in 1898. Despite the alliances with France and now Russia, despite *Dreadnought*, nothing had changed in the way Britain was seen as uniquely bully-able because uniquely on the lookout for her selfish interests:

> Every Englander today knows ... that London itself would, very shortly after the outbreak of the war, be exposed to the danger of bombardment from German air-vehicles ... as soon as the German armies have completely or partially occupied the coast from Ostend to Calais all available rigid and semi-rigid air-vehicles will be sent across the Channel.[503]

And what would the Englanders do, knowing of this threat to do to London from the air what the cannons had done to Paris in 1871? Why, they would swiftly abandon their profitless alliances and turn to Germany, of course! It would be 'a far quicker and more effective way of attaining the important goal of a German–English alliance than every assurance of friendliness towards England'.

A page from this year from Germany's most prestigious satirical magazine sums up the whole, long story of the last 150 years from the German point of view. Here is the tale of those alleged relations, the Britons and the Germans, as told by *Simplicissimus*:

The poor Cousin

A rich man called John Bull had a poor cousin called Michel Tschoerman, whom he often and gladly praised for his modesty. He purchased this relation's sons whenever he needed to fight a war anywhere in the world, and watched in comfort as the brave young men fought so well for him. Sometimes he did a deal with the good Michel for one of his handsome princes, to improve his own high family. And he was particularly happy to send his spare princesses to live with his poor cousin. But now that has all sadly changed, and Mr Bull is quite outraged that Mr Tschoerman has been so bold as to give up his poverty.

And here is the picture that went with it:

Der arme Vetter

(Zeichnungen von O. Gulbransson)

Der reiche Herr John Bull hatte einen armen Vetter, Michel Tschörmen, und er lobte ihn oft und gerne wegen seiner Bescheidenheit.

Auch kaufte er ihm seine Söhne ab, wenn er irgendwo in der Welt Krieg führen wollte.

und sah behaglich zu, wie die braven jungen Leute für ihn so tapfer fochten.

Manchmal handelte er dem guten Michel auch einen hübschen Prinzen ab zur Aufbesserung seiner hohen Familie.

Und besonders gerne schickte er dem armen Vetter überständige Prinzessinnen ins Haus.

Das hat sich alles leider geändert, und Mr. Bull ist sehr entrüstet, daß sich Mr. Tschörmen erlaubt hat, seine Armut aufzugeben.

With this story, or some variant of it, almost universally accepted in Germany as the historical truth, it is small wonder that no one, after 1908, had a hope in hell of swinging the wheel there.

Britain's choice

In 1908, Britain at last made the choice she had been faced with ever since 1879. By then, British convictions about what the Germans were like had changed not a jot since the 1870s, having already solidified, even among those essentially well-disposed to Germany, into the vision we know from a hundred twentieth-century war movies:

> Before you have been in Germany a fortnight the Police expect to know all about you. You have to give them your father's Christian name and surname, and tell them how he earned his living and where he was born, and your mother's Christian and maiden names, and where she was born. You must declare your religion and if married give your husband's Christian and surname and where he was born, and what he does for a living ... You are well looked after, but if you are used to England you never quite lose the impression in Germany that if you are not an official or a soldier you must be a criminal and that if you move an inch to the left or the right of what is prescribed, you will hear of it. [504]

The book-reading British public having just made Le Queux rich by buying his *Invasion of 1910* in such numbers, their theatre-going compatriots next poured money into the box office of Wyndham's Theatre to see *An Englishman's Home*, in which a blithely sport-loving, middle-class British family argue about whether a crowd might jeer a referee, and lazily debate Lord Roberts's advice to get trained for war, until they are sneaked up upon, out of a thick fog, by brutal Nearlanders. In case there was the slightest doubt who was actually being referred to, the producers advertised the play by employing extras dressed in jackboots and spiked helmets to parade around central London.

In the end, British pluck naturally triumphed and Lord Roberts ('Bobs – bless his heart') was vindicated. In a strangely accurate pre-echo of the decisive Battle of the Marne in 1914, the day was saved by a reserve army hurried out in 'motors, busses, every blessed thing that could move'. But this salvation came off-stage, and was merely reported: the final actual image of the play, the emotional sting in the tail, the picture that the packed houses went home with night after night, was that of the Nearlanders still in possession of the suburban English home, having just shot the owner for resisting them.

The play hit the national mood, and hence the jackpot, spot-on. The *New York Times* described 'Cabinet Ministers and army officers going repeatedly as if fascinated' and announced that universal conscription was now certain in Britain:

NEED OF DEFENSE STIRS ENGLAND

Only in Time of War Has the Nation Been So Seriously Excited.

NAVY NOT TO BE RELIED ON

In No Condition to Defend the Coast — Army Greatly Reduced and Lacks Officers.

UNIVERSAL SERVICE SURE

Du Maurier's Play, Which Brought Agitation to a Head, Prepares Public Mind for Compulsory System.

The play did such business that, almost uniquely, it ran in two West End theatres simultaneously. When Katherine Mansfield's first book, *In a German Pension*, appeared the next year, she did not have to explain what play she meant when her heroine was mockingly grilled in chapter one by overbearing Germans (whose table manners had evidently got no less ghastly since Henry Mayhew's visit in 1864):

"If I drink a great deal of Munchen beer I sweat so," said Herr Hoffmann. "When I am here, in the fields or before my baths, I sweat, but I enjoy it; but in the town it is not at all the same thing." Prompted by the thought, he wiped his neck and face with his dinner napkin and carefully cleaned his ears. A glass dish of stewed apricots was placed upon the table.

"Ah, fruit!" said Fraulein Stiegelauer, "That is so necessary to health. The doctor told me this morning that the more fruit I could eat the better." She very obviously followed the advice. Said the Traveller: "I suppose you are frightened of an invasion, too, eh? Oh, that's good. I've been reading all about your English play in a newspaper. Did you see it?"

"Yes." I sat upright. "I assure you we are not afraid."

"Well, then, you ought to be," said the Herr Rat. "You have got no army at all – a few little boys with their veins full of nicotine poisoning."

"Don't be afraid," Herr Hoffmann said. "We don't want England. If we did we would have had her long ago. We really do not want you."

Some British leaders, Lloyd George and Winston Churchill notable among them, still worked to find a peaceable solution. But by now the very word 'German' was used as an insult by powerful sections of the British press, just as to call something 'English' had for years been more or less a term of abuse to many people in Germany. Anyone who wanted peace with Germany – and more German-style state spending! – was something close to a traitor. A Conservative poster from

1909 showed 'Herr von Lloyd George' bombing British prosperity from a Zeppelin.

Soon, even the best-intentioned British politicians were giving up. On a visit in 1909, Churchill was struck deeply by the 'mighty engine' of the German Army, and the utterly split nature of German society, and began to change his tune.[505] In his Mansion House speech of 1911, Lloyd George amazed his pacifist electors, and confounded his Tory enemies, by formally warning Germany not to go too far.

No man worked harder than Lord Haldane to avoid the collision – so hard, indeed, that he was publicly reviled in Lord Northcliffe's papers as pro-German. But by 1911, even Haldane saw the relationship between Britain and Germany more in terms of anthropology or of a dysfunctional family than those of normal diplomacy. The Germans were so superficially like us – yet they had turned out so utterly different:[506]

LORD HALDANE IN OXFORD.

GREAT BRITAIN AND GERMANY COMPARED.

" A STUDY IN ETHNOLOGY."

LORD HALDANE'S ADDRESS.

LORD HALDANE pointed out that while it was never easy to make a satisfactory appreciation of a country to which one stood in the relation of a foreigner, Germany was for Britons a specially difficult country to understand. Its people possessed traits so like those of our own that we were apt to overlook those other traits in which they were profoundly unlike.

Haldane's mission of 1912 really was the last gasp. He went to Germany, that place 'so like' and yet so 'profoundly unlike' Britain, with a pretty spectacular offer: that if Germany would merely 'not increase' her naval expenditure any further, Britain would discuss almost any other conditions Germany wanted.

Would this offer actually have stuck with the British public? Probably not. But we shall never know, because Haldane's advance was turned down flat by Wilhelm. Why did Britain still think it could dictate Germany's naval spending? Why would the British never treat the Germans as real equals? If Britain came to the table with such an offer, that was simply proof that the policy of threat was working, just as predicted. So the way to improve Britain's offer still further, to make her back down even more, was obvious: increase the pressure!

Even now, after the agreements with France and Russia, and after perfectly clear evidence that Britain was not going to back down from the naval arms race, a close and senior colleague of Tirpitz's remained absolutely certain that their old analysis was still correct:

> We hold the trumps, not England. We only have to wait patiently until our present Navy law is carried out. Then England will see things far more clearly than now. England must and will opt for Germany over France in the course of the next few years, because it is obviously in England's interest [this last sentence is doubly stressed in the margin of the original] ... Our position must be: show England the cold shoulder and don't chase after her! England must and will come to us.[507]

But the myth was wrong. England was not going to come to Germany. Britons at the polls would happily rubber-stamp an amicable agreement with France; they would praise the statesmen who came to agreements with Russia, even if that involved a clear degree of yielding; they would not bat an eyelid at the more or less blatant ceding of precedence to America in various distant regions of the globe; but they were by now convinced that Germany was going to make a bid to destroy them – or rather, was already making that bid:

P I P

IS ENGLAND FULL OF GERMAN SPIES? A GERMAN CHIEF OF POLICE FOR ENGLAND

By MAJOR DE BREZE DARNLEY STEWART-STEPHENS.

Many people have puzzled over the fact that so many Britons volunteered to fight in the Great War, but there is really nothing mysterious at all about it. The young men who flocked to the recruiting offices in 1914 were not blindly or stupidly obeying a blanket appeal from King & Country to go to any old war, but signing up, quite specifically, for a war *against Germany* which they had seen coming for years, felt certain had been forced upon them, and believed would, if lost, mean the end of everything.

This was no longer a place where rational calculations applied. As Salisbury had put it way back in 1864, at the time of the first confrontation: 'Governments can do so little and prevent so little nowadays. Power has passed from the hands of statesmen. It is all pure drifting.'[508]

Drifting to Armageddon

And drift things did, undesired by the leaders on both sides but unstoppable, towards 1914. One side or the other had to back down. Neither side could, because, by 1908, any German party or government which back-tracked from the challenge would have been doomed, and so would any British party which did not respond to the music-hall demand to keep building more dreadnoughts than the Germans: 'We want eight and we won't wait!'

Worse, these febrile electorates of young males were courted on both sides by men who themselves had no understanding of the real position:

the leaders of Britain and Germany were in thrall, just as much as any man on the Clapham omnibus or the Friedrichstrasse S-Bahn, to the false lights of national myth.

Ever since the slaying of Daniel Eugene Ott, the most strikingly obvious, easily comprehensible and media-friendly symbol of the difference between Britain and Germany had been the sabre-rattling Prussian von. The ABC Memorandum of 1901 firmly stated that Anglophobes were 'usually of the Agrarian class' and Sir Edward Grey operated right up until the end on the assumption that the trouble was being incited by a small and mysterious 'war party' of Junkers who were pushing the Kaiser towards confrontation. In fact, the military Junkers were the least Anglophobic class in Germany and would gladly have clawed back funds from the Imperial German Navy in order to concentrate against France and Russia – indeed, they partially succeeded in 1913–14, to Tirpitz's despair. Given half a diplomatic chance, the scar-faced Prussian generals would actually have been, in practice, Britain's best friends.* British leaders, however, could not rid themselves of the fatuous ideology which said that supporters of Progress were necessarily a Good Thing: they simply could not see that, in Germany, it was not the forces of aristocratic reaction, but those of a radical modernity which were implacably and specifically bent on disputing Britain's position in the world.

To Germans, the story was just as clear, and just as false. They had known, ever since 1864, that Britain was ready to do anything to stop Germany – anything, that is, *except* go to war, fair and square, and risk, like any decent continental power, a hecatomb of her own sons. The British might try sneakily to wipe out the German fleet, before it got too strong, in a surprise attack *à la* Copenhagen – that would indeed be in the national character, and the possibility genuinely obsessed the German Navy – or they might enlist dupes to do her work. But Britons actually *fight*? Since when? As one leading MP put it in the Reichstag, Britain would and could never raise a big conscript army, since she was 'ruled by the stock-exchange'.[509]

---

* Just as they would have been in 1938 and 1944.

The very obviously ungentlemanly Englishman declares: 'For five shillings we can hire people to fight the greatest wars for the honour of our nation. No English gentleman would ever lower himself to such a trade.' In the widespread Treitschkean myth, England's 'civilisation' was that of the money-obsessed shopkeeper (posing for the time being as a gentleman).

So even if they did join in, what could contemptibly army-less Britain actually do?* The legendary Schlieffen Plan did indeed admit the possibility that some British troops might appear on the scene, but its author had such a low opinion of the British Army that he allotted no time at all to its defeat, merely stating that this would make no difference whatever to his timetable.[510] General Bernhardi, coiner of the all-or-nothing mantra 'World Power or Downfall' ('Weltmacht oder Untergang'), warned his countrymen that black African troops would make many excellent divisions for France, but thought it 'very questionable whether the English army is capable of effectively acting on the offensive against Continental European troops'.[511]

'The Duty of Others'. The smug Englishman declares: 'Very good thing, this universal conscription; it means the others can really protect one.' It remained an article of faith to many German opinion-formers that the British would never raise their own decent army, and hence that in a short, swift war it would not matter even if the Englanders did for once – unlikely as it seemed – stick with their allies.

* The Kaiser's famous statement about Britain's 'contemptibly small army' needs reading with careful regard for grammar. It did *not* mean that he thought the BEF in itself contemptible, but that *Britain as a nation* was contemptible for having such a small army.

Edward (by now widely seen as the heart of all anti-German intrigue) is taken aback by 'Haldane's standing army'.

Treated everywhere as second class citizens, the English regular army consists of hirelings ... the British uniform is not the King's coat, but the livree, bought by the taxpayer, in which those who hire themselves out for service are dressed up.[512]

The fatal double error was set: the Englanders would always break their word to their supposed friends if they thought they might profit by it – and it would not even matter if they didn't. Thanks to this compound miscalculation, even those Germans who did not actually want war with Britain did not think her involvement would make much difference.*

By 1912, it only needed the spark. In December, Germany rattled her sabre at Russia. Haldane and Grey made it absolutely clear to the German Ambassador that Britain would not sit and watch France be further humbled if it came to a general war. They were merely stating

---

* Long myths die hard: extreme German leaders made exactly the same lunatic miscalculation about the 'Anglo-Saxons' in 1917, and again in 1941.

what had obviously been the case since 1904, or by 1908 at the latest, but this was not how England was *supposed* to behave. For every other power to stick by its promises was honourable – but, uniquely, for England to do so was treachery.

Treachery to nature. Furiously, Wilhelm scribbled in the margins of the report from London on 8 December 1912. His rage was driven by that decades-old conviction that for England to be hostile to German ambitions was somehow *unnatural*:

England is definitely going to stand by France and Russia against us, out of envy and hatred against us. In the event of the battle for existence which the Germanic people of Europe (Austria, Germany) will have to fight against the Slavs (Russia) supported by the Romans (Gauls), the Anglo-Saxons will be on the side of the Slavs. The reason: envy and fear of us becoming too great! [513]

The Kaiser immediately summoned the infamous War Council of December 1912, which many eminent historians see as the actual point at which the German leadership decided on war at the next best opportunity. Tirpitz begged for a delay of eighteen months to get the fleet ready (to which Moltke, like a good Junker, scornfully replied that the navy would not be ready to face the Englanders even then, so why wait?). Wilhelm and his military cabal pencilled in a short, sharp war for the summer of 1914, their main concern being that it could be presented to the German socialists as a defensive struggle against backward Russia.

Sarajevo and its aftermath fitted the bill. It was not an attack on Germany as such, but still, a vile Slav assassin had murdered a German-speaking prince. And now things fell out exactly as, why and where thinking people had known since 1879 that they probably would. Austria-Hungary sought to permanently neuter Serbia; Serbia called on Russia, who felt that she could not back down as she had done in 1908 without forever giving up all claim to influence in the region; Austria invoked support from Germany against Russia; the German generals thought it would be their best chance to beat Russia before modernisation and sheer numbers made her invincible, so the Kaiser issued Vienna with the famous 'blank cheque' of which the Austrian military elite had been dreaming ever since 1879; France saw, in a full-scale Russo-German war, the only chance she would ever get to win back what she had lost in 1871.

The war had been so long in the coming, and so often flagged by politicians on all sides for their own tactical reasons, that when it did come at last, most of Europe's innumerable young men greeted the prospect of a swift, great showdown with a relief that was – as relief often is – hard to tell from joy.

Yet on 3 August 1914, Britain and Germany were still at peace, as they had always been. If things had stayed that way, as many in both camps confidently expected or secretly feared that they would, European history would have ended, and not in a vale of tears.

Blaming one country when two go to war is a bold thing, and it's very tempting to leave it all implied and to say, like Gibbon, that 'the duty of an historian does not call upon him to interpose his private judgement in this nice and important controversy'. But let's not beat about the bush. There's no question whatever that Germany forced Britain's hand. Almost no Britons, and none of their political leaders, wanted a war with Germany, ever, even after 1908. Many Germans, and even some of their leaders, by 1908, thought a war with Britain inevitable or even desirable. In the end, Britons, who would have been very happy to sit peaceably on their laurels and their empire, were forced to choose between rolling over and standing up.

This is not a question of morality, but one of judgement. Take the obvious modern parallel. If China (a fast-rising power with a com-munitarian, state-based vision of societal fulfilment) were to physically contest the Pacific with America (a declining hegemon with a univer-sal ideology of individual freedom), the aggressor in regard of the status quo would undoubtedly be China. But the Chinese would cer-tainly point out, as did countless German writers between 1864 and 1914, that an imperium assembled by buccaneering endeavour, eco-nomic power and sheer physical force can hardly object on *moral* grounds when it is threatened with revision by exactly the same means.

What would be the outcome of that attempt is another question. If there is one lesson to be taken for today from the whole fatal Anglo-German tale, it may be that a rising power should beware lest its heady sense of destiny blind it to the remaining strength of the declining hegemon.

Germany called it wrongly, with disastrous consequences for everybody. Britain did not go quietly; she went in, and the young men who were supposedly so averse to a manly fight raced, completely of their own free will, to take up arms. Their contribution – their deaths – so levelled the odds that a European war which would have ended with total victory for Germany and Austria by Christmas 1915, if not earlier, turned into a Great War so inconclusive that it would all have to be gone through again in another twenty years. By the time the issue was beyond any doubt, the world had learned the words *Lenin*, *Stalin*, *Hitler*, *Auschwitz*, and Europe was a corpse-filled rubble-tip, half of it at the mercy of Russia, the rest of it, including an exhausted Britain and what was left of Germany, begging helplessly to America.

The German myth of British decadence, the story that had been told ever since 1864, had at last been tested, and it turned out to have been both generally right and fatally wrong: Britain's age as the great world power was indeed over, but her final strength was enough to make sure that her mantle did not pass, after all, to the country which she by now saw as fundamentally inimical to everything she stood for.

The mighty, fallen (but still bickering)

Today, it's hard to imagine that one of H. G. Wells's Martians, looking across space with icy calculation in June 1914, would have been pushed to decide whether the next century on planet Earth was going to belong to the culture of Marx and Nietzsche, of Klimt and Kafka, of Mahler and Max Planck, of Krupp, Thyssen and Siemens, of Freud and Einstein – or to that vast, free-trading, ocean-going, cricket-playing empire which Karl Peters so admired and so dreaded.

Germany now has a worldwide cultural reach approximately that of Sweden and, like Holland, might almost as well declare English her official second language, while Britain now obscures her true status, at least to herself, by acting as principal sidekick of a power to whom the Special Relationship is a mere sideshow.

No one anywhere trembles at the thought of the German Army; no one anywhere worries about what the British Navy might do. Many people around the world buy cars made in Germany, and many people around the world invest their money through British banks, but the corridors of global diplomacy scarcely wait with bated breath for the latest hint from the Kanzleramt or Downing Street. If China ever decides to tighten the screws on Japan, if Pakistan and India go to war, if Israel is threatened with annihilation, what Germany or Britain say or do will be of pretty much no account whatever to anyone. Yet there are two countries in the world for whom Germany and Britain loom very large indeed: Britain, and Germany. And the way in which they figure to each other is really quite extraordinary.

We still cannot resist presenting each other as polar opposites. If you follow the British media for a month or two, it's a safe bet you'll find unsubtle hints that the Germans are incurably hard-wired towards constructing a European super-state, run from Berlin and arranged for the benefit of German industries which claim to have found the secret of competing on sheer quality against the low-wage economies of Asia, but have, in fact, been covertly state-aided, as usual, in this case by the cunning way the Germans have spread and run the euro.

Track the German media, and you are just as likely to come across equally bald suggestions that the British, possibly because they are averse to real work, are inexplicably wedded to an all-out version of globalisation, driven by short-term 'Anglo-Saxon' financial wheeler-dealing and underpinned by a basic cultural one-ness with America, making them fundamentally untrustworthy partners for the mature and care-requiring economies of the Continent.

It's very handy to say that this is all just the fallout from the propaganda of the twentieth century's wars. The happy implication is that as the physical scars of those wars finally heal and the last memories of them become history, so too the Anglo-German distrust will dissolve all by itself. The far less easy truth is that when German and British 'analysts' say these things about each other, as they still do, what they are parroting is not the war propaganda of 1914–18, or of 1939–45, but voices from each side which were widely accepted even before 1900.

By the time Tirpitz and Wilhelm drew up their first Navy Bill, an entire generation of Britons and Germans – the first generation born in the age of the mass-read press and mass electorates – had come to age having imbibed a consistent, and consistently negative, view of each other. By 1897, it was already common in Britain to view Germany, and in Germany to view Britain, rather as Spain was seen by the Elizabethans and Revolutionary France by the Georgians, as communists and capitalists would see each other after 1945 (and, perhaps, as Americans and Chinese see each other today): not simply as a possible diplomatic adversary, not just as a direct economic competitor, and not even merely as a potential enemy in the field, but as a fundamentally alien polity, the triumph of whose values over ours would mean little less than national-cultural extinction.

Incredibly, that view is still common on both sides today. Here, then, is the simple but unwelcome point to this study of long-dead people and their opinions: the notion of an irreconcilable difference, which still plagues Anglo-German relations, is not the *product* of the twentieth century's great disasters, but was one of the *causes*. Those old 'analyses' from our great-great-grandfathers' days are still copied and pasted, again and again – and if we are not careful, they will destroy the one institution which gives either of us any real, remaining say in the world: the EU.

There are Britons who argue loudly that the vestiges of empire could provide a real future outside the EU, as money-launderer to the world and bag-carrier for America; there are Germans (though they are as yet neither so many nor so loud) who maintain that one might slough off ungrateful, insulting southern Europe, the better to embrace Berlin's natural hinterland, middle Europe, where enthusiasm for all things German is becoming a true phenomenon. They are all deluded. Neither of us counts for anything much, alone in today's world.

Anyone who doubts that there tens of millions of Britons who, if things go on as they are, really would – will – vote to leave the EU outright at the earliest opportunity must be blind and deaf; anyone who forgets that Germany has a tried and tested ability to get on with business while completely re-jigging its national currency has little memory of European history since 1918. The fall of the EU may seem unthinkable, but such things have a habit of seeming unthinkable until the moment they happen, at which point they immediately seem to have been inevitable.* Britons and Germans may have little power in the wider world today, but the future of the Old Continent still hangs, as it has done ever since 1879, on whether they can ever see eye to eye.

---

* On 5 November 1915, in Prague, Dr Franz Kafka, a deeply educated lawyer, a fast-track high-flyer in the service of his state, co-owner of an asbestos factory and newly announced winner of Berlin's biggest literary prize, concluded that the Germanic victory he desired was now certain. He therefore rationally and freely chose to enhance his future wealth by putting about £30,000 in today's money into a rock-solid vehicle: Austrian 5.5 per cent fifteen-year bonds. It was not a prophetic call: three years later, the Habsburg Empire defaulted on its centuries-old sovereign debt by the simple, if drastic, method of ceasing to exist.

NOTES

1 War between Britain and Germany was 'unthinkable' as late as 1890 (Ramsden); 'deep roots' favoured entente even in the 1900s (Ferguson); Germany's first colonies were acquired 'with British encouragement and assistance' (Massie). Simon Winder's wonderful *Germania* sums up the general idea: 'If anyone had carried out opinion polls in 1890 the idea of an Anglo-German war would in both countries have seemed ludicrous.'

2 John Keegan, *An Illustrated History of the First World War*, London, 1991, p. 17.

3 These terms are from Fritz Fischer and Ludwig Dehio. German historians disagree mainly on whether, and how far, Kaiser Wilhelm II was personally to blame. Was he a 'missing link, as it were, between Bismarck and Hitler' (Roehl) or a mere 'shadow Kaiser' who presided in name only over a clique of militarists and industrialists (the so-called 'Bielefeld School')? One way or another, though, they would all pretty well agree with Roehl that 'an accommodation with the English Empire could have been had right up to the last minute ... a very few men in Berlin, with no good reason, without even truly understanding what they were doing, flung the old Europe into the abyss'.

4 There's no doubt that this story, whose presiding deity is Jürgen Habermas, is the received wisdom in modern German schools and universities. See e.g. the widely used textbooks: Beate Althammer, *Das Bismarckreich 1871–1890* (Heidelberg, 2009), p. 83; Volker Ullrich, *Die nervöse Grossmacht: Aufstieg und Untergang des deutschen Kaiserreichs*, p. 99.

5 Christopher Clark, *The Sleepwalkers: How Europe Went to War in 1914* (London 2012), p. 147.

6 *The Times*, 23 May 1864.

7 *House of Commons Debate, 4 March 1864, vol. 173, cc1475–95.*

8 William Thackeray, *Vanity Fair*, vol. 2 (London, 1886), p. 291.

9 *Observer*, 16 June 1888.

10 Henry Mayhew, *Scenes from German Life* (London, 1864) pp. 121–7.

11 Written by Karl Marx on 15 March 1865, first published in *Der Bote vom Niederrhein*, no. 57, 13 May 1866.

12 *Daily News*, 17 August 1865.

13 *Reynolds's Weekly Newspaper*, 6 November 1864.

14 Günter Ogger, *Die Gründerjahre* (Munich, 1982), p. 39.

15 Stefan Keppler-Tasaki, 'Prussian Anglophilia', in *German Life and Letters* (2012), p. 430.

16 Andreas Dorpalen, *Heinrich von Treitschke* (Yale, 1957), p. 43.

17 Walter Bussmann, 'Treitschke als Politiker', in *Historische Zeitschrift*, vol. 177, part 2, (1954), p. 261.

18 *Die Gartenlaube* (1866), no. 12, p. 183.

19 Otto von Bismarck, letter of 2–4 May 1856, quoted in Jonathan Steinberg, *Bismarck: A Life* (London, 2012), p. 129.

20 Morier Papers, Balliol College Archive, box 1, letter of November 1860.

21 William F. Bertolette, 'German Stereotypes in British Magazines', thesis submitted to California State University (2004), p. 155.

22 Henry Vizetelly, *Berlin Under the New Empire*, vol. 2 (London, 1878), p. 395.

23 Tracey Reimann-Dawe, 'The British Other on African Soil', in *Patterns of Prejudice*, vol. 45, no. 5 (2011).

24 Mayhew, op. cit., p. 559.

25 *Handbook for Travellers on the Continent* (John Murray, London, 1843), p. 197.

26 Mayhew, op. cit., pp. 36, 85.

27 *Handbook for Travellers*, op. cit., p. 197.

28 Mayhew, op. cit., 117.

29 Sabine Baring-Gould, *Germany, Present and Past* (London, 1879), p. 1.

30 Edmund Spencer, *Germany from the Baltic to the Adriatic* (1867), p. 112.

31 Mayhew, op. cit., p. 41.

32 Mayhew, op. cit., p. 186.

33 'The Season at Baden-Baden' in the *Illustrated London News*, 19 August 1865.

34 Spencer, op. cit., pp. 265–80.

35 Ibid., p. 292.

36 Mayhew, op. cit., p. 362.

37 *Pall Mall Gazette*, 5 August 1865.

38 *The Times*, 23 September 1865.

39 *Liverpool Mercury*, 30 September 1860.

40 Baring-Gould, op. cit., foreword.

41 Mayhew, op. cit., p. 365.

42 Mayhew, op. cit., pp. viii–ix, 117.

43 *The Times*, 18 September 1865.

44 Mayhew, op. cit., p. 117.

45 Mayhew, op. cit., p. ix.

46 *Daily News*, 31 December 1863.

47 *Daily News*, 21 January 1864.

48 See Matthew P. Fitzpatrick, *Liberal Imperialism in Germany: Expansionism and Nationalism 1848–1884*, (Berghahn, New York, 2008).

49 Hegel, *Philosophy of Mind*, trans. Wallace and Miller (Oxford, 2007), p. 241.

50 William H. Dawson, *Bismarck and State Socialism* (London, 1891), p. 85.
51 Christopher Clark, *Iron Kingdom: The Rise and Downfall of Prussia* (Penguin, London, 2003), p. 544.
52 Ibid., p. 431.
53 Ralph Raico, *Die Partei der Freiheit* (Stuttgart, 1999), p. 188.
54 *Pall Mall Gazette*, 8 February 1879.
55 Brian Vick, 'Imperialism, Race and Genocide at the Paulskirche' in *German Colonialism and National Identity*, eds Perraudin/Zimmerer (Routledge, New York, 2011), p. 14.
56 Daniel Snowman, *The Hitler Emigrés* (Pimlico, London, 2003), p. 3.
57 'A scrutiny of the most prominent liberal thinkers of the nineteenth century and early twentieth century, as well as an observation of many of liberalism's most prominent political figures, illustrates quite overwhelmingly that Germany's liberals had been positing imperialism on the English model as the basis of a modern liberal nation for almost a century before [1933].' Matthew P. Fitzpatrick, *Bürgertum ohne Raum* (University of New South Wales, 2005).
58 See Fitzpatrick, op. cit.
59 Denkschrift über die Errichtung einer deutschen Flotte, Kiel 1848, p. 9.
60 Lawrence Sondhaus, *Preparing for Weltpolitik: German Sea Power Before the Tirpitz Era* (US Naval Institute, Annapolis, 1997), p. 65.
61 Fitzpatrick, op. cit., p. 104.
62 Quoted in Ulrike Kirchberger, *Aspekte deutsch–britischer Expansion* (Stuttgart, 1991), p. 455.
63 Ibid., p. 424.
64 Friedrich Althaus, *Englische Charakterbilder* (Berlin, 1869), p. 488ff.
65 Quoted in Fitzpatrick, op. cit., p. 104.
66 Richard J. Evans, *Death in Hamburg* (Penguin, London, 1987), p. 11.
67 Vizetelly, op. cit., p. 107.
68 *The Times*, 14 February 1877.
69 Klaus Hildebrand, *No Intervention: die Pax Britannica und Preußen 1865/66–1869/70* (Oldenbourg, Munich, 1997), p. 116; Dora N. Raymond, *British Policy and Opinion During the Franco-Prussian War* (Yale, 1921), p. 30.
70 *Daily News*, 21 January 1864.
71 *The Times*, 8 January 1864.
72 *The Times*, 2 January 1864.
73 *Preussische Jahrbücher* (1864), pp. 506, 522.
74 *The Times*, 5 January 1889.
75 Ibid.
76 Walther G. Oschilewski, *Zeitungen in Berlin* (Berlin, 1975), p. 62.
77 *The Times*, 7 May 1878.
78 Moshe Zimmermann, *Wilhelm Marr: The Patriarch of Anti-Semitism* (Oxford, 1986), p. 61.
79 Heinz-Dietrich Fischer, *Handbuch der politischen Presse in Deutschland* (Düsseldorf, 1981), p. 406.

80 *New York Times*, 2 January 1893.
81 Geoff Eley, 'Society and Politics in Bismarckian Germany', in *German History*, vol. 15, no. 1 (1997), p. 111.
82 Hegel, op. cit., pp. 241, 244.
83 Ibid.
84 *Neue Preussische Zeitung* ('*Kreuz-Zeitung*'), 13 July 1865.
85 Bismarck on 18 June 1864, cited in Hildebrand, op. cit., p. 115.
86 *Provinzial-Correspondenz*, 6 July 1864.
87 *Quarterly Review*, July 1864, quoted in Sir L. Woodward, *The Oxford History of England: The Age of Reform* (Oxford, 1938), p. 121.
88 *New York Times*, 3 March 1864.
89 *Fun*, 28 May 1864.
90 *Era*, 13 November 1864.
91 *Era*, 4 December 1864.
92 *Freiburger Zeitung*, 5 November 1864.
93 *Guardian*, 25 August 1865.
94 *Standard*, 17 August 1865.
95 Thomas Parent, 'Die Kölner Abgeordnetenfeste im preussichen Verfassungskonflikt', in Duedij/Friedmann/Muench (eds), *Öffentliche Festkultur: Politische Feste in Deutschland* (Hamburg, 1988), p. 259.
96 *Freiburger Zeitung*, 8 August 1865.
97 Gustav Freytag to Moritz Busch, quoted in Peter Sprengel, *Der Liberalismus auf dem Weg ins 'neue Reich'*, in Wagner (ed.), *Literature und Nation* (Cologne, 1996), p. 161.
98 *Neue Preussische Zeitung*, 18 July 1865.
99 *Heidelberger Zeitung*, 8 August 1865.
100 *Morning Post*, 12 June 1865.
101 *Pall Mall Gazette*, 6 June 1865.
102 Cole and Postgate, *The Common People* (London, 1961), pp. 392–3.
103 *Reynolds's Weekly Newspaper*, 12 August 1865.
104 *The Times*, 30 August 1865.
105 Queen Victoria, letter of 3 August 1865.
106 *Daily News*, 23 August 1865.
107 *Observer*, 3 September 1865.
108 Vizetelly, op. cit., p. 6.
109 *Ludgate's Monthy*, 6 November 1893.
110 *Freiburger Zeitung*, 8 August 1865.
111 William Howitt, *The Rural and Domestic Life of Germany* (1842), p. 32.
112 *Kölner Zeitung*, 7 August 1865.
113 *Pall Mall Gazette*, 26 August 1865.
114 *Pall Mall Gazette*, 7 September 1865.
115 *Examiner*, 9 September 1865.
116 *Penny Illustrated Paper*, 9 September 1865.
117 *Observer*, 10 October 1865.
118 *Lloyd's Weekly*, 10 September 1865.

119 *Guardian*, 3 October 1865.

120 Russell to Clarendon, 30 March 1866; Clarendon to Victoria, 31 March 1866.

121 Lord Napier, letter of 5 January 1866, quoted in Hildebrand, op. cit., p. 112.

122 *Reynolds's Weekly Newspaper*, 3 April 1864.

123 *Reynolds's Weekly Newspaper*, 8 April 1866.

124 Eley, op. cit., p. 111.

125 Morier Papers, Balliol College Archive, box 1, draft of *The Reconstruction of Germany* (dated 1867 but begun earlier).

126 *Chambers's Journal* (1866), p. 519.

127 *Daily News*, 7 September 1866.

128 *Guardian*, 17 July 1866.

129 Raymond, op. cit., p. 99.

130 *Graphic*, 23 July 1870.

131 *New York Times*, 13 October 1870.

132 *Cornhill Magazine*, vol. 22, pp. 566–79.

133 Lord Edmond Fitzmaurice, *The Life of Granville*, vol. 2 (London, 1905), p. 66.

134 *Observer*, 11 October 1870.

135 Robert Morier, quoted in Ian Colvin, *The Safety of the Nation* (London, 1919), p. 99.

136 *Pall Mall Gazette*, 1 September 1870, cited in Raymond, op. cit., p. 136.

137 *New York Times*, 2 September 1870.

138 Raymond, op. cit., p. 86.

139 *John Bull*, 20 August 1870.

140 *Gentleman's Magazine* (1871), p. 107.

141 *Gentleman's Magazine* (1870), p. 635.

142 *Graphic*, 27 August 1870.

143 *Graphic*, 19 November 1870.

144 *Gentleman's Magazine* (1870), p. 565.

145 *The Times*, 22 December 1870.

146 Bodleian Library, (oc) 200 h.89(8), p. 14.

147 Frederic Harrison, 'Bismarckism', in the *Fortnightly Review*, December 1870, p. 638.

148 *The Times*, 6 January 1871.

149 *Judy*, 25 January 1871.

150 *Gentleman's Magazine* (1871), p. 14.

151 *Cornhill Magazine* (1871), p. 484.

152 *Pall Mall Gazette*, 17 January 1871.

153 *Observer*, 11 June 1871.

154 *Gentleman's Magazine* (1871), p. 299.

155 Bodleian Library, (oc) 200 h.89, *Historical Pamphlets, Franco–Prussian War*, p. 20.

156 *Gentleman's Magazine* (1871), p. 107.

157 *Graphic*, 18 May 1871.

158 *Guardian*, 15 August 1871.

159 *The Times*, 4 September 1871.

160 *New York Times*, 26 June 1871.

161 *Freiburger Zeitung*, 30 August 1870.

162 *Freiburger Zeitung*, 4 September 1870.

163 *Freiburger Zeitung*, 11 September 1870.

164 Herbert Tuttle, *German Political Leaders* (New York, 1880), p. 17.

165 *Gentleman's Magazine* (1875), p. 50.

166 *The Times*, 18 November 1872.

167 Colvin, op. cit., p. 98.

168 *Economist*, 27 March 1875.

169 *Nineteenth Century*, February 1878, p. 416.

170 Geoff Eley, *From Unification to Nazism* (London, 1986), p. 210.

171 *Provinzial-Correspondenz*, 13 May 1874.

172 *Examiner*, 19 October 1878.

173 Papers of the Prussian Crown Council (Kronrat), November 1874–January 1875.

174 *Examiner*, 19 October 1878.

175 *Pall Mall Gazette*, 18 January 1875.

176 W. F. Monypenny, *The Life of Disraeli*, vol. 4 (London, 1929), p. 421.

177 Disraeli to Derby, 18 April 1875.

178 Disraeli to Derby, 6 May 1875.

179 Bismarck, letter to Emperor William, cited in E. T. S. Dugdale, *German Diplomatic Documents 1871–1914*, vol. 1 (London, 1928), p. 8.

180 Bismarck, letter to Count Münster, 3 June 1875.

181 Dugdale, op. cit., p. 8.

182 Queen Victoria to Emperor Wilhelm, 20 June 1875.

183 *Manchester Weekly Times*, 29 May 1875.

184 The cartoon is sadly not of reproducible quality, but may be found at the University of Heidelberg's wonderful digital edition of *Kladderadatsch*: KLA_1875_0767.

185 *Graphic*, 17 July 1875.

186 *Fortnightly Review*, 1 July 1875.

187 Dugdale, op. cit., pp. 53–4.

188 *Die Gartenlaube* (1872), p. 594.

189 J. Fear and C. Kobrak, *Origins of German Corporate Governance and Accounting 1870–1914* (XV International Economic History Congress, Helsinki, 2006), p. 12.

190 Ogger, op. cit., p. 202.

191 See 'England's Iron Trade with Germany', in *The Times*, 4 February 1879.

192 *Blackwood's Magazine* (1876), p. 316.

193 *Athenaeum*, February 1876.

194 Baring-Gould, op. cit., p. 412.

195 Dawson, op. cit., pp. 39–44.

196 *The Times*, 24 August 1881.

197 Tuttle, op. cit., p. 686.

198 *Standard*, 19 July 1890.

199 Tuttle, op. cit., p. 241.

200 Friedrich Paulsen, *An Autobiography* (New York, 1906), cited in Gordon Craig, *Germany 1866–1945* (New York, 1978), p. 205.

201 Treitschke, letter of 5 July 1876, quoted in Walter Bussmann, 'Treitschke als Politiker', in *Historische Zeitschrift*, vol. 177, part 2 (1954), p. 267.

202 *Pall Mall Gazette*, 17 September 1879.

203 Ulrich Langer, *Heinrich von Treitschke* (Düsseldorf, 1998), p. 137.

204 *Preussische Jahrbücher*, vol. 41, p. 104.

205 *The Times*, 4 February 1877.

206 Vizetelly, op. cit., p. 391.

207 *Daily News*, 8 July 1876.

208 *The Times*, 8 May 1878.

209 *Pall Mall Gazette*, 6 May 1878.

210 *The Times*, 7 May 1878.

211 *Morning Post*, 14 July 1876.

212 *Pall Mall Gazette*, 10 July 1876.

213 Treitschke quoted in *Pall Mall Gazette*, 17 December 1871.

214 *Saturday Review*, 1 June 1878.

215 Münster to Bülow, 25 February 1878, cited in Dugdale, op. cit., pp. 68–9.

216 *Graphic*, 20 April 1878.

217 *The Times*, 5 January 1878.

218 *Observer*, 24 February 1878.

219 *New York Times*, 11 May 1878.

220 *The Times*, 29 May 1878.

221 *The Times*, 7 May 1878; *Standard*, 15 May 1878.

222 *Guardian*, 17 March 1876; *Observer*, 21 October 1877.

223 *The Times*, 3 April 1878.

224 *Pall Mall Gazette*, 16 April 1878.

225 *Observer*, 5 May 1878.

226 Bodleian Library, (oc) 200 h. 88.10.

227 *Guardian*, 28 December 1871.

228 *Guardian*, 19 April 1872.

229 *London Review*, 13 April 1872.

230 *Guardian*, 22 October 1872.

231 *Guardian*, 2 July 1874.

232 *Guardian*, 10 July 1874.

233 *Guardian*, 23 July 1874.

234 *The Times*, 22 September 1874.

235 *York Herald*, 4 February 1875.

236 *The Times*, 2 June 1877.

237 *The Times*, 29 November 1877.

238 *Standard*, 14 June 1878.

239 *Blackwood's Magazine*, October 1879, p. 468.

240 *Standard*, 7 February 1880.

241 *The Times*, 7 September 1875.

242 Tuttle, op. cit., p. 7.

243 *The Times*, 22 September 1879.

244 *Blackwood's Magazine*, October 1879.

245 *Pall Mall Gazette*, 23 October 1879.

246 *The Times*, 3 April 1880.

247 *Bismarck-Album des Kladderadatsch* (Berlin, 1894), p. 244 (see footnote).

248 *Neue Preussische Zeitung*, 14 November 1879/11 December 1879/19 December 1879.

249 Treitschke, *Unsere Aussichten*, in *Preussische Jahrbücher*, November 1879, various pages.

250 *Die Gartenlaube* (1874), p. 789.

251 *Allgemeine Zeitung des Judenthums* (1879), p. 370.

252 *Macmillan's Magazine*, July 1880.

253 *Examiner*, 4 December 1880.

254 *Guardian*, 6 January 1880.

255 *The Times*, 6 June 1884.

256 Evans, op. cit., pp. 1890–91.

257 *Guardian*, 18 March 1880.

258 *The Times*, 21 October 1879.

259 *Guardian*, 17 March 1880.

260 *The Times*, 18 March 1880.

261 *The Times*, 9 February 1880.

262 *Saturday Review*, 11 October 1879.

263 *Examiner*, 7 February 1880.

264 *Contemporary Review*, April 1880.

265 *The Times*, 3 April 1880.

266 *The Times*, 1 May 1880.

267 *Guardian*, 20 May 1880.

268 *Guardian*, 12 May 1880.

269 *Guardian*, 20 May 1880.

270 *Guardian* 28 December 1880.

271 Vizetelly, op. cit., p. 14.

272 Mrs Alfred Sidgwick, *Home Life in Germany* (London, 1908), p. 34.

273 Vizetelly, op. cit., p. 129.

274 Baring-Gould, op. cit., preface to 1879 edition.

275 Vizetelly, op. cit., p. 157.

276 Ibid., p. 19.

277 R. S. Baker, *Seen in Germany* (New York, 1902), p. 27.

278 Baring-Gould, op. cit., p. 46.

279 See the debate in the Staatsministerium, 1 February 1885.

280 'Home Life in Germany', in *Fraser's Magazine* (1875).

281 Baker, op. cit., p. 17.

282 Vizetelly, op. cit., p. 79.

283 Ibid., p. 196.

284 Ibid., p. 80.

285 *All the Year Round*, 6 August 1881.

286 Ibid., p. 87.

287 Ibid., p. 196.

288 Ibid., p. 100.
289 Ibid., p. 88.
290 Ibid., p. 78.
291 Ibid., p. 79.
292 *The Times*, 7 November 1878.
293 Vizetelly, op. cit., pp. 110–12.
294 Baring-Gould, op. cit., p. 414.
295 Vizetelly, op. cit., p. 113.
296 Ibid., p. 386.
297 *Pall Mall Gazette*, 10 June 1878.
298 Baring-Gould, op. cit., p. 308.
299 Baker, op. cit., p. 14.
300 Vizetelly, op. cit., p. 102.
301 Ibid., p. 228.
302 Ibid., vol. 2, p. 11.
303 Ibid., vol. 1, pp. 13, 24.
304 Ibid., pp. 384–91.
305 *Fraser's Magazine* (1875).
306 *Saturday Review*, 27 November 1880.
307 Vizetelly, op. cit., pp. 292–5, 347.
308 *The Times*, 4 January 1884.
309 Baring-Gould, op. cit., p. 378.
310 Ibid., p. 185.
311 Ibid., p. 56.
312 Violet Hunt, *The Desirable Alien at Home in Germany* (London, 1913), p. 113.
313 Baring-Gould, op. cit., p. 189.
314 Vizetelly, op. cit., p. 105.
315 Baring-Gould, op. cit., p. 189.
316 Vizetelly, op. cit., p. 14.
317 Baring-Gould, op. cit., p. 56.
318 Vizetelly, op. cit., p. 105.
319 'The persecution of the Marxists, and of democrats in general, tends to obscure the fundamental fact that National "Socialism" is a genuine socialist movement, whose leading ideas are the final fruit of the anti-liberal tendencies which have been steadily gaining ground in Germany since the later part of the Bismarckian era, and which led the majority of the German intelligentsia first to "socialism of the chair" and later to Marxism in its social-democratic or communist form.' (Hayek, 1933, Hayek Papers, box 105, folder 10, Hoover Institution Archives.)
320 *Daily News*, 24 September 1878.
321 *Guardian*, 4 September 1874.
322 *The Times*, 10 October 1884.
323 *Westminster Review*, January 1880, p. 157.
324 *Saturday Review*, 25 May 1878.
325 *Fortnightly Review*, vol. 1 (1885), p. 676.
326 *Saturday Review*, March 1890, p. 272.

327 Sidney Whitman, *Imperial Germany* (Leipzig, 1888), pp. 24, 296.

328 Vizetelly, op. cit., p. 395.

329 Paulsen, op. cit., p. 205.

330 Althaus, op. cit., p. 7.

331 L. F. C. C. von Ompteda, *Neue Bilder aus dem Leben in England* (Berlin, 1882), p. 412.

332 Althaus, op. cit., p. 212.

333 L. F. C. C. von Ompteda, *Bilder aus dem Leben in England* (Berlin, 1881), pp. 125–7, 133, 151.

334 *Vossische Zeitung*, 11 April 1875.

335 Althaus, op. cit., p. 4.

336 'German Life in London', in *The Nineteenth Century* (May 1887), p. 732.

337 Sigdwick, op. cit., p. 27.

338 Ibid., p. 730.

339 Ibid.

340 Ibid., p. 732.

341 Ompteda, op. cit. (1881), p. 120.

342 *York Herald*, 9 June 1888.

343 Panikos Panayi, *Germans in Britain Since 1500* (London, 1996), p. 44.

344 Althaus, op. cit., p. 5; Ompteda, op. cit. (1881), p. 234.

345 Ompteda, op. cit. (1881), p. 19.

346 Ompteda, op. cit. (1882), p. 263.

347 Ompteda, op. cit. (1881), p. 276.

348 Ibid.

349 Ibid., p. 263.

350 Ibid., pp. 19, 263.

351 Ibid., p. 269.

352 Sidgwick, op. cit., p. 54.

353 Karl Peters, *England und die Engländer* (Berlin, 1904, 1915 edition), p. 1.

354 Ompteda, op. cit. (1882), p. 263; op. cit. (1881), p. 19.

355 Ompteda, op. cit. (1881), p. 19.

356 Althaus, op. cit., p. 281.

357 Ompteda, op. cit. (1881), p. 28.

358 Althaus, op. cit., p. 440.

359 Ibid., p. 424.

360 Ibid., pp. 433, 462.

361 Friedrich Fabri, *Bedarf Deutschland der Colonien? Eine politisch-ökonomische Betrachtung*, 1879.

362 Bismarck in the Staatsministerium, 8 December 1884.

363 Thomas Pakenham, *The Scramble for Africa* (London, 1991), p. 204.

364 Paul Kluke, 'Bismarck und Salisbury', in *Historische Zeitschrift*, Bd. 175, H.2 (1953), p. 288 (author's translation).

365 War Office to Mr Lister, 2 May 1884.

366 Bismarck in the Reichstag, 23 June 1884.

367 *House of Commons Debate, 9 March 1885.*

368 Inclosure 3 in no. 47 Correspondence Respecting Affairs in the Cameroons, February 1885, p. 48.

369 *The Times*, 10 October 1884.

370 *The Times*, 21 November 1884.

371 *The Times*, 5 January 1885.

372 Paulsen, op. cit., p. 205.

373 *Pall Mall Gazette*, 21 January 1885.

374 *Pall Mall Gazette*, 10 March 1885.

375 *The Times*, 15 December 1884.

376 *Neueste Mittheilungen*, 7 February 1885.

377 British Consulate, Samoa, 28 October 1884.

378 *Pall Mall Gazette*, 26 July 1890, cited in William F. Bertolette, 'German Stereotypes in British Magazines' (thesis submitted to California State University, 2004).

379 *New York Times*, 12 February 1885.

380 British Consulate, Samoa, 18 October 1884.

381 P. M. Kennedy, 'Bismarck's Imperialism: The Case of Samoa, 1880–1890', in *The Historical Journal*, vol. 15, no. 2 (June 1972), pp. 261–83.

382 *Neueste Mittheilungen*, 23 June 1885.

383 *Guardian*, 13 January 1886.

384 Whitman, op. cit., pp. 10, 232, 234, 303.

385 Whitman, op. cit., p. 105.

386 Ibid., p. 271.

387 *Neueste Mittheilungen*, 7 August 1888.

388 *Morning Post*, 8 October 1889.

389 Thorstein Veblen, *Imperial Germany* (1915), p. 197.

390 Baker, op. cit., pp. 91, 103, 114, 116, 121.

391 *House of Commons Debate, 2 April 1886.*

392 *Der Spiegel* (1967), no. 21, p. 76.

393 J. C. G. Röhl, *Young Wilhelm: The Kaiser's Early Life, 1859–1888* (London, 1998), p. 646.

394 *The Times*, 10 June 1887.

395 *Der Spiegel*, op. cit.

396 *New York Times*, 2 August 1903.

397 Röhl, op. cit., p. 678.

398 *The Times*, 27 October 1887.

399 Röhl, op. cit., p. 692.

400 Philip Eulenburg quoted in *Der Spiegel*, op. cit.

401 Röhl, op. cit., p. 691.

402 *Neueste Mittheilungen*, 18 October 1888.

403 *The Times*, 16 March 1888.

404 Treitschke, *Politische Schriften* (Berlin, 1907), p. 316.

405 J. C. G. Röhl, *Wilhelm II: The Kaiser's Personal Monarchy* (New York, 2004), p. 37.

406 *Saturday Review*, 23 June 1888.

407 *Guardian*, 16 June 1888.

408 *Reynolds's Weekly Newspaper*, 20 November 1887.

409 Röhl, *Young Wilhelm*, p. 679.

410 *Guardian*, 16 June 1888.

411 *The Times*, 9 November 1887.

312 *The Times*, 5 January 1889.

413 *Pall Mall Gazette*, 30 April 1889.

414 'German Life in London', in *The Nineteenth Century* (May 1887).

415 Salisbury to Paget, 16 October 1888.

416 *Neueste Mittheilungen*, 30 July 1889.

417 *The Times*, 3 August 1889.

418 Wilhelm II to Sir Edward Malet, 14 June 1889, cited in Keppler-Tasaki, op. cit., p. 422.

419 *The Times*, 3 August 1889.

420 Röhl, *Wilhelm II*, p. 106.

421 Ibid., p. 346.

422 *London Daily News*, 11 July 1891.

423 *The Times*, 29 September 1889.

424 *Daily News*, 23 April 1891.

425 *Contemporary Review*, April 1892.

426 Ibid.

427 *Fun* – see illustration.

428 *Contemporary Review*, April 1892.

429 Craig, op. cit., p. 244.

430 Ibid., p. 245.

431 *Contemporary Review*, April 1892.

432 See I. V. Hull, *The Entourage of Kaiser Wilhelm II* (Cambridge, 1982).

433 *The Times*, 19 January 1896.

434 *The Times*, 12 June 1884.

435 *Fun*, 13 October 1896.

436 *Morning Post*, 2 March 1895.

437 *The Times*, 21 November 1894.

438 Tirpitz to Stosch, 13 February 1896.

439 Ibid.

440 J. Lepsius et al. (eds), *Die Große Politik der europäischen Kabinette 1871–1914*, vol. 11 (Berlin 1922–7), pp. 31–2.

441 *Standard*, 14 January 1896.

442 *New York Times*, 16 November 1896.

443 *New York Times*, 27 January 1896.

444 *The Times*, 9 January 1896.

445 *Pall Mall Gazette*, 13 January 1896.

446 *Daily News*, 23 April 1891.

447 *Lloyd's Weekly Newspaper*, 10 May 1891.

448 *Daily News*, 23 April 1891.

449 E. E. Williams, *Made in Germany*, (London, 1896, fourth edition), p. 18.

450 Ibid., p. 167.
451 Ibid.
452 Ibid., p. 61.
453 *The Times*, 9 January 1896.
454 *Pall Mall Gazette*, 13 January 1896.
455 Ibid.
456 *The Times*, 29 December 1896.
457 *The Times*, 6 March 1897.
458 *The Times*, 14 August 1897.
459 *The Times*, 27 September 1897.
460 H. A. Winkler, *Der lange Weg nach Westen* (Munich, 2000), p. 273.
461 Memo by Captain August von Heeringen, 24 September 1900, Bundesarchiv/ Militärarchiv, RM 3/9551. Cited in Volker Berghahn and Wilhelm Deist, *Rüstung im Zeichen der wilhelminischen Weltpolitik: Grundlegende Dokumente 1890–1914* (Düsseldorf, 1988), pp. 201–11.
462 Roderick R. McLean, *Royalty and Diplomacy in Europe* (Cambridge, 2007), p. 90.
463 *The Times*, 28 March 1898.
464 *New York Times*, 6 July 1989.
465 *The Times*, 24 April 1899.
466 *New York Times*, 26 November 1898.
467 *The Times*, 7 February 1899.
468 Ibid.
469 Memorandum by Bernhard von Bülow, 14 March 1899.
470 *New York Times*, 14 January 1902.
471 *New York Times*, 12 December 1899.
472 *Pall Mall Gazette*, 13 March 1900.
473 *The Times*, 20 November 1901.
474 Ibid.
475 Röhl, *Young Wilhelm*, p. 125.
476 Barbara Tuchman, *August 1914* (London, 1980), p. 83.
477 *Spemanns goldenes Buch der Sitte* (Berlin, 1901), section 1005, by Count Wolf Baudissin.
478 Heiner Gillmeister, *Tennis: A Cultural History* (London, 1998), p. 265.
479 F. Prezinsky, *Lawn Tennis* (Leipzig, 1907), foreword.
480 Dr H. O. Simon, *Tennis als Spiel und Sport* (Leipzig, 1912), foreword.
481 *Fortnightly Review*, 1 June 1896.
482 General Friedrich von Bernhardi, trans. A. H. Powles, *Germany and the Next War* (London, 1912), p. 128.
483 Peters, op. cit., p. 249.
484 Ibid., p. 250.
485 Ibid., p. 248.
486 Ibid. p. 246.
487 'Lookout' (pen-name, author unknown), *Englands Weltherrschaft und die deutsche 'Luxusflotte'*.

488 Julius Stettenheim, *Der moderne Knigge*, vol. 2 (Berlin 1905), pp. 4–6.

489 Bernhardi, op. cit., p. 43.

490 *The Straits Times*, 6 November 1902.

491 *The Times*, 7 March 1900.

492 *House of Commons Debate, 21 March 1900*.

493 *The Times*, 9 April 1900.

494 *National Review*, November 1901.

495 Baker, op. cit., p. 46.

496 *New York Times*, 2 December 1902.

497 Volker Berghahn, 'Zu den Zielen des deutschen Flottenbaus unter Wilhelm II', in *Historische Zeitschrift*, Bd. 210, H.1 (February 1970), p. 29.

498 Ibid., p. 38.

499 Austin Harrison, *England and Germany* (London, 1907), pp. 4, 19, 140, 164.

500 *Harmsworth History of the World*, vol. 42 (London, 1909), p. 5354.

501 *The Times*, 7 September 1908.

502 *The Times*, 1 November 1908.

503 Rudolf Emil Martin, *Deutschland und England: ein offenes Wort an den Kaiser* (Berlin, 1908), pp. 12, 80, 82.

504 Sidgwick, op. cit., pp. 61, 71, 75.

505 Churchill, letter to Clementine, 15 September 1909.

506 *The Times*, 4 August 1911.

507 Vice-Admiral Eduard von Capelle, October 1911, quoted in Walter Hubatsch, *Die Ära Tirpitz: Studien zur deutschen Marinepolitik 1890–1918* (Göttingen, 1955), p. 92.

508 Hildebrand, op. cit., p. 61.

509 Von Kardorff in the Reichstag, quoted in *The Times*, 29 March 1900.

510 Brian Bond, *The Pursuit of Victory, from Napoleon to Saddam Hussein* (New York, 1996), p. 92. Quoted in Major Craig O. Petersen, unpublished thesis, USMC Command and Staff College, April 2008.

511 Bernhardi, op. cit., p. 79.

512 *Die Woche* (1902), nr 10, p. 434.

513 J. C. G. Röhl, *Kaiser, Hof und Staat* (Munich, 1987), p. 187.

SELECT BIBLIOGRAPHY

Althaus, Friedrich, *Englische Charakterbilder* (Berlin, 1869).

Baker, R. S., *Seen in Germany* (New York, 1902).

Baring-Gould, Sabine, *Germany, Present and Past* (London, 1879).

Bechthold, Elske, *Burenagitation und Anglophobie: Das Bild von England in der deutschen Öffentlichkeit während des Anglo-Burenkrieges 1899–1902* (unpublished thesis, University of Hamburg, 2008).

Berghahn, V., 'Zu den Zielen des deutschen Flottenbaus unter Wilhelm II', in *Historische Zeitschrift*, Bd. 210, H.1 (February 1970).

Berghahn, V., and Deist, W. (eds), *Rüstung im Zeichen der wilhelminischen Weltpolitik: Grundlegende Dokumente 1890–1914* (Düsseldorf, 1988).

Bertolette, William F., 'German Stereotypes in British Magazines' (thesis submitted to California State University, 2004).

Bismarck-Album des Kladderadatsch (Berlin, 1894).

Bodleian Library, (oc) 200 h.89, Historical Pamphlets, Franco-Prussian War.

Bond, Brian, *The Pursuit of Victory, from Napoleon to Saddam Hussein* (New York, 1996).

Bussmann, Walter, 'Treitschke als Politiker', in *Historische Zeitschrift*, vol. 177, part 2 (1954).

Clark, Christopher, *Iron Kingdom: The Rise and Downfall of Prussia* (London, 2003).

Cole, G. D. H., and Postgate, Raymond, *The Common People* (London, 1961).

Colvin, Ian, *The Safety of the Nation* (London, 1919).

Craig, Gordon, *Germany 1866–1945* (New York, 1978).

Dawson, William H., *Bismarck and State Socialism* (London, 1891).

Der Spiegel, 1967, no. 21.

Dorpalen, Andreas, *Heinrich von Treitschke* (Yale, 1957).

Dugdale, E. T. S., *German Diplomatic Documents 1871–1914*, vol. 1 (London, 1928).

Eley, Geoff, *From Unification to Nazism* (London, 1986).

Eley, Geoff, 'Society and Politics in Bismarckian Germany', in *German History*, vol. 15, no. 1 (1997).

Evans, Richard J., *Death in Hamburg* (London, 1987).

Fear, J., and Kobrak, C., *Origins of German Corporate Governance and Accounting 1870–1914* (XV International Economic History Congress, 2006).

Ferguson, Niall, *The Pity of War* (London, 2009).

Fischer, Heinz-Dietrich, *Handbuch der politischen Presse in Deutschland* (Düsseldorf, 1981).

Fitzmaurice, Lord Edmond, *The Life of Granville*, vol. 2 (London, 1905).

Fitzpatrick, Matthew P., *Bürgertum ohne Raum* (University of New South Wales, 2005).

Fitzpatrick, Matthew P., *Liberal Imperialism in Germany: Expansionism and Nationalism 1848–1884* (New York, 2008).

'German Life in London', in *The Nineteenth Century* (May 1887).

Gillmeister, Heiner, *Tennis: A Cultural History* (London, 1998).

Harrison, Austin, *England and Germany* (London, 1907).

Harrison, Frederic, 'Bismarckism', in *Fortnightly Review* (December 1870).

Hegel, *Philosophy of Mind*, trans. Wallace and Miller (Oxford, 2007).

Hildebrand, Klaus, *No Intervention: die Pax Britannica und Preußen 1865/66–1869/70* (Munich, 1997).

'Home Life in Germany', in *Fraser's Magazine* (1875).

Howitt, William, *The Rural and Domestic Life of Germany* (1842).

Hubatsch, Walter, *Die Ära Tirpitz: Studien zur deutschen Marinepolitik 1890–1918* (Göttingen, 1955).

Hull, I. V., *The Entourage of Kaiser Wilhelm II* (Cambridge, 1982).

Hunt, Violet, *The Desirable Alien at Home in Germany* (London, 1913).

Keegan, John, *An Illustrated History of the First World War* (London, 1991).

Kennedy, P. M., 'Bismarck's Imperialism: The Case of Samoa, 1880–1890', in *The Historical Journal*, vol. 15, no. 2.

Kennedy, P. M., *The Rise of the Anglo-German Antagonism* (London, 1980).

Keppler-Tasaki, Stefan, 'Prussian Anglophilia', in *German Life and Letters* (2012).

Kirchberger, Ulrike, *Aspekte deutsch-britischer Expansion* (Stuttgart, 1991).

Kluke, Paul, 'Bismarck und Salisbury', in *Historische Zeitschrift*, Bd. 175, H.2 (1953).

Langer, Ulrich, *Heinrich von Treitschke* (Düsseldorf, 1998).

Lepsius, J. et al. (eds), *Die Große Politik der europäischen Kabinette 1871–1914* (Berlin, 1922–7).

Lookout (pen-name), *Englands Weltherrschaft und die deutsche 'Luxusflotte'* (Berlin, 1912).

McLean, Roderick R., *Royalty and Diplomacy in Europe* (Cambridge, 2007).

Martin, Rudolf Emil, *Deutschland und England: ein offenes Wort an den Kaiser* (Berlin, 1908).

Massie, Robert K., *Dreadnought* (London, 1991).

Monypenny, W. F., *The Life of Disraeli* (London, 1929).

Morier Papers, Balliol College Archive, Oxford.

Murray, John (ed.), *Handbook for Travellers on the Continent* (London, 1843).

Ogger, Günther, *Die Gründerjahre* (Munich, 1982).

Oschilewski, Walther G., *Zeitungen in Berlin* (Berlin, 1975).

Pakenham, Thomas, *The Scramble for Africa* (London, 1991).

Parent, Thomas, 'Die Kölner Abgeordnetenfeste im preussichen Verfassungskonflikt' in Duedij/Friedmann/Muench (eds) Öffentliche Festkultur: Politische Feste in Deutschland (Hamburg, 1988).

Paulsen, Friedrich, An Autobiography (New York, 1906).

Peters, Karl, England und die Engländer (Berlin, 1904, 1915 edition).

Petersen, Major Craig O., unpublished thesis (USMC Command and Staff College, April 2008).

Prezinsky, F., Lawn Tennis (Leipzig, 1907).

Raico, Ralph, Die Partei der Freiheit (Stuttgart, 1999).

Ramsden, John, Don't Mention the War (London, 1996).

Raymond, Dora N., British Policy and Opinion During the Franco-Prussian War (Yale, 1921).

Reimann-Dawe, Tracey, 'The British Other on African Soil', in Patterns of Prejudice, vol. 45, no. 5 (2011).

Röhl, J. C. G., Kaiser, Hof und Staat (Munich, 1987).

Röhl, J. C. G., Wilhelm II: The Kaiser's Personal Monarchy (New York, 2004).

Röhl, J. C. G., Young Wilhelm: The Kaiser's Early Life, 1859–1888 (London, 1998).

Sidgwick, Mrs Alfred, Home Life in Germany (London, 1908).

Simon, Dr. H. O., Tennis als Spiel und Sport (Leipzig, 1912).

Snowman, Daniel, The Hitler Emigrés (London, 2003).

Spemanns goldenes Buch der Sitte, section 1005, by Baudissin, Count Wolf (Berlin, 1901).

Spencer, Edmund, Germany from the Baltic to the Adriatic (London, 1867).

Sprengel, Peter, 'Der Liberalismus auf dem Weg ins neue Reich', in Wagner (ed.), Literature und Nation (Cologne, 1996).

Stettenheim, Julius, Der moderne Knigge (Berlin, 1905).

Thackeray, W. M., Vanity Fair (London, 1886).

Treitschke, Politische Schriften (Berlin, 1907).

Treitschke, 'Unsere Aussichten', in Preussische Jahrbücher (November, 1879).

Tuchman, Barbara, August 1914 (London, 1980).

Tuttle, Herbert, German Political Leaders (New York, 1880).

Veblen, Thorstein, Imperial Germany (1915).

Vizetelly, Henry, Berlin Under the New Empire, 2 vols, (London, 1878).

Von Bernhardi, General Friedrich (trans. Powles, A. H.), Germany and the Next War (London, 1912).

Von Ompteda, L. F. C. C., Bilder aus dem Leben in England (Berlin, 1881).

Von Ompteda, L. F .C. C., Neue Bilder aus dem Leben in England (Berlin, 1882).

Whitman, Sidney, Imperial Germany (Leipzig, 1888).

Williams, E. E., Made in Germany, (London, 1896, fourth edition).

Winkler, H. A., Der lange Weg nach Westen (Munich, 2000).

Woodward, Sir L., The Oxford History of England: The Age of Reform (Oxford, 1938).

Zimmermann, Moshe, Wilhelm Marr: The Patriarch of Anti-Semitism (Oxford, 1986).

TEXT AND PICTURE PERMISSIONS

p. 53 (1864) John Bull gets a black eye from Germany.
http://digi.ub.uni-heidelberg.de/diglit/kla1864/0124

p. 54 (1864) John Bull the gutless money-bag.
http://digi.ub.uni-heidelberg.de/diglit/kla1864/0144

p. 109 (1870) Britain sells munitions to France.
http://digi.ub.uni-heidelberg.de/diglit/kla1870/0508

p. 162 (1878) Disraeli and Britain's big mouth.
http://digi.ub.uni-heidelberg.de/diglit/kla1878/0004

p. 162 (1876) Disraeli the cunning shopkeeper.
http://digi.ub.uni-heidelberg.de/diglit/kla1876/0334

p. 163 (1877) Disraeli as a monkey.
http://digi.ub.uni-heidelberg.de/diglit/kla1877/0278

p. 235 (1878) Germany the last country without colonies.
http://digi.ub.uni-heidelberg.de/diglit/kla1878/0416

p. 235 (1884) Still no German colonies.
http://digi.ub.uni-heidelberg.de/diglit/kla1884/0298

p. 246 (1884) The fat John Bull shown off by Gladstone.
http://digi.ub.uni-heidelberg.de/diglit/kla1884/0466

p. 247 (1884) Europe niggles Britain.
http://digi.ub.uni-heidelberg.de/diglit/kla1884/0234

p. 247 (1883) John Bull nets colonies as Europe wrangles.
http://digi.ub.uni-heidelberg.de/diglit/kla1883/0416

p. 251 (1884) Gladstone claims Bismarck is the devil.
http://digi.ub.uni-heidelberg.de/diglit/kla1884/0244

p. 253 (1885) The right way to deal with Britain in the colonies.
http://digi.ub.uni-heidelberg.de/diglit/kla1885/0385

p. 253 (1885) Germany wants Heligoland.
http://digi.ub.uni-heidelberg.de/diglit/kla1885/0028

p. 254 (1890) John Bull shakes his fist in vain.
http://digi.ub.uni-heidelberg.de/diglit/kla1890/0160

p. 302 (1899) How to treat the British Lion.
http://digi.ub.uni-heidelberg.de/diglit/kla1899/0572

p. 333 (1901) Britain in pain.
http://digi.ub.uni-heidelberg.de/diglit/kla1901/0372

p. 333 (1901) Britain dances with death.
http://digi.ub.uni-heidelberg.de/diglit/kla1901/0223

p. 338 (1900) Germany truckles to Britain.
http://digi.ub.uni-heidelberg.de/diglit/kla1900/0561

p. 339 (1902) Edward VII in Hell.
http://digi.ub.uni-heidelberg.de/diglit/wj1902/3664

p. 340 (1902) The British Lion has the German eagle shackled.
http://digi.ub.uni-heidelberg.de/diglit/wj1902/0234

p. 341 (1899) A nasty shock for John Bull.
http://digi.ub.uni-heidelberg.de/diglit/wj1899/3119

p. 341 (1899) Britain's money factory.
  http://digi.ub.uni-heidelberg.de/diglit/wj1899/3130
p. 342 (1900) John Bull in Nelson's day – and now.
  http://digi.ub.uni-heidelberg.de/diglit/wj1900/3170
p. 343 (1902) Edward VII and his army of donkeys.
  http://digi.ub.uni-heidelberg.de/diglit/wj1902/3791
p. 344 (1903) England's dupe, Mommsen, pours the milk of human kindness.
  http://digi.ub.uni-heidelberg.de/diglit/kla1903/0547
p. 379 (1908) The German policeman sees a conspiracy.
  http://digi.ub.uni-heidelberg.de/diglit/kla1908/0477
p. 381 (1908) The ideal nephew.
  http://digi.ub.uni-heidelberg.de/diglit/kla1908/0297
p. 382 (1909) Edward VII outplays the Kaiser,
  http://digi.ub.uni-heidelberg.de/diglitData/image/kla1909/1/kla1909
p. 383 (1908) The Kaiser should throw off his Englishness.
  http://digi.ub.uni-heidelberg.de/diglit/kla1908/0193
p. 385 (1908) Relics of Bismarck.
  http://digi.ub.uni-heidelberg.de/diglit/kla1908/0515
p. 387 (1908) Edward VII's feast.
  http://digi.ub.uni-heidelberg.de/diglitData/image/kla1908/1/KLA_1908_0523.jpg
p. 399 (1908) Edward VII's toy army.
  http://digi.ub.uni-heidelberg.de/diglit/kla1908/0481

By kind permission of *Simplicissimus*:

p. 331 (1899) The British Army flees in panic.
  http://www.simplicissimus.info/typo3temp/pics/bf83b8143d.jpg
p. 332 (1901) British Concentration Camps.
  http://www.simplicissimus.info/typo3temp/pics/0039dcdf55.jpg
p. 332 (1901) Edward VII is taken to hell.
  http://www.simplicissimus.info/typop/pics/de1f397537.jpg
p. 334 (1899) 'If only it been made in Germany!'
  http://www.simplicissimus.info/typo3temp/pics/a267cb0822.jpg
p. 337 (1901) The German and British dogs.
  http://www.simplicissimus.info/typo3temp/pics/f9045e4c0a.jpg
p. 337 (1901) The Boer deputation is turned away.
  http://www.simplicissimus.info/typo3temp/pics/f551378cd0.jpg
p. 338 (1901) The British murder, the Kaiser looks on.
  http://www.simplicissimus.info/typo3temp/pics/dede962d97.jpg
p. 359 (1902) A German couple visit Britain.
  http://www.simplicissimus.info/typo3temp/pics/b85cd2426a.jpg
p. 374 (1902) Tommy dances with his black ally.
  http://www.simplicissimus.info/uploads/tx_lombkswjournaldb/1/07/07_53_006.jpg

p. 374 (1906) Germany's colonial troubles are 'Made in England'.
  http://www.simplicissimus.info/uploads/tx_lombkswjournaldb/1/10/10_02_022.jpg
p. 375 (1906) A black guerrilla in Britain's pay.
  http://www.simplicissimus.info/typo3temp/pics/623c5e830c.jpg
p. 375 (1906) Britain arms the blacks.
  http://www.simplicissimus.info/typo3temp/pics/5921141d9b.jpg
p. 384 (1908) The Kaiser is all wrapped up by Edward VII.
  http://www.simplicissimus.info/uploads/tx_lombkswjournaldb/1/12/12_38_635.jpg
p. 384 (1909) The Kaiser welcomes his prodigal uncle.
  http://www.simplicissimus.info/typo3temp/pics/a4625c060d.jpg
p. 386 (1909) A Zeppelin bombs the Royal Navy.
  http://www.simplicissimus.info/typo3temp/pics/490038a707.jpg
p. 387 (1909) Edward VII writhes in the shadow of a Zeppelin.
  http://www.simplicissimus.info/typo3temp/pics/ba562154f0.jpg
p. 389 (1912) The poor cousin grows big.
  http://www.simplicissimus.info/typo3temp/pics/9e946f2def.jpg
p. 397 (1901) British 'gentlemen' refuse conscription.
  http://www.simplicissimus.info/typo3temp/pics/a4a6a3b460.jpg
p. 398 (1912) 'The Duty of Others'.
  http://www.simplicissimus.info/typo3temp/pics/f72655205c.jpg

By kind permission of Special Collections and Archives, Cardiff University:

pp. 6 and 121 (1878) The Last German, *The Graphic*, 18 March 1878.
p. 62 (1864) British tars laugh at Germany, *Punch*, 2 July 1864.
p. 118 (1871) A shell-smashed room in Paris, *The Graphic*, 18 February 1871.
p. 120 (1871) The First German, *The Graphic*, 18 March 1871.
p. 141 (1873) A German in clubland, *Punch*, 22 February 1873.
p. 180 (1878) The Last of the *Grosser Kürfust*, *The Graphic*, 9 June 1878.
p. 364 (1901) Lord Roberts copies the German army, *Punch*, 10 September 1902.

By kind permission of Worcester College, Oxford:

p. 346 (1901) Breeches, *Spelmann's Goldenes Buch der Sitte*, Leipzig.
p. 348 (1898) Rugby for German readers, *Fusslümmelei*, Leipzig.
p. 349 (1898) The drop kick described, *Fusslümmelei*, Leipzig.

INDEX

Page references followed by fn indicate a footnote on that page